Beyond Redemption

AMERICAN BEGINNINGS, 1500–1900
A series edited by Edward Gray, Stephen Mihm, and Mark Peterson

ALSO IN THE SERIES:

The Republic Afloat: Law, Honor, and Citizenship in Maritime America
by Matthew Taylor Raffety

Conceived in Doubt: Religion and Politics in the New American Nation
by Amanda Porterfield

Beyond Redemption

*Race, Violence, and the
American South after the Civil War*

CAROLE EMBERTON

The University of Chicago Press   Chicago and London

The University of Chicago Press, Chicago 60637
The University of Chicago Press, Ltd., London
© 2013 by The University of Chicago
All rights reserved. Published 2013.
Paperback edition 2015
Printed in the United States of America

24 23 22 21 20 19 18 17 16 15   2 3 4 5 6

ISBN-13: 978-0-226-02427-1 (cloth)
ISBN-13: 978-0-226-26999-3 (paper)
ISBN-13: 978-0-226-02430-1 (e-book)
10.7208/chicago/9780226024301.001.0001

Library of Congress Cataloging-in-Publication Data
Emberton, Carole.
  Beyond redemption : race, violence, and the American South after the Civil War / Carole Emberton.
     pages. cm. — (American beginnings, 1500–1900)
     ISBN 978-0-226-02427-1 (cloth : alk. paper) —
ISBN 978-0-226-02430-1 (e-book) 1. Reconstruction (U.S. history, 1865–1877). 2. Violence—Southern States. 3. Southern States—Race relations. I. Title. II. Series: American beginnings, 1500-1900.
E668.E49 2013
973.8—dc23   2012045014

♾ This paper meets the requirements of ANSI/NISO Z39.48–1992 (Permanence of Paper).

For Darrell, and for my mother and father,

Joyce and Charles Emberton

Contents

Introduction 1

1 Reconstruction as Redemption 11
2 The Politics of Suffering 36
3 Wounds and Scars 73
4 The Militarization of Freedom 102
5 Ballots and Bullets 136
6 The Violent Bear It Away 168

Epilogue 206
Acknowledgments 217
Notes 221
Index 271

Introduction

"Finally, finally, finally," exhaled Jim Prince, editor of the *Neshoba Democrat*, in June 2005, when he learned that Edgar Ray Killen had been convicted of manslaughter in the shooting deaths of three civil rights workers near Philadelphia, Mississippi, forty-one years earlier. A sawmill operator, part-time preacher, and former Ku Klux Klansman, Killen was long suspected of orchestrating the kidnapping and murder of James Earl Chaney, who was a local African American organizer, and two white Congress of Racial Equality (CORE) volunteers from New York, James Goodman and Michael Schwerner, in 1964. The men disappeared on their way to investigate a local church bombing on the night of June 21, Father's Day; their bodies were found buried in an earthen dam almost six weeks later. Despite considerable national attention, including a prolonged federal investigation, justice for the dead men and their families remained elusive. Killen had been indicted in 1967 on a federal conspiracy charge, but the all-white jury was deadlocked allowing Killen and seven coconspirators to remain free until the state of Mississippi reopened the case in 1999. For those like Prince who rejoiced at the verdict, Killen epitomized Mississippi's bloody history as well as the hope for a new beginning. At eighty, Killen sat in a wheelchair, a decrepit old man unable to walk. Thin plastic tubes brought oxygen to his nose from a tank attached to the back of his wheelchair. It was as if the hate that Killen had preached and lived might very well be choking the life right out of him. Whether it was his violent racism or a lifetime inhaling sawdust and cigarette smoke that crippled his lungs was unknown, but to many observers

INTRODUCTION

the almost pitiable image of the broken old man hauled before the bar of justice—finally, finally, *finally*—represented the South's redemption from a long and violent past.¹

Not everyone shared in Prince's hopefulness, however. For Ben Chaney, James Chaney's younger brother, who was only eleven years old when his brother disappeared on a dark Mississippi highway, Killen's trial did not provide peace of mind. Nor did he believe it would help Mississippi "move forward" as the prosecutors had maintained. "There won't be closure," he declared in an interview during the trial. "This is not an attempt at real justice; what's taking place now is a simple whitewash," he said, alluding to his belief that there were others, including members of law enforcement and state government, as guilty as Killen if not more so. "What people in Mississippi are doing is a fraud," Chaney said. "They went after one individual, the most unrepentant individual. Yet the people involved in the cover-up have not been brought to trial. So no, this is not closure. It's more like the Civil War is being fought again."²

Ben Chaney's invocation of the Civil War escaped comment in the mainstream media coverage of the Killen trial, yet it remains a piercing criticism of the monumental efforts to tell a redemptive narrative about racial justice in the modern South. It is not only that Chaney recognized how the roots of the violence that claimed the lives of his brother and the other two men lay tangled up with the South's military defeat, the destruction of slavery, and the attempts to bring biracial democracy to the former Confederacy during Reconstruction. It is not simply that he wanted the public to understand that his brother was part of what historians now call the "long civil rights movement" that connected the grassroots organizing in the 1960s with similar movements led by freedpeople and their white allies a century earlier. His words were much more disconcerting than this. By invoking the Civil War as the historical precedent to what he considered the trial's fraudulent claims to atonement and justice, Ben Chaney exposed the troubling role narratives of redemption have played in America's struggle to come to terms with the legacy of slavery, racial oppression, and violence, not only in the South but in the entire nation.³

Beyond Redemption is a study of the making of manhood, freedom, and citizenship in the aftermath of one of the most destructive wars in human history. Not only did the Civil War destroy more than half a million human beings, it also destroyed an extraordinarily lucrative system of forced labor whose cultural power far exceeded its monetary value. It was in the wake of such unfathomable destruction that the language of redemption, a familiar idiom in American political culture, attained a new explanatory power to help Americans come to terms with their world's violent transformation. Yet even as the language of redemption often spoke to a desire to transcend the violence of the past, the struggles over its meaning revealed the centrality of violence to American political life.

Redemption is a powerful trope in American history. Long before the recent "atonement trials" for the violence Edgar Ray Killen and others committed in the 1950s and 1960s, Americans often understood their politics, religion, and social organization in redemptive terms. Other scholars have explored the importance of regeneration metaphors to American history, and while the trope of redemption can encompass images of rebirth, its meaning runs deeper. An idea that denotes both a hope for deliverance from sin, corruption, and death as well as reclaiming something lost or taken away, redemption holds both religious and secular meanings that have created an important political language in the United States. In fact, it is that blending of religious and political imagery that leads critic George Shulman to argue that that the language of redemption in America has created "a vernacular for ordinary as well as political life, providing the stories and the narrative frameworks by which people—singly and collectively—give purpose to life." After the Civil War, redemption provided the key to the creation of a civic theology that, while grounded in evangelical Christianity, infused the revolutionary legal and political changes that gripped the nation.[4]

Redemption held a number of different but closely related meanings. As the context of its use shifted, the emphasis shifted as well. One scholar notes that the word's Latin root had little of the religious connotation it would later acquire. Meaning to purchase a slave out of bondage, *redemptio* denoted a cash payment, a ransom for freedom. That original meaning is important because it reminds us of the centrality of slavery to America's redemption stories. The language of payment and indebtedness would play an important part in the telling of those stories, especially when freedpeople spoke of the government's obligation to protect them from violence. It also spoke to their belief that they had a right to the land and were owed compensation for their years of unrequited toil.[5]

In Christian theology, redemption signified both the promise of deliverance from suffering and violence as well as the wrath of God's punishment for sin and corruption.[6] Both meanings would inspire mid-century Americans in their views of violence. Radical Republicans premised their reconstruction plans as a way to atone for the sin of slavery and give meaning to the sacrifices soldiers had made on the battlefield. Their aim was to stop the violence plaguing the former Confederacy. To be sure, their motivations included securing their party's ascendency in the South as well as the nation's salvation; the two goals were one and the same. White Southerners, however, increasingly sought deliverance from their suffering through violence. Guided by an understanding of violent atonement embedded within Christianity, white Southern men legitimized their armed assault on freedpeople and Republican officials as a kind of punishment for the corruption unleashed by emancipation and Union victory. *Redemption*—the self-proclaimed movement by Southern whites to take back their state governments from federal control—represented a powerful and lasting narrative about the role of violence in American politics.[7]

However, it should not be understood as a perversion of *true* Christian or democratic values. Both as a religious and a political language, redemption entailed a deep ambivalence about violence. Redemptive language helped Puritan settlers make sense of their violent encounters with Native Americans and allowed their descendants to justify their purification of the frontier. Similarly, redemption narratives inspired antebellum reformers to strive to perfect individual spirits and bodies, laying the evangelical foundations for perfectionist politics, including the antislavery movement. For early African Americans, the promise of redemption from their earthly bondage and oppression animated not only the formation of a distinctive religious practice but also of a subaltern political culture on Southern plantations that would enable slaves to take their freedom long before the Union army begrudgingly offered it to them. Neither the forces of racist dispossession nor egalitarian perfectionism could lay sole claim to redemption's beautiful cogency and dynamism. By the mid-nineteenth century, redemption had become a multivalent discourse that gave voice to disparate movements and agendas that simultaneously sought redemption *from* violence as well as redemption *through* violence.[8]

In the wake of the Civil War, as the nation reeled from violence committed on a scale unimaginable by most nineteenth-century standards, the language of redemption took on even greater significance. As Charles Royster notes, "It was to be a redemptive war, a transformation of society—a sacrifice, like Christ's, full of blessings and ordained by God."[9] By providing a familiar idiom through which people could come to terms with the horrors of war and the uncertainty that lay ahead, redemption offered postwar Americans a meaningful way of narrating their recent history that forged the spiritual with the political. In 1865, Americans grappled not only with how to comprehend the deaths of more than 600,000 of their best young men but also with the emancipation of some four and a half million slaves. The destruction of slavery, as Herman Melville noted, was itself the result of "agonized violence," and the terrible reverberations of this destruction would continue well beyond the formal declarations of peace. Redemption narratives made the staggering loss of life more bearable, made the grieving meaningful, and in the eyes of some, demanded a reevaluation of the basic principles of American democracy. For others, redemption inspired recalcitrance, intransigence, and resistance to any attempt to empower ex-slaves. White supremacists in the 1870s did not choose the name of their movement haphazardly. They called themselves Redeemers because of the important religious and political connotations the word held and the depth of commitment it inspired.[10]

Although seemingly distinct from one another, these views shared a preoccupation with the role of suffering in the nation's spiritual and political redemption. Recently, historian Drew Faust has argued that the Civil War created a culture of "shared suffering" that served as a basis for sectional reunification after the war was over. "At the war's end," she writes, "this shared suffering would override persisting differences about the meaning of race, citizenship, and nationhood to establish sacrifice and its memorialization as the ground on which North and South would ultimately reunite." Yet not all suffering received equal sympathy in the emerging postwar political culture. While images of suffering slaves had inspired the antislavery movement and laid the foundations for a legal revolution in human rights, racialized understandings of freedom and citizenship complicated the politics of suffering for African Americans. Narratives of suffering worked to reunite whites, but they did so at the expense of blacks. Not only were black soldiers and their families often denied the benefits of a military pension, and not only did they receive significantly less for their sacrifice, the images and representations of black suffering that proliferated in the postwar battles over Reconstruction entailed contradictory results for the African American freedom struggle. Certain images of black suffering were marshaled to justify the policies of Radical Reconstruction, including the nationalization of citizenship and civil rights as codified in the Fourteenth and Fifteenth Amendments, thereby ushering in a new era of state activism on behalf of African Americans. However, ideas about the necessity of black suffering as a condition of freedom, a painful but requisite part of making slaves into good citizens, circumscribed the expansion of the body politic and the narrative of freedom that postwar Northern Americans liked to tell about the war (and still do today).[11]

The impulse to protect freedpeople from abuse and intimidation by their former masters competed against an equally strong impulse to discipline ex-slaves, to reform their degraded spirits and control their

INTRODUCTION

laboring bodies. While the language of universal, national citizenship offered freedpeople the hope of transcending the physical scars of slavery and protecting them from future violence, the state's ability to provide physical security was limited by a number of conditions, including its need to maintain a reliable workforce. Take, for instance, the constant admonitions to work hard and obey their employers federal agents gave to freedpeople in response to their complaints of abuse. The federal government assured a skeptical workforce that planters would not rely on violence because it would corrupt labor and make the workers fearful and drive them away. This was, after all, the primary economic argument that liberals had made against slavery before the war: it was inefficient and ultimately untenable as a form of modern labor extraction. Such naïveté revealed how deeply Northern officials misunderstood the importance of violence not only to Southern ideas of labor but also to their ideas of race and self.[12]

But if the federal government was ill-prepared to effectively counter the overwhelming personal and political violence that plagued freedpeople, perhaps it was because some shared the Southern worldview more than even they imagined. When a Northern journalist overheard a group of white Southerners who were watching the procession of an Alabama chain gang proclaim, "That's the beauty of freedom! That's what free niggers come to," his initial outrage eventually turned to sympathy for the Southerners' point of view. Whites in both sections shared a belief in the necessity of physical coercion, and with it suffering, to limit the dangers too much freedom posed. Many Freedmen's Bureau agents, the guardians of freedpeople's well-being and safety, agreed with former slaveholders that whipping, imprisonment, and compulsory apprenticeships might be necessary in order to transform freedpeople into productive citizens. Freedpeople were caught between the law and the lash—by efforts to supplant the power of white planters, on the one hand, and to regulate and discipline black bodies and labor, on the other.[13]

As a result, the idea of redemption produced a divided legacy for former slaves in their attempts to reimagine themselves as free. They celebrated the end of slavery as a time of "Jubilee," the divinely ordained moment when their suffering would be redeemed. Ex-slaves also invoked the violence they had endured as slaves and still experienced as free persons to make important claims as citizens, including a right to own land, to vote, and to be protected from violence. Yet speaking of violence entailed certain risks. To a great extent, whites controlled the discourse of Southern violence and its impact on Reconstruction. Whether in the halls of Congress, on the pages of newspapers, or at the local Freedmen's Bureau office, whites dictated who spoke, what their words meant, and even how (or if) those words would be recorded. Therefore, African Americans who managed to testify before a congressional investigating committee or make a complaint to a local agent struggled against the narrative structures imposed by bureaucratic systems as well as the frameworks of race and gender that mediated the reception of their stories. White ideas about black dependency, promiscuity, and criminality often made it difficult for their stories of deprivation, rape, or assault to be taken seriously. Thus, to speak of those violent experiences risked reinforcing the negative ideas whites harbored about them. Repetitions of "terrible spectacles" like whipping could inure white audiences to black pain and make them into objects of a perverse spectatorship that enjoyed such displays even as it professed to abhor them.[14]

The words former slaves found (or did not find) to talk about their violent experiences paint a complicated and compelling picture of a how people, both individually and collectively, deal with trauma. A vibrant literature in the fields of anthropology and literary studies endeavors to understand how people in various cultures and states process and overcome experiences with systematic violence, such as civil war, ethnic cleansing, and genocide. Yet many historians remain wedded to an empirical ideal that shuns the emotional life of our subjects as unknowable, particularly when the feelings displayed run counter to our intellectual and political commitments to respect and recover the agency of the oppressed. Freedpeople's responses to violence revealed not only moments of astonishing defiance and resistance but also wrenching expressions of fear, vulnerability, resentment, rage, and perhaps most tellingly of all, silence. These responses call into question the redemptive narrative of citizenship and equal rights as told by Reconstruction-era lawmakers, Freedmen's Bureau officers, and other reformers.[15]

The words of former slaves testify to the centrality of violence to American politics and force us to ask new questions about an old subject. The question of why the Reconstruction South experienced so much violence has long fascinated historians, but that question presumes the era to be unique, a regional aberration in the general trend of American politics toward peaceful deliberation and consensus, or a political tool used periodically when the state is weak. But what if we begin to see violence as providing "the threads that weave . . . history together," a foundational element in the construction of ideas of American citizenship instead of a repudiation of them?[16]

Reconstruction awakened Americans to the formative role violence played in the development of their politics and national identity. While they might come to understand the Civil War as a tragic rupture of their mostly peaceable history, Reconstruction revealed how images, symbols, and languages of violence, as well as its methods, informed the very definition of what it meant to be an American. Violence ordered life in the United States, not just the South, in important ways, but its influence tended to go unspoken. As Homi Bhabba writes, national histories often involve "a strange forgetting . . . a minus in the origin" that obscures, diminishes, or otherwise denies the role of violence in "establishing the nation's writ."[17] Reconstruction precipitated a naked confrontation between the exalted status accorded the rule of law and nationalized citizenship, on the one hand, and punitive racial policies, militarized notions of freedom and citizenship, and a hypermasculine, aggressive political style, on the other.

As historians have long pointed out, there was nothing new per se about the explosion of postwar violence in the South. In many ways, white assaults against freedpeople and their white allies replicated antebellum traditions of rough justice and racialized violence grounded in slavery.[18] What was new, however, in addition to the scale of the violence, which contemporary observers found shocking, was its unfolding relationship to politics and citizenship both on the local and national levels as well as how Americans reckoned with those connections. Violence posed the biggest stumbling block to the redemptive story of freedom, not simply because Southern whites wielded it so successfully, or even because the government was structurally too weak to stop it. Rather, the problem of violence created a "crisis in legitimacy" for Republicans because its existence exposed the inconsistencies within the liberal ideology guiding Reconstruction.[19]

Not only did many white Americans view freedpeople's redemption from slavery as requiring certain forms of coercion and even violence in order to make them into good, productive citizens, their views of freedom as a violent struggle also risked the goal of pacifying the South. The postwar "obsession with manhood" equated freedom with fighting, and while the discourse of martial valor redeemed enslaved black manhood, enhanced black veterans' claims on the state, and paved the way for black enfranchisement, it also put freedpeople at considerable risk. In the South, where the paramilitary political tradition was particularly strong, the equation of freedom with fighting, of voting with self-defense, and manhood with citizenship, contributed to the explosion of violence in the late 1860s and throughout the 1870s that would claim countless black lives and reverse black Americans' hard-won political gains.[20]

By examining the relationship between violence, manhood, and politics, this book contributes to the history of American manhood as well as the history of Reconstruction. While many scholars detect a rise in the idea of martial or "primitive" masculinity at the end of the nineteenth century, I trace its origins to midcentury, when the war, emancipation, and Reconstruction produced a political culture that idealized military valor and sacrifice as the ultimate expression of American citizenship. Reconstruction was nothing if not a struggle to overcome the ambivalence that had characterized antebellum notions of masculinity and violence. While this glorification of war and soldiering hardly went uncontested, it nonetheless shaped the visions of freedom and manliness among both blacks and whites. The ideal of martial manhood, much like the discourse of suffering, held contradictory meanings for African American men. The "right to brutality" driving the martial vision of emancipation was reserved for white men only; black men's claims to it challenged a basic tenet of white supremacy, resulting in an escalation of collective violence that inaugurated the horrific reign of Jim Crow lynchings. The ritualized violence typically associated with later decades, in fact, grew out of the contests over manhood during Reconstruction.[21]

Redemption, the self-styled movement to deliver the South from the throes of tyranny and dispossession, was not just a Southern story. Long before white paramilitaries undertook their armed assaults against freedpeople and their Republican-led governments in the Deep South in the mid 1870s, the North's need to write its own redemption narrative implicated those who claimed friendship with former slaves in their reenslavement. The drive to stop Southern violence and bring about a peaceful political transformation was compromised by the discourse of martial manhood that reduced freedom to a violent struggle between men. Although the Redeemers succeeded in driving federal authority from the South and reestablishing "home rule," they did so by using a language that all Americans could appreciate.

Thus, the title of this book contains a double meaning. First, it alludes to the prevailing idea that the South was a distinctively violent place that was *beyond redemption*. By drawing connections between structures of violence and coercion that spanned regional boundaries, this book argues that the Reconstruction-era Southern violence both reflected and reinforced well-established cultural patterns and ideological imperatives within the larger nation. It also reveals how the naturalization of Southern violence and a belief in the inevitability of black suffering emerged out of the particular historical context of Reconstruction.

Second, the title asks the reader to push past the conventional geographic and temporal boundaries of Reconstruction narratives and to think *beyond Redemption*, the white counterrevolution that swept the last vestiges of biracial democracy from the South in the 1870s. Insofar as historians of the South and Reconstruction have interrogated the idea of redemption, they have done so only through that specific political movement. Redemption is understood as marking the end of Reconstruction, not as an integral part of it.

While it might be easy to look at the end of Reconstruction and the restoration of white home-rule as the ultimate victory of redemption through violence, the story does not end there. The struggles of Reconstruction over the place African Americans would occupy in the body politic and the protections that the government owed its citizens did not end in 1877 despite the "hands off" policy the Hayes administration adopted in exchange for Democratic support in the contested presidential election. The fruits of those early efforts to secure physical protection can be traced to recent hate-crime legislation and other protective measures that recognize a federal obligation to uphold a citizen's physical security, such as the Violence Against Women Act. Moreover, African Americans and a small cadre of white allies conducted smaller-scale redemptive strategies that challenged the regenerative narratives of white supremacy, the results of which can be found in local Emancipation Day celebrations, the lessons taught to children in black schools, and a rich literary tradition that continues to struggle with the legacy of slavery and racist violence. Often these smaller-scale redemption projects remained doubtful of the possibility or even desirability of complete redemption from violence. They did, however, offer ways of coping, of moving forward, of lessening the emotional burdens of historical trauma and suffering.

Writing the history of violence and its redemption is a struggle to maintain a sense of contingency. The South was not destined to give way to violence by fate, "nature," or some other inevitable force. The violence of the Reconstruction years was the consequence of a thousand individual choices that actors perhaps justified as being unavoidable but were far from so. Reconstruction captured a moment when Americans could imagine a more peaceable, less violent society where physical safety would become a right of all citizens. This is the story of their struggle to achieve that vision. But just as we cannot reduce Reconstruction to an exercise in futility, we cannot rest satisfied with the image of Edgar Ray Killen wheezing his last hateful breath in jail and believe in *finally*. As redemption goes, the search is long, arduous, and unfinished even if we look for shortcuts whenever we can.

ONE

Reconstruction as Redemption

They shall build up the ancient ruins; they shall raise up the former desolations; they shall repair the ruined cities, the desolations of many generations. ISAIAH 6:4

"What like a bullet can undeceive?" HERMAN MELVILLE[1]

The trial and execution of Mary Surratt was a spectacle to rival any in our present time. Found guilty of being one of John Wilkes Booth's coconspirators in the assassination of President Lincoln, Surratt was the first woman put to death by the federal government. Along with four others on a blistering July day in 1865, Surratt mounted the gallows at the Old Capital Prison as throngs gathered outside the prison yard hoping to catch a glimpse of the execution. The crowd sweated and cursed, angry that only a select few Congressmen and military officials had been allowed inside. They had been willing to pay hundreds of dollars, some of them, to see justice done to one of the most notorious criminals of the nineteenth century. The fact that a woman was among the condemned only intensified their curiosity. Up until the moment the trap door was opened beneath her feet, few expected she would actually hang. Surely the president would pardon her. A special guard of federal soldiers was stationed nearby ready to usher the woman back to safety should a last minute reprieve be issued. But no reprieve came. As the executioner tied the cotton strips around her arms and skirt, to stop her legs from flailing and her petticoats flying up, the irony of the man's concern for the dignity of the woman he was about to kill must have seemed a cruel joke to her supporters who steadfastly maintained her innocence to the last. Her daughter, who watched from below, collapsed with grief. For a brief moment, the five convicted assassins stood together with their nooses in place, "equal in justice." But it was Mary Surratt's last words that would ring in the ears of all those who watched the event or read about it in the following days: "Don't let me fall."[2]

Mary Surratt's execution for her role in the assassination of President Lincoln marked a pivotal moment in the history of violence in the United States. Never before had the federal government put a woman to death, and the state's exercise of its raw power over an individual citizen's life was a cause of great concern to many—even those who believed Surratt to have been John Wilkes Booth's "anchor." Over the previous four years, the government had consolidated its vast economic, political, and legal authority to build the greatest killing machine ever assembled at that point in time, the Grand Army of the Republic. That consolidation did not go uncontested, and the work of justifying the consumption of hundreds of thousands of young men proved one of the most difficult aspects of waging civil war. What difference, then, could the death of one woman make? In the agonizing figure of Mary Surratt, gripped by fear on the scaffold, Americans recognized a part of themselves, also gripped by fear, not only of the secret plottings of wild assassins but also the seemingly unstoppable force of the nation-state. Like Surratt, they feared falling into a chasm of violence that seemed to open up beneath their feet, and they sought redemption from four long years of civil war. Government officials professed to close the chasm by punishing the "deep dyed villains" who had perpetrated the most egregious act of violence imaginable—killing the president. But could they close the chasm, or did they simply tear it wider? Advocates for Surratt's execution argued that it opened a pathway to peace and national reunification. Justice, they argued, necessitated Surratt's death, although horrible—as well as the punishment of others responsible for the war. Her supporters, on the other hand, decried her execution as "judicial murder" and condemned the government for enacting such "stupendous a retribution" for Lincoln's death. Arguing that her conviction had been a foregone conclusion given the high passions surrounding the assassination, critics of the military tribunal that judged the conspirators believed the usurpation of civil due process made a mockery of the law. These competing interpretations stemmed from questions far greater than simply Surratt's guilt or even the propriety of hanging a woman. The trial and execution of Mary Surratt and the other Lincoln conspirators was but one incident in a long and torturous history of the government's efforts to control both the meaning and the means of violence within American society.

The Civil War problematized violence in new and frightening ways. Americans wondered if the war had so demoralized society that the war's violent reverberations might still be felt long after it was over. It also implicated the national government in perpetrating violence so brutal that it called into question the legitimacy of the war and its outcomes, including emancipation. Unitarian minister John Weiss summed up the anxiety over the new forms of violence the war had created and their long-term impact on American society when he declared that the United States had become "the most dangerous country on the face of the earth."[3]

As Americans emerged from the devastation of the Civil War, violence became central to their hopes and concerns about the nation. Violence had nearly destroyed it and continued to threaten the fragile reunion of North and South. Postwar Americans, however, were not concerned just with events in the defeated South. They were worried about the war's effects on their own society and the growing power of the federal government. They also sought meaning in the war's destruction. To many, the war had purified the nation, creating new opportunities to remake the United States into the ideal republic that they believed it was meant to be. Melinda Lawson argues that the Civil War "redefined the relationship between the individual and the national state, presenting the sate as a benefactor, no threat to individual Americans." But that transformation progressed unevenly, for although many Americans viewed the war as fulfilling America's redemptive promise, there remained considerable ambivalence with regard to the growing coercive power of the nation-state. While many looked to the national government as the new protector of individual rights, others feared that this new mission might endanger the republic rather than rejuvenate it.[4]

Reconstruction and Redemption are typically viewed as opposing forces, two endpoints on the timeline of the United States during the mid-nineteenth century. The former, historians tell us, denotes the efforts by freedpeople and their white allies to bring biracial democracy and free labor to the former Confederacy. The latter is the term chosen by white supremacists to lend religious as well as political legitimacy to their violent opposition to freedpeople's quest for full citizenship.[5] That white Southerners would choose such a word to cloak their hateful, undemocratic agenda rankles some, such as Vernon Burton, who refuses to allow the enemies of freedom the protection he understands as implicit in the word's meaning. "Redemption," Burton writes, is "a beautiful term of religious faith that would be a better label for the promising years from the early 1860s through the early 1870s than so grossly to misconstrue the decades that follow."[6]

Burton's point is well taken. The efforts to reconstruct the slave South were in no small part driven by the same evangelical ethos that had driven the antislavery movement and laid the foundations to a nascent conception of human rights. The language of perfectionism, purification, and atonement for the sin of slavery remained a vital component to the reconstructing impulse that would help Radical Republicans wrest control of the South from the more conservative elements in American government, including the president himself. The mingling of religious and political ideologies—nothing new to American politics—created a new civic theology that imagined the newly reinvigorated nation as a powerful protector of individual rights, an identification that would soon be codified in the Fourteenth Amendment to the US Constitution. The martyred Abraham Lincoln would not be alone in his apotheosis. The iconography of this new civic theology elevated the institutions of American governance, its symbols, and some of its leaders to almost godlike status. To reconstruct the South was to redeem the nation.[7]

Violence remained central to this mission. One major aspect of the South's so-called Redemption that Burton and other historians deplore was, in fact, integral to Reconstruction itself. In seeking redemption from the war's violence, slavery's brutal legacy, and the continuing upheaval in the postwar South, Americans confronted the unsettling possibility that more violence might be necessary in order to ensure the past four years of suffering and death would not have been in vain. Questions about the necessity of Confederate punishment and the use of other coercive methods to extract a modicum of contrition, humility, and regret from errant Southerners exposed the paradox of redemption: redemption *from* violence easily became redemption *through* violence. The language of redemption provided a thread that would run through the course of the 1860s and 1870s, uniting people who viewed themselves as enemies in a common dialogue about violence, its role in the political process, the limits of state intervention to protect certain classes of citizens from it, and the right of some of those citizens to employ it under certain conditions. While not everyone agreed on these issues, and much blood would be spilled in the process of addressing them, redemptive discourse made the tumultuous and violent decades of the 1860s and 1870s legible both for those who lived through them as well as for those of us endeavoring to understand them today.

Rituals of Redemption

The threat of rain on March 27, 1865, did not dampen the resolve of black Charlestonians to enact a dramatic and emotional performance of their redemption from slavery. Although General Robert E. Lee's official surrender was still over two weeks away, Confederate forces had evacuated the cradle of secession a month prior as General William T. Sherman's troops pushed northward from Savannah. The fleeing Confederate troops had set fire to the cotton warehouses, and flames had spread throughout the town, leaving much of the city a charred shell of its former self. Amid the rubble, however, the city's black population gathered not to mourn the destruction but to celebrate it. A correspondent from the *New York Tribune* who witnessed the event stood in awe of the two-and-a-half-mile parade that snaked through Charleston's streets from the Citadel Green and back again. "Upward of ten thousand persons were present," he wrote in his report to the *Tribune*, "colored men, women and children, and every window and balustrade overlooking the square was crowded with spectators." They carried a myriad of handmade banners bearing slogans such as "Our Past the Block, our Future the School" and "Massachusetts Greets South Carolina as a Child Redeemed (Wendell Phillips)," no doubt having been aided in their production by the sea of Northern missionaries already flowing into the lower South. Among the participants were companies of United States Colored Troops (USCT), some of whom had liberated the city and its inhabitants, as well as an impressive organization of Charleston's black workingmen who carried the tools of their trades (the masons carried trowels, the barbers carried shears, the painters their paintbrushes, and so on) along with banners welcoming the Union forces to South Carolina. In claiming their place as skilled workingmen, the laborers rejected the characterizations of them typically associated with slavery. These laboring men wanted to be seen not as driven brutes but as the skilled and expert craftsmen they were. They marched to redeem their city and their place within it.

As profound as this statement was, it was not the most impressive, according to the *Tribune* correspondent. The "most original feature" of this "celebration of . . . deliverance from bondage and ostracism," this "jubilee of freedom," was a large horse-drawn cart carrying an auctioneer's block and a black man reenacting one of slavery's archetypal scenes. As the cart rolled through the streets following the procession of workers, the man performed a mock auction, ringing a bell and calling out to the crowd, "'How much am I offered for this good cook? She is an 'xlent cook, ge'men ... 200's bid ... 250, 300, 350, 400, 450, who bids 500?'" Behind the auction cart marched a solemn coffle of sixty men tied together at the wrists "on their way from Virginia to the sugar-fields of Louisiana," representing the internal slave trade. That the actor playing the auctioneer and the men in the coffle all "had been sold in old times" spoke of the personal as well as collective redemption enacted in their movements. After the coffle came a hearse with the words "Slavery is Dead," written on the sides with chalk. Fifty women dressed in black but "with joyous faces" walked behind the hearse in pretend mourning. Indeed, the black residents of Charleston and throughout the rest of the dying Confederacy became slavery's pallbearers that spring. In similar rituals of redemption in cities and towns throughout the South, freedpeople enacted "Jubilee"—their earthly deliverance from bondage like that of the Jews of the Old Testament.[8]

The assassination of President Lincoln on April 14 marred the celebratory atmosphere surrounding the Confederacy's defeat. Spasms of shock and grief gripped Northerners as they mourned their president, more beloved in death than in life. Redemption continued to serve an important function, giving greater meaning to a seemingly senseless act of violence. "Redemption is a mystery," confessed a Presbyterian minister to his congregation in Bedford, Pennsylvania, who wondered how Lincoln's death could possibly fit into God's plan for the nation's salvation after four bloody years of war. Despite the difficulty in understanding how the Almighty could allow the death of the "Uniter and Liberator of America," the image of Christ's blood sacrifice, central to the Christian notion of redemption, proved useful. "Our national unity is perfected by the martyrdom of our President," assured A. G. Thomas, chaplain of the Filbert Street Army Hospital in Philadelphia. Ministers like Thomas delivered funeral eulogies and remembrances that drew analogies between Lincoln and the great Redeemer, Jesus Christ, a comparison made easier by the fact that the assassination had taken place on one of the holiest of Christian holidays, Good Friday. That day became "the Good Friday of American Redemption," according to one Baptist minister in Philadelphia. Others also spoke of Lincoln's death as the nation's atonement for slavery. Recalling Lincoln's emotional second inaugural address some weeks earlier, in which he reminded the nation of the enormous debt it owed to freedpeople, Methodist minister Gilbert Haven remarked, "How sadly it prophesies his own fate! His too much be of the blood which God requires from the sword to repay that drawn by the lash." For Haven, Lincoln's death, like the war itself, was but another installment in the payment of that debt.

Haven also elevated Lincoln to a pedestal of American statesmanship once reserved only for the nation's earthly father. In Haven's eyes, Lincoln's accomplishments put him on equal footing with, if not exceeding, George Washington. "The one liberated three millions of his own race from foreign despotism," Haven said of Washington. "The other," meaning Lincoln, "liberated another people than his own—four millions of bound and bleeding victims—from a despotism infinitely more horrible." The United States thus had "two creators and redeemers," Haven told the crowd gathered in Boston for Lincoln's funeral on April 23, and "the influence of both shall go forth for the redemption and regeneration of all lands."[9]

Other eulogies focused on the tasks still remaining before Congress if Lincoln's martyrdom were to result in national redemption. Connecticut congressman Henry Champion Deming informed a meeting of the state legislature gathered in Hartford to mourn the "the elect of liberty" that he had died for "the redemption of a long suffering race." Mingling political and religious imagery, Rev. Frank L. Robbins of Philadelphia believed Lincoln's martyrdom had assured "the redemption of the liberties of mankind," while Haven concluded that in death Lincoln had found "everlasting redemption and equal citizenship with the unfallen angels of God." In their efforts to channel the nation's grief and rally support for some legal guarantees for black civil rights, these ministers expanded the notion of redemption to include political as well as spiritual rejuvenation.[10]

The redemptive visions of emancipation and Lincoln's martyrdom imbued the nation's political culture with a new impetus toward institutional reform. The importance of this transition cannot be overstated. Reform movements in the United States enjoyed a long and varied history, seeking to perfect the human condition, and in some instances, institutions of law and government. However, there existed within the evangelical culture that spawned antebellum reform movements a tension regarding the state both as a target of reform work and its role in promoting perfectionist politics. Garrisonians viewed institutions as inherently corrupt *and* corrupting. They eschewed political parties, campaigning, and voting as means for reform. Suspicious of the government's capacity for corruption and violence, they insisted that "moral suasion," focused on individual atonement and purification, was the only way to enact true, lasting change in social behavior. Who could blame them? The history of political compromise and protection for slavery and the interests of slaveholders in the national government could be told as a kind of morality play about corrupting influence of power, greed, and self-interest. Although political abolitionists steadfastly opposed any further compromise on the issue of slavery's expansion into the western territories, the Republican Party's "white manism," as Garrison called it, gave little cause for hope. Racism and self-interest, not moral opposition to slavery or concern for one's fellow man, drove white men into the Free Soil and then Republican parties. They could not be trusted to uphold their commitments if doing so became disadvantageous to their personal aims. Nonetheless, the Garrisonians' anti-institutional stance failed to deter politically minded reformers, such as the abolitionists who formed the Liberty Party, from seeking more immediate, practical applications of their evangelical ideals.[11]

The issue of slavery rested at the core of this controversy over reform. Could the problem of slavery be solved through legal changes alone, or would deeper cultural, religious, and social reforms be necessary in order to redeem the nation from slavery's corrupting power? The war's blood sacrifice appeared to offer the answer. Lincoln himself had done much to create a memory of the war as a sanctifying event that justified the unprecedented consolidation of federal power, the most important act of which was emancipation. In both the Gettysburg Address and his second inaugural, Lincoln tied the nation's redemption to the deaths of soldiers and the suffering of slaves. In particular, the second inaugural, given just weeks before his death, invoked an apocalyptic image of the war as divine retribution for the national sin of slavery:

Fondly we do hope—fervently we do pray—that this mighty scourge of war may speedily pass away. Yet, if God wills that it continue, till all the wealth piled by the bond-man's two hundred and fifty years of unrequited toil shall be sunk, and until every drop of blood drawn with the lash, shall be paid by another drawn with the sword, as was said three thousand years ago, so still it must be said 'the judgments of the Lord, are true and righteous together."

The metaphor of blood sacrifice sanctified the war as the proper atonement for a sin belonging not just to the South but the whole nation. By "asking the entire nation to confront unblinkingly the legacy of the long history of slavery," Lincoln made atonement for slavery central to the nation's redemption and recovery.[12]

"The First Object of Government"

Lincoln was not alone in his belief that the war provided an opportunity to atone for the government's long history of inaction and complicity with regard to slavery. In fact, it arose from a well-established idea that the state bore an obligation to protect its citizens. Its basis lay in social contract theory and English common law tradition, both of which influenced the formation of American political theory in the eighteenth century. In return for the government's protection, citizens pledged their allegiance to the state and promised to abide by its laws. "Each individual of the society has a right to be protected by it in the enjoyment of his life, liberty, and property, according to standing laws," asserted the Massachusetts state constitution in 1780. "He is obliged, consequently, to contribute his share to the expense of this protection; to give his personal services, or an equivalent, when necessary," and to otherwise abide by the laws the state enacted in order to protect the rights and property of others. Other early American state constitutions echoed this claim, and soon the reciprocal obligations of allegiance and protection became axiomatic of American citizenship.[13]

Not simply a limitation on the state's interference with private property, the axiom of protection as it emerged in the legal culture of the Early Republic required positive action on the government's part to ensure the conditions of freedom, including physical safety. To act as a corrective to man's aggressive nature, argued James Madison, was "the first object of government." Madison took a Hobbesian view of human nature and understood the function of the state as a corrective to the more nasty and brutish aspects of human existence. "So strong is this propensity of mankind to fall into mutual animosities," he advised, "that where no substantial occasion presents itself, the most frivolous and fanciful distinctions have been sufficient to kindle their unfriendly passions, and excite their most violent conflicts." Like most other governmental functions, the United States Constitution divided the obligation to protect between the federal government and the states, placing most of the burden on the individual states. While the document charged the national government with the duty to protect against foreign invasion and "domestic Violence," the states were left to be "the immediate and visible guardians of life and property." Through the administration of civil and criminal courts, as well as other methods of law enforcement, the states maintained the primary duty to protect citizens in their daily lives. Only

CHAPTER ONE

in extreme circumstances would the duty of the federal government supersede that of the states.[14]

As reform movements aimed at perfecting man's nature as well as his body blossomed in the antebellum period, the state's obligation to ensure citizens' physical safety expanded. Beginning in the 1830s, local governments began passing antiriot laws that required states and municipalities not only to prosecute breaches of the public peace but also to actively work to prevent such outbreaks from occurring. These laws established some of the first police forces in the United States. States also expanded their regulatory powers to provide for the public safety by enacting fire and building codes, legislating penalties and fines for those who failed to abide by the codes or enforce them, and mandating that cities and towns form fire companies as well as purchase firefighting equipment and fire insurance. State legislatures also invoked their duty to protect the public from contagion and began to issue quarantine, port, and pilot regulations for water vessels. Other reform movements, such as antivice, antiprostitution, and temperance campaigns, also employed the discourse of public safety and protection to justify their intrusion into "private" life. In addition to commerce, public safety became the overriding concern of the state's regulatory impulse in the nineteenth century and justified a host of intrusive state actions.[15]

The civil rights legislation enacted in the wake of emancipation, however, far surpassed these earlier attempts to protect the lives and property of citizens. By making the national government the supreme protector, it redrew the boundaries of federalism. Equally important, these new laws aimed specifically at correcting the wrongs of slavery and securing the protection of former slaves, thereby expanding the scope of civil rights and the nature of citizenship itself. Whereas Garrisonians had rejected the idea of constitutional reform, by war's end calls for amendments abolishing slavery and guaranteeing equal rights for blacks rang out across the North. In Cleveland, a self-styled group of "Radical Germans" demanded "a revision of the Constitution in the spirit of the Declaration of Independence." This had been Lincoln's strategy a few months before at Gettysburg when he invoked the spirit of the Declaration of Independence as the foundational document for his "new birth of freedom." Rather than abandoning the Constitution, however, Civil War–era Americans increasingly believed they could correct its mistakes. The Constitution was not a "divine book," wrote one Republican who stressed the document's flexibility and impermanence. Accepting its fallibility did not diminish its importance but rather enhanced the document's ability to aid in reform.[16]

The movement to amend the Constitution also reflected an expanded view of emancipation informed by redemptive language. After enumerating the many sacrifices and valorous achievements of black soldiers in the Union Army, Radical Congressman Isaac Arnold equated the Thirteenth Amendment with the creation of "a new nation" where "equality before the law is to be the great cornerstone." No doubt referencing Alexander Hamilton Stephens's infamous 1861 speech in which he repudiated the idea of equality as a founding principle by pronouncing slavery to be the "cornerstone" of the Confederate nation, Arnold called for the nation to be made anew by expunging slavery from its governing document. The theme of rebirth seemed appropriate to several of those who had participated in the amendment's creation. "It seemed to me that I had been born into a new life," recalled Senator George Julian thirty years later. Another congressman, Martin Russell Thayer of Pennsylvania, considered Americans to now be "a regenerated people" and claimed that as he and his colleagues emerged from the House of Representatives that day, the sun broke through the clouds, which he took as Divine approval for what they had accomplished. Even William Lloyd Garrison changed his tune. For Garrison, the Thirteenth Amendment transformed "a covenant with death" into a "covenant with life." Satisfied that his life's work had finally been accomplished, he promptly (and prematurely, critics contended) called for the American Anti-Slavery Society to disband. Not immune to "amendment fever" even the Democrats, whose avowed purpose had been to keep "the Constitution as it is," came around to the political promise that an antislavery amendment held once it became popular. However limited their specific views may have been with regard to black political rights, the amendment revealed how postwar Americans ritualized certain aspects of redemption as an atonement for slavery. Emancipation became more than just a temporary policy based upon military necessity; it became a lasting tribute to the belief that specific policies could be changed, and that the government not only could *do* better, but also that it could *be* better. It was a way to redeem the debt owed freedpeople and regenerate the national mission. Despite its shortcomings, the Thirteenth Amendment represented "a new departure" in American political culture. Rather than seeing the Constitution and the government it created as an impediment to freedom, Americans would begin to see it as "an unequivocal charter for freedom."[17]

In his celebratory engraving entitled "Emancipation" (fig. 1.1), cartoonist Thomas Nast captured the redemptive vision of freedom that so moved Garrison. First published in *Harper's Weekly* to celebrate the enactment of the Emancipation Proclamation on January 1, 1863, the

CHAPTER ONE

FIGURE 1.1 Redemption from the violence of slavery. Thomas Nast, "Emancipation" (Philadelphia: S. Bott, 1865). Wood engraving. Courtesy Library of Congress.

engraving tells the story of freedom as a triumph of good over evil as a black family featured in the center frame enjoys the peace of a free home. On the left side of the engraving, a series of images depicting the sin of slavery, overseen by none other than Satan himself, represents the dark past out of which the family has emerged. The horrors of the auction block and the whipping post, where a woman is tied, stripped, and flogged, signify slavery's corruption and brutality. After emancipation, however, the schoolhouse replaces the auction block and whipping post, becoming a symbol of freedom. Nast tells a redemptive story where children go to school, parents work and receive wages, and families build respectable homes. With the degradation of slavery and its myriad abuses erased, ex-slaves are redeemed through a combination of state support (represented by Lincoln's portrait), education, and hard work.

The government's new charter was hardly complete. In November, eight months after the amendment's passage, a public celebration in Harrisburg, Pennsylvania, to honor returning black soldiers began with a simple prayer: "Hasten, O God, the glad day of universal liberty, when all men, equal before God in their creation and redemption through Christ, may be recognized as equal before the law." Invoking the Crucifixion, the group spoke of their faith in redemptive suffering, specifically the sacrifices of black soldiers. They hoped that the soldiers' sacrifices and the constitutional amendment abolishing slavery would be "the star of our redemption" leading to other changes in the country's political and legal system.[18]

With the Thirteenth Amendment's ratification in December 1865, African Americans were guaranteed the right of habeas corpus, which had previously been denied to them under the Fugitive Slave Law. However, this change seemed to have little effect on the treatment Southern blacks received from whites, many of whom seemed determined to resurrect the violent customs of mastery despite its legal demise. Thus, within a month of the constitutional abolition of slavery, Radical senator Lyman Trumbull of Illinois introduced the most direct articulation of protection yet.

A lengthy and detailed piece of legislation, the Civil Rights Act (CRA) made the "security of person and property" a right of American citizenship. With a total of ten sections and more than two thousand words, the final version of the CRA, passed in April 1866, endeavored to make African Americans national citizens and delineated the specific rights of American citizenship, including the right to own property, sue, make contracts, testify in court, and "be subject to like punishment, pains, and penalties" before the law. The CRA also established federal authority to police the states with regard to their treatment of black citizens and made the interference with such authority or any other infringement of the rights of black citizens a federal crime. Finally, the act gave the president the authority to use the military, if necessary, to enforce the act. Any one of these tasks by itself was gargantuan, but taken together they represented the most ambitious and audacious expression of federalism, anchored by the sentiment of protection, ever imagined. While opponents to the bill claimed that the Thirteenth Amendment was protection enough for freedpeople and that the CRA went too far, Trumbull insisted that it was necessary to secure "practical freedom" for the several million former slaves living in the South. "There is very little importance in the general declaration of abstract truths and principles," Trumbull explained, "unless they can be carried into effect."[19]

The first section, which Trumbull argued laid the foundation for the entire bill, established birthright citizenship regardless of race or "any previous condition of slavery or involuntary servitude." Although not a part of the initial bill he introduced on January 12, Trumbull put forth an amendment adding the citizenship clause on January 29 because he believed it was the only way to guarantee the protection of black lives and legitimize federal authority over them. In the South, state legislatures had passed "Black Codes" that, among other things, restricted the movement of African Americans, designated special punishments for black criminals, and barred the testimony of blacks in courts. The fact that they were nominally free meant little to the experience of life after slavery in the South for Southern blacks. "The right of American citizenship means something," Trumbull declared during the stiff debates over the act's provisions. Federal protection provided that meaning. Trumbull understood protection as a distinct right of citizenship, not a "generic reference" to unspecified benefits. Relying upon a common-law conception of natural rights, Trumbull argued that the rights to "personal security," "personal liberty," and "to acquire and enjoy property" were the "absolute rights" of all individuals regardless of any other political rights they might be granted, such as the right to vote—the bugbear of conservative criticisms against Reconstruction. The CRA, he insisted, went only so far as to secure and protect those natural rights, what in today's language are called human rights. Federal protection gave American citizenship meaning, Trumbull believed. Otherwise, a citizen would be "left entirely to the mercy of State legislation." Without the uniformity of protection embodied in the CRA and cemented in the idea of national citizenship, membership in the American nation would be meaningless and without benefit. "American citizenship would be of little worth if it did not carry protection with it," Trumbull declared in his final push for the act's passage.[20]

Although they employed a language of universality and "natural rights" to persuade their colleagues that the CRA was in line with republican values, Trumbull and the act's other supporters justified its expansiveness based upon the specific vulnerability of former slaves and other racially marginalized people in the United States. The CRA also instilled agents of the Freedmen's Bureau with federal police powers to arrest any person suspected of violence or intimidation against freedpeople. Senator Jacob Howard of Michigan admonished opponents to the bill for their naïve belief that the Thirteenth Amendment was any real guarantee of freedom. Calling it "mockery emancipation," Howard described the freed slave as "a waif upon the current of time." At the mercy of those who despised him, the enemies of freedom, the freedman suffered from poverty, deprivation, and violence. Invoking once again the stark image of the suffering body, Jacob implored his colleagues in the Senate to understand that the freedman "has nothing that belongs to him on the face of the earth except solely in his naked person." Because of the particular vulnerability of the freedman, Howard believed the government should not "abandon the poor creature we have emancipated."[21]

Jubilee parades, mock-funerals for slavery, the mourning of a fallen president, amending the Constitution—these rituals of redemption put to work notions of atonement, martyrdom, and suffering to advance the causes of Reconstruction and legal reform. This redemptive narrative created a persuasive rationale for institutional change in the weeks and months after the war's official end. Americans answered the war's spiritual challenge of death and violence in both religious and political terms, beginning the process that would transform the state's role in their everyday lives.

Not surprisingly, defeated Confederates did not speak of redemption in the same way their Northern neighbors did. In 1865, redemption was primarily the victors' language. Wallowing in grief, self-pity, and despair, white Southerners found it very difficult to imagine their own redemption as resulting from such degradation and loss. Yet ideas of atonement, suffering, and deliverance also enabled them to makes sense of their devastating and baffling defeat. Like freedpeople, white Southerners compared themselves to the Israelites who endured enslavement and deprivation while awaiting God's deliverance. They saw in the war dead Christ's Passion, a "baptism in blood," that would lead to the perfection of their society. Military defeat became transitory, a trial from God meant to test their faith and resolve in anticipation of their "final triumph." Although they grieved for the loss of their slaves and feared the upending of their way of life, white Southerners could find scraps of encouragement in the redemptive idiom. Just days after Lee's surrender, South Carolinian Emma LeConte wrote in her diary of a sermon that gave her hope. "Dr. Palmer this morning preached a fine and encouraging sermon. He says we must not despair yet, but even if we should be overthrown—not conquered—the next generation would see the South free and independent." In the meantime, they would have to demonstrate their endurance of God's—and the federal government's—chastisement. Southern rituals of redemption included the repatriation of the war dead, the decoration of their graves, and the building of public memorials to the Lost Cause. In time, other rituals would be added to the litany of Southern Redemption.[22]

"A Wilderness of Death"

Even as redemptive language provided a kind of glue that enabled Radical Republicans to keep hold of Reconstruction, there remained considerable ambivalence about these redemptive visions and the violence they portended. As the freedpeople of Charleston enacted their deliverance from slavery, some white missionaries who fancied themselves as overseers of the celebration fretted that a group of black children wanted to sing "We'll Hang Jeff Davis on a Sour Apple Tree," a variation of the popular tune "John Brown's Body."[23] Although their teacher, who was from Massachusetts, had supposedly taught the children this version of the song, the superintendent opposed capital punishment and ordered the teacher and his students not to sing it on parade. Children being children, they did the opposite of what they were told, and sang it so loudly that "no other sound could be heard." The superintendent's opposition to the song most likely stemmed from a number of reasons aside from his moral aversion to capital punishment. The sight of black schoolchildren singing a song of retribution so joyously, so openly, might have alarmed white onlookers. The missionaries' efforts to keep the parade orderly and dignified, a feat that so impressed the *Tribune* correspondent that he felt compelled to comment upon it throughout his report, might be impeached by the raucous celebration of Davis's hanging. It is also possible that the violence embedded within the redemptive narrative of war and emancipation proved too discomfiting. This little controversy hinted at a much larger problem as well—whites' struggle to control not only freedpeople's behavior but also the meaning of freedom.[24]

Although many Americans glorified the war's regenerative purpose, they also felt ill at ease with the violence it unleashed. Ministers preached its righteousness, counseling prospective combatants that it was not immoral to kill another human being in cases where "lawful war calls for the slaying of our country's foes." Billy Yank and Johnny Reb both were holy crusaders in the cause of human liberty, however they defined it. Poets and essayists exalted the soldier's bravery and sentimentalized his sacrifice. In imagery soaked with blood and "patriotic gore," American writers, diarists, and orators created a redemptive war that promised to remake themselves and their nation even if it first required, quite literally, their unmaking. The fervor with which men and women took to war-making might seem astonishing for those lingering under the assumption that Victorian Americans were a restrained and passive bunch. But as Anne Rose points out, Victorians nurtured a deep desire for "vigorous strife" and excitement that enabled them to make war so greatly and so easily. "The mixed attractions and torments of both civilian and army life" caused them to be simultaneously horrified and fascinated by the business of killing.[25]

Their horrified fascination with the war's effects continued into the postwar period. Encouraged by the news media and its sensational reporting of crime and mayhem, many Americans believed they were witnessing the negative effects of the war all around them.²⁶ "Wife-murder, husband-poisoning, fratricide, homicide, parricide, infanticide—in short, every conceivable form of murder"—seemed to be on the rise. Newspapers around the country began printing "calendars of crime" that detailed the state of lawlessness that existed in the usual places, like New York City, as well as formerly quiet locales, like East Saginaw, Michigan, where two young brothers were arrested for murdering the entire Donnelly family over the Canadian border in Ontario. Reformers also noted the increased rates of incarceration for women, not including the most famous female inmate of the century, Surratt. The increase in "female crime" disturbed veteran prison officials, most notably the "tendency to abortion" by women left destitute after their husbands had gone to the army. Having "lapsed from virtue," such women turned to prostitution and desired to "obliterate the evidence of their guilt." But a lack of parental affection and devotion appeared to be a more general problem. Infamous child murders made national headlines with their shocking exposés on the abject cruelty of parents who attempted to starve their children to death in places like Norwich, Connecticut—the heart of old New England. Once believed to be characteristic of the "dangerous classes," these violent behaviors were no longer confined to the lowest strata of society.²⁷

The concern about violent crime, particularly in growing urban areas, predated the war and emancipation, but the tenor of the lamentations in 1865 was different.²⁸ The postwar years seemed to bring about a "universal turmoil of American life, the upturning of everything," which threatened a degree of social discombobulation to rival the war itself. The African American *Christian Recorder* viewed the situation within a millennialist framework and spoke of "an irrepressible feeling of apprehension arising from the comparative frequency of great crimes in our cities and our country at large which is deepened by frequent earthquakes, volcanic eruptions, conflagrations on land and water, and other disasters, unusually destructive of precious human lives." The United States had become a "wilderness of death" from which there was no easy escape.²⁹

Recent studies have concluded that the postwar crime-wave panic was largely unfounded. In fact, large urban areas like New York City experienced a relatively peaceful postwar period. Given the paucity of reliable statistics regarding homicide and other violent crime in the nineteenth century generally, it is difficult to determine with any certainty whether postbellum America experienced any more violent crime than antebellum America. Still, the question remains: why did so many people believe violent crime was on the upswing *everywhere* after the Civil War?³⁰

There are several answers to that question. One is that the methods and frequency of reporting in the news media had changed significantly during the war. Just as the military mobilized hundreds of thousands of men to fight, news agencies also engaged armies of correspondents to follow the war's unfolding both on the battlefield and at home. Perfection of communication technologies such as the telegraph made it possible to transmit news hundreds, even thousands, of miles with the click of a few keys. Sensational reporting, a staple of antebellum journalism, continued to be as much about entertainment and profits for publishers as it ever was, and now it was possible to draw in non-urban readers like never before. Reports of family killings in out-of-the-way places in rural Michigan or New Mexico Territory surely reflected these tendencies even as commentators pondered the implications of such violence for the entire nation. In a sense, stories like these broke down traditional community barriers that separated rural and urban Americans, making violence a shared trait that could defy class and region. Products of new technology and media culture, stories of violence became the foundation for a popular, print-based nationalism.[31]

Although no one could point to a singular cause for what seemed to be a general debasement of human life and its subsequent proliferation in violent crime, most observers agreed that the war exacerbated the violent tendencies within American society. There seemed to be a loss of control; moral barriers had been breached. Social degradation had ensued. Some argued that women's entry into the political realm, specifically their wartime work in soldiers' aid societies and sanitary commissions, had caused them to neglect their duties to the family, and in extreme cases, to murder their own children. Others believed that the great influx of unwashed immigrants into the cities and the US Army had precipitated a rise in crime among demobilized soldiers. If innovations in news reporting could make it *seem* that violence was on the rise, it is little wonder that a country still reeling from a bloody civil war would fear the proliferation of violence outside the boundaries of conventional warfare. The Civil War had, in fact, spilled over into the yards and homes of noncombatants in countless ways. With the lines between battlefield and home front blurred, even obliterated throughout much of the former Confederacy, survivors questioned the long-term effects of "hard war" on civil society.[32]

The official cessation of the conflict provided little reassurance. Reformers worried that demobilized soldiers, scarred by the experience of combat, would find it difficult to readjust to civilian life. Those worries were not unfounded. The army actively "recruited" from the ranks of the incarcerated offering freedom to petty criminals in exchange for military service. Some worried that the army had made soldiers of more violent offenders when the calls for additional manpower increased after the war's first two years. This was a special concern in the South where Confederate provost marshals practically emptied prisons and jails to fill the depleted ranks. The increased violence reported among demobilized soldiers signaled trouble, according to the nation's leading prison officials. They noted that like the Mexican War, the Civil War had produced a "demoralization" that led to drinking, robbery, fighting, and even rape and murder. High rates of morphine addiction (the "soldier's disease") and alcoholism exacerbated the social dislocation of veterans who began to fill prisons north and south.[33]

However, a few more general apprehensions about the militarization of society animated the discourse about returning soldiers. Writing in 1862, Nathaniel Hawthorne frowned upon the increasing militarization of civilian life and the growing power of military leaders. "Military notoriety," Hawthorne feared, "will be the measure of all claims to civil distinction." "One bullet-headed general will succeed another in the Presidential chair," reducing the United States, Hawthorne worried, to a democracy in name only. Hawthorne recoiled at the masses of soldiers he saw lining the streets on a visit to Washington, DC, and wondered, "Will the time ever come again in American, when we may live half a score of years without once seeing the likeness of a soldier, except it be in the festal march of a company on its summer tour? Not in this generation, I fear, nor in the next." Hawthorne may have been motivated by selfishness; he declared that the coming of the war signaled the end of his career, as he had to suspend his "contemplation of certain fantasies" that had been his "harmless custom" before the conflict. He felt that he had lost his audience who were now engrossed in their "violent, but misdirected sympathies" with causes and characters he found uncomfortable. It was an era for Homer, not Hawthorne. His audience now craved "the exhilarating sense of danger—to kill men blamelessly, or to be killed gloriously—and to be happy in following out their native instincts of destruction, precisely in the spirit of Homer's heroes." In his mind, society had regressed to a state of precivilization where his intellectualism had no place. "It is so odd," he wrote, "when we measure our advances from barbarism, and find ourselves just here!"[34]

Echoing Hawthorne's concerns about the potential political leadership of "bullet-headed generals," John G. Nicolay and John Hay, Lincoln's personal secretaries, wondered if "a million men, with arms in their hands, flushed with intoxicating victor, led by officers schooled in battle" would be willing to lay down their weapons "and go to work again at the bidding of a few men in Washington?" With Lincoln dead, Nicolay and Hay questioned if "the tailor from Tennessee," referring to Andrew Johnson, had enough gumption to "direct these myriads of warriors to lay down their arms and melt away into the everyday life of citizens." "Familiarity with deeds of violence and destruction," another report surmised, "leaves its impression after the one is over the and the other disbanded." Some advocated diligent prosecution of soldiers charged with crime and long prison sentences to serve as "a terror" to those men tempted to reject authority and continue in their violent habits. More sentimental reformers worked to obtain medical treatment for imprisoned veterans whose ill health made it difficult for them to obtain steady work—a key factor, they noted, in the men's turn to crime. Regardless of what sympathy there may have been, one thing was clear. Having served "an apprenticeship to the trade of war," the figure of the Civil War veteran could be as menacing as he was valorous.[35]

Despite the public's concern that the war had ruptured the ligaments of individual morality, dissolved fragile social bonds, and empowered militant and despotic men within the central government, Radical Republicans argued that it was a lack of government control rather than an excess of it that threatened the nation's future. Some observers who worried that crime was on the rise reckoned that the criminal justice system, having been neglected for four years of war, had become too soft, failing to exact adequate retribution from those who violated the laws. The *Nation*, the Republican Party's fledgling political magazine, argued that President Johnson's generous Confederate amnesty plan contributed to a debilitating leniency within the criminal justice system. "The wholesale way in which the President and many governors of late have been pardoning criminals," the paper wrote, had made pardoning so fashionable that clergymen everywhere "attach their signatures to petitions for the pardon of anybody who has strong claims on their sympathy." If ex-Confederates, who had brokered treason and civil war, expected pardons for their crimes, so could the average robber, murderer, or any other lawbreaker expect to find someone to take up his cause and win his release from prison based upon "his own professions of sorrow as proof of reformation." These "sham penitents" duped the softhearted and took advantage of lax standards for clemency, giving rise to more violent crime both north and south.[36]

The postwar crime-wave panic suggests some far-reaching social and political implications of wartime violence. In their hand-wringing over a perceived increase in crime, the threats posed by demobilized and demoralized soldiers, and a weakened judicial system, Northerners expressed anxiety about the war's long term effects on everyday social life. They also feared that a highly militarized government might not make the transition to peace very easily. Yet it also appeared that President Johnson could use a lesson in military justice when it came to his haphazard amnesty policy. This tension reflected a society at odds with itself over the role violence played in the formation of a new national identity. The war supposedly "redeemed and regenerated" the country's long history of complicity with and violence in support of slavery, according to one of the foremost authorities on redemptive imagery, Harriet Beecher Stowe. Yet it seemed to have opened up a chasm of violence that might be impossible to close up again. Invoking apocalyptic imagery, Stowe praised the war as the fulfillment of the "prophetic visions of Nat Turner, who saw the leaves drop blood and the land darkened." While it brought comfort to Stowe, this was precisely the kind of redemptive imagery that haunted many postwar Americans.[37]

The Great Crime

The fear that emancipation would unleash a wave of violence in the South animated white Southerners' complaints to army officials in the summer and fall of 1865. From Memphis to Mobile, whites complained of the growing problems of freedom. "Insolence, violent and obscene language, idleness and pilfering are rapidly growing vices among the negro population of the county," wrote a white resident of Pulaski, Tennessee, the same town where the Ku Klux Klan would emerge a few months later. With their labor "no longer organized by the intelligence and capital of [their] master," whites believed freedpeople had fallen victim to their own propensity for vice and crime. Planters complained that freedmen had set up "dram shops," where they made and sold liquor, and drank too much. They perpetrated "all kinds of misdemeanors" such as being drunk, not working, and being disrespectful of whites. That disrespect was exhibited in a variety of ways, including asking for higher wages or time off, refusing to sign a work contract, leaving the plantation altogether, or "talking back" to their employers. Refusal to move off the sidewalk or tip a hat to a white person, as was the custom before emancipation, became yet another sign that freedpeople were quickly becoming uncontrollable. "If some steps are not taken," the white residents of Mecklenberg County, Virginia, wrote to the Bureau's chief in Richmond, "the whites will not be able to live much longer in the County."[38]

As shrill as their cries may seem, federal agents often took white Southerners' complaints that freedmen posed a danger to them seriously. The assistant quartermaster at City Point, Virginia, W. Storer How, drafted a speech to the area's freedpeople advising them of the consequences for being "bad men." Rejoicing in their new status was expected, even encouraged, he said, but "taking revenge on your old masters . . . is wrong." "You are only free from the one unjust law that made you slaves," he wrote, but "all the other laws you must obey . . . The bad men are idle, or steal, or do other wicked things and get punished for breaking the laws." How laid the responsibility for their own protection at the freedmen's feet: "You are free, but your future welfare and prosperity all depend upon how you shall use your Freedom."[39]

Southerners' fear of freedmen was part of a much larger apprehension about the effects of emancipation on social order. To many, the freeing of some four million slaves had raised a troubling question in relation to crime and disorder: had the war and emancipation, in breaking the bonds of slavery, also severed the bonds of morality that had connected individuals with each other and maintained the delicate balance of social relations that, although hierarchical, reflected the "natural" order of things?

Because slavery had been the foundation of the Southern political and social order that allowed all white Americans, especially white workers, to define themselves as "freemen" and citizens against the representations of black slaves, its dissolution produced serious anxiety about how well the bonds of white society could withstand such a momentous rupture. The stock representations of African Americans as shiftless, dishonest, and prone to outbursts of violence so common in antebellum culture continued to inform public perceptions of black life after freedom.[40] Not surprisingly, slavery's old apologists became sirens of impending disaster. Proslavery ideologue George Fitzhugh, writing in *DeBow's Review*, claimed that "all good sensible people, North and South, have always dreaded abolition, more on account of the collisions between the black and white race . . . than for any other reason." Fitzhugh claimed that prior to emancipation, the South enjoyed peace and tranquility in contrast to the urban North where "bloody fights between mobs of whites and blacks were of frequent occurrence." Fitzhugh declared emancipation to be "the great crime" that precipitated all others, and called its architects "fiends in human form" who had unleashed a "war of the races" onto the whole of American society. For decades, proslavery thinkers like Fitzhugh had credited slavery with the South's presumed lack of crime. In some sense, they were right. The mechanisms of control slavery required—the slave patrol, local militias, individual surveillance, and punitive justice for even the most minor offenders—resulted in a discernable lack of popular unrest of the kind that plagued urban areas like Philadelphia and New York City. Moreover, transgressions were often matters of individual honor and settled accordingly outside the realm of the courts. Of course, Fitzhugh did not consider the brutal treatment inflicted upon slaves to be "criminal" in any sense of the word he was familiar with. Nevertheless, the labeling of emancipation as a crime signified the fluidity of meaning surrounding the concept of freedom, a fluidity that would come to have significant implications for the process of Reconstruction.[41]

Although Fitzhugh's flair for exaggeration marked him as a an extremist even among slavery's most ardent apologists, his claims that a "war of races" threatened the United States seemed plausible to a wide audience who also worried about crime and social dislocation. Many Northern whites feared an influx of former slaves over the Mason-Dixon line, not only because of the economic threat thousands of hungry workers might pose to white jobs and wages, but also because of the perceived criminal threat of "contrabands" and free blacks. Democratic politicians had played to these fears in the hope of gaining an advantage against Republicans in the national elections since 1864.[42] Not surprisingly, opponents to Radical Reconstruction resurrected the specter of black violence to warn against the exigencies of emancipation and the inherently violent nature of African Americans. More curiously, some advocates of greater federal oversight in the South used similar arguments to advance the Radicals' agenda.

In October of 1865, a rebellion in Jamaica fueled the old arguments that emancipated blacks posed a danger to society. When black workers marched a police station to protest the unfair jailing of black workers for petty crimes, British troops responded with brutal force that left some 500 black Jamaicans dead. Another 349 were executed later for inciting rebellion. Hundreds more were publicly flogged and given long prison sentences. Not surprisingly, Southern observers responded to the events at Morant Bay with warnings about black savagery. But while Southerners (and most British officials) viewed the violence in Jamaica as evidence that emancipation had failed, Republicans saw it as an example of a failed reconstruction. They used the massacre to demonstrate the exigencies of withholding full citizenship from former slaves and allowing their former masters to oversee the transition from slavery to freedom. Despite these divergent takes on Morant Bay, white Americans in both regions and both parties could agree that postemancipation societies were powder kegs whose fuses must be dampened. Republicans acknowledged an impending race war but argued that it could be avoided by recognizing black "manhood" and giving freedmen the right to vote, hold property, and pursue their own livelihoods.[43] Massachusetts senator Charles Sumner claimed that the United States risked its own Morant Bay—or worse—by leaving the black men of the South unfulfilled and resentful. The danger was in withholding civil rights from former slaves, who Sumner believed would respond accordingly. Although they spoke of "justice" to freedpeople and the dangers of failing to uphold the "national charge" of emancipation, these arguments did not explicitly challenge what Southerners maintained was the "incurable ferocity of negroes." In June 1865, Sumner's fellow abolitionist Richard Henry Dana had addressed a mass meeting in Boston's Faneuil Hall and agreed that plans to give freedpeople the franchise were revolutionary but asked the crowd, "Do you want, some years hence, to see a new revolution?—the poor, oppressed, degraded black man, bearing patiently his oppression until he can endure it no longer, rising with arms for his rights?" While Republican observers hesitated to use Morant Bay to impugn the character of Jamaican blacks, they nonetheless exhibited a growing unease about the state of affairs in the South and the likelihood that blacks would respond violently if left unsupervised.[44]

Freedpeople were Southerners, too. That fact threatened Republicans' emancipatory visions of African American life. Carl Schurz expressed his apprehension of black violence on his tour of the South shortly after the war. Although he was convinced that "the negro, in his ordinary state, is docile and good-natured," he feared that "once engaged in a bloody business" his "hot impulses" might override everything else.[45] In its discussion of a duel between two freedmen near Savannah, Georgia, *Harper's Weekly* lamented the "renewed degradation of manhood" that accompanied emancipation. In an illustration, well-dressed black gentlemen gather for an afternoon's delight in the South's favorite pastime (fig. 1.2). The men's clothing denotes their rise in social and economic class, but their participation in the duel suggests the poverty of their moral education. These freedmen enact violent social rituals as if they were badges of freedom.

Republicans were just as concerned with containing black freedom as they were protecting black lives in the South. The fear of slave rebellion that gripped white Americans for at least two centuries instructed Republican lawmakers that federal intervention in the South was necessary to protect whites as well as blacks. The old specter of Saint-Domingue and more recent reports of violence from Jamaica sparked concerns that the American South also might be on the verge of an uprising. Furthermore, racist ideas about black criminality exploded after emancipation, not only among white Southerners but whites in the North as well, setting

RECONSTRUCTION AS REDEMPTION

FIGURE 1.2 "Black Men Duel near Savannah." *Harper's Weekly*, June 27, 1868.

the stage for the South's Redemption in the mid-1870s. By then, events in the former Confederacy seemed to prove that freedom had been the "great crime" that George Fitzhugh claimed.[46]

While the language of redemption helped assuage the grief, uncertainty, and guilt many Americans felt surrounding the war and emancipation, leading lawmakers to pass the nation's first civil rights legislation, there remained a troubling ambivalence about the growing power of the federal government as well as some uncertainty about ex-slaves' peaceful incorporation into the nation. A growing concern about reestablishing social order, not only in the South but also throughout the country, cast an ominous cloud over the joyous emancipation celebrations that marked the end of the war. In this context, the idea of redemptive suffering could circumscribe rather than enhance former slaves' quest for freedom. As the question of what freedpeople were to be redeemed from—white violence or themselves—began to circulate among those in charge of overseeing the transition from slavery to freedom, the prospects for federal intervention to protect freedpeople diminished. Thus, even at the moment when the nation appeared to be most sympathetic to the plight of freedpeople, the process of nation building and the imperatives of economic reconstruction compromised that sympathy.

TWO

The Politics of Suffering

"When danger or pain press too nearly, they are incapable of giving any delight, and are simply terrible; but at certain distances, and with certain modifications, they may be, and they are delightful." EDMUND BURKE, 1757[1]

"Suffering may result from this course to some extent, but suffering is preferable to slavery, and is to some degree the necessary consequence of events." GEN. OLIVER OTIS HOWARD, COMMISSIONER OF THE BUREAU OF REFUGEES, FREEDMEN, AND ABANDONED LANDS, 1865[2]

"We want these freedmen protected . . . Let the men of the rebel States realize the condition of affairs and accept the adjustment that gives security to man and property." REP. HENRY WILSON (R-IOWA) IN SUPPORT OF THE FREEDMEN'S BUREAU ACT, 1866[3]

"In an instant the man vanished and the slave appeared." This declaration punctuates a pivotal scene in Louisa May Alcott's 1863 short story "My Contraband." After seeing a slave's physical wounds up close, Alcott's fictional alter ego, Claire Dane, confronts the reality of slavery and her own ideas about a slave's humanity. Based upon Alcott's time as a Union Army nurse, the story follows Nurse Dane and Robert, the contraband working as her orderly. Upon first being "given" Robert by the hospital's commander, Dane finds him sitting in silence, apparently daydreaming and unaware she is watching him. She finds herself inexplicably attracted to the man, "a fine mulatto fellow," whose physical features from a distance elicit the dutiful nurse's womanly admiration. "He was more quadroon than mulatto," Dane observes, "with Saxon features, Spanish com-

plexion, darkened by exposure, color in lips and cheek, waving hair . . . "
Obviously enamored by his pleasing near-white physical features, Dane insists that her interest is also drawn to "an eye full of the passionate melancholy which in such men always seems to utter a mute protest against the broken law that doomed them at their birth. What could he be thinking of?" Watching the man deep in his own thoughts, Dane imagines a number of different scenarios: that he is brooding over some "deep wrong or sorrow"; or perhaps mourning over his dead master "to whom he had been faithful to the end"; or that he missed a loved one still held in bondage. From a distance, Robert fulfills all of Dane's romantic abolitionist fantasies.

Those fantasies quickly evaporate. Overcome by her desire "to know and comfort him," Dane touches Robert on his shoulder to rouse him from this thoughts only to see the "ghastly wound" that had left its mark across his check and forehead. "Being partly healed, it was no longer bandaged, but held together with strips of that transparent plaster which I never see without a shiver and swift recollections of the scenes with which it is associated in my mind," Dane reports, her fascination turning to disgust. Confronted with the gruesome physical evidence of Robert's subservience and inequality, Dane can no longer imagine the man in the heroic manner that she had seconds before. Instead, Robert represents "a far more striking type of human suffering" that reduces him to an object of pity rather than admiration. Dane, too, is transformed. No longer the icon of selfless sacrifice, the army nurse embodies all that she believed she stood against. "By one of those inexplicable processes that often teach us how little we understand ourselves," Dane muses, "my purpose was suddenly changed, and though I went in to offer comfort as a friend, I merely gave an order as a mistress."[4]

Like many Civil War–era representations of black suffering, *My Contraband* highlights the problematic nature of white sympathy and calls to mind Edmund Burke's observations about how we tend to view the pain and suffering of others. At a certain physical and intellectual distance, it can be *sublime*—a source of pleasure, amusement, and self-absorption. The images of the suffering slave that had fed Nurse Dane's own sense of self as an abolitionist and war worker, however, cannot withstand the horror of Robert's wounds. Up close, the scars disrupt the romantic narrative Dane had created about herself and her relationship to Robert. Similarly, when reformers, lawmakers, and army officials confronted contrabands up close as they began to pour over Union lines in great numbers, they often found ex-slaves' behavior and appearance appalling. In order to redeem them from the legacy of slavery, white reformers embarked upon a civilizing mission that stressed the importance of discipline, and at times, even suffering, as a necessary condition of freedom.[5]

The impulse to discipline freedpeople, command their labor, and order their social existence rubbed painfully against the protective impulse to shelter them against cruelty and abuse. Although free labor advocates denounced physical compulsion, it remained an integral part of the civilizing process that followed emancipation. Missionaries, government agents, and planters were united in their efforts to discipline freedpeople and correct their presumed misunderstandings regarding freedom, labor, and politics. While Northern emissaries of democracy and free labor saw their project as one guided by enlightened benevolence aimed at making the slave into a good citizen, theirs was a mission steeped in violence both brutal and "tender." The languages of free labor, dependency, and manhood, which treated freedpeople as targets of civilization and reform, made such violence seem natural, necessary, and legitimate—all in the name of protecting freedpeople not only from racial prejudice, but more importantly, from themselves. Frederick Douglass recognized this paradox in 1881 when he looked back on Reconstruction and considered its shortcomings. "In the hurry and confusion of the hour, and the eager desire to have the Union restored," Douglass told a crowd gathered in Elmira, New York, that August to celebrate the anniversary of West Indian emancipation, "there was more care for the sublime super-structure of the Republic" than for the well-being of former slaves. Although freedpeople could no longer be bought and sold, whites retained the "power to starve them to death." The language of freedom and redemption softened the raw power Douglass pointed to, and its "misrecognition" remains one of the most troubling aspects of Reconstruction.[6]

Despite the recent attention it has received from Civil War historians, important questions remain about the politics of suffering in the age of slave emancipation: Whose suffering mattered and why? How were certain types of suffering politicized? What meanings did Civil War–era Americans derive from their suffering and the suffering of others?[7] These questions interrogate the troubling role black suffering has played in the "great American tragedy" of slavery and the Civil War. As literary critic Elizabeth Spelman advises, it is important for us to reflect on the way suffering grabs our attention and the lessons it presumes to tell. Not only do we tend to create hierarchies of suffering that rank some people's suffering more tragic and therefore more worthy of our grief than others, Spelman argues that the compassion images of suffering invite can reinforce relationships and systems of domination and submission. Instead of relieving or ending pain, the proliferation of such images and narratives can numb us to the pain of others, making us emotional voyeurs who derive pleasure from others' pain as it becomes self-referential. Saidiya Hartman also cautions us against the "prurience" that is bound up with historical representations of black suffering. The highly sexualized images of pain and torture that animated the antislavery movement of the nineteenth century coldly objectified the bodies of enslaved people, creating a "benumbing spectacle" that could serve to titillate white audiences while alerting them to the horrors of slavery. Furthermore, whites' recognition that blacks could feel both physical and emotional pain (a question up for much debate before antislavery images of slave suffering), opened up new possibilities for racial oppression. As Hartman asks, "What if the presumed endowments of man—conscience, sentiment, and reason—rather than assuring liberty or negating slavery acted to yoke slavery and freedom? Or, what if the heart, the soul, and the mind were simply the inroads of discipline rather than that which confirmed the crime of slavery and proved that blacks were men and brothers?"[8]

The reforming impulse guided both the antislavery movement and the post–Civil War efforts to establish a contractual system of free labor governed by consent instead of force. It also shaped the legal codification of a notion of civil rights belonging to all citizens regardless of color, but ideas of reform remained wedded to racialized notions of suffering that often devalued blacks' experience of pain and violence both in slavery and afterward. Despite the language of protection that animated the passage of postemancipation civil rights legislation and the establishment of social welfare organizations such as the Freedmen's Bureau, the need to discipline freedpeople's bodies in order to make them labor in Southern fields formed a bridge that linked the antebellum and postbellum worlds. In both eras, images of beaten, raped, and terrorized black bodies formed a spectacle of violence that both demanded white sympathy and reinforced the social distance between those empowered middle-class and elite whites at whom such images were targeted and the objects of their pity, thus compromising the promise of redemption on which Radical Reconstruction was built.

Emancipating the Suffering Slave

Ideas of black suffering played an important role in the abolition of slavery and the formation of a theory of human rights in the midnineteenth century. According to historian Elizabeth Clark, images of slave suffering "took on a revolutionary quality" as abolitionists used them to invoke feelings of sympathy among white audiences, breaking down racial prejudices that held black slaves were incapable of feeling pain. Abolitionists set out to document with irrefutable proof the horrors of personal violence through engravings of slavery's "instruments"—shackles, chains, whips, collars, and firsthand testimony of visitors to the South and the autobiographies of former slaves. Abolitionist literature confronted people both visually and rhetorically with the hope of igniting the fires of moral outrage, indignation, and sympathy within their hearts. To a great extent, they succeeded. The antislavery movement in the United States fomented a "reinterpretation of human pain" that distinguished between "unavoidable" suffering, such as sickness and disease, and intentional cruelty, of which slavery became the most horrific example. The sentiment of protection that arose out of this growing aversion to cruelty and avoidable suffering not only galvanized the antislavery movement but also laid the groundwork for an eventual legal revolution in human rights during Reconstruction.[9]

Images of black suffering continued to play an important role in the politics of Reconstruction. As their abolitionist predecessors did before them, Radical Republicans cultivated images of black suffering in the hope of rallying popular support for their political platforms. With the help of the pictorial press, namely the Republican favorite *Harper's Weekly*, they developed an iconography of Reconstruction to help readers understand the magnitude of the Southern hatred of freedpeople and their unrepentant natures. *Harper's* led a reinvigorated attack on Southern violence against freedpeople through its publication of images that depicted violated black bodies broken and mutilated by vengeful Southern whites. The editors of *Harper's* saw themselves and their publication as part of the nineteenth century's larger reform mission, and their images of freedpeople's suffering nurtured the protectionist sentiment and helped Radical Republicans denounce President Andrew Johnson and his plans for a quick restoration, place the South under military supervision, and pass the nation's first civil rights legislation.[10]

Thomas Nast, the nation's leading political cartoonist and engraver, became the paper's most valuable artistic asset. A pioneer of the politics of the "bloody shirt," Nast employed images of violence and violated black bodies to draw a sharp contrast between slavery and freedom. Nast's iconography tapped into a sentimental tradition that employed pain and suffering to demonstrate the government's failure to live up to its obligation of protection. Like his 1863 engraving "Emancipation," which linked the past of slavery with the future of freedom in violent

THE POLITICS OF SUFFERING

FIGURE 2.1 "Slavery Is Dead (?)" *Harper's Weekly*, January 12, 1867.

terms, Nast reminded his audience on emancipation's four-year anniversary that freedpeople were still at risk for cruelty and violence. In an engraving entitled "Slavery Is Dead (?)" (fig. 2.1), Nast exposed the naïveté of those who presumed the war's end meant an end to servitude and violence. Once again blurring the lines between past and present, Nash depicts slavery's violent legacy as alive and well in the Reconstruction South by illustrating newspaper reports of men being sold and whipped for punishment for alleged crimes. The sadistic Legree-like character reappears with whip in hand as white men from both classes (symbolized by their headwear) watch in delight. In the picture on the left, Justice shares a sympathetic look with the black man being sold but can do no more. Maryland's Black Codes have incapacitated her. Justice is blindfolded in the second image, where the stripped freedman stifles his own screams. Nast's trademark sarcasm comes through in the two inscriptions in the lower corners of the frame: "Land of the Free" and "Home of the Brave."

While "Slavery Is Dead (?)" drew on familiar antislavery images, other Nash engravings utilized different motifs while maintaining the focus on black suffering. In the hard-hitting caricature style that would become Nast's signature, the illustrator sharpened his pencil on President Johnson as he battled Radicals for control over Reconstruction. "Andrew

CHAPTER TWO

FIGURE 2.2 Playing Iago to America's Othello: A wounded black Union veteran. *Harper's Weekly*, September 1, 1866.

Johnson's Reconstruction and How It Works" (fig. 2.2) clothed Johnson in Elizabethan dress as Shakespeare's Iago goading Othello, a black Union veteran, into abandoning his desire for civil and political rights. The veteran's bandaged arm symbolizes the sacrifice black soldiers had made on the battlefield and makes Johnson's duplicity all the more reprehensible. This central image is flanked on either side by images of the recent riots in Memphis and New Orleans, where freedpeople were shot, beaten, and burned out of their homes. Again, Nast chose to insert a historical reminder of slavery's recent past and its continuing influence. At the top of the picture rests a box portraying the slave market and the whipping post with the caption "Southern rights" meant to chide Johnson and his policy of amnesty with a full restoration of ex-Confederates political rights.

THE POLITICS OF SUFFERING

FIGURE 2.3 "The Virginia Elections." *Harper's Weekly*, August 19, 1865.

Black bodies in pain represented some of the most potent images of postwar American political culture. Just as it had been emblematic of slavery, whipping remained an important motif in the iconography of Reconstruction, a rallying point for the Republican Party. For Congressional Republicans facing a monumental struggle to control the war's meaning, whipping represented the best evidence of Southerners' unreconstructed spirits. On both the local and national levels, whipping provided Republicans with an image of a violent, dangerous South that continued to threaten their goals of national redemption and reunification. An illustration entitled "The Virginia Elections" (fig. 2.3), published in August 1865 in *Harper's Weekly*, shows Johnson's gullibility in offering amnesty to former Confederates. With a whip protruding from his pocket, a sulking Southerner stands on the Thirteenth Amendment as well as his pardon, while another ex-Confederate whips a freedman in the background.

CHAPTER TWO

FIGURE 2.4 "Whipping a Negro Girl." *Harper's Weekly*, September 14, 1867.

As the 1868 presidential election approached, Republican papers painted Democrats as members of the party of "tyranny and despotism" who would "go back if they could to the local statutes of the South which authorized the sale of men on the auction block; which punished with the lash, at the whipping post, men, women and children; and imprisoned any who dared to teach the colored man to read the scriptures." During the fall congressional elections in 1867, *Harper's* ran a lithograph of a freedwoman being whipped by a crowd of jeering "unreconstructed Johnsonians," whose obvious delight in her suffering symbolized the failure of presidential Reconstruction (fig. 2.4). Repeating the familiar flogging motif that had played such a prominent role in the antislavery campaign, Radical Republicans used images of beaten black bodies to communicate an important political message to white audiences.[11]

The meanings Northern politicians invested in whipping recognized the invaluable cultural currency the act held for former slaveholders. According to Josiah Millard, an Internal Revenue assessor in Loudon County, Virginia, "the point of mortification" among his white neighbors was that they could no longer lawfully whip black people. He had seen whites "performing it [whipping] as if it were a luxury," and they detested being deprived of it as they did good whiskey, fine cloth, or three meats at Sunday dinner. As an emblem of mastery, the whip enabled former slaveholders to reenact scenes of submission that rebuked slavery's destruction. Through their performance of this ritualized violence, white Southerners attempted to reinscribe the pain of racial inferiority onto the bodies of their former bondsmen and women. Although they could no longer claim to be legal proprietors of black bodies, whites still maintained their right to control and brutalize them.[12]

White Southerners insisted that the lash was necessary for social order and scoffed at Northern criticism that called it a "relic of barbarism." A North Carolina planter warned a local teacher against coddling the "lazy niggers" he believed would not work without physical inducement. "You had better whip them and send them to work instead of giving them clothing," he said. Without the lash, the planter warned, freedpeople would be ungovernable. "None of you don't know how to manage and treat the niggers," he exclaimed. "We can teach you that!" During presidential Reconstruction, provisional Southern state governments passed new Black Codes, many of which allowed flogging as punishment for most petty crimes, such as larceny. Florida went the furthest, prescribing a set number of stripes (thirty-nine) as an "alternative punishment" to fine or imprisonment to be determined at the jury's discretion. Likewise, South Carolina allowed local courts to choose corporal punishment among a number of penalties. Most commonly, stripes could be substituted for fines in cases where fines (usually five dollars or more) could not be paid. Needless to say, freedpeople, who were cash poor, could not buy their way out of a whipping. In Virginia, local magistrates administered "whippings by consent" where a freedperson charged with a petty crime could choose to take a whipping in lieu of a trial, which could take months, and in the meantime the accused would be kept in jail. The Black Codes also maintained an employer's right to "moderately chastise" his or her underage apprentices.[13]

While some state codes were "colorblind" in making stripes a lawful punishment for both blacks and whites, others reserved corporal punishment exclusively for freedpeople. As they hashed out the details of their new postwar penal code, the South Carolina legislature expressly stated, "No punishment more degrading than imprisonment shall be imposed on a white person for a crime not infamous." ("Infamous" crimes included rape and murder). Although the Virginia legislature amended their laws so that its language was colorblind, in reality very few white men were lashed, and when they were, according to one Freedmen's Bureau agent in Albermarle, the whip barely touched their backs. In fact, public whippings helped white Southerners recreate their tattered communities through ritualized brutality that prefigured the lynching spectacles of the future. In Raleigh, North Carolina, witnesses reported crowds as large as 500 gathering outside the courthouse to see black convicts lashed in the public square and then "sold at auction" for three-year periods. These daily gatherings, which recreated iconic scenes of slavery, allowed large numbers of white North Carolinians to witness the physical subordination of the newly freed and through "exultant" revelry be elevated themselves. As it had done before emancipation, whipping helped reestablish the South's racial hierarchy after the war.[14]

However, whipping also symbolized the national commitment to white supremacy. Whipping marked—quite literally—the unfree, marginalized, and disenfranchised in a dialectical performance of domination and submission that had become increasingly problematic in the decades leading up to the Civil War. In the first half of the nineteenth century, reformers committed to ending corporal punishment in schools, prisons, and the navy protested against flogging not simply because it was cruel but also because it was emblematic of slavery, and thus, racial degradation. That it was a staple in American institutions, namely schools and the navy, threatened to shatter the thin façade of white unity that masked deep rifts in American society.

In the debates over flogging in the navy in the early 1850s, the problem of corporal punishment became increasingly sectionalized as well as racialized. With Northern lawmakers unanimously opposed to flogging, and Southerners almost unanimous in favor of its continuation (two border-state senators from Missouri and Kentucky would eventually side with the antiflogging contingent), the debate in late September 1850 rekindled sectional animosities that had driven the contentious arguments over the Fugitive Slave Act and Kansas-Nebraska Act just a few weeks earlier. The question of flogging allowed Congress to take up once again the issue of the Slave Power and denounce its influence on American institutions. New Hampshire senator John Parker Hale, the first US senator elected on an antislavery ticket, introduced the bill to abolish flogging aboard naval ships. Still reeling from defeat in their efforts to keep slavery out of the western territories ceded from Mexico and the strengthening of the federal fugitive slave law, Hale and his colleagues turned their attention to flogging. "We have been engaged now nearly the whole session for interests of another character, and for those that are subjected to a discipline of another kind," announced Hale as brought the issue up for a

FIGURE 2.5 Whipping symbolized the South's dominance of national politics in the 1850s. "The Democratic Platform Illustrated" (1856) equates South Carolina Representative Preston Brooks's infamous caning of Massachusetts Senator Charles Sumner, on the left, with the slaveholder's domination of his slaves with a whip, on the right. Courtesy Library of Congress.

vote on September 28. "I do ask that, when we have done so much to heal the 'bleeding wounds' of a violated Constitution," Hale said, mocking Southerners' previous arguments that banning slavery in the territories violated constitutional protections of private property, "the Senate of the United States will not consent that the bleeding wounds of the lacerated backs of the white citizens of this republic shall be longer submitted to this brutalizing punishment." For Hale, flogging represented a debasement of Americans' racial and civic identity. Similarly, senator Robert F. Stockton of New Jersey, himself a former naval captain who sang the heroic praises of American sailors, reduced the issue to a question of race. Would the sailor "be entitled to all his rights as an American citizen" or "whether, freeman as he is, shall be scourged like a slave?" Stockton allowed that lashing might be a suitable punishment for the Southern slave "when he deserves it," but maintained that it was too degrading for white sailors on American ships.[15]

Thus, it was not physical cruelty or pain, per se, that galvanized the antiflogging movement in the early nineteenth century. Because of its close connection with slavery, whipping compromised a recipient's racial status, thereby threatening the myth of white men's unity in the North. If white men could be whipped, then the subjugation of African Americans, on which the foundations of white republicanism rested, became less meaningful. For poor and working-class white men, the navy "tars," and other petty criminals who found themselves tied to the pillory, their whiteness could not shield them from the sting of the lash.[16]

The universalizing language of cruelty and humane treatment obscured the racialization of corporal punishment. For instance, prison reformers who decried the use of the lash against white prisoners admitted it might be the only punishment for "depraved and abandoned" black prisoners. At Sing Sing, reformers noted that black prisoners "from the stews and brothels of our large cities" were "lost to all sense of shame and impervious to all good impressions." No religious training or appeals to their conscience seemed to work. The New York State Senate issued a report on female prisoners that found black female inmates incorrigible and permitted the use of whipping, straitjackets, and gags on them. What constituted cruelty to whites appeared to be the only viable option for restraining and reforming African Americans. While white suffering was to be avoided, black suffering was welcomed.[17]

Despite the focus on black whipping instead of white, the postwar movement against corporal punishment also resulted from mixed motivations. While many observers were clearly concerned with improving the quality of life for Southern blacks, others were more troubled by the blatant challenge to federal authority that whipping and other forms of violence posed. This was a prominent concern for the Joint Committee on Reconstruction (JCR), which convened late in 1865 to determine the proper course Congress should take with regard to the former Confederacy. The Committee called hundreds of witnesses, the overwhelming majority of whom were white, who detailed not only the mistreatment of freedpeople but also the persecution of white Unionists and federal agents. Witnesses reported brazen attacks on army officers and Freedmen's Bureau agents as signs that that hostility toward the federal government was as fresh in 1866 as it had been in 1861. As the only law enforcement in the backcountry areas, US soldiers performed a dangerous duty. Local bands of "late rebel soldiers" targeted Union officers and soldiers, and their actions met with tacit approval if not outright applause from their neighbors.

In October 1865, a group of local men killed three Union soldiers who were guarding a fifteen bales of confiscated cotton at Brown's Ferry on the Savannah River, on the border between South Carolina and Georgia. One of the men, Crawford Keyes, claimed ownership of the cotton, and liberating it was the pretense for the midnight raid that claimed the soldiers' lives. However, the group's actions called their motive into question. A witness claimed to have heard Keyes and his men announce to the soldiers, "God damn you, we have come to throw you in the river" as they approached the young privates. The next morning, the soldiers' bodies were found floating in the river. All three had been shot in the head. The men's hair was burned around the wounds, suggesting that they had been executed rather than killed in a skirmish. Their horses, arms, and ammunition had been stolen, but most important, the cotton that Keyes claimed to have been liberating, was left undisturbed. Army officials reported similar incidents across the South. A former Union scout was ambushed and murdered near Goldsborough, North Carolina, after he assisted federal soldiers in arresting local men wanted for robbery and murder. When a Pitt County, North Carolina, man accused of "outrages on freedmen and Union men," including several murders, shot an army lieutenant as he attempted to arrest the suspect, no one gave the dying officer and his comrades shelter or treatment. Neighbors refused the wounded man admittance to their houses. The lieutenant's men were forced to transport him several miles back to town, where he died four days later. Dexter Clapp, the Freedmen's Bureau agent who reported this incident, cautioned against the belief that local people were afraid to help the lieutenant because of the threat of retribution from the person responsible. He believed that excuse was "exaggerated" and that it was equally the case that local citizens were disinclined to assist the government because they wanted to mock it and drive out federal agents. Maj. Gen. George Thomas, stationed in Tennesssee, concurred with Clapp. "There is no doubt but what there is a universal disposition among the rebels in the south," he informed his committee, "to embarrass the government in its administration, if they can, so as to gain as many advantages for themselves as possible."[18]

To the extent that white violence against Southern blacks embarrassed the federal government by highlighting its inability to rein in the rebelliousness of ex-Confederates, black suffering became a centerpiece in the struggle over Reconstruction waged by Radical Republicans against

President Johnson and the more conservative wing of their party. Even at the nadir of national outrage over Southern violence in the summer of 1866, after the Memphis and New Orleans riots, the primary focus was not on the brutal treatment of freedpeople but rather on the precariousness of federal authority and the threat of general social disorder. The national press referred to both events as "massacres" that were "inconceivably brutal," but according to the *Nation*, "brutality was, after all, not the most remarkable thing about it." The "most novel and striking" aspect of the violence in both cities "was that the police headed the butchery." Because "the sworn guardians of the public peace" appeared to have planned and carried out organized violence against civilians and the national government, the riots looked like a renewed rebellion. The committee investigating the Memphis riots was shocked to learn that the white mob included some two hundred deputized members of a "posse comitatus" that was "under the protection and guidance of official authority." The mob targeted their aggression first at black soldiers stationed at nearby Fort Pickering but soon focused their attacks against the whole of black Memphis. The committee discounted the "great efforts . . . made by the citizens to belittle [the violence] into a simple row between some discharged negro soldiers and the Irish police." It was not a "nigger riot," as the conservative Memphis press alleged, but rather a "well-appointed thing" that the police and city officials "had been working on . . . for a long time."[19]

The same was true in New Orleans, where the murder of Rev. Jotham Horton—a white New Orleans Republican and leader of the ad hoc convention that had gathered to discuss the adoption of the new state constitution—became symbolic of the threat of organized Southern violence posed to the nation-state. According to eyewitness accounts, when white rioters overran the Mechanics' Hall where the convention met, the unarmed Horton attempted to surrender to the mob. Witnesses remembered him descending the building's staircase and announcing to the crowd that he was unarmed only to be gunned down in cold blood. The illustrator for the *Harper's* re-creation of Horton's death scene (fig. 2.6) gave Horton an American flag to dramatize the moment further and suggest that the killers attacked not just an individual but rather the entire nation.

"Yet where does the slave stand in relation to the violence inflicted by white men on white men . . . ?" asks critic Marcus Wood in his study of antislavery imagery. The same question can be asked Reconstruction-era images of black bodies in pain. As Wood notes, images of the suffering slave asked white audiences to consider the degradation of white society

FIGURE 2.6 Murder of Rev. Horton at New Orleans—an attack on the nation. *Harper's Weekly*, August 25, 1866.

and the harm slavery inflicted on white sensibility rather than simply opening white hearts to the pain that freedpeople endured. In 1866, the terrible assaults on freedpeople in Memphis and New Orleans represented the renewed threat of war and the dissolution of white Americans' fragile Union. Insofar as images of black suffering reflected this fear, then those images contained a powerful emotive force. However, nothing was said of the trauma, grief, and dislocations that white violence inflicted on black victims and their families. Thus, it was not black pain alone that galvanized the antislavery movement or the first civil rights movement after the war but rather the total "melodramatic fantasy" that presented the suffering slave as an imaginative vehicle for white moral and social transformation.[20]

Although Radicals' victory over President Johnson and the advent of Radical Reconstruction suggests that images of black suffering were influential in convincing the nation that more stringent measures were needed to bring recalcitrant ex-Confederates to heel, the proliferation of such images also could undermine the cause of civil rights. The history of the visual representations of African Americans in the eighteenth and nineteenth centuries is one of intense objectification, where black bodies became templates for a myriad of object lessons for white audiences. Stripped of individuality and agency, black characters in antislavery representations were presented as passive recipients of either white brutality or benevolence. Even in the new medium of photography, which allowed white audiences to see flesh-and-blood black bodies instead of artistic fascimiles of them in engravings or lithographs, their objectification remained constant, rendering the meanings contained within the images unstable.[21]

The political commodification of black bodies in pain that resulted from the Radical Republican campaign to defeat presidential Reconstruction and later to elect Ulysses S. Grant as president in 1868, depersonalized freedpeople's suffering, creating stock images that could be used interchangeably. The white discourse surrounding Southern violence in this period objectified freedpeople and their suffering, making them into examples of the dangers of Democratic electoral victories. "One Vote Less," another Nast engraving (fig. 2.7), depicts the murdered body of a black man strewn across rubble that by the inscriptions on the rocks represents the Democratic presidential platform of that year. Acting as his headstone, the rocks are inscribed with the words "Negro Killed," "Seymour," and "Ratification" (referring to Democratic presidential candidate Horatio Seymour's opposition to the Thirteenth and Fourteenth Amendments), and "KKK" (Ku Klux Klan). With the bullet wound in the murdered man's forehead visible, the viewer is meant to associate the freedman's death with Democratic opposition to Radical intervention in the South and Democrats' tacit approval of Klan vigilantism, which resulted in the freedman's murder. The barren landscape suggests that a Seymour presidency would leave the South in total ruin.

Depersonified and disempowered, the dead freedman represents a national political crisis created and controlled by whites. White sympathy seemed to require black passivity. The Joint Committee and other congressional investigating bodies severely limited freedpeople's participation in the construction of the postwar narrative of Southern violence. When the JCR convened in Washington in December 1865, it failed to call a single black witness. Fortunately, a black convention met in nearby

FIGURE 2.7 "One Vote Less." *Harper's Weekly*, August 8, 1868.

Alexandria, Virginia, at the same time, and seven representatives presented themselves to the committee to testify. Of the 144 witnesses deposed, these were the only black voices heard by Congress at this critical moment in the debates over Reconstruction. Later hearings into the Ku Klux Klan's activities and other violent outbreaks in the South called more black witnesses; however, when allowed to testify to their own experiences, Southern blacks did so only within very tight parameters set by the congressional investigating committees, who often made it clear that they found black voices unrealiable or even unbelievable. As Hannah Rosen notes in her study of black women's testimony to Congress in this period about the sexual violence they experienced, investigators routinely impugned the women's virtue, reputations, and truthfulness. Although African Americans challenged the presumption that they were prostitutes or had somehow invited their assaults, the tone of the questioning remained hostile to their claims of abuse. Presumptions about black women's "depravity" and black criminality undermined freedpeople's ability to claim protection from the federal government, which became increasingly difficult to do as time went on. In other words, so long as white lawmakers and politicians could control the meaning of black suffering, then such images were useful. As it became more difficult to maintain this control, they relied on them less as a marker of the South's reconstruction.[22]

The larger cultural context within which white audiences, including congressional investigating committees, received images and testimony of black suffering shaped their responses to it. Perhaps even a "pornographic impulse" guided white representations of black suffering, which would further complicate the political usefulness of such images. Representations of black men and women whipped, tied up, and held down formed a critical yet conflicted motif within antislavery and Reconstruction-era propaganda. The sexualized nature of many Reconstruction-era assaults increased the potential for white male audiences in Congress to find these images and narratives pleasing at some level, even as they disavowed the behavior of their Southern counterparts. The possibility of white titillation underlying protestations of "outrage" at black victimization calls into question the popularity of these images in both the antebellum and postwar periods and their function on the American political landscape. Sexual voyeurism may also help explain the fleeting utility the images had with regard to securing long-term guarantees of civil rights protections for African Americans. Images such as "Whipping a Negro Girl" (fig. 2.4) conjured up a number of possible meanings, including latent beliefs about black women's sexual availability, their illicit relationships with white men, and their unfitness for freedom and citizenship.[23]

The proliferation of images of black suffering also risked normalizing the very thing Republicans claimed they wanted to stop. At what point would the Northern public become immunized to the horrors of Southern violence? Might these images be read as evidence of freedpeople's unfitness for freedom, or of the inevitability of violent racial conflict? Would white "home rule" then be understood as the only viable alternative to an internecine race war? President Grant's infamous response to Republican governor Adelbert Ames's continual request for federal troops to combat white paramilitaries in Mississippi gives some indication of the unreliability of white sympathy for black suffering. "The whole public are tired of these annual autumnal outbreaks in the South," Grant proclaimed in September 1875 when Mississippi verged on collapse. In less than a decade, the images of black suffering had lost their shock value.

With their ability to elicit outrage in white audiences gone, only boredom, frustration, and disillusionment remained.[24]

Furthermore, representations of extreme violence could also increase the imaginative distance between audience and subject, as few Northern whites at whom such images were aimed could imagine facing such physical insecurity themselves. Like many antislavery narratives of the suffering slave, postwar narratives of the suffering freedman focused on the particular helplessness of freed slaves and their dependency on the federal government. The physical pain freedpeople suffered could separate them from the audience instead of drawing them closer together, thereby disrupting the process of identification necessary for sympathy and compassion to emerge within the hearts of the white audience. Scenes of black victimization and submission could also reinforce ideas of racial hierarchy among whites. As Kathleen Brown observes in her study of cleanliness in early America, the black body historically represented dirtiness, disease, and disgust in an age when cleanliness and purity became markers of civilization and citizenship. The scars freedpeople bore on their bodies marked their dependency and inequality in ways that conflicted with the redemptive promise of Reconstruction.[25]

The pity that images of black suffering might arouse proved an unstable foundation on which to build a new world of freedom. "I sympathize with the negroes natural condition," wrote one white Southerner in the wake of emancipation. "I believe that God Almighty designed him as an object of pity. He can only bring on himself the ill will of Southern white men by unreasonable demands." Yet if pity could mediate white violence in the South, it brought out a latent disgust among Northern whites. Like Nurse Dane in Alcott's short story, white audiences viewed black suffering in relation to white suffering, and while Dane steadied herself to care for white soldiers' ghastly war wounds, the sight of Robert's unhealed scar made her sick. In either case, pity and citizenship were incompatible.[26]

Suffering Freedom

In June 1865, Capt. Charles Soule, the Freedmen's Bureau agent in Orangeburg, South Carolina, called the freedpeople in his district together to "disabuse" them of the "false and exaggerated ideas of freedom" they seemed to possess. "You are talking too much; waiting too much; asking for too much," Soule admonished. Irritated by the fact that freedpeople demanded shorter workdays, provisions of food and clothing, as well as shelter and medical care, Soule warned them that deprivation and suffering were inevitable. Freedom, in fact, might be worse than slavery, at least for a while. He endeavored to explain to the crowd the difference between slavery and freedom as he understood it:

> You are now free, but you must know that the only difference you can feel yet, between slavery and freedom, is that neither you nor your children can be bought or sold. You may have a harder time this year than you have ever had before; it will be the price you pay for your freedom.

According to Soule, the line between slavery and freedom was a fine one indeed. The only thing separating the two was the custom of attaching "money value to the former slaves." Although they could not longer be bought and sold as property, their expectations that they should receive some reprieve from the endless work they had endured as slaves was outrageous. "If you get through this year alive and well," he told them, "you should be thankful."[27]

It was not as if freedpeople imagined their postemancipation lives to be free from labor. Their desires to have more control over their work and time, along with access to, if not outright ownership of, the land and its resources, were the same modest aspirations most working people held in the nineteenth century. Soule and many other government officials, however, interpreted these aspirations as a threat to the South's economic reconstruction as well as the safety of whites throughout the region. In a letter to his commander, O. O. Howard, explaining his rationale for addressing the freedpeople in Orangeburg, Soule expressed his belief that the protectionist impulse in Washington risked doing more harm than good. Soule told Howard of the importance of "restraint and fear of punishment" in securing both freedpeople's diligent labor and good behavior. He blamed the "ignorance, the prejudice, the brutality, and the educated idleness" of freedpeople for the "increase in vagrancy" in his district. Soule proved sympathetic to whites' response to this state of affairs, assuring Howard that even extreme "cases of flogging and shooting" freedmen were justifiable as "self-defence." The problem was not white violence, Soule explained, but that many of his fellow agents were "very liberal" in treatment of freedpeople. When they worked to secure food and clothing to black workers and their dependents, they robbed the freedman of his obligation to support his family and his need to work. Protecting them from the harsh conditions that in Soule's mind characterized the transition from slavery to freedom encouraged laziness, impudence, and "false pride." Soule concluded that "only actual suffering, starvation, and punishment will drive many of them to work."[28]

Although Howard corrected Soule's sympathetic portrayal of Southern whites, reminding him that "the sophistries of the planters are often insidious and hard to refute," the commissioner remained silent on his agent's belief in the necessity of suffering, punishment, and restraint. Howard's tacit approval of Soule's brand of discipline stemmed from the anxieties emancipation and the protectionist imperative produced. While Congress worried about "outrages" against freedpeople, the flagrant physical abuses that typified the slaveholding mentality and posed a significant threat to federal authority in the South, lawmakers and their agents also feared that too much freedom might be as detrimental as not enough. Not only did the CRA and the Freedmen's Bureau call into question the limits of federalism, these protective measures also stirred up criticism of "class legislation." Opponents, including some within their own party, accused Radical Republicans of legislating preferential treatment for African Americans and providing them with benefits not afforded whites. Reaction to these measures also revealed a deep suspicion toward what twentieth-century sociologist T. H. Marshall termed "social citizenship." While freedpeople argued that economic welfare and physical security went hand in hand, and that the federal government bore an obligation to aid them in attaining both, many whites feared doing so threatened both the regional and national reconstruction programs. As important as it was to convince white Southerners that it was no longer acceptable for them to chain, whip, or kill blacks, it was also imperative to discipline freedpeople's "exaggerated ideas of freedom."[29]

Captain Soule was not alone in his belief in the redemptive value of suffering for freedpeople. Fearful that a shortage of labor stemming from former slaves' suspicion of the contract system would endanger agricultural production, Freedmen's Bureau agents throughout the South implemented a variety of coercive policies aimed at reducing dependency on government support and ensuring the freedmen's cooperation with the free labor enterprise. Commissioner Howard ordered his assistants to take steps to eliminate "the false pride which renders some of the refugees more willing to be supported in idleness than to support themselves." According to many of those agents, the distribution of rations engendered this sentiment, so Howard instructed them to reserve the monthly allotment of one bushel of corn and eight pounds of pork for only the "aged and infirm" and half that amount to very young orphans, both of whom were incapable of labor and self-support. In both of those cases, relatives or caretakers could claim rations for those indigent individuals.

All "able-bodied" freedpeople were to be denied assistance in the hope of inducing them to sign contracts and go to work. Although some agents protested that without rations starvation was certain, Howard assured them in Circular No. 11, issued in August 1865, that "suffering is preferred to slavery, and is, to some degree, the necessary consequences of events." Within a year, Howard would halt all rations except for "the sick in regularly organized hospitals" and children confined to orphan asylums. Because of suspicions that freedpeople were cheating the system and claiming rations for people who could actually work, family and friends could no longer claim assistance for the elderly, sick, and very young living in their homes. While Howard understood his actions as beneficent and integral to the Bureau's larger civilizing mission to teach ex-slaves the duties of freedom, the policy gave them a dubious choice: work or starve.[30]

And starve many of them did. Edward O'Brien, the agent at Mount Pleasant, South Carolina, informed his commander at Charleston that in order "to prevent actual starvation" the people in his district were living on green corn, pond lilies, and when lucky, the occasional alligator. O'Brien worried about the coming winter and predicted that the people did not have "corn enough to feed themselves until Christmas." He made requisitions for clothing, blankets, and undergarments in anticipation of the cold weather. "I hope," he wrote, "that some plan may be adopted to aid the suffering poor." J. E. Cornelius also needed new, clean clothing to combat a smallpox epidemic that swept through the Sea Islands in the summer of 1866, threatening the freedpeople under his command, who numbered more than 8,000. Most of the people had only the clothing on their backs, which in many cases had become contaminated and needed to be burned. Those spared the smallpox outbreak suffered a myriad other debilitating physical ailments: hernias, deformed or missing limbs, ulcerated wounds that refused to heal, blindness, and mental illness. Other conditions proved much harder to document. Charlotte Lewis suffered from "paroxysms" that she maintained inhibited her from obtaining employment. The Bureau physician could find not physical cause for the severe "fevers and chills" she claimed to suffer from, and therefore he refused to give her a certificate of disability. However, her destitute appearance persuaded him to recommend rations for her on account of her "special complaint." How many others like Charlotte, devoid of the irrefutable "proof" provided by a gaping wound or other acute physical symptom of disease, were turned away by a less-sympathetic surgeon? The irony is that Charlotte's well-being continued to depend on the pity she could arouse in a white man empowered to examine her body and determine her worthiness for assistance—just as it had during slavery.[31]

Not surprisingly, crops suffered from lack of attention due to the rampant sickness and disability among freedpeople. In the fall of 1866, South Carolina agents reported an "unfavorable season" due in part to a drought that damaged both the cotton and corn crops. Freedpeople's shares would be small, if any, thereby compounding the crisis that left many impoverished and destitute. Agents also noted that often the seed was old and required "three or four seedings before a fair stand could be had." This meant that crops were late and vulnerable to seasonal damage, if not complete ruin, from autumn rains and frost. F. W. Liedtke, the agent at Monck's Corner, noted that many freedpeople were already trapped in a vicious cycle of peonage. Because freedpeople lacked subsistence, planters agreed to advance the necessary provisions at the start of the season so that the workers could devote their full time to the cotton crop. However, the cost of those provisions had to be repaid out of the workers' shares, which in the case of a bad crop like the one in 1866 left freedpeople with little if anything to show for their labor. Many began the next season already indebted and unable to look for better terms elsewhere.[32]

Extreme poverty, sickness, and destitution—not laziness and ignorance—caused the free labor crisis that plagued South Carolina and many other parts of the South in 1866. Yet even as they acknowledged the trying conditions plaguing freedpeople's efforts to become self-supporting, including planters' efforts to swindle and abuse them, Bureau agents insisted that freedpeople themselves were largely to blame for their own suffering. Edward O'Brien, who feared starvation among the freedpeople in his district, understood that desperation drove many of them to steal equipment and machinery from the plantations and sell to traders in the area. "Everything finds a ready sale," he wrote, adding that he believed freedpeople used the money they received to buy "whiskey, powder, and shot and the most hurtful articles that can be found" instead of more useful items such as food, clothing, and better seed. The agent at Columbia blamed freedpeople's prejudice against white planters and their mistrust of the contract system as the root of the problem. Because they refused to trust their employers and insisted upon bargaining too hard for higher wages and time off, they brought on their troubles themselves. Their hard-headedness, the agent reported, resulted in "idleness, vagrancy and theft, and was the main cause of half the destitution that existed throughout the District during the year." John W. De Forest, who had grown tired of freedpeople's complaints, likewise dismissed their destitution as the inevitable result of their own laziness. "Regular labor is the only thing that will keep you from suffering," he informed the people in his district.[33]

De Forest typified the ambivalence with which many Bureau agents viewed their jobs. Reports from the field routinely expressed concern for freedpeople's impoverishment and outrage at the treatment they received at the hands of their former masters but at the same time condemnation for what agents perceived as ignorance, laziness, and dishonesty. De Forest showed particular sympathy for ill-clothed children without proper winter gear and fought to secure clothing, shoes, and blankets from the army. However, he felt rations of food were "demoralizing" and begrudged anything to those he described as "the notoriously idle, the habitual beggars, the thieves, and prostitutes." Recalling the chaos that would erupt on "draw days," when rations were distributed, De Forest derided the "pauper classes" who "made for me like pigs for an oak tree in autumn."[34]

De Forest's hostility toward the poor was not uncommon. As Chad Goldberg notes in his study of social welfare programs in the United States, "traditional poor relief tended to conflate poverty with deviance and criminality," and often assumed a "rehabilitative function" that could be simultaneously paternalistic and callous. Modern efforts to establish a rational system of government-sponsored social welfare, of which the Freedmen's Bureau was the first, were no less susceptible to the class and racial prejudices of their predecessors. Despite the Bureau's attempts to standardize the aid process and the guiding belief that the organization functioned as a protective force that was indispensible to the South's reconstruction, agents like De Forest remained suspicious of certain aspects of the government's intervention, particularly its material support of freedpeople. As a matter of "general principle," De Forest felt it necessary to be "merciless toward the few for the good of the many" by "refusing to feed the suffering lest I encourage the lazy."[35]

The impulse to reform and discipline made protection a double-edged sword for the South's freed population. Although they often admonished planters for their insistence that freedpeople would not work unless compelled to do so, the government's actions nonetheless reflected its larger civilizing mission that shared many of the planters' assumptions. Not only did the Bureau support the restriction of rations, vagrancy laws, the formation of "pauper colonies," the apprenticeship of children, and at times even fines or imprisonment to compel freedpeople's labor, administrators and agents understood these coercive methods as essentially beneficial to Southern blacks. Stuart Eldridge, the agent in charge at Vicksburg, Mississippi, referred to these methods of compulsion as "appliances of freedom" that would be used "to ameliorate the condition of the people and to meet the many demands of their new state." Orlando Brown, who oversaw the Bureau's operations in Virginia, ordered his district superintendents to "look after the vagrants" and turn those who refused to sign contracts "over to work under some military guard, without payment, until they are ready to work for themselves." Brown then instructed his agents to "consider [freedpeople] under the same common laws that govern free laborers throughout the North." Brown's understanding of equality exposed the important role compulsion played in white notions of freedom. These methods fostered considerable suffering and deprivation among freedpeople, but in Commissioner O. O. Howard's words, suffering was "the necessary consequence of events."[36]

At times, the desire to discipline the freed population produced the kinds of violence that ostensibly negated the conditions of freedom. Planters were no longer allowed to beat or whip black workers, but army and Bureau officials sometimes found corporal punishment to be another "appliance of freedom." In Georgia, any punishment short of whipping was allowed, and so long as the whipping did not appear excessively cruel, or was reserved solely for black offenders, then corporal punishment still might be justified. Davis Tillson, the state's commissioner, advised his agents "that punishments should contemplate the reparation of the injury done ... rather than the infliction of mere cruelty." Whipping was officially forbidden, however Tillson recommended that Bureau officers follow the conditions prescribed in Georgia's 1844 state code governing the relations between employers and free apprentices that allowed the master to "use the same amount of force to compel obedience, which a father may use with his child." While leaving the door open for corporal punishment, Tillson encouraged his officers to use other means of correction, including "fines, loss of wages ... imprisonment at hard labor, solitary confinement on bread and water for a limited period" and "in extreme cases, labor with ball and chain, or in chain gang." Tillson expected that these methods of "practical and reasonable punishment" would have "a most salutary influence."[37]

When agents doubled as planters, their reliance on physical coercion became more direct. In May 1866, Andrew Johnson appointed two army generals, James Steedman and J. S. Fullerton, to investigate allegations of abuse and malfeasance against Freedmen's Bureau agents. Whereas some historians have dismissed the investigation as a partisan ploy to discredit the Radical Republican agenda, the generals' report listed widespread accusations, often made by freedmen themselves, against Bureau agents who, in addition to their government jobs, had taken up planting as a side business. The report reveals, at the very least, a serious conflict of interest with the potential to further blunt an already dull sense of obligation toward the freed population. Two cases in particular stood out. In North Carolina, a Bureau superintendent known as Rev. Fitz, who supervised a freedmen's settlement on the Trent River and claimed to be a former army chaplain (but was later revealed to have been only a quartermaster's clerk), was accused of tying freedmen up by their wrists and sentencing them for long terms of imprisonment for minor offenses. Perhaps driven by religious zealotry, "Rev." Fitz was said to have imprisoned a group of children for ten days simply for playing on the Sabbath. Generals Steedman and Fullerton reported that "four intelligent ladies from the North, who are teaching school in the settlement," corroborated freedpeople's claims to have suffered "revolting and unheard-of cruelties" at Fitz's hands. Fitz also levied a "tax" on all occupants of the settlement and threatened to "turn out" any resident who did not pay it. He also collected taxes on all business transactions between the residents, as well as on their fishing boats, horses, and carts. The generals could not determine where the money collected went and implied that it ended up in Mr. Fitz's pockets. In his defense, Fitz claimed that his commander informed him that he must collect a thousand dollars a month from the settlement to be turned over to the commanding officer for what purposes he did not know.[38]

The second case proved even more disturbing. Freedmen near New Bern accused the state's assistant commissioner, Eliphalet Whittlesey, of covering up the murder of a freedman who attempted to escape Whittlesey's plantation in rural Pitt County. Whittlesey and another agent, Horace James, had organized the operation ostensibly as a good-faith effort to prove to local whites that free labor could be a success. James had charged a freedman named Keel with stealing from the plantation's stores, and in his capacities as the local Bureau agent had tried the man and convicted him in a special freedman's court. James sentenced Keel to "dig ditches" on Whittlesey's plantation. When Keel ran away, James and his clerk pursued him, and as the fugitive attempted to cross the river in an old canoe, James ordered his clerk to shoot him. The clerk fired a shot, and Keel fell into the river and was never heard from again. The clerk believed the shot hit Keel and presumed that he had died. When James reported the event to Whittlesey, he assured his business partner that there was nothing to worry about. Since "the affair seems to have occurred at night," Whittlesey wrote in his report, "and as the body of the negro has not been discovered, it does not appear certain that the shot took effect. No further action in the case seems to be called for." Two weeks later, the freedman's body was found and a formal investigation commenced, which resulted in a finding of "justifiable homicide." According to Steedman and Fullerton, the freedmen in and around New Bern "expressed dissatisfaction at the manner in which this case had been passed over," but the generals themselves found the plantation too remote to visit and see the conditions firsthand. Eventually, Whittlesey was court-martialed for the way he managed his "model plantation" but was acquitted of all wrongdoing. He left North Carolina but continued working for O. O. Howard, who maintained that his favored agent was "a brave Christian gentleman" who had been a pawn in the political game between Radical Republicans and the president over control of Reconstruction.[39]

Howard's suspicions about what ultimately drove Steedman and Fullerton's investigations were undoubtedly warranted. By the spring of 1866, when Steedman and Fullerton issued their report, President Johnson and Radicals in Congress were in the throes of political warfare. Evidence of mismanagement and abuse within the Freedmen's Bureau might dissuade moderate Republicans from supporting such measures and ignite a public outcry against Radicalism. If Whittlesey was a pawn in that game, so were freedpeople, and they had much more to lose. Had the generals been concerned with actual conditions on Whittlesey's and other Bureau-operated plantations, might they not have made the time and arranged a visit even to the most remote areas? Yet despite its undeniable partisan perspective, their report reveals a number of internal problems that compromised the Bureau's protective mission. First, a lack of direct supervision, stemming in part from the Bureau's manpower shortages as well as from the lack of adequate transportation and communication lines, allowed abuses of power to take place in backcountry locations. Manpower shortages meant that the Bureau frequently relied on "citizen agents" like Horace James. To these men the government subcontracted the work of distributing rations, supervising labor contracts, and adjudicating disputes in freedmen's courts. When men like James, who were often planters themselves, were empowered to supervise their own labor contracts and employees, the Bureau's ostensibly disinterested status became compromised.

These problems resulted from more than just poor management, however. A deep-seated aversion to the working poor fed a belief in the necessity of physical coercion that compromised the government's free labor principles. As vehement as many free labor acolytes were in their insistence that wages alone guaranteed ex-slaves' labor and obedience, their actions often spoke otherwise. An army district commander in western Tennessee explained his reasons for siding with local planters in order to deal with the "gravity of evils which have arisen from the new status of the negro." Among these "evils" the commander listed "a growing spirit of restlessness and disaffection" that made freedpeople "an incubus on society" that was "vicious and unsafe." "They think they are free to do what they please," he scoffed, "free to expect and demand support from their former masters without compensation, free to enter into contracts for their labor . . . perfectly free to violate such contracts, and abandon their employers whenever they choose to do so." The commander's solution was to "protect with force the negro in the full enjoyment of his rights as a free man, and to compel him to the performance of his engagements with this employer." In this formulation, citizenship and bodily autonomy for freedpeople occupied contradictory positions.[40]

In his assessment of how the Freedmen's Bureau should handle the "evils" of emancipation, the commander identified a central tension in the story of freedom. Emancipation created an imperative to protect freedpeople from violence and intimidation, on the one hand, and a need to ensure their labor and productivity, on the other. The belief that some form of compulsion—whether in the forms of contracts and wages or in some instances corporal punishment—was necessary to guarantee black labor and the South's economic reconstruction united Northern capitalists and Southern planters in a common endeavor. Although the law had replaced the lash as both the symbol and substance of the region's political and social institutions, compulsion in its various forms remained at the heart of things. When a Northern journalist overheard a group of white Southerners who were watching the procession of an Alabama chain gang proclaim, "That's the beauty of freedom! That's what free niggers come to," his initial outrage eventually turned to sympathy for the Southerners' point of view. The system of convict leasing, what David Oshinsky calls the "new American gulag," took hold in the South under the watch of Republican governors as a way to relieve their states' massive wartime debts while simultaneously dealing with the growing problem of "black crime." White Republicans, like Mississippi governor James Lusk Alcorn, may have abhorred the sight of chain gangs as an affront to their liberal humanitarian pretentions, but they tolerated them nonetheless as an effective means of labor control and punishment. Why shouldn't they? After all, the Thirteenth Amendment allowed slavery or involuntary servitude "as punishment for crime." Freedpeople were caught between the law and the lash—by efforts to reform Southern penal law and supplant the power of white masters, and to regulate and discipline black bodies and labor.⁴¹

"The Negro Nursery"

In 1866, George Fitzhugh, slavery's erstwhile apologist, penned an exposé of the Freedmen's Bureau in Richmond that predicted the government's eventual abandonment not only of the Bureau but the entire project of Reconstruction. "This Negro Nursery," as Fitzhugh called the Bureau, "is an admirable idea of the Federals, which, however, they stole from us. For we always told them the darkeys were but grown-up children that needed guardians, like all other children." Rehashing the argument that drove his 1857 proslavery diatribe *Cannibals All!*, Fitzhugh infantilized freedpeople, painting them as ignorant and incapable of self-support. The government had realized this, Fitzhugh argued, and set up the Freedmen's Bureau to replace the masters who had previously "nursed" them. Unlike their former masters, however, the government imagined they could raise former slaves to a level of equality with white men, a proposition Fitzhugh found ridiculous. Chiding the government's "hopeless attempt to make citizens of negroes," Fitzhugh wrote that ex-slaves "must first be made men, and the Bureau is a practical admission and assertion that they are not men." As vitriolic as Fitzhugh's antiblack and antigovernment sentiments were, his ideas were far from marginal. To Fitzhugh and many other white Southerners, the Freedmen's Bureau was a symbol of dependency, proof positive that Southern blacks were unfit for freedom much less political rights. Furthermore, his prediction that Northerners would soon enough come around to his way of thinking proved accurate. In a few years time, he presaged, "they will discover that their pupils are irreclaimable '*mauvais sujets*,' and will be ready to throw up 'in divine disgust' the whole negro-nursing and negro-teaching business, and to turn the affair over to the State."⁴²

Tangled up in the essay's caustic tone was a curious argument. Fitzhugh claimed that the government "stole" the idea for the Freedmen's Bureau from Southern slaveholders. In his vision of slavery as a paternalistic, beneficent system of caregiving for "grown-up children," this made sense. While proslavery apologists like Fitzhugh had long maintained that slavery was a humane institution, more humane than Northern free labor, these arguments took on new meanings in the postemancipation period. By claiming that the protectionist impulse had originated in the slaveholding South, Fitzhugh cleverly began to rework the narrative of freedom that Radical Republicans and freedpeople had constructed. According to Fitzhugh, protection was neither a constituent element of freedom nor a right of citizenship. Instead, protection represented the well-meaning but defeated impulse behind slavery. Freedom demanded that the remnants of the past be discarded, yet the Freedmen's Bureau seemed to confirm what Fitzhugh and other slaveholders had known all along. Scoffing at the "hopeless attempt to make citizens of negroes," Fitzhugh insisted that "they must first be made men, and the Bureau is a practical admission and assertion that they are not men." It appeared to Fitzhugh that the government had instituted a separate set of laws and institutions for freedpeople that, instead of recognizing their particular and acute vulnerabilities, reflected a tacit admission of their irredeemable inferiority. "They are our fellow-beings, children," Fitzhugh remarked, "not men, and therefore to be compassionated and taken care of."[43]

According to Fitzhugh, freedom and protection were incompatible. Although few others articulated it with the same animosity that Fitzhugh did, the idea gained popularity in the postwar years. The meaning of freedom underwent a redefinition during the late 1860s. Due in part to the growing acceptance of Darwinian evolutionary theory and its popularization by theorists such as Herbert Spencer, the belief that freedom was best understood as a "struggle for existence" gelled quite nicely with Fitzhugh's overwrought narrative about the downfall of slaveholding paternalism. Freedpeople needed competition, not protection, to undo the debilitating effects of slavery. Many might suffer, even die, as the result of being thrust into the "natural" conditions of life, but that must not be legislated against. Suffering would bring about the elevation of the race if, in fact, the race could be elevated. Fitzhugh doubted it. So did renowned scientists such as Harvard's Louis Agassiz, who, in a letter to Samuel Gridley Howe, the head of the American Freedman's Inquiry Commission, predicted that the freed population would soon die out without the protection offered to them under slavery. Howe had asked the United States' most eminent scientist if there was any scientific evidence to support the notion (often touted by proslavery thinkers like Fitzhugh) that slaves could not survive if cast out on their own. Agassiz believed that the high rate of "amalgamation" in the South left the race as a whole weaker and incapable of reproduction. Only considerable interference from the government would save them from eventual extinction, a policy that Agassiz warned strongly against lest the white population fall victim to the same "degradation." Although he may have rejected Darwin's theory of a single line of ancestry for all mankind, Agassiz (like Spencer) was won over by the cold violence they saw in natural selection. It enabled them to justify the existence of social hierarchies among humans and naturalized the often-brutal maintenance of those hierarchies. For opponents of Reconstruction and its protective policies toward freedpeople, the language of struggle infused their opposition to the Freedmen's Bureau as well as the Civil Rights Act, the Fourteenth Amendment, the Enforcement Acts, and other attempts to protect freedpeople and establish their claims to civil and political rights.[44]

Nathaniel Shaler, a student of Agassiz and a Union veteran who would eventually become dean of sciences at Harvard, began commenting on Southern affairs during the 1870s as the Ku Klux Klan crisis captivated national attention. A native of Kentucky, Shaler published an essay entitled "An Ex-Southerner in South Carolina" in the *Atlantic Monthly* in the summer of 1870 that critiqued the government's intervention on behalf of freedpeople using explicitly Darwinian reasoning. Calling the freedman the "heir to the ignorance and superstitions of that original chaos of humanity, Africa," Shaler denounced attempts by Northern philanthropists, missionaries, and the government to provide education and other vestiges of white civilization to him. Shaler pitied "the devoted Northern woman who toils her life away under the delusion that she can fight all Africa with a spelling-book and multiplication table." It was a simple fact, according to Shaler, that the "African" could not achieve much in the way of intellectual advancement. "Unless the negro, therefore, can handle something requiring more art than a hoe," the naturalist concluded, he had no role in the South's reconstruction other than to perform agricultural labor. Instead of "seeking to ease the hard road he [the freedman] has to travel," Shaler advised that the protective mechanisms employed by the government on his behalf be withdrawn. "Every move of the government has been clearly against the negro," Shaler argued. The misguided emphasis on education as well as the confiscation of rebel property, the disenfranchisement of whites, and the enfranchisement of black men had denied them the hard lessons of freedom they needed. The government's protection had "fixed in the negro the belief that if he will just sit still and open his mouth, Uncle Sam will see that he is fed." And now that Southern whites had moved to halt these unnatural and dangerous policies, Uncle Sam had sent troops to shield Southern blacks from the natural consequences of their behavior. Having thrust the "final product of our national growth" upon a race unfit to wield such power, it was little wonder that there existed so much turmoil and violence in South Carolina. The "savage life of a hundred generations" dictated such an outcome.[45]

CHAPTER TWO

Although critics might argue that Shaler bastardized Darwin's theories, the fact remains that the discourse of struggle, competition, and natural violence contributed to the antiprotectionist views that arose during the 1870s. E. L. Godkin, publisher of the *Nation*, which had once been the organ of Radical Republicanism, also employed Darwinian imagery to attack federal intervention in the South. Godkin blamed the "intermingling of the diverse races" in government affairs for the upheavals in the South. He urged legislators to study advances in "social science" to find solutions to the problem. "The fundamental fact," Godkin wrote, "brought about by the researches of Mr. Darwin is that any characters which have been the property of a group of animals for a long time tend to perpetuate themselves." For blacks, these characteristics included indolence, dishonesty, and thievery, which now threatened to corrupt the nation's political system. They had already destroyed South Carolina's government. The culminating violence between the races, therefore, was to be expected. In order to stop it, the government must pull back and allow the black man to be taken out of the system of governance. Biology demanded it. "In our effort to do the best for ourselves and for them," Godkin advised, "we should remember that, for the bottom to the top of the animal kingdom, allied races are invariably enemies; they dislike each other's very smell, and find that it is an excuse for war." Godkin believed that it was "probably this animal instinct which makes it difficult to mingle races without having castes."[46]

According to Shaler and Godkin, as well as those for whom evolutionary "struggle" seemed to define freedom in the postemancipation age, Southern blacks were destined for a state of "natural" dependency and subservience. Although they lamented that the government's protection had encouraged idleness and vagrancy among the freed population, they did not envision—nor did they desire—actual self-sufficiency and independence among freedpeople. They imagined ex-slaves as nothing more than "unskilled" agricultural workers, cultivating cotton, rice, tobacco, and sugar just as they had before emancipation. While they did not wish to see them dependent upon government support, they had no problem with them being bound to the lands of their former (and sometimes new) masters, drawing subsistence from white employers who, in turn, used those distributions to entrap them in a cycle of debt and poverty that in many ways resembled the kind of servitude that the war and emancipation ostensibly had ripped apart. Now the servitude was contractual and "voluntary." Work and suffering were unavoidable. "They are perhaps less merry than before," wrote Shaler of the freed slaves he recalled from his Kentucky youth. "The careless laugh of the old slave is now rarely heard, for it belonged to a creature who had never pondered the question of where his next meal was to come from." Freedom was a curse.[47]

The specter of dependency haunted postemancipation efforts to reimagine a world without slavery and establish legal protections for African Americans in areas of civil and political rights as well as a modicum of social support for the impoverished masses of freedpeople in the former Confederacy. Longstanding fears about dependency, which were bound up with presumptions about civic virtue and who was or was not worthy of citizenship, informed how many midcentury white Americans interpreted the protective impulse emanating from Washington during the heady days of Radical Reconstruction. For some, inferiority—not equality—demanded protection. "If [the black man] is, as it is claimed, an inferior being and unable to compete with the white man on terms of equality," declared Radical Congressman Ignatius Donnelly in support of the Civil Rights Act, "surely you will not add to the injustice of nature by casting him beneath the feet of the white man." Donnelly's attempt to persuade opponents of the bill that their insistence upon black inferiority demanded that they support protective measures undermined his colleagues' efforts to make protection an attribute of equal citizenship. Despite those efforts, protection and dependency clung together with an inescapable stickiness that seemed to get worse the harder freedpeople struggled against it. Not only were efforts to provide for their basic needs like food, clothing, and medical care interpreted as an admission of their unfitness for freedom, those services were often given only grudgingly if at all. Those charged with freedpeople's protection understood suffering to be a necessary, if unfortunate, aspect of freedom and their larger civilizing mission. Like a tar baby, the government's efforts to protect too often entrapped freedpeople in new systems of oppression and servitude that belied the triumphant narrative of freedom that Bureau agents and other insisted upon telling.[48]

Frederick Douglass had predicted the dangers embedded within white benevolence in 1862. Frustrated with whites wringing their hands over the issue of emancipation, Douglass curtly answered the question about what was to be done with freed slaves: "do nothing with them." "Your doing with them is their greatest misfortune," Douglass informed his white readers and antislavery colleagues. "They have been undone by your doings, and all they now ask, and really have need of at your hands, is just to let them alone." Douglass did not object to legal efforts, such as the Civil Rights Act or the Fourteenth Amendment, which attempted to establish "equal protection" for African Americans. He opposed any legislation that made attempts to discriminate against blacks or interfere with their right to work, own property, go to school, or vote. However, he was skeptical of white efforts to reform freedpeople. "We would not for one moment check the outgrowth of any benevolent concern for the future welfare of the colored race," he wrote, "but in the name of reason and religion, we earnestly plead for justice before all else." Although he would have been loath to ally himself with George Fitzhugh, Douglass nonetheless expressed a similar sentiment. He feared that plans to reform black behavior, to civilize the slave into a free person, risked objectifying him or her as inferior and unfit for citizenship. Knowing the hostility with which many Americans viewed the poor, not to mention the black poor, Douglass anticipated how instruments of protection could be wielded against them. He recognized that although antislavery advocates had helped bring about the institution's demise there still remained much "negro hate" among those who claimed to be the freed slave's best friends. "Is the presence of a black freeman less agreeable than that of a black slave?" Douglass asked them. Douglass sensed that white sympathy was fleeting and tempered with racial and class-based animosity.[49]

What Douglass called the "unholy alliance between negro hate and antislavery" preceded the advent of evolutionary science but nonetheless reflected a belief in the necessity of violent, aggressive struggle in the natural word. Although he had been an outspoken and energetic critic of slavery, radical abolitionist minister Theodore Parker's sympathies did not extend to emancipated blacks. Writing in the in late 1850s, Parker expressed an underlying belief in the corrective value of competition, struggle, and natural violence for the lower classes. Seething in his animosity for "Paddies" as well as "Africans" who refused to work and took charity, Parker once remarked, "I hate lazy people, and should (perhaps) see an idle Irishwoman *starve and die* with no compunction at all." Parker praised "the chaotic condition of our social system" and declared that through its "antagonistic competition . . . a better state of things will come." He saw in abolitionism an end to the "negro problem." Foreshadowing Darwinian concepts, Parker wrote in 1858 that the "curious law of nature," which held that "the strong replaces the weak," would determine the struggle between the races in the United States. Parker did not need Darwin's *Origin of the Species*, which would be published the following year, to prove this point. He had all of American history to support his theory. "The white man kills out the red man and black man," he stated. "When slavery is abolished the African population will decline in the United States, and die out of the South as out of Northampton and Lexington."[50]

No scientific or sociological treatise was needed to advance the "natural law" of American history. The frontier struggles against the Indians seemed to reflect the validity of Malthusian, Spencerian, and Darwinian theories all in one. Writing in 1863, Rev. J. M. Sturtevant, president of the abolitionist Illinois College, articulated the problem facing the county in the wake of emancipation:

> How can the public mind be assured that to emancipate the enslaved race, to confer on them all the moral rights of humanity, does not involve by any necessity, or even remote possibility, either an internecine war of races on our own soil, or the fusion of the two races into one homogeneous people?

According to Sturtevant, white Americans sought an alterative solution to the prospect of either race war or "amalgamation." That solution, Sturtevant promised, could be found in the "great law of population" that dictated "the inevitable extinction of the weaker race by the competition of the stronger." Instead of embarking upon a lengthy explanation of Malthus, however, Sturtevant used examples that would be immediately familiar to his readers. "I must assume the reader is sufficiently versed in American history to know that even the Indian perishes," he explained, "not by the sword or the rifle of the white man, but by the simple competition of civilization with the Indian's means of subsistence." Of course, his readers were well aware of the role the "sword and rifle" played in the conquest of native peoples, but Sturtevant assuaged any latent doubt they might have about the fairness of such competition by crediting "civilization" over "subsistence." It was the Indians' dependency, ignorance, and primitive ways that led to their destruction. The same would be true of emancipated slaves who, like the Indians, could not compete with the whites' aggressive progress. Their "inevitable extinction" solved the problem of what to do with the emancipated slaves.[51]

Even within the discourse of protection, redemptive violence provided the idiom through which many Americans viewed the transition from slavery to freedom. Although Radical Republicans premised their advocacy of civil rights legislation as a means to eradicate the violent legacies of slavery, the larger project of Reconstruction seemed to depend upon the use of coercive and often violent strategies to discipline freedpeople's bodies and minds. In order to teach them the duties of freedom, Freedmen's Bureau agents, along with white planters, used freedpeople's susceptibility to suffering to leverage their submission to the contract system. While they justified their actions as the best remedy for dependence, which jeopardized freedpeople's assimilation into the body politic, government agents effectively created a system of labor that trapped Southern blacks in a cycle of poverty and dependence that circumscribed their freedom instead of enlarging it. Underpinning these methods was a belief in the necessity of competition and struggle as a solution to the tough social and political questions emancipation posed. The violence of the natural world, as seen through the lens of Darwinian evolutionary theory and its various reformulations, reinforced what many whites already understood as America's special destiny of conquest and expansion. A hodgepodge of scientific and historical reasoning naturalized violence, suffering, and conflict, making the protective impulse seem at once antiquated and incredibly misguided.

Rather than securing freedpeople's physical security as a basic right of citizenship, the revolution in sentiment that made black suffering both recognizable to whites and the centerpiece in antislavery reform also worked to make ex-slaves' health and safety conditional upon their obedient performance of agricultural work. The proliferation of images of black bodies in pain may have inured Northern whites to black suffering and naturalized the violent racial conflict that plagued the postwar South, but it was also the case that suffering became a tool of reform itself, a way to teach ex-slaves the responsibilities of freedom. By viewing pain as instructive rather than destructive, those men in charge of overseeing the transition from slavery to freedom created another redemptive narrative that presented the forceful, sometimes violent, control of black bodies as a positive good, leaving Southern blacks the painful task of authoring their own redemptive narratives.

THREE

Wounds and Scars

"Oh, deep in my heart I do believe We shall overcome some day."[1] CIVIL RIGHTS MOVEMENT ANTHEM

"Stretching out beyond this there exists an interpretive void that engulfs the irrecoverable thoughts and feelings of the hundreds of thousands of real slaves who had to live out the liberator's fantasy." MARCUS WOOD, *THE HORRIBLE GIFT OF FREEDOM*[2]

In mid-October 1865, Henry Bram, Ishmael Moultrie, and Yates Sampson, three former slaves, penned a petition to General Oliver Otis Howard, the head of the newly established Freedmen's Bureau, on behalf of their friends, neighbors, and relatives living on Edisto Island, South Carolina. Union forces had occupied Edisto and the other Sea Islands for much of the war. As a result, the plantations had long been abandoned by their white owners, and the slaves had been left to fend for themselves and cultivate the land. The Sea Islands were sites of the first experiments in free labor, and by all accounts, the islanders performed superbly. However, by the fall of 1865, the absentee planters had returned to the island, emboldened by President Johnson's amnesty proclamation, and demanded that the freed community relinquish the lands and contract to work for them, their former masters. To complicate matters, general William Tecumseh Sherman had issued Special Field Order No. 15 back in January officially confiscating the plantations along the sea coast of South Carolina and Georgia and ordering them to be divided among the area's 400,000 former slaves. The planters' return engendered much tumult and animosity within the Sea Island community over the rightful ownership of the land. Despite Sherman's order and the freedpeople's physical possession of the land, the War Department demanded that the plantations be turned over to their former owners, a message that Gen. Howard, as commander of the Freedmen's Bureau, was obliged to convey to the Sea Islanders. Desperate to hold on to their homes and independence, the Edisto Islanders chose Bram, Moultrie, and Sampson to make their case to Gen. Howard. The petition, penned in Bram's rough script and signed with Xs by the other two men, reveals the importance of land to freedpeople's ideas of freedom, but it also illuminates the interconnection between land, labor, and physical safety in the postwar freedom struggle. While the Edisto Islanders' claims were premised both on the decades of unremunerated toil they had performed and their loyalty to the Union during the war, land also provided them with physical security by allowing them to work independently of white supervision, and if possible, away from whites altogether.[3]

The petition quivers with the apprehension that the very recently enslaved felt about their former masters. "We are at the mercy of those who are combined to prevent us from getting land enough to lay our Fathers bones upon," the petitioners wrote. The only options left to them as they saw it was to "Step Into the *public road or the sea* or remain on them working as In former time and subject to thire [sic] will as then." With little means and fearful of leaving the only homes they had ever known and striking out "on the road," the petitioners lamented having to choose between the sea and slavery. Having to make such a choice made a mockery of their so-called freedom: "You will see this Is not the condition of really freemen."[4]

One of the petition's most significant elements comes in its invocation of the brutality they had suffered under slavery. Howard's suggestion that they should forgive their former masters particularly galled Bram who wrote that he could not forgive "the man who tied me to a tree & gave me 39 lashes & who stripped and flogged my mother & my sister" and who still "tries to keep me In a condition of Helplessness." Although Howard assured the islanders the "whipping post of which you complain is abolished forever," Bram saw no radical break with the past. "Here is where secession was born and Nurtured," he reminded Howard, and "Here is were [sic] we have toiled nearly all Our lives as slaves and were treated like dumb Driven cattle." The Freedmen's Bureau reports of abuse, whipping, apprenticeship, pass systems, patrols, and other forms of surveillance, intimidation, and violence supported the petition's claim that Sea Island freedpeople were still treated as slaves, and that the spirit of mastery among the white planters flourished.[5]

As the petitioners made clear, violence remained an integral part of Southern life despite war, abolition, and Confederate defeat. Its presence shaped not only what happened at the polling place but also in homes, yards, and neighborhoods where the importance of questions such as who would be the next congressman or governor paled in importance to questions about how often the silver should be cleaned, and how much someone should be paid to do it. Violence settled political disputes, but it also brokered relationships in the fields and households throughout the former Confederacy. Its everydayness threatened to erase the line between slavery and freedom that Howard and other federal agents attempted to draw.[6] Violence disrupted the celebratory atmosphere surrounding slavery's destruction. While there was much cause to rejoice, the continued predation from Southern whites dampened an otherwise jubilant moment. Freedpeople began to question the nature of freedom as well as the authority of the federal government. What good was freedom if it did not include some level of physical safety? How could a government demand their allegiance and obedience when it did not have the will or the power to protect them? How could they be expected to work, save their wages, and obey the law if the law offered little or no recourse to them? These questions pushed at the limits of the Republican vision of a free-labor society.

The petition opens up space to wonder how freedpeople's lived experiences of violence, both in slavery and after, shaped their expectations of freedom, the state, and their place within it. By examining the claims ex-slaves made on the government to protect them, we begin to uncover the intimate relationship between violence and the rights of citizenship—land, labor, family, and voting. What also emerges from these claims is the creation of a unique political subjectivity rooted in violence and cognizant of the physical vulnerability of the newly free—and of the negative representations of them as dishonest, lazy, and in need of physical and moral correction. Freedpeople's articulation of the linkage between citizenship and protection reflected what legal historian Hendrik Hartog calls a "continuing pragmatic tradition of care and responsibility" that had informed America's regulatory and reform movements throughout the nineteenth century. In this pragmatic tradition, the issue of vulnerability was balanced with individuals' desire for autonomy. Claimants typically positioned themselves as vulnerable and dependent upon the state for protection as a means to advance their desires for rights as citizens. Acknowledging vulnerability, Hartog argues, did not necessarily undermine a claim for autonomy. Instead, it informed the expansion of ideas of public welfare and laid the foundations for workers', women's, and children's rights. It also laid the foundations for black civil rights, both in the nineteenth and twentieth centuries.[7]

Yet while freedpeople articulated a sophisticated revision of Reconstruction's liberal promise based upon their continued subjection to white violence and coercion, there remained something unspeakable about those experiences. The language of rights, citizenship, and redemption obscured the fragmentation, dissemblance, and grief that also characterized black visions of freedom. If we accept the idea that slavery (and include with that the continued terrorization of freedpeople during Reconstruction) was a form of large-scale institutionalized torture, then Elaine Scarry's assertion that torture aims not merely to inflict physical pain or even death but to rob victims of their ability to speak of their pain, and thus denying them their own subjectivity, points to an unsettling aspect of emancipation that does not fit easily within the conventional political narratives of Reconstruction that define black agency as active resistance to white domination, political resilience, and revolutionary social transformation.[8] The process of becoming free also entailed reclamation of voices lost, and finding ways to express the inexpressible and to live in the shadow of trauma that revealed the limits of redemption as a purely political act symbolized by laws and ballots. And while there is ample evidence of freedpeople's defiance, determination, and redemptive spirit, there is also evidence of their dejection, dislocation, and dependence. While the latter parts of this chapter are in no way intended to be a comprehensive examination of these less often acknowledged responses to pain, they are meant to be suggestive of some of the limitations of history as a discipline when it comes to writing about violence. As Karl Jacoby explains, "the historian's responsibility to create a single, authoritative narrative of the past" makes it difficult to know what to do with the kind of evidence (or lack thereof) that a history of violence invariably produces. In order to appreciate the effects of violence on black lives in the nineteenth century and of freedpeople's efforts to overcome it, we must examine not only the narratives of escape and transcendence but also the ruptures in those narratives that appeared when the memories of suffering and loss splintered the story of freedom.[9]

"This is our home"

As the Edisto Island petition reveals, freedpeople harbored a close association between land, labor, and physical safety. Land became the primary impulse guiding freedpeople's efforts to rebuild their lives after slavery not because they were good Jeffersonians but because they wanted to be safe. The autonomy that land ownership provided was a shield to the abuses they had endured in slavery. This simple, almost commonsense observation, however, obscures a complex social reality that deserves further elucidation.

First, land represented a sense of place, of belonging, of *home*. Home included a social landscape as well as a geographical one. Home meant family and community. Having a place to gather together satisfied freedpeople's spiritual as well as material needs. The land housed kin, both living and dead, and thereby linked past with present, providing a sense of continuity and familiarity that could soothe the painful memories of slavery as well as the challenges of freedom. Freedpeople's affinity for the old "home place" baffled some Northerners who assumed that it only represented pain and suffering. When the Edisto Islanders complained of being driven off the land, they feared not only the loss of their crop and livestock but also the dissolution of their families and their connections to the past. "This is our home," they declared, "were [where] we have toiled nearly all Our lives." They needed "land enough to lay our Fathers bones upon," pointing to the generational ties they had to the plantations. To be driven from "the Homes we Have lived In In the Past" signified a spiritual and communal separation they could hardly endure.[10]

Access to land and kin often meant the difference between life and death. Land produced economic independence and subsistence in the form of gardens, poultry, and livestock. Land provided families with the means to care for their relatives and those in the community who could not care for themselves. The postwar South was a dangerous place for a single person. This was especially true for women and children, who suffered destitution and starvation when alone. As Susan O'Donovan explains in her study of emancipation in southwestern Georgia, when planters cast single women and their small children off plantations because they could not produce, they were left to wander the backcountry searching for support where they could find it. These homeless women flocked to Freedmen's Bureau offices, asking for rations, and when denied, left their children in overcrowded orphanages or apprenticed them to white planter families. Delicia Patterson and her three-month old infant "wandered from place to place, working for food and a place to stay." Her husband, a member of the USCT, had been killed in the war, leaving Delicia and the child destitute. At the mercy of their former owners or over-worked and unsympathetic government agents, both of whom demanded control over their labor, single women experienced a kind of physical vulnerability that is difficult to imagine.[11]

Although their attachments to the "old home place" may have run deep, those attachments rarely extended to their former masters. Freedpeople wasted little time putting as much physical distance between themselves and their white neighbors as possible. When General Sherman met with a delegation of Savannah's black ministers shortly after he occupied that city in January 1865, to find out the condition of the area's ex-slaves and their expectations from the government, the group's spokesperson, Garrison Frazier, a sixty-seven year old former slave who was an ordained Baptist minister, informed the General that they wanted to live in colonies away from whites. "We would prefer to live by ourselves," Frazier explained, "for there is a prejudice against us in the South that will take years to get over."[12]

Another member of the group, a twenty-six year old missionary from Baltimore, James Lynch, who had also urged freedpeole to forget the horrors of slavery, disagreed with Frazier and insisted that the best way to overcome racial prejudice would be to live among whites. However, none of the other ministers shared his belief in the power of integration. Having only been in the South for two years, and that time spent only in Union-occupied areas largely free from white violence, Lynch had not experienced slavery firsthand, and having spent much of his life in the North, he did not know white Southerners very well. Thus, he did not anticipate the resistance freedpeople would face from their former masters. To the other ministers, most of whom were former slaves like Frazier, he surely seemed naïve. However, Frazier's request to live in black colonies away from whites did not fit in with the liberalizing mission Reconstructionists in Washington were beginning to sketch out. More in line with Lynch's belief in the restorative power of industry and free labor, most plans for Reconstruction hinged their success on the South's economic rejuvenation, which required integrating black agricultural workers into the market networks of production and sale. The idea that former slaves would work productively if not supervised closely by whites remained untenable to many despite the success of Sea Islanders in maintaining productive plantations throughout the war. Many of their supposed "protectors" viewed freedpeople as "an incubus on society, a helpless, useless, unproductive class," recalling the words of the army commander in west Tennessee, "there [was] danger of its soon becoming vicious and unsafe to communities." With views such as these rife among government officials in charge of ironing out the details of Reconstruction, Frazier's call for independent black colonies away from the dangers of racial prejudice and violence went unheeded.[13]

Nonetheless, freedpeople sought control over the spatial geography of their local communities to counteract the threat of violence. Ulysses Houston, another of the Savannah ministers, led 1,000 blacks to Skiddaway Island, Georgia, where they established a self-governing community and elected Houston governor. Eventually forced to abandon their land, Skiddaway's ex-slave population, like others on the Sea Islands, continued their quest for physical distance and safety in other ways.[14] Across the South, freedpeople fled the countryside for the protection afforded in towns and cities like Richmond, Mobile, Nashville, New Orleans, and Atlanta. Despite large-scale riots in New Orleans and Memphis in 1866, which targeted African Americans in those cities, urban areas generally were safer, policed by Union soldiers, many of who were black, and later black policemen as well. There was also safety in numbers. "They leave the country in many instances because they are outraged, because their lives are threatened; they run to the cities as an asylum," surmised Henry McNeal Turner in his testimony to Congress in 1871. Abram Colby, a black Republican from Greene County, Georgia, echoed Turner's conclusions about this first Great Migration. According to Colby, freedpeople from his area went to cities like Atlanta "for protection" because "the military is here and nobody interferes with us . . . we cannot stop anywhere else so safely."[15] Although violence was just one factor among many that drove freedpeople off the plantations and farms, it is clear that freedpeople went to great lengths to put themselves out of their former masters' reach and avoid the violence that flourished in the backwoods.

Life in postwar Southern cities presented its own challenges. Immigrants from the countryside endured unsanitary living conditions, intense overcrowding, disease, inadequate housing, and poverty. Their white urban neighbors were far from welcoming as were the cities' freeborn black population, who sometimes regarded the new arrivals as "ignorant country darkies" who threatened the fragile balance of power and social status free blacks struggled to maintain. But for the thousands who flocked to the South's cities and towns, it seemed safer and more hospitable than the rural areas they left behind. The "rival geography" slaves created in their quarters, and in woods and swamps, to minimize slavery's brutality seems to have shifted from the countryside to the city after emancipation.[16]

The diffuse and often unpredictable nature of postwar violence, however, made it difficult to find refuge from the barrage of insults and assaults that came at freedpeople from all directions. The "outrage reports" from the Freedmen's Bureau list attackers ranging from Union military personnel, former owners, paramilitary "patrols" and other quasi-law enforcement officers, to "unknown." Often, however, freedpeople knew who assaulted them and named them publicly either to a Bureau officer or in court. The personal nature of much of the violence recorded by the Bureau attests to both its pervasiveness in postwar society as well as the indeterminacy of power relations in everyday life.[17]

When Hickory Foster left Charleston for Mount Holly, South Carolina, he hoped to find work as a carpenter, carrying two planes with him on the train north from the coast. As he disembarked the train in Mount Holly, he set down his bundle and planes, the sight of which caught the attention of a white man named John Hamlin. Perhaps Hamlin was also a carpenter, or maybe he just bristled at the sight of a newly arrived freedman in his town, but for whatever reason he picked up Foster's prized tools and smashed them against the railroad cars. Hamlin then cussed Foster and stamped his foot. Although Foster reported the incident to the Bureau headquarters at Moncks Corner, it is unknown if he received any kind of restitution from Hamlin for his destroyed property or the assault on his person. This relatively minor incident may not compare in horror to the innumerable of rapes, beatings, and murders that litter the pages of the Freedmen's Bureau reports, or the spectacular "massacres" in Memphis, New Orleans, Camilla, Colfax, and Hamburg that captured the nation's attention throughout the period, but it is important nonetheless. Hickory Foster endured some of the "small, endless, mean little injustices of everyday" that, according to Chicago *Tribune* correspondent Sidney Andrews, "most wronged the negro" and eventually would "kill him off." Although Foster did not know Hamlin prior to his arrival in Mount Holly, he found himself the object of the white man's personal bitterness and hostility. For reasons not entirely clear, Foster was subjected to a minor but violent assault (the stamping of his foot) and forced to watch his livelihood broken to shards against the side of a train car. No doubt, this was the most damaging aspect of Hamlin's assault on Foster, although who can measure the toll taken by countless cussings or hungry bellies denied even the most meager of federal rations?[18]

Among the other assailants often listed in Bureau records but less frequently discussed among historians were freedpeople themselves. A brief survey of cases brought before the Freedmen's Courts in Virginia reveals the prevalence of domestic and intraracial violence among former slaves. On July 4, 1866, Charlotte Revis brought charges against her husband Adam for "beating and abusing her and allowing others to beat her" in Charlottesville. Ten days later, Hester Ann Burwell charged Celia Franklin, another freedwoman, for beating her "without cause or provocation" in the same court. At the same time, Charles Lennox assaulted Martha Cosby, his sister-in-law, when she tried to visit her sister's children. Cosby appealed to the court for protection not only for herself but for the children as well. In August of the next year, two freedmen with the same surname, Ben and Barry Davis, were charged with "violating and ravishing" a black woman named Chany Stevens in Danville. In Winchester, Caroline Jenkins charged James Hawkins with repeatedly trying to sleep with her, and when she refused, drawing a revolver on her in an attempt to force her to have sex with him. Hawkins went into hiding and the court officials were unable to locate him. Court records are replete with similar cases of spousal violence, family quarrels, and other black-on-black assaults. Although Southern white critics of Reconstruction would often point to such cases as evidence that blacks were unfit to be free, much less enjoy any political or civil rights, we should not downplay their existence or underestimate their impact on freedpeople's everyday lives. Home was not always the safe haven the Edisto Islanders imagined it to be.[19]

"We is come to the law now"

Perhaps one of the most striking aspects of slavery's fitful demise is the surprising lack of interest among freedpeople in exacting some kind of retribution from their old masters for the physical violence they had endured. Whites certainly expected it. Their fears of insurrection among their former slaves, recorded in the reports of Freedmen's Bureau agents of white militias terrorizing and abusing freedpeople and letters to provisional governors asking that the whites be allowed to arm themselves to put down the threat, represented whites' anticipation of their chickens coming home to roost. The Freedmen's Bureau agent in Magnolia, Mississippi, summed it up nicely: "a man seldom fears a man with whom he deals justly, while he does fear the man whom he has wronged, in proportion to the wrong sustained. To fear the negro insurrection then is to confess the negro outraged, and violence is apprehended as the result." White Southerners were not alone in their anticipation of violence from the freedmen. In the Emancipation Proclamation itself, Abraham Lincoln felt compelled to advise freedpeople "to abstain from all violence, unless in necessary self-defence." Likewise, orders from military commanders and the Freedmen's Bureau routinely warned Southern blacks against seeking a pound of flesh from those who had wronged them. An army quartermaster at City Point, Virginia, took it upon himself to address the freedmen about their proper behavior. "What next—taking revenge on your old masters who have separated families, whipped and otherwise abused you?" he asked them, acknowledging the emotions that might lead to fantasies if not acts of revenge. "If you do that," he warned, "that is wrong, as you know, and besides against the *Law* and you must not break the law."[20]

For the most part, freedpeople took the quartermaster's advice to follow the law. To the extent that they had imbibed the tenets of liberal democracy, most freedpeople acquiesced to the law's authority and welcomed it as a replacement to the impunity of their former masters. "We have no massa now—we is come to the law now," declared Florida freedmen. Despite the violence they continued to endure from whites who struggled to maintain domination over them, many freedpeople endeavored to live up to the ideals of a free society which meant letting the courts decide personal disputes and punish those who might violate one's person or property. As the most local representatives of the law, Freedmen's Bureau agents received the bulk of freedpeople's complaints and grievances. Agents oversaw the formation of tribunals, known as "freedmen's courts," to ensure that Southern blacks received fair trials. They adjudicated not only disputes regarding labor arrangements but also personal disputes between individuals over any number of matters including assault and battery. The local agent was, according to Eric Foner, a "diplomat, marriage counselor, educator, supervisor of labor contracts, sheriff, judge, and jury." While more serious crimes, such as murder, were usually sent to a provost martial or the state courts if they accepted black testimony, the thousands of cases brought before the freedmen's courts across the South demonstrate the willingness of most freedpeople to let the law take its course.[21]

Freedpeople were sensitive to charges that they harbored violent intentions toward whites. Members of Wilmington's Equal Rights League protested against charges that they were a secret organization bent on intimidating freedmen into voting the Republican ticket or violently opposing whites. "We disclaim the remotest intention of enforcing our claims by violence," William Cutler, the League's president, declared in an open address to citizens of the Wilmington area. "Does anyone *suggest* insurrection! We frown upon him; we denounce him," Cutler insisted. Members did not, as some whites claimed, hoard weapons and ammunition in preparation for a race war. "Arms can do nothing for us," Cutler added, "our appeal is to the minds and hearts of free American citizens." A meeting of black citizens in Norfolk likewise vehemently denied accusations of violence made against them. Many of these men and women had witnessed nearly three years earlier the spectacle of violence left by local whites after the Emancipation Day parade—dead horses with their eyes cut out. Indignant that such charges should be made against them, a mass meeting convened to denounce attempts to discredit them and sully their legitimate, peaceful organizing efforts. Calling such accusations "vile falsehoods designed to provoke acts of unlawful violence against us and bring about the very evils they affect to deprecate," the citizens opened their meetings to the public and invited those concerned about their intentions to come and see for themselves. The meeting then affirmed their "faith in God and our Country and in the justice and humanity of the American people for redress of grievances" and promised to "labor in all lawful and proper ways for equal rights as citizens." Subsequent mass meetings in Hampton and Williamsburg adopted similar resolutions condemning violence and affirming their faith in the law.[22]

In making their claims to citizenship and protection, freedpeople looked to balance their particular vulnerability as a race with their rightful possession of citizenship rights enjoyed by all Americans. In doing so, they questioned the nature of the relationship between the physical body and the body politic. The Edisto Islanders pointed to the physical abuses they had endured as slaves in order to remind General Howard of the government's obligation to them. "You ask us to forgive the land owners of our Island, *You* who only lost your right arm," they wrote, implying that Howard, who lost his arm at the Battle of Seven Pines in 1862, failed to understand the gravity of their situation. Howard's war wound did not compare to having been systematically tortured, tied to a tree and flogged, and having to watch mothers and sisters "stripped & flogged" as well. The wounds white Americans suffered "In war," the Islanders concluded, might allow for forgiveness, but the abuses of slavery did not, at least not without some form of compensation—land. The Islanders demanded that Howard recognize the special nature of their past suffering and their continued physical vulnerability.[23]

Other groups of freedpeople around the South made similar claims that questioned the radical break with the past that Howard and other government agents believed emancipation represented. In June 1865, blacks in Richmond met to consider the state of affairs facing the newly freed and expressed their "sad disappointment" with their present condition. In a petition to President Johnson, the Richmond community informed the executive that their lives were now "in many respects worse than when we were slaves, and living under slave law." The committee pointed out with irony, "Under the old system, we had the protection of our masters, who were financially interested in our physical welfare."

CHAPTER THREE

Freedom, however, stripped their former masters of any incentive to care for black people. "That protection is now withdrawn," the delegation told the president, "and our old masters have become our enemies, who seek not only to oppress our people, but to thwart the designs of the Federal Government and of benevolent Northern associations in our behalf." The petition recounted instances of physical abuse that betrayed the promise of emancipation—whippings, forced labor, and men being arrested and jailed for not carrying passes. The petitioners pointed out the defunct state of Southern civil society and the unreliability of institutions that Northern politicians took for granted. They informed the president, "We cannot appeal to the laws of Virginia for protection, for the old negro laws still prevail . . . so that we have nowhere to go for protection and justice but to that power which made us free."[24]

A group of ten freedmen from Lincoln County, Tennessee, repeated the black Richmonders' claim that slavery had provided them a modicum of protection that freedom did not. "In our former condition as slaves, we had the protection of our masters, and it was to their interest, at least, to consult for, and secure our physical welfare," the freedmen explained in a petition to the Assistant Commissioner for the regional Freedmen's Bureau. Emancipation had severed the old ties between master and slave, but the state's civil institutions had yet to be radically transformed, leaving the freedmen in a dangerous limbo with nowhere to turn but to "the United States Authority," which the men deemed their "only other recourse, besides God." Not only had their employers whipped them and withheld their wages, the freedmen were prohibited from bringing a case to court or seeking redress in normal civil or criminal channels. By pointing out the dramatic incongruity between their former masters' bare economic interest in their physical protection and the government's apparent indifference to them, the freedmen aimed to shame officials into acting on their behalf. They also invoked the language of loyalty to compel the Bureau officials to recognize their claims:

During the continuance of the war, we have not been engaged in insurrection, or in any way been insubordinate to constituted authority: and in the future, as in the past, we propose to be a law abiding people. As in the past, we have by our labors enriched our masters, in many instances, besides supporting ourselves and our families. We now, simply ask that we may be secured as others, in the just fruits of our toil: protected from unjust, and illegal punishments, and we are sure we will keep our families from want, and do our part as good citizens of the United States to add to the wealth and glory of the Country. We are recognized as men by the Constitution of the land: we only ask to be treated as such, and we will, in the future as in the past, be law abiding men.[25]

The Tennessee freedmen reminded Bureau officials of their uncompromising devotion to the Union cause during the war. Their former masters, who now enjoyed the protection of the law, had "engaged in insurrection." They asked only for what their former masters could expect and enjoy—"that we may be secured . . . in the just fruits of our toil: protected from unjust, and illegal punishments." The freedmen also demonstrated their clear understanding of the reciprocal duties of protection and allegiance, promising "to do our part as good citizens of the United States to add to the wealth and glory of the Country." They also reminded the Bureau, however, that their allegiance was conditional. "We are recognized as men by the Constitution of the land: we only ask to be treated as such, *and we will, in the future as in the past, be law abiding men."*

"We feel, unsettled as Sheep Without a Shepard," wrote another group of former slaves, members of the Medway Church near Savannah, Georgia. Their words demonstrated a keen understanding and appreciation of the dynamics of power at play in the postwar South. Without a protective authority that could shield them from the greed, avarice, and sheer meanness of their former masters, freedom remained a theoretical abstraction. The Liberty County delegation recognized the tentative nature of freedom when they remarked that slavery was the condition "that we have *Just to some extent* Been Delivered from." Like the freedmen from Virginia and Tennessee, the Georgians recounted abuse they sustained from private citizens, namely their former owners, as well as local and state officials who enacted laws, commonly known as the "Black Codes," which denied them access to the courts or sentenced them to long jail terms or stripes for the slightest offenses. Others were less deferential and more demanding in their petitions for protection. "Can it be possible that we are to be kicked and cuffed about in this manner and no one to protect us?" asked South Carolina freedmen of their local Bureau agent. Unsatisfied with his response, the men mocked the government, saying, "We have no protection from this So Called State."[26]

As the ultimate symbol of slavery's continued influence, violence represented the government's lack of power in the immediate postwar South. By repeatedly invoking the state's obligation to protect them, freedpeople called upon notions of reciprocity that were in some ways reminiscent of slavery's paternalistic ethos. Slaves often used a language of obligation and reciprocity to compel their masters to grant them a variety of privileges due to them by virtue of the lopsided power relation of the master-slave relationship. Humane treatment, including protection from physical abuse, was but one of a number of benevolent gifts slaves attempted to make into customary rights albeit with limited success.

Nevertheless, power rested in the hands of he who could protect as well as punish, and it seemed in the early days of Reconstruction that the federal government could do neither.[27]

Freedpeople demanded a show of force as proof of the power that the state claimed to possess. It is evident from reading those letters and petitions to Southern governors and to the Freedmen's Bureau that without such a demonstration the vision of liberal citizenship that Bureau agents and other state officials had to offer was in serious jeopardy. Those agents spoke in an abstract language of rights that contained little specific information about what ex-slaves were entitled to or could expect from the government except their "right" to work for wages. They promised that hard work, thrift, and faithful passivity would bring freedom's rewards. Freedpeople were encouraged to "wait patiently until you know what your rights are" and that the free market would correct any abuses they might suffer in the meantime. General Howard's reassurance to the Edisto Islanders when they told him of being whipped and thrown off of the plantations by their former owners seemed out of touch and naïve, at best. Howard insisted, "The old master would be very foolish to try a system of oppression as it would ruin them forever . . . If the planters combine as you think, they will soon be able to get no labor." Howard's faith in the power of free labor made him dismissive of the Islanders' fears and their knowledge of the continued power of physical coercion and domination.[28]

The abstract, disembodied notion of citizenship and free labor that Howard expressed derived from both the republican tradition as well as antislavery and women's rights discourse. The universal language of citizenship, based upon the idea of self-ownership, what John Locke identified as "property in one's person," provided the theoretical underpinnings of American political culture from the Revolution through the antebellum period. In antislavery discourse, ideas of universal personhood translated into the belief that the slave's physical deprivation and suffering could be transcended. The Civil War's nationalizing impulse further empowered the drive to make ascriptive, physical qualities irrelevant to citizenship. In 1866, when the American Equal Rights Association announced their campaign to "bury the woman in the citizen," Radical Republicans also commenced a movement to bury the slave in the citizen by erasing the "badges and incidents of slavery" as they applied to African Americans' political status. Turning on its head chief justice Roger Taney's embodied, historical narrative of American citizenship that belonged to whites only, Republicans hoped that their universal, abstracted citizenship would open the doors to African Americans that the Supreme Court had closed on Dred Scott.[29]

That vision of the disembodied liberal citizen, however, stood in stark contrast to the physical, embodied experiences freedpeople articulated in their complaints. Rather than appeal to ideas of belonging removed from the physical experience of slavery, the petitions reveal how the pain and suffering endured before emancipation continued to inform freedpeople's understanding of where they stood in relation to the nation-state. As slaves, their bodies had been marked not only by color but also by physical punishment. In much the same way that the disability rights movement would demand recognition of physical vulnerability and a readjustment of the rights of citizenship for the disabled in the late twentieth century, ex-slaves created a radical political discourse that placed bodies marked by violence and race within the American liberal democratic tradition. In so doing, they revealed the "unacknowledged embodiment of all citizens" even as some bodies (white, male) enjoyed a kind of "invisible neutrality" that allowed them to stand in for the idealized public body of the citizen.[30]

By creating a historical narrative of physical vulnerability to justify their inclusion in the national body politic, freedpeople embarked upon an innovative but risky journey. "Remembering bondage was tricky," as Kathleen Clark reminds us, and while freedpeople sought to establish their physical and political autonomy, they did so using the language of obligation and dependence. The themes of abuse and homelessness that gave their petitions such moral currency were also registers of racial inferiority. Given the postwar anxieties about black bodies and their presumed propensities for violence and disorder, demonstrations of physical depravation and victimization could reinforce rather than break down negative racial stereotypes that excluded African Americans from the body politic.[31]

Militias

Dependency did not define all aspects of freedpeople's political claims. Despite the Wilmington Equal Rights League's hesitancy to be associated with militant resistance, emancipation and military service opened up the possibility of collective self-defense, which gave black Southerners hope. Across the South, freedpeople petitioned officials to organize local militias, many of them led by black veterans. After their discharge from the army, eight soldiers from the 34th Regiment petitioned to form a militia company in Jacksonville, Florida, in order to protect the city's "peaceable citizens." On Fenwick Island, South Carolina, five former members of the United States Colored Troops (USCT) were charged with illegally organizing a militia company and acting as a local police force. When a military commander ordered their leader to disband his regiment, he "positively refused." The men of this company retained their Union Army insignia and uniforms. Another former soldier asked the military commander of Atlanta for permission to form a quasi-military company he wished to call the "Lincoln Blues" in celebration of the Fourth of July in 1867. Likewise, a group of South Carolina freedmen asked that the "African United Blues" be allowed to bear arms for the Independence Day celebration in 1868. The "Lincoln Reserves" in Washington, DC, also asked the War Department for arms. Both groups were denied. So were the men who formed "Lincoln's Georgia Cavalry" near Savannah. In Richmond, a group of black men asked governor Francis H. Pierpont to give them a "lawful commission" to drill as the "National Guards" in order to "become efficient in military tactics, to the end that we might elevate our race." No record of Pierpont's response remains, but it is likely that their request met with the same denial as their counterparts in DC and Savannah. When Maj. Gen. Lorenzo Thomas notified his superior officer, Gen. Ulysses S. Grant, that freedmen in the vicinity of Georgetown, near the nation's capital, had organized a militia and called themselves the "Independent Zoaves," Grant informed him that it was "inexpedient" to allow them to drill.[32]

While some companies petitioned for official recognition, many others were ad hoc and cared little whether or not the government sanctioned their actions. In Jacksonville, another "several hundred" freedmen armed themselves after a rumor circulated that workers on a nearby plantation would be sold as slaves to Cuba. In response to their plan to "free the captives" with armed force, the local Freedmen's Bureau agent eventually succeeded in convincing them that the rumor was false. Freedmen in Georgetown, South Carolina, solicited contributions from the community for ammunition and formed armed companies to aid in their negotiations with employers, and they enjoyed some success. They negotiated contracts in which they worked two days for their employers, three days for themselves, and had both Saturday and Sunday off. Freedpeople argued that forming militias in their own communities was the best way to keep the peace. In Edenton, North Carolina, they attempted to raise a company for protection as well as to police their own members. "We don't wish to rebeal [sic]," they assured their Freedmen's Bureau agent, "we only wish to restrane [sic] those that wish to rebeal [sic]."[33]

In the early days after emancipation, drilling, parading, and wearing militia-style uniforms held symbolic importance for freedpeople who wished to express their newfound freedom. Freedpeople used militias as a vehicle to move between the spheres of what Dylan Penningroth identifies as the legal and extralegal political institutions of the postwar South. Penningroth argues that to establish a new political identity freedpeople utilized many "extralegal forums" in addition to the more formal arenas that became available to them during Reconstruction. Church meetings, community "clubs," and public arguments may have been as important as provost courts and the Freedmen's Bureau as venues in which freedpeople aired their grievances, settled disputes among one another or with whites, or made claims against the government. By providing freedpeople with a recognizable organizational structure, a highly visible mode of display and public recognition, and a rich playbook of symbolic rituals from which to enact a very potent image of emancipation, militias became one of the most popular political forums in the South. Later, after Southern governments decided to re-arm their state militias, these local black regiments became part of a larger legal institution sanctioned by the state government and armed—literally—with the power to enforce and interpret the law, and thereby live out their notions of justice. Furthermore, black militias represented freedpeople's "aggressive determination" to defend themselves against white violence and assert their right to political participation as key to the struggles of Reconstruction.[34]

The association of black militias with the performance of overtly political rituals at election times, however, obscures the importance these quasi-military groups and individuals with military credentials had in freedpeople's everyday lives. Black soldiers and militiamen became freedpeople's unofficial protectors in the postwar South. Henry McNeal Turner wrote Edwin Stanton that the presence of black troops curbed the discourteous behavior whites often displayed toward freedpeople. "The fact is," Turner explained, "when colored Soldiers are about they are afraid to kick colored women, and abuse colored people on the Streets, as they usually do." Another white officer attested to the security black troops brought to neighboring black communities. "The Freedpeople feel secure and protected, and are little molested by the Whites," he reported to his commander in response to complaints headquarters had received about the presence of black soldiers in the area. Black soldiers also performed important community-building work. In Helena, Arkansas, black troops built an orphanage, not only clearing the ground, but also erecting "four substantial buildings" and collecting money to support the children to be housed there. Because they received wages from the army, however unequal or irregular, black soldiers in the postwar South represented the tangible benefits of a cash economy thereby attaining a position of economic importance among freedmen. Likewise, many black soldiers had learned to read and write while in service, and as a result, they became a bridge to the bureaucratic world of the federal government that now governed Southern life. Erasmus Booman, a Virginia freedman, wrote to secretary of war Edwin Stanton on blue-lined paper given to him by a black soldier. Black soldiers also wrote letters for freedmen seeking lost family members or government assistance. Edwin O. Latimer, an army captain stationed in Wilmington, North Carolina, complained to his superiors that freedpeople looked to black soldiers to solve disputes with their former masters and that the soldiers readily "assume the responsibility of redressing their wrongs." This was certainly true of Sgt. E. S. Robison, a member of the 102nd USCT stationed in Columbia, South Carolina. Robison wrote to the Department of the South on behalf of local freedmen whom he found to be "Shamefuly abused." He told of how white men searched without warrant the home of Andrew Lee "with a pretinse [sic] of searching for a hog that they Claimed to have lost." The men broke open Lee's belongings and ransacked his house. When Lee complained to the post commander, the officer dismissed Lee and told him that the men had a right to search his house, and that if he protested further, he would be put "in the Guard house." Robison was irate at this injustice. "I could not hold my temper After fighting to get wrights [sic] that White men might Respect By Virtue of the Law," he declared, and asked that the matter be investigated. After Reconstruction, militias continued to play important roles in the lives of local people in some areas. In the Louisiana sugar parishes in the 1880s, militias protected black workers from exploitation and defended them when they struck for better wages.[35]

For many Southern blacks struggling against the violence aimed at curtailing their freedom, an expanded sense of what it meant to "come to the law" included militia organizing and other means of collective self-defense. While they insisted that such actions were legitimate and necessary, in an attempt to distinguish themselves from their white paramilitary counterparts, such as the Ku Klux Klan, freedpeople nonetheless maintained that having access to a means of organized violence was crucial for their survival as well their economic and political independence. Yet this was not simply acquiescence to the nature of paramilitary politics in the Reconstruction South; it was also a commentary on the essence of political legitimacy everywhere.[36]

The political career of Texas freedman Matt Gaines illustrates this point well. Born a slave in Louisiana, Gaines made numerous escapes, a habit that eventually led to him being sold to a Texas cotton planter in 1863. A lay preacher, Gaines possessed extraordinary oratorical skills that gained him a large grassroots following in Washington County, in the eastern part of the state's "hill country."[37] The pulpit and the podium were often one and the same for Gaines, who used his authority to persuade his parishioners to support the Republican Party. But it was Gaines's advocacy of armed self-defense for freedpeople that makes him a notable figure for this story. As a member of the legislature in 1870, he supported the militia bill in the hope of protecting black lives and voting rights as well as staving off a race war. In response to members of the Democratic opposition who foreshadowed that "the old Dead Confederate spirit of Vicksburg would rise up again" if the bill passed, Gaines warned that if the bill did not pass, "the dead spirit of those [blacks] who were massacred at Fort Pillow would also rise," referring to the slaughter of black soldiers by Nathan Bedford Forrest and his Confederate cavalry.[38] Gaines was unafraid to buck the Republican Party when necessary to advance his primary concern of protecting black lives. "We will arm old women with ax and hoes and our young men with double barrel guns and clean them up," Gaines declared although it was unclear whether he meant white terrorists or his own Party. Gaines did not support the Republican candidate for Congress, William Clark. Gaines wanted a black candidate, and in his unwillingness to push his considerable support for Clark, he had rankled many in his own party, including governor Edmund Davis. Gaines feared that his outspokenness had placed his life in jeopardy. "If I die I pray that you who are present today will take seven fold vengences [sic] for me," he told his audience at a pre-election rally. "If they want to fight the war [there is] no better time than now," and with this Gaines made perfectly clear the lengths he was willing to go to ensure black security and political independence.[39]

Governor Davis and other party leaders had good reason to believe that Gaines was not alone in his militancy. While freedpeople overwhelmingly supported Davis, they nonetheless demanded that he either protect them against the Klan and other violent actors or enable them to protect themselves. Perhaps the most foreboding advice came from D. F. Davis of Waco, who wrote to Governor Davis imploring him to recognize the heavy responsibility of leadership during such perilous times:

All desire that you may not fall like . . . all other men who have dared forsake the <u>vilent force</u> [*sic*] of the times. It is that force of which you at present are the honored Representative which has been voted up. Men are no more feathers in a wind unless they truthfully represent it. It was that force which causes your constituency to swim rivers upon rafts and to through the Eon to vote for you . . . If you for a moment depart from that <u>force</u> all that you friends can do will not be able to hold you up.[40]

The "vilent force" that D. F. Davis spoke of is only implied, but can we doubt that it is more than mere metaphor? Ideas about citizenship or equality meant little in Reconstruction-era Texas without the necessary force to back them up. Should the governor fail to buttress his philosophy with action, his failure would be assured. Davis ended his letter with one final, ominous warning: "Let the old ideas survive and you perish with the new."

Davis's recognition that force played a central role in democratic governance highlights an otherwise invisible element buried in the notion of "popular sovereignty." As Edmund Morgan points out, "Government requires make-believe," and the notion that the consent of the governed laid the foundation of the American state became one of its founding myths, a myth that buried the nation's reliance on violence and coercion as a means to expand and legitimize its own existence. Even in ostensibly modern, peace-loving, democratic nations, political legitimacy rests upon the control of both the means and the meaning of organized violence. To make it appear as though the people willingly give that power to the state is an act of sheer wizardry. Men like Gaines and Davis had the audacity to pull back the curtain.[41]

Slavery's Long Shadow

Although land, autonomy, and family were central to freedpeople's own sense of redemption from slavery, there remained the troubling possibility that some things would not be easily overcome, if at all. If history has been a burden for white Southerners who have struggled to cope with the poverty, disillusionment, and guilt that resulted from losing the war, then black Southerners likewise have wrangled with the past and memories of pain and loss. Saidiya Hartman writes about the unbearable weight of this history when she tells the story of her paternal grandparents, immigrants from the former Dutch slave colony of Curaçao, whose "losses were too immediate" to speak of slavery, and whose new lives in America failed to offer much solace, despite their best hopes. "Nostalgia or regret could kill you in a place like America," Hartman writes, realizing that her grandparents' disengagement with the past was a form of self-protection. "When it became clear that they would never return home, my grandparents erected a wall of half-truths and silence between themselves and the past," she recalled. "They parceled time, lopping off the past as if it were an extra appendage, as if they could dispose of the feelings connecting them to the world before this one . . . In time, they decided the present was all they could bear."[42]

History could be dangerous. Like a venomous reptile, it had to be handled gingerly. Worried that a focus on slavery's abuses might strengthen ideas of black degradation, some freeborn African Americans were hesitant to bring up the past. Instead, they encouraged freedpeople to look forward and forget the physical suffering they had endured as slaves. James Lynch, the AME missionary from Baltimore who opposed the idea of separate freedmen's colonies, used the Biblical story of Exodus to stress freedpeople's deliverance from bondage in a Fourth of July speech he gave in Augusta, Georgia. "Slavery is no more," he declared, and he encouraged Southern blacks to rejoice in their liberation, rather than stew in hatred and bitterness. Lynch encouraged a spirit of reconciliation among white and black Southerners that painful memories would impede. "Now that the thunderings of artillery are no longer heard . . . and the constitutional amendment stands like a rainbow in the national sky, let North and South, white and black shake hands—join hearts—shout for joy . . . ," Lynch proclaimed, diminishing the importance of slavery's negative effects on blacks as well as whites. Henry McNeal Turner, a black chaplain with the colored troops and later speaking among coastal Georgians, also urged reconciliation. Although Turner used the memory of violence to impugn the very idea of white supremacy, he nonetheless recognized that he walked a fine line. Turner issued a disclaimer that the violence of the past need not impede the future: "Let me say that I have not referred to the cruelty of slavery to incite your passions against the white people . . . To the contrary, let us love whites . . . neither taunt nor insult them for past grievances. . . . Let us show that we can be a people, respectable, virtuous, honest, and industrious, and soon their prejudice will melt away . . . " By reminding blacks of horrific brutality, slavery's memory threatened Turner's invocation to respectability and good will.[43]

The hesitation that Lynch and Turner expressed about invoking slavery's violence in the postemancipation world is understandable. Sensitive to images of black degradation, men like Lynch and Turner worried that such talk might not only reinforce white racial prejudice but also inflame the hostilities of Southern whites. By calling for reconciliation and a limited amnesia with regard to slavery's many cruelties, both Lynch and Turner hoped to smooth over racial antagonisms that jeopardized blacks' safety and well-being in the postwar South. Some freedmen also wished to put the horrors of the past behind them. In a letter to his missing sister whom he had not seen for more than twenty years, Hawkins Wilson coyly described his life in Texas after being sold away from his family in Virginia as a young boy. Avoiding all mention of slavery, Wilson's letter instead informs his sister that he has married "a Texas girl" and has "learned to read, and write a little." He tells her of the Sunday school class he teaches and that he is a sexton in the Methodist Episcopal Church in Galveston. Despite his long list of accomplishments and his assurance that he is well and happy, Wilson's letter is heavy with the burden of his family's separation so long ago. Although a grown man, Wilson refers to himself as "Your little brother Hawkins" who "is trying to find out where you are and where his poor old mother is." Like a lost child, Wilson clings to the painful memories of their separation and relives them. "I shall never forget the bag of buiscuits [sic] you made for me the last night I spent with you," he writes. Wilson also reveals that his life since their parting, especially his religious enthusiasm, has focused on a solitary goal: reuniting his family and healing the pain of their separation. "Your advice to me to meet you in heaven has never passed from my mind," he informs the sister who most likely would never receive her brother's loving report, "and I have endeavored to live as near to my God, that if He saw fit not to suffer us to meet on earth, we might indeed meet in Heaven." Wilson's upbeat demeanor masks the pain he has endured since being sold away to Texas. He tells her that he had "a hard road to travel since I parted with you," but he stopped well short of naming any specific physical cruelties he endured as a slave. However, the pain of familial separation, felt thousands of times over throughout the South, left its own special, if invisible, scars.[44]

Wilson's letter is not unique. Despite the writer's particular historical context as a former slave searching for his lost family in America, it shares similar characteristics with personal correspondence contained in archives everywhere; in particular, Wilson's negotiation of the "epistolary relationship" between himself and his beloved sister demands that he be less than fully open with her about the past. In his study of immigrant letters in the late nineteenth and early twentieth centuries, David Gerber argues that such correspondence should be read for their silences as much as for the often-mundane details of everyday life that they contain. Letter writers consciously chose what stories to tell with an eye toward not only how those stories reflected their own sense of self but also the effect they would have on the recipient, usually a family member with whom the writer had a close relationship. "Precisely because the psychological and practical stakes are highest of all in dealing with such significant others," Gerber explains, "it may well be the case that the costs of 'clarity and truth' are sometimes deemed much too high. At our bests, most of us wish to be honest, but the consequences of being so, both for ourselves and for those dearest to us, often exact anguish and pain." In choosing not to include the details of his life growing up as a slave, Wilson spares both himself and his sister the pain that recounting them would cause.[45]

Slavery's historical record groans under the weight of this pain. As former slaves struggled to come to terms with slavery's myriad traumas, they searched for language to describe the indescribable. "Dem times," "unmerciful times," and "pitiful times"—these were the euphemisms they used to recall slavery. Clara Allen stopped herself from using the word "slave" to describe herself and other black people. "When de sla— colored folks go ter be old an' couldn't work much longer, their masters would sell um to keep from buryin' um," she recalled. Struck by the look in her eye or the twist of her mouth, the interviewer noted that "floods of ancient hatred for somebody or the whole white race" seemed to rush over Allen as she spoke. Others' reticence may have resulted from embarrassment. "My folks don't want me to talk about slavery," Sarah Debro informed the interviewers who came to collect her story. "They's shame niggers ever slaves."[46]

Shame, however, was not the primary obstacle impeding ex-slaves' efforts to speak of the past. Other emotions—sadness, grief, and pain—fragmented their memories. Although they often described routinized if not at times ritualized whippings and other punishments, their recollections sometimes shifted uncomfortably from the painful feelings they had about those encounters to a flatter, more ordinary description of the objects used to inflict punishment. For example, Charles Crawley recalled witnessing a slave sale in Petersburg, Virginia, and spoke of the slaves crying and kicking as they were dragged away from their loved ones. They were "lak crazy folks," Crawley said, and "it was pitiful to see 'em." That memory nearly overpowered Crawley, who abruptly stopped his story. "I don' like to talk 'bout back dar," he said. "It brung a sad feelin' up in me." However, he continued to talk about violence, describing in great detail the "cat nine tails" used to whip disobedient slaves. "Honey, dis strop was 'bout broad as yo' hand from thum' to lil finer, an' 'twas cut in strips." Perhaps it felt safer, easier to talk about an inanimate object than the desperate, flailing, wailing bodies of those struggling to hold on to their families. Straps, sticks, canes, whips, flyswatters, brooms, hands—the instruments of punishment make up a common motif in the postemancipation slave narratives as they occupied a place of prominence in the memories of those who endured them.[47]

When the flocks of Works Progress Administration (WPA) historians descended upon their homes in the 1930s to record their memories, many former slaves found it difficult to speak of slavery and give the kind of personal details that the interviewers wanted.[48] "I don't like to think about them times, much less talk about 'em," declared Beverly Jones when interviewers arrived at his home near Gloucester Court House, Virginia. "They over now, an' it ain' no point in worryin' 'bout 'em." Others shared Jones's reluctance. "You want me to tell yer 'bout slavery days? Well I kin tell yer, but I ain't," Elizabeth Sparks informed Claude Anderson when he came to her home in rural Virginia on a cold January day in 1937. Sparks was glad for the company, and welcomed Anderson and his assistant into her home. Unlike their counterparts in other Southern states, the Virginia interviewers were all black, which altered the dynamic between them and their subjects. Sparks, for instance, seemed torn between her desire to fulfill the young men's request and a wish to protect them from what she had seen. "S'all past now," she told them, "so I say let 'er rest; 's too awful to tell anyway. Yer're too young to know all that talk anyway." Sparks finally relented and promised to give them something to "put in yer book," but insisted, "I aint'a goin' tell yer the worse."

Yet she told them plenty. She told them about being beaten by both her master and mistress, taking to the woods to escape the punishment, and being constantly hungry. She told about how her mistress, "a good woman," she insisted, made her aunt Caroline stand up and knit when the woman got too sleepy late at night to continue. When Caroline would nod off standing up and begin to drop her needles, the mistress would take a switch across her hands. Sparks interrupted her own narrative continuously, at war with herself over the story she told: "But I aint'a goin tell yer nuffin'. No, I ain't. Tain't no sense fur yer to know 'bout all those mean white folks." She started to tell them of "much wrongness" her master committed but thought better of it, saying, "I couldn't tell yer all of it." But once she got started, she found it hard to stop. A slave girl named Betty Lilly, who "always had good clothes an' all the privlileges," was his favorite, Sparks explained, but that was as far as she could go, again insistent that she "cain't tell all!" Finally Sparks ended the interview. "Now yer tak dat an' go," she told Anderson. "Put that in the book. Yer kin make out wif dat. I ain't a-gonna tell you no more. No sir."[49]

Not surprisingly, rape and sexual abuse proved the most difficult to thing to talk about. Like Sparks, other female ex-slaves bore the memories of their sexual vulnerability close to them—a woman might speak only of refusing "to be wife" to the master, of white men trying to "throw" her, or of a young girl being put in the Big House "where the young masters could have the run of her." Minnie Folkes's mother had warned her of the danger of being young and female. "Don't let nobody bother yo' principle," she said, "'cause dat wuz all yo' had." Folkes took her mother's admonitions about sexual purity to heart. Married at fourteen, Folkes delighted in keeping her husband's house, cooking for him, and performing all her wifely duties, save one. After three months of marriage, her husband complained and she relayed to him her mother's warning. He convinced her to seek her mother's advice, and when Folkes told her that she wouldn't allow her husband to "get close" to her as her mother had advised, her mother corrected her gently and praised her daughter for being "a pu'fect lady."[50]

In a rare but nonetheless guarded moment, Robert Ellet recalled when he had "eight hundred dollars in bank notes and silver laid on my head" when he was eight years old by a white man who wanted to buy him. To Ellett, this was evidence of "what a find looking lad I was." The white man "said there was something in me that he wanted." *What would a man want with an eight-year-old boy?* Ellet appears to be asking himself this question as he tells this story, for his next statement, "Of course I was only eight, but I was strong and was working in the fields," is contradicted by the fact that he had accompanied his master to town, as well as his master's refusal to sell him because Robert had been bequeathed to his wife and could not be sold out of the family, suggesting he had lived in the main house. Therefore, it is unlikely that the buyer would have encountered the boy working in the fields. Furthermore, Ellet had previously told of growing up with the master's sons as playmates. "I played with them, ate with them, and sometimes slept with them. We were pals," he said. Could Ellet's self-proclaimed prowess at killing tobacco worms been what the man "saw" in him? Maybe. A healthy, young male slave certainly would bring a high price at auction some day. Or maybe the buyer had sexual designs on the young boy. Ellet's own doubts seem to seep through his otherwise ordinary story of a potential sale.[51]

Slavery's physical scars haunted some ex-slaves' spoken memories. Many recall being beaten or whipped with brutal regularity, and even those who claimed never to have been whipped themselves still could envision the checkerboard patterns left on other slaves' backs. The memory of it made Arthur Greene "shudder" when he described it to Susie Byrd in 1937. Katie Blackwell Johnson declared that her "Uncle" Lewis was whipped so many times that "when he went to Gawd he didn't have the skin he was borned with." Henrietta King took her interviewer's hand and placed it on her deformed face, which had been crushed years before under her mistress's rocking chair for stealing candy, so that they could feel "what slave days was like." Yet for others, the scars that remained after all those years were written on hearts instead of skin.[52]

The passing of time could not heal the pain of family separations. At ninety-seven years old, Ellaine Wright recalled with vivid detail the day her mother was sold away from her. According to the WPA interviewer who wanted to know Wright's memories of the Civil War, "just this one important thing clings to her memory—her parting with her mammy." Only four at the time, Wright remembered the last words her mother spoke to her: "Ellaine, honey, momma's goin way off and ain't never goin to see her baby agin." "An I can see myself holding only my momma and both of us cryin," Wright recalled, her emotion unnoted by the interviewer but seeping through her words. "And then she was gone and I never seed her since." Her mother's abrupt departure created a fissure in Wright's sense of time, a chasm too wide and painful to be bridged. Yet like Hawkins Wilson, Wright's religious faith provided her with hope for redemption. "I hopes I goin to see my good mamma some day, I do. Yes, I goin to do it son," she assures the interviewer (and perhaps herself as well), "I sure is, yes indeed."[53]

Memories could provide solace as well as grief. When the interviewer admired Clara Allen's hand knit counterpane bedspread and suggested she sell it, Allen flatly refused. "Naw'm I wouldn't part wid dat. I knit dat at de old place an those what show me is dead an' gone," she explained. "Dats all I got lef uf um." Charles Crawley found comfort in the home he and his mother bought when they became free. Proud of the fact that that he had managed to retain ownership after all those years, Crawley announced that his mother had died in her own home, and "Ise livin' in dis same house, dat she an' us all labored an' worked fer by de sweat o' our brow, an' wid dese hands." Like the Edisto Islanders, who sought protection both physical and spiritual in land and home, Crawley found peace in his house and the memories it sheltered.[54]

Hawkins Wilson may have wanted to spare his sister the knowledge of his physical suffering. He may also have heeded the advice of ministers like James Lynch who "prescribed a preventative does of forgetfulness" as a way to cope with the acute sense of loss he obviously felt. Whatever the reason, Wilson chose to evade the subject of violence altogether, but not all freedpeople were able to carry the pain of the past with such forbearance. Charlie Moses was eighty-four years old when in 1938 the WPA interviewer asked him about slavery. "Slavery days was bitter," Moses said, "an' I can't forgit [sic] the sufferin'. Oh, God! I hates 'em, hates 'em." He may have been bedridden with the infirmities of old age, but Moses's recollection of the abuse he and other slaves suffered at the hands of their master remained sharp. "I can tell you plenty 'bout the things he done to us poor Niggers," Moses informed the interviewer. "He whipped us 'til some jus' lay down to die. It was a poor life." Like Lynch, Moses had been a preacher, but he found little solace in the message of Christian forgiveness. Unable to let go of the hunger, deprivation, and punishment, even after all those years had passed, Moses exclaimed, "I knows it ain't right to have hate in the heart, but, God almighty! I prays to the Lord not to let me see him [his former master] when I die."[55]

Thomas Hall, an ex-slave living near Raleigh, North Carolina, also held onto the pain of the past, in no small part because the pain of the present demanded it. Hall mocked the WPA interviewer and his seemingly innocent request for his memories of slavery. If the interviewer expected to find the friendly, conciliatory, welcoming elderly ex-slave he found on other occasions, his shock at what Hall had to say is unrecorded. "When I think of slavery, it makes me mad. I do not believe in giving you my story," Hall informed the white man sitting in his house with tape recorder, "because with all the promises that have been made, the Negro is still in a bad way in the United States, no matter in what part he lives, it's all the same." Hall recounted a long history of whites' efforts to shape the memory of slavery to suit themselves. Harriet Beecher Stowe received the brunt of Hall's annoyance. He believed she wrote *Uncle Tom's Cabin*, a book commonly credited with helping to bring the conflict over slavery to a head in the 1850s and at the time hailed for its sympathetic depictions of slaves and their suffering, "for her own good." Hall explained, "She had her own interests at heart, and I don't like her, Lincoln, or none of the crowd." Hall saw the white WPA interviewer as part of "the crowd." "Now you may be all right; there are a few white men who are," Hall told him, "but the pressure is such from your white friends that you will be compelled to talk against us and give us the cold shoulder when you are around them, even if your heart is right toward us." Impatient with the interviewer's desire to *know* about slavery, Hall berated the man for his ignorance:

You are going around to get a story of slavery conditions and the persecutions of the Negroes before the Civil War and the economic conditions concerning them since that war. You should have known before this late date all about that. Are you going to help us? No! You are only helping yourself. You say that my story maybe put into a book, that you are from Federal Writer's Project. Well, the Negro will not get anything out of it, no matter where you are from. Harriet Beecher Stow wrote *Uncle Tom's Cabin*. I didn't like her book, and I hate her. No matter where you are from, I don't want you to write my story, because the white folks now and always will be against the Negro.[56]

Against his wishes, Hall's words were included in the WPA slave narratives, and I include them here because his anger, resentment, and bitterness are so palpable. Although I risk reproducing the same kind of interpretive theft that Hall recognized in Stowe's work as well as in the WPA narratives, I value his emotive response as an indictment of the transcendent stories of overcoming that he hated so much. *You should have known before this late date about all that.* Hall cannot tolerate the willful ignorance he sees in the interviewer's lack of knowledge about what he and other former slaves endured. *You are only helping yourself.* Hall knew that in telling the story of slavery and black suffering, whites had ulterior motives that often conflicted with the needs and desires of their black subjects. *I don't want you to write my story.* He wanted to retain authorship of his own history, disbelieving that anyone other than himself could write it, much a less a white person.

Neither Thomas Hall nor Charlie Moses experienced the kind of redemptive suffering that abolitionists had promised. Seventy-three years had neither eased either man's pain nor blurred their memories of slavery's violence. Unlike Hawkins Wilson, they were unwilling to push those memories down and incapable of the forgiveness that James Lynch encouraged. A fleeting glimpse into the inner life of a former slave, Hall's and Moses's words suggest the profound difficulty many like them must have had finding solace in the redemptive narrative of freedom. Their feelings of anger and resentment were difficult for freeborn men like Lynch, and later W. E. B. DuBois, to accept.

In *The Souls of Black Folk*, DuBois recalled meeting a "big red-eyed black" along the roadside in rural Georgia. The man had stopped them to ask about a recent incident in nearby Albany, where a white policeman had shot and killed a black boy for talking too loudly. Enraged by the continued violence leveled against him and his neighbors, DuBois recounted how the man vowed to kill any white man who touched him. DuBois, a meticulous chronicler of black life in the urban North as well as the rural South, recognized the "hot anger" that simmered close to the surface in many of the black folk he met, yet he could not allow the man to express his pain openly. When he began to recall slavery and seeing his father whipped and his mother working in the cotton fields "till the blood ran," DuBois quickly pulled away. Leaving the man in midsentence, the scholar who would become one of the leading spokesmen for the black race in the early twentieth century could not at that moment witness such pain.[57]

That pain has since been translated into other forms of cultural memory: protest literature, art, film, blues music, hip-hop. Through these mediums, African Americans have interrogated the idea of redemption, sometimes revising it, other times denouncing it altogether. For freedpeople, their belief in redemption was rooted in land, home, and family. But those dreams could not be separated from the terror and violence of slavery. The ballot and other political rights might ease the pain for some, but for others, their suffering had been so great that the promise of redemption could not be fulfilled.[58]

Freedpeople's understanding of redemption—and its limits—often stood at odds with the vision whites had for them. Although they certainly valued land, control over their labor, and cash wages, the value freedpeople placed on these aspects of freedom reflected the ways that violence had shaped their lives. Premised upon the recognition of their own physical vulnerability and the way that race contributed to their continued risk for violence, freedpeople's conception of rights was anything but disembodied or colorblind. In addition to their strivings for legal status and political rights, freedpeople also pursued paths to personal autonomy and physical safety that belied their faith in the liberal dogma of republicanism. The importance of local militias and, as we shall see in the following chapters, the organizing power of martial culture, revealed the importance of violence to the democratic transformation in Southern society that Republicans and freedpeople alike endeavored to make. Not only was it necessary to have access to the means of organized force, it was also incumbent upon freedpeople and their white allies to articulate a justification for employing those means that did not ignite the fears of slave rebellions and "race war" that haunted many white Americans both north and south.

FOUR

The Militarization of Freedom

"A man without force is without the essential dignity of humanity."
FREDERICK DOUGLASS, *MY BONDAGE AND MY FREEDOM*

"How extraordinary and what a tribute to ignorance and religious hypocrisy, is the fact that in the minds of most people, even those of liberals, only murder makes men." W. E. B. DUBOIS, *BLACK RECONSTRUCTION* (1935)

On July 4, 1863, *Harper's Weekly* published a triptych representing "A Typical Negro" in his transformation from slave to citizen (fig. 4.1). The first panel in the triptych featured a ragged contraband called Gordon who, the reader is told, escaped his brutal master in Mississippi and found his way to Union lines near Baton Rouge that spring. "With clothes torn and covered with mud and dirt from his long race through the swamps and bayous," the contraband Gordon represented the destitute and dependent condition of escaped slaves reaching Union lines as well as the lengths they were willing to go to get there. The central panel revealed the man's horribly scarred back, the product of years of physical abuse that army doctors found when they administered a physical examination for Gordon's induction into the service. The final panel shows a clean-shaven, smiling Gordon, nearly unrecognizable in his crisp, new Union Army uniform. The figure in the third panel, no longer a slave, shows none of the deprivation or suffering of the figures in the previous two. His scars covered by the uniform,

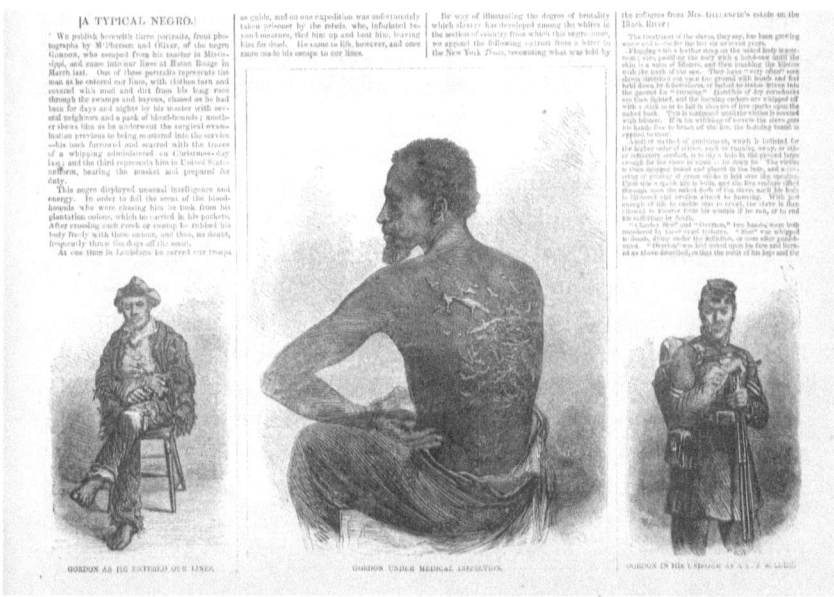

FIGURE 4.1 Gordon's transformation from slave to soldier. *Harper's Weekly*, July 4, 1863.

Gordon's image represented the promise of manhood and citizenship for black men who enlisted to fight for the Union.[1]

The center triptych of the *Harper's* study reproduced an already popular carte de visite entitled "The Scourged Back," the proceeds of which were said to benefit the education of freedpeople in the Department of the Gulf. Reproductions of the image proliferated after the *Harper's* expose. Gordon's image became a touchstone not only for the antislavery cause, the Union war effort, and black citizenship, but also the British workingman's movement, which used the scars to illustrate the need for laborers to unite against the ravages of wage slavery. More importantly, Gordon's transformation from slave to soldier epitomized the militarized vision of freedom that had begun to dominate the discourse surrounding emancipation in the United States.[2]

The vision of martial manhood that guided Gordon's transformation from ragged contraband to respectable soldier played an important role in the redemptive narrative of the war, emancipation, and Reconstruction. For many white abolitionists and Republican lawmakers, black soldiers represented not only a crucial military advantage over the Confederacy but also an ideal of independent manhood that seemed to answer the problem of dependency that clouded the dawn of freedom. For African

Americans, who longed to prove their manhood, and thus their worthiness to be included in the body politic as full citizens, the military offered respect, honor, and political enfranchisement. No longer suffering, supplicant slaves, black soldiers seized their freedom and demanded the rights of citizenship.

The image of the slave-turned-soldier, however, proved troubling for a society haunted by the specter of black violence and uncertain about the amount of independence that could be afforded the newly free. Gordon's image offered reassurances that black men would make obedient soldiers whose violence could be controlled and channeled to appropriate ends. The soldier Gordon leans unobtrusively on his upturned musket, his hand covering the barrel. This soldier could be trusted to use his musket wisely and not to fire it in revenge for the abuses he had endured. The army uniform covered Gordon's physical scars, ostensibly erasing them and his suffering. Through his military service, the illustration argued, Gordon transcended his slave past. Gordon's triptych assured white readers that the recruitment of black men into the army would not result in a second Saint-Domingue.

This chapter follows two distinct yet often intertwined paths, both of which emerged out of the swirl of anxieties and ambiguities that surrounded the recruitment of black men into the Union Army and their subsequent fight for "manhood rights." The first path questions the relationship between manhood, citizenship, and violence on which those claims for political rights were based. The triumphant story of black martial valor in the face of discrimination, unequal pay, and death on the battlefield obscures the gendered politics of emancipation that reduced freedom to a violent struggle between men. What one scholar terms the "obsession with manhood" not only relegated women to the sidelines of the era's political history but also masked critical aspects of the black military experience that circumscribed freedpeople's aspirations at the same time it opened up new possibilities. The limitations of martial manhood as a vehicle for freedom, however, remain largely unacknowledged. As the editors of the Freedmen and Southern Society Project's multivolume *Freedom: A Documentary History* series argue, "The achievements and pride engendered by military service helped to make the new world of freedom."[3]

Yet if military service ushered in a new world of freedom, it did so unevenly. Despite evidence of the growing acceptance of and admiration for black soldiers both within the army and among the Northern public, there remained troubling contradictions within the popular representations of black soldiers that countered the narratives of black martial valor and circumscribed the liberalizing effects that many believed military service would have on African American claims to citizenship. Military service also replicated aspects of violence and coercion that characterized a vision of freedom uncomfortably close to slavery. Forced enlistments, corporal punishments, and violent death—often stripped of the glory typically associated with battlefield sacrifice—also represented the black military experience during the Civil War. The coercion and violence inherent in military service intensified the racial politics of emancipation, reinforcing images of blacks as subservient, passive, and inferior. Despite republican ideology of the citizen-soldier, the nature of military service did not rule out forms of bondage and servitude either within the army or outside of it. Moreover, the term "citizen" can be misleading. Lawmakers may have acquiesced to the idea that black soldiers might well be citizens, but what rights that title entailed were unclear. After all, women and children could be citizens, too. Despite the universalizing language, not all citizens enjoyed equal civil or political rights. This may help explain why the gains black soldiers won, namely the right to vote, receded so quickly after the war was over. As Mary Frances Berry notes in her study of how the legal status of African Americans changed as a result of their Civil War service, when black soldiers were no longer needed to secure a military victory for the Union, the impetus to sustain their rights as citizens faded. While the Thirteenth, Fourteenth, and Fifteenth amendments represented revolutionary changes to the American body politic that would eventually overturn the racial restrictions of the Jim Crow era, the fact remains that the rhetoric of martial manhood employed by black veterans and their allies to win their rights in the 1860s did not sustain the larger projects of either Southern or national reconstruction.[4]

The chapter's second path traces the ambivalence that surrounded black soldiers and their violent performance of manhood. For while white reformers encouraged black enlistment as an important disciplinary and civilizing measure, they feared the other lessons black men might learn in the ranks. Advocates of black enlistment had to reconcile an effeminized image of enslaved black men as lacking the courage and intelligence necessary to become warriors with the murderous violence required of soldiers. In other words, slaves had to be violent enough to become good soldiers but not *too* violent. Such a refiguring of black masculinity entailed serious consequences for the process of Reconstruction, which would come to depend so heavily on black veterans and local militias for its grassroots survival. Black military service buttressed the redemptive narrative of freedom that abolitionists, veterans, and historians have told about the Civil War and emancipation. However, this narrative relied upon violent rituals of war and remembrance that created a highly gendered vision of freedom and citizenship. In turn, this militarization of freedom contributed to the explosion of racial and political violence that ultimately brought Reconstruction to such a dispiriting end.[5]

Resistance and Respectability

Although he was one of the most vocal proponents of the view that fighting would make slaves into not only men but also citizens, Frederick Douglass was hardly the first American to posit this theory. Historian Francois Furstenberg traces its origins to the American Revolution and finds that the relationship between freedom and violent resistance was grounded in the "peculiar combination of liberal and republican ideology" that justified armed struggle against Britain as a noble and virtuous act. The belief that "'nations were as free as they deserved to be'" translated to individuals as well and "made it possible to blame a *person* for his or her enslavement." Continued enslavement proved a person's unwillingness to resist, but resistance for black slaves was a tricky matter. Furstenberg relates the eighteenth-century folk story of Quashi, a slave who would not be whipped and after a violent struggle subdues his master at knifepoint. But instead of killing his master and fleeing, Quashi cuts his own throat rather than take the life of the man who enslaved him but whom he nonetheless loves "as [him]self." Furstenberg argues that Quashi's story prescribed the proper course of action for a "virtuous slave": suicide. Resistance that took the lives of white masters was inconceivable. Thus, the stories whites told about real-life slave rebels, such as Gabriel Prosser and Nat Turner, emasculated the men by portraying them as fearful and submissive once captured by authorities. Had they been "virtuous" like Quashi and truly undeserving of their enslavement, they would have killed themselves.[6]

Black abolitionists rejected the notion that a slave could prove his virtue only through death, but they maintained the link between freedom and violence. Frederick Douglass's unstinting faith that military service would result in freedom for slaves and political rights for all black men stemmed not only from the citizen-solider ideal that penetrated so much of American political culture since the revolutionary era but also from his own deeply transformative experience with violence. True freedom, according to Douglass, did not come as the result of a simple exchange of services—a kind of quid pro quo–but rather emanated from within. In his autobiography, he provided his readers with the most dramatic example of the power of fighting back. His refusal to submit to the efforts of the overseer Covey to break him marked a "turning point" in Douglass's life as a slave. Douglass wrote that the two-hour ordeal in which he and Covey fought "rekindled in my breast the smouldering embers of liberty . . . and revived a sense of my own manhood. I was a changed being after that fight. I was *nothing* before; *I was a man* now." His willingness to fight, to hazard the risk of death (either Covey's or his own), "recalled to life my crushed self-respect, and my self-confidence, and inspired me with a renewed determination to be a free man." Before the fight with Covey, Douglass had taken to the woods in fear of the slave driver's excessive cruelty. Wanting nothing more than to escape the beatings, Douglass had been cowed and found himself sleeping on the woodland floor, covered in leaves so as to escape detection. He recalled the feelings of helplessness and inadequacy, as he lay motionless in the dark, waiting for nearby footsteps to move on. He could not run much less fight. He could only hide and wait in what had become "the dark and pestiferous tomb of slavery," a tomb from which the fight with Covey would resurrect him. Lying in the woods, covered with leaves as well as his own fear, Douglass realized that "a man without force is without the essential dignity of humanity." This became for Douglass the very essence of slavery's effect on the human spirit. A slave was *a man without force*. To reclaim his humanity, Douglass used personal violence to make a symbolic break with his slave identity. Fighting back, striking out with force, drawing the master's blood: all of these symbolized Douglass's denial of his position of servitude and his demands for recognition as an individual. "When a slave cannot be flogged," Douglass argued, "he is more than half free." In the war, Douglass saw an opportunity to channel the desire to fight back—that he felt both as a slave and a free, yet marginalized, black man in the North—into a collective struggle for manhood and with it civil and political inclusion.[7]

Reiterating the themes of his autobiography, in which a moment of violence enabled Douglass to break the mental and eventually physical bonds of slavery, he told Northern crowds throughout 1863 that black men must "know that those who would be free, themselves must strike the blow, and they long for the opportunity to strike that blow." He chided those who believed that the recruitment of black soldiers was "only a military necessity," insisting, "it has a higher significance. It is a grand moral necessity." Douglass created a millennial vision of freedom that emerged from the Emancipation Proclamation and the enlistment of black men into the army. Together, these two things enabled African Americans to realize their full humanity by uniting their physical liberation with their spiritual one. This was, in his mind, the "the final perfection of the race."[8]

That perfection lay in the attainment of manhood and respect. Military service not only fulfilled black men's inner strivings but also rehabilitated the feminized image of enslaved men held by many whites, including those opposed to slavery. The specter of slavish passivity continued to haunt Douglass and other black abolitionists who endeavored to prove that African Americans did not deserve their enslavement. Military service legitimated the taking of white lives, a manly duty denied Quashi and other slave rebels. The Civil War represented the pinnacle for African Americans in the long journey toward freedom that began with Crispus Attucks and the Revolutionary War's "colored patriots." While everyday acts of resistance and self-defense provided African American men the means through which to assert their manhood, military service formalized these acts. The Civil War's scale provided black men an unprecedented opportunity to battle collectively for the emancipation of their race and with the sanction of state authority. As such, the sacrifices of the few might translate into rewards for the many. Douglass and his likeminded colleagues who aggressively campaigned for the inclusion of black men within the ranks of the Union Army responded to a fundamental if untested relationship between military service and citizenship. The Constitution recognized arms bearing as a protected right of citizens. It was the denial of that right to African Americans that Chief Justice Roger Taney pointed to in his infamous rejection of Dred Scott's citizenship claims. The fact that black men were barred from militia duty and restricted in their personal possession of firearms led Taney to conclude that they did not possess "any rights a white man was bound to respect."[9]

For Douglass, Taney's harsh words crystallized the importance of military service for black men: "let him get an eagle on his button, and a musket on his shoulder, and bullets in his pocket, and there is no power on the earth or under the earth which can deny that he has earned the right of citizenship in the United States." When Douglass proclaimed these words to a Boston crowd in July 1863, he referred not to the mere material possession of weaponry but rather to the authority and prestige they bestowed on their holders. Douglass aspired to that previously unattainable condition that Justice Taney so flippantly identified: respect. Likewise, when he surmised that there existed "something ennobling in the possession of arms," he looked beyond the instrument itself to the feelings its possession inspired in the holder as well as those who witnessed him.[10]

Douglass was not alone in his advocacy of military service as a vehicle for black liberation. Many radical abolitionists shared his vision of freedom as a violent process of man-making. Their perceptions of slavery's cruelty reflected the "foundational premise that slavery had emasculated

African American men." White and black abolitionists alike critiqued slaveholding by focusing the un-manning of enslaved men and its effects on individual development as well as the family. One prominent strain within this discourse focused on the inability of enslaved men to protect and defend their female kin. William Wells Brown expressed his tearful lament of having watched his mother being beaten and being helpless to stop it. "Experience has taught me," Brown wrote, "that nothing can be more heart-rending than for one to see a dear and beloved mother or sister tortured, and to hear their cries and not be able to render them assistance. But such is the position the American slave occupies." According to Brown, the "American slave" was male and the most "heart-rending" cruelty he had to endure was the emasculation of being denied protective authority over women's bodies. Women also decried their loss of men's protection. Even as she exposed slavery's attack on womanhood, Harriet Jacobs linked her own sexual vulnerability to the absence of male protectors. Her father was absent, and even had he been available to her, he could have done little to stop the lecherous advances of her master. The slave whom she loved likewise was unable to make her his wife. Her chosen lover, a white man who promised to free her and their children, was unreliable. Without any male figure to depend upon, Jacobs took to the attic.[11]

Enslaved men's inability to claim traditional patriarchal authority over the bodies of their female kin became part of a broader discourse about slaves' presumed passivity. In their attempts to paint a sentimental picture of the American slave with whom a wider public could sympathize, white abolitionists stressed enslaved men's natural docility and their Christian forbearance of slavery's brutality. In a sermon aimed to enlighten antislavery audiences to the dehumanization of Southern slaves as well as counter the charges that the antislavery movement aimed to foment a race war in the South, abolitionist minister Theodore Parker referred to them as "feeble" people who were naturally less aggressive and less vengeful than whites, while the poet Theodore Tilton described all blacks, not just the enslaved, as a "feminine people" who possessed "that strange moral, instinctive insight" typically ascribed to women. The white antislavery movement romanticized enslaved people as morally superior to the whites who held them in bondage, but like Harriet Beecher Stowe's Uncle Tom, they remained physically passive and essentially nonviolent.[12]

As the sectional conflict over slavery intensified, ideas of manly violence became increasingly important to radical abolitionism. Antislavery rhetoric became steeped in masculine bravado and bloody imagery.

Not only did abolitionists see slavery as a "state of war" that justified arming free-state settlers in Kansas, violence also became a regenerative force capable of wiping away the stain of slavery. Manly violence became an important corrective to the imagined docility of the enslaved. Black radical abolitionists rallied against the sentimental feminization of black men and called on their audiences to prove their physical commitment to the cause of liberty. Douglass began to imagine a "day of judgment" when God would exact vengeance for the slave; others, like David Walker and Henry Highland Garnet, worked to ensure that that day would come sooner rather than later. "Let your motto be RESISTANCE! RESISTANCE! RESISTANCE!" concluded Garnet in a rousing speech entitled "An Address to the Slaves of the United States of America," which he delivered to the American Anti-Slavery Society's national convention in 1843. According to Garnet, the mark of the slave was his unmanly submissiveness. "You act as though you were made for the special uses of these devils. You act as though your daughters were born to pamper the lusts of your masters and overseers," Garnet declared. Slave rebellion, whether imagined as in Frederick Douglass's novel *The Heroic Slave*, or actual as in John Brown's calamitous raid at Harper's Ferry, provided a means to collective and personal re-masculinization, and thus liberation, while at the same time uniting white and black men across racial lines in the cause of liberty.[13]

Black women abolitionists insisted upon equal representation within the antislavery movement as organizational leaders, speakers, and decision makers. However, the double bind of race and respectability in which they found themselves placed a premium on male authority and measured racial progress in masculine terms. As a result, black women abolitionists often echoed the wider concerns about the manhood of the race and saw their future tied to that of black men. Maria Stewart, one of the earliest and most militant black abolitionists, challenged the "Sons of Africa" to stand up for their manhood rights and "flee from the gambling board and the dance-hall." In a speech to a crowd gathered at Boston's Masonic Hall in February 1833, she chastised black men for neglecting their families and communities in pursuit of "frivolous amusement," ordering them out of the gambling dens, dance halls, and saloons. She implored them to remember their forebears who "bled and died in the revolutionary war" and those other black men who "fought bravely under the command of Jackson, in defense of liberty."

Stewart often invoked the memory of black patriots and their military sacrifice as a model of service to which African Americans could aspire. According to Stewart, progress and respectability reflected in the behavior of men, and she found little to admire in the apathetic and hedonistic attitudes she saw around her. She believed black men should devote themselves to the cause of "African rights and liberty" by forming temperance societies and schools, and becoming more militant in their resistance to discriminatory legislation that kept them out of the legislative halls and voting booths. Inspired by David Walker's *Appeal*, she also believed Southern slaves would rise up in violence against slavery, thereby exacting a divinely sanctioned retribution for the sin of slaveholding. Like other militant abolitionists, Stewart viewed slavery and the struggle against racist discrimination as a war that required much sacrifice and quite possibly some bloodshed. Although she viewed herself and other black women as equal participants in the war against slavery, she nonetheless portrayed manhood as the hinge on which the door to the future opened.[14]

Nat Turner vs. Uncle Tom

The vision of freedom as fighting posed a conundrum for black abolitionists and their white allies: how to counter the image of docility that inhibited their push for black enlistments in the Union Army while reassuring lawmakers and the public at large that black soldiers could be controlled? This contradiction within emancipationist discourse regarding black men and their potential for violence proved troublesome indeed. First, black men needed to demonstrate that they were not too docile, passive, or dim-witted to withstand the test of battle or life as free men. Thomas Wentworth Higginson, who had been one of John Brown's secret financiers, believed that this perception of the slaves' unmanliness lay at the root of much racial prejudice. "The Anglo Saxon habitually despises the negro because he is not an insurgent," Higginson wrote in 1861 as the debates over enlisting black men into the army began to swell. Higginson advocated for allowing black men to fight so that they might gain whites' respect. According to Higginson, army life could correct blacks' docility and submissive nature. "Our race," said Higginson, meaning whites, "does not take naturally to non-resistance, and has far more spontaneous sympathy with Nat Turner than with Uncle Tom."[15]

At the same time, however, black men had to demonstrate restraint, obedience, and control. Making black men, particularly slaves, agents of state-sponsored violence posed a most troubling scenario for congressional lawmakers struggling to weigh the costs of waging war with emancipation. Fearing that the war to save the Union was fast becoming a *servile war* "with its necessary accompaniments in the shape of murder, rape, outrage, rapine, and incendiarism," one Kentucky congressman declared, "I would as soon think of enlisting the Indian, and of arming him with the tomahawk and scalping knife, to be let loose upon our rebellious countrymen, as to arm the negro in this contest." Kentucky's senior senator, Garrett Davis, invoked the memories of Saint-Domingue and Southampton, where armed blacks had used "red-hot pincers" on their white captives before "roasting them over a slow fire." Davis warned that armed blacks would become the "destroying scourge of the cotton States." The specter of slave rebellion, however, was the not simply the produce of overactive white imaginations. Frederick Douglass had invoked it as a recruiting tactic, encouraging Northern black men to "Remember Denmark Vesey . . . remember Nat Turner."[16]

Of course, it could be argued that as representatives of slaveholders still in the Union, the Kentucky delegation manipulated the fear of slave insurrection to limit the effects of Lincoln's emancipation, and therefore their cries of "servile war" were little more than the desperation of men faced with the inevitable loss of their slaves. However, some nonslaveholding representatives concurred with their Border State colleagues. Senator John Sherman of Ohio, brother of General William T. Sherman, admitted that recruiting blacks into the Union Army was "shocking to our sense of humanity" and would not sign on to the policy "unless disciplined and under complete control, and never as armed men." Sherman could only imagine arming blacks if forced "to choose between their employment and the destruction of this country." Another Ohioan, Rep. William Allen, deemed the proposition of arming slaves to be the "'crowning act' of that folly and madness which seem to have taken possession of the Government." He urged Congress to consider "what gloomy hope" would remain if the army inducted one hundred fifty thousand black men. "When are we to expect peace . . . before a peace is conquered on the terms of the radicals?" he wondered. "Is the war thus to continue, and *these soldiers* to be the guardians of our liberties in the future?" Not a slaveowner himself, Allen did not utter desperate pleas to maintain a feeble grasp on his personal property. Nonetheless, the Ohioan feared an army that had "at its command half a million of ignorant, vicious, negroes with arms in their hands." Allen seemed to predict the struggle that would ensue when Reconstruction governments attempted to use black soldiers, policemen, and militias to fulfill law enforcement duties. His fear that "they may become potent in the hands of tyrants" foreshadowed Democratic criticisms of Republican Reconstruction.[17]

Commanders like Higginson attempted to reassure a skeptical public that black soldiers could be controlled. While lauding their courage under fire, white advocates of black enlistment praised the "absence of revenge and blood-thirstiness" among recruits. In his diary, Higginson wrote of his troops' enormous "capacity of honor and fidelity" as well as their deep religiosity, which conditioned them to obedience and restraint. Higginson noted the frequency of prayer meetings and spiritual singing as a sign that black soldiers adhered to the same moral code as white soldiers. As sentinels in camp, Higginson observed no "upstart conceit" but rather "steady, conscientious devotion to duty." He also dismissed any notion that black troops would take revenge on civilians. "I would far rather enter a captured city with them than with white troops, for they would be more subordinate." Notwithstanding his praise for their obedience, Higginson noted a decided lack of sympathy among his soldiers for the physical suffering of others. Having endured so much cruelty and hardship themselves, Higginson believed the recruits had become hardened, which in his mind made them all the more valuable as soldiers. "If I ordered them to put to death a dozen prisoners," Higginson admitted, "I think they would do it without remonstrance." General Rufus Saxton echoed Higginson's evaluation, remarking on black troops' "fiery energy" and that "it requires the strictest discipline to hold them in hand." Despite his professed faith in his troops' obedience and restraint, Higginson's opinion that slavery had blunted black soldiers' ability to empathize with the sufferings of others left open the frightening possibility that black soldiers might perform their duties too well.[18]

The question of whether or not slaves would make good soldiers occupied much of the investigations of the American Freedmen's Inquiry Commission (AFIC), a War Department committee formed of leading white abolitionists including Samuel Gridley Howe, James McKaye, and Robert Dale Owen charged with determining the conditions necessary for the former slave to fully reap the benefits of freedom and lead a "civilized life." Although the AFIC strongly supported enlisting refugees as both laborers and soldiers, they were concerned about arming slaves and looked to head off potential criticism from political opponents. In their interviews with military officials, missionaries, and other freedmen's aid workers, the commission asked about freedmen's "quarrelsome" reputations, their propensity for anger, and their desire for revenge against whites. Most respondents reassured the commission that although freedmen may be quick tempered and "passionate," they showed few signs of hatred for whites and did not speak of revenge. Witnesses stressed the freedmen's "docility" and submissiveness, especially if shown kindness and concern. The AFIC concluded that good officers who treated their men with respect and fairness would be the key to ensuring a disciplined force of black troops.

CHAPTER FOUR

A commander like Higginson, who was also a minister, might be able to steer his troops in the right direction away from wanton violence. A less scrupulous commander might well bring out the worst in his soldiers. Such was the case with Colonel James Montgomery, commander of the 2nd South Carolina, a regiment of freed lowcountry slaves. Better known as "Bushwhacker Montgomery," the 2nd regiment's commanding officer was a Kansas jayhawker who had cut his military teeth fighting as a Free State guerilla in the 1850s. John Brown, who knew Montgomery in those days, called him "a natural chieftain," but others were put off by his style of "frontier" fighting, including his old friend Col. Higginson. Higginson feared that Montgomery's use of black soldiers as raiding parties threatened the respectability he so desperately wished to maintain. Furthermore, Montgomery's policy of executing deserters worried Higginson, who knew that black regiments often faced high desertion rates.[19]

Montgomery harbored few of Higginson's paternalistic feelings toward his troops, a fact that put him at odds with other white officers over his "expeditions." One regimental leader under Montgomery's command reported that the Kansan had "disregarded all the rules of civilized warfare" and that his black troops had "acted more like fiends than human beings." Colonel Robert Gould Shaw, leader of the 54th Massachusetts, butted heads with Montgomery when Shaw was ordered to have his troops burn the town of Darien, Georgia, in June 1863. Shaw was pleased that his troops, composed primarily of freeborn Northern blacks, did not take part in the "pillage" until Montgomery ordered them to do so. Montgomery's justification—"We are outlawed," referring to the Confederacy's refusal to recognize black soldiers as legitimate combatants, "and therefore are not bound by the rules of regular warfare"—did not convince Shaw, who found the looting and burning of private homes "revolting." Shaw warned his wife not to tell anyone of the raid for fear that it would "harm the reputation of black troops and of those connected with them." The town had been deserted, Shaw told her, but for "two white women and two negroes." These individuals posed no tactical threat to the troops and put up no resistance. "There was not a deed performed, from beginning to end, which required any pluck or courage," he said. Even the property they took had no military value "excepting that we can now sit on chairs instead of camp-stools." Shaw felt "ashamed" and hoped for the day his troops could perform their duty in a more honorable manner. Montgomery's actions cast doubt on the army's ability to channel and discipline the aggression that liberated slaves might harbor against whites. After the Darien incident, Col. Charles Russell Lowell commiserated with his friend Shaw over the behavior of Montgomery's slave-soldiers. "Instead of improving the negro character and educating him for civilized independence," Lowell wrote to Shaw's sister, "we are redeveloping all his savage instincts."[20]

Others shared Lowell's apprehensions. When Louisa May Alcott's fictional alter ego, nurse Faith Dane, finds the contraband Robert preparing to kill a wounded Confederate soldier who turns out to be his half-brother and former master, Dane pleads with Robert to let go of his anger at least momentarily and focus his energies on his military training. Robert relents and becomes a soldier, an in an ironic and highly sentimental twist, dies at the hand of the white brother he spared. Yet in his sacrifice, Robert "found . . . eternal liberty and God." With the promise of sanctioned violence against masters and their emissaries on the battlefield, Alcott, like other advocates of black recruitment, hoped to harness black violence for the sake of national struggle and the redemption of the entire race.[21]

John Eaton, a chaplain and superintendent of the Tennessee Freedmen's Department, believed he knew the best way to control black troops. Like Higginson, Eaton believed that their experience as slaves had hardened them to violence. Because the slave "is used to suffering," Eaton wrote, "and to seeing his own blood flow, he will not be now so easily shocked and dismayed by carnage, as those of more delicate sensibilities." Eaton viewed this as a beneficial characteristic of black soldiers, but he suggested taking certain precautions against slaves' propensities toward violence. Eaton advised military officials to reject "the lowest types of the inferior tribes," or the "purely black," who were more difficult to control. White officers should not fear trusting their lives to armed soldiers of "the better types of superior tribes," as Eaton called mulatto, or mixed race, African Americans. Eaton noted the existence of some regiments that included men who looked white but had lived "all their lives slaves" and encouraged efforts to form new regiments of mixed-race soldiers who could "not be distinguished by any African characteristics."[22]

Despite their enthusiastic support for black enlistment, the AFIC struggled to reconcile the image of effeminized, docile slaves with the deep-seated fear they shared with Southerners about slaves' propensity for violence. "There can be no doubt the rebels would have armed them long ago had they dared put weapons in their hands," Eaton told the commission. The time had come to do away with "that prejudice," Eaton proclaimed, just as Washington and Jackson had done when they armed small numbers of black men in the American Revolution and War of 1812, respectively. Still, the idea of arming tens and perhaps hundreds of thousands of black men, many of whom were "purely black" and perhaps lacking in the sentiments and self-restraint that presumably came with the admixture of European blood, proved unnerving. Striving to balance the need for discipline with black men's desire for liberation, the AFIC assured the War Department and Congress that black soldiers could be controlled and that arming them would not put the lives of their white officers and fellow troops at risk.

Citizen Soldiers?

Even more than the church and the schoolhouse, the army provided "the most efficacious" means of disciplining the troublesome population of refugees growing within Union lines. The AFIC concluded that strict military discipline would help slaves unlearn certain "vices," such as lying, stealing, and promiscuity, and instill in them the virtues of honesty, hard work, and fidelity. The discipline of military life stood in bold contrast to the presumed life of idleness Southern slaves had led. According to the AFIC, men in contraband camps would be encouraged not only to enlist in the army but also to marry the mothers of their children and establish proper families. With his wages, he could support his dependents, and if he refused to marry, he nonetheless would be "compelled to contribute to their support." The army would provide not only the material means by which newly freed men would support their families and assume their rightful place as head of household, it also gave them the "self-respect and self-reliance" on which their domestic authority depended. When he was a slave, the black man's family had not been permitted to take his name, the report explained. "He did not eat with his children or with their mother," and because slave marriages, such as they were, were ruled not by any idea of "religious duty" but by profit, partnerships changed frequently, and there was little shame in illegitimacy. The combination of marriage and military service would combat the "disintegration of the family" and establish proper domestic relations between men and women.[23]

What former slaves needed was "judicious management," and the military ensured that the growing population of refugees "need not be, except for a brief period, any burden whatever on the Government." Drilling, marching, and parading in uniform, even if it was only for show, instilled in refugees a sense of purpose and honor. It also made them more willing to perform the kinds of manual labor the army required. "The organization of freedmen employed as military laborers into brigades, with badges around their hats, labeled 'United States service,'" the commission reported, succeeded in making sure that "the men marched regularly to and from work." The AFIC hoped that the training and dis-

FIGURE 4.2 "The Man Who Won the Elephant at the Raffle." This 1863 broadside illustrates the enormous problems military service posed for the army. Would slaves make good soldiers? What should be done with the thousands of women and children who followed the men to Union lines? How could freed people be disciplined and controlled? The questions suggest that the pitfalls of assuming military service represented a linear, unproblematic path to national citizenship. Courtesy American Antiquarian Society.

cipline black men received in the military would gain them "respect and decent treatment in their social relations with whites." But short of this rather vague proclamation about respect and decent treatment, the AFIC's report did not issue any specifics regarding the postwar political status of freedpeople. Military service might help the emasculated slave gain his manhood but it did not automatically result in the accumulation of political citizenship. The remunerations for military labor and soldiering were rations and wages. Just days after the Emancipation Proclamation went into effect, *Harper's Weekly* surmised, "We shall have to feed and clothe the emancipated negroes, and there is no present way of making them earn their living except by making them garrison our forts." The calculations were clear: instead of military service functioning as a way to earn citizenship, it became a way to pay back the favor of freedom. The military *could* be a vehicle for freedom, but more pressing to the nation's immediate concerns, it also became tool of management for the growing population of refugees crowding in Southern army camps. The report's full title says as much: "On the condition and management of emancipated refugees." Although the commission concurred with Douglass that soldiering provided freedpeople some of the manly attributes required of free men, nowhere in the report did they entertain the idea that military service alone would result in the full inclusion of African Americans in the body politic.[24]

As the long, global history of arming slaves indicates, making slaves into soldiers did not necessitate making them into citizens, at least not the *kind* of citizens—full, equal, empowered with a wide range of individual rights—that Douglass imagined. Nor did it require a reevaluation of slavery itself. In the classical age, Athenians begrudgingly bestowed freedom and a limited citizenship to slaves as a last, desperate measure in the Peloponnesian Wars, and then the privileges accorded them quickly receded. If for no other reason, freedom and rights to slaves often proved transitory because the endless cycle of war and conquest might soon nullify recent manumissions by a defeated power. Whatever the case, classical states remained fully committed to slavery as a social and political institution despite regular arming of slaves. In fact, as one scholar notes, the use of slaves as soldiers may have in fact contributed to a "demotion of the importance of military virtues" in Grecian politics.[25]

Even when slave-soldiers became a revered class, they remained subservient to the individual rulers or states that owned and employed them. This was the case of the Chikunda of southern Africa in the eighteenth and nineteenth centuries. The Chikunda enriched their Porturgeuse *prazeiros* by conducting slave raids, collecting tributes from local peasants, suppressing resistance, and protecting the frontier estates. In gratitude, the *prazeiros* doled out generous bounties to their warrior-slaves as well as giving them land and captives of their own. Despite these privileges, however, the Chikunda remained slaves, subject to flogging from their masters and prohibited from choosing their own places of residence or disposing of their property. Although their renowned military skills made them invaluable to the project of Portuguese colonialism, it did not make them free or guarantee them any formal, legal rights within that society.[26]

Although the mobilizations of citizen-soldiers in the French Republic during the tumultuous 1790s and early 1800s may have transformed the ideological relationship between freedom, citizenship, and military service in ways that inspired black abolitionists in the United States, more recent and local histories than those of ancient Greece or Portuguese southern Africa should have left them wary of staking too much on their performance of martial manhood. The praise of "colored patriots" in the American Revolution and the War of 1812 resulted in only a handful of individual manumissions. At no point did it seem possible that the service of a few might mean liberation of the many. Douglass did hope that the larger numbers of black recruits in the Union Army would bear more fruit than earlier American conflicts. If that were to happen, the Civil War would represent an exception to the general rule of arming slaves while maintaining fundamental systems of hierarchy and exclusion.[27]

The discourse of national citizenship that emerged during the Civil War, particularly around the issue of black enlistment, was infused with the language of obligation. Instead of premising the rights of black soldiers, calls for black troops focused instead on black men's obligations to defend their country, destroy slavery, and support their families. "Who is a citizen?" rhetorically asked attorney general Edward Bates in his treatise on the matter. His answer would not have pleased Frederick Douglass and others who argued that military service entitled black men to full and equal citizenship with white men. While Bates denounced Chief Justice Taney's earlier pronouncement against black citizenship in the Dred Scott decision, he nevertheless limited his definition to exclude "certain rights and privileges" that he felt were erroneously equated with national citizenship, including "voting and office holding." According to Bates, citizenship denoted the most general "political quality" of being a member of the body politic "and bound to it by the reciprocal obligation of allegiance on one side and protection on the other." Insofar as they were citizens, a status they shared with "paupers, lunatics, all females, and all minor males," African Americans bore an obligation to uphold the nation, share in its national defense, and according to the AFIC, not to be a burden to it. National citizenship, then, reflected a general status without clear meaning, one that was hardly incompatible with exclusion based on either race or gender. Thus, while black veterans would employ rights-talk to define national citizenship as entailing specific political activities, such as voting and office holding, the language of obligation would remain a potent weapon in the arsenal of those who wished to restrict black participation and access.[28]

In one sense, however, Douglass was right. A revolution was afoot in the United States. Emancipation and eventually Reconstruction would codify a new legal definition of political belonging based upon individual rights. Although the details remained sketchy, the "theoretical individual," to borrow Laura Edwards's phrase, endowed with "a full array of rights . . . held great promise" for former slaves who could now demand recognition of their rights in unprecedented ways. However, as Edwards notes in her discussion of antebellum Southern law, a legal system focused on individual rights was not incompatible with institutions of pronounced hierarchy, coercion, and violence that often belied the rhetoric of full, democratic citizenship. The army was one such institution.[29]

The reality of military life often fell short of Douglass's manly aspirations. Soldiering did not always offer black men either the esteem they sought or the tangible relief they needed. Lack of adequate compensation, denial of rightful bounties, neglect, and impressment characterized the black military experience alongside the glory of battlefield exploits. Black recruits often performed the same menial duties they had as slaves, acting as body servants or valets to white officers. As one black soldier put it, "It is retten that a man can not Serve two master But it Seems that the Collored population has got two a rebel master and a union master." Douglass's belief in the citizen-soldier ideal blinded him to the continuum of coercion and unfreedom that shadowed his visions of jubilee.[30]

For the most part, white officers proved naïve, at best, and often dismissed their recruits' concerns about coercion and abuse. When a company within his regiment gained a new captain and lieutenant, Higginson found the men's reaction "childish." Although they had complained that their former officers had mistreated them, they continued to protest against the new ones "in a state of utter wretchedness." Higginson tried to explain to the men that the new officers would be better, and that other companies had received new officers and their condition had improved. But only the commander's promise that the new officers would not be "savage to we" assuaged their apprehension. Better the devil you know than the one you don't—this was surely the case in the soldiers' eyes, but Higginson failed to grasp the weight of the men's concerns. Perhaps his belief that they were "blunt" to physical pain and deprivation impeded his ability to sympathize with the people over whom he and the other white officers wielded so much power.[31]

Army life *was* savage. Not surprisingly, it sometimes proved difficult to convince potential recruits that the army held the keys to freedom. Neither the promise of wages nor the lure of arms seemed tempting enough to many Northern blacks who were skeptical of the army's intentions. Some men exhibited mild interest in joining regiments based near their homes but were reluctant to leave their families to join the organizing efforts in Massachusetts or Pennsylvania, where the first infantries were

FIGURE 4.3 "What do I want, John Henry?" Submission and subservience continued to define the black military experience during the Civil War. Courtesy Library of Congress.

raised. With all the talk of black soldiers being used as cannon fodder, it is little wonder that enlistment efforts in the North got off to a slow start. Moreover, the bounty hunters "who prowled the country under various names and pretended military titles," cajoled black men into service, and then took their enlistment bounties stained the entire recruiting enterprise's reputation hardly before it began.[32] Soon, Northern governors like Massachusetts's John Andrew, whose gregarious organizing efforts had given birth to the soon-to-be-famous Massachusetts 54th, called upon well-known black orators like Douglass and Martin Delany to aid them in the search for black enlistees when "the response proved less than encouraging."[33]

Although "freedom provided the most powerful stimulus to enlistment," it did not always translate so clearly for Southern blacks sensitive to any hint of coercion or force. Among contrabands, especially those residing on or near abandoned plantations, enlistment efforts also met with resistance. General John Dix related how freedmen "preferred working on the plantations, or otherwise to enlisting." Not only was pay irregular and unequal, army life also replicated the brutality and degradation freedpeople hoped to leave behind. "Press gangs" operated as a

CHAPTER FOUR

recruitment mechanism within Union lines. In the border states and on the coast in Union-occupied Mississippi and Louisiana, soldiers—often members of the United States Colored Troops (USCT)—attempted to persuade contrabands and fugitives to join the army. When they hesitated, potential recruits were threatened or forced into service. When they resisted, men were kidnapped and locked up until they relented. Even men already employed by the army as laborers on fortifications were not safe from the press gangs. "My men, Colonl, *have not been drafted. They have been kidnapped in the night,*" complained an army engineer stationed in Florida in a letter to his superior. Men living near Fort Leavenworth in Kansas testified to being "knocked down and beaten like dogs" and imprisoned until they joined the service. Those who refused were tied up and held under water or "tied up by the thumbs all night" until they relented.

Statements made by impressed black soldiers suggest the pervasiveness of the practice throughout the South and the hardship—physical, emotional, and financial—impressment caused its victims. John Banks was cutting wood for his family in the woods of eastern Virginia when a squad of ten armed black soldiers approached him and asked him to enlist. "I told them that I could not enlist because I was obliged to do the work for my family," Banks reported. Disregarding his excuse, the party took the man off to camp "surrounded by armed soldiers, just though I was a prisoner." He was allowed five minutes to say his goodbyes to his family. H. Ford Douglas, a black recruiter from Illinois, complained that the families of impressed men were left to starve in the middle of winter without the support of their fathers, brothers, and husbands. Another Virginia man relented to enlist with a group of USCT only because "I thought dey might kill me; I was green and ignorant." Ignorance aside, the man had good reason to be fearful of the armed men who persuaded him to enlist. John Banks recalled hearing stories of "men being obliged to 'tote' [cannon] balls because they refused to enlist and also of their being confined in the guard house on hard bread & water." So when Banks arrived at camp, he "did not dare remonstrate but accepted the five dollars bounty and my uniform and clothing and performed the duty of a soldier." A soldier guarding impressed men at camp in Newport News, Virginia, told them that if they didn't enlist "he would put the contents of his musket" into them.[34]

Press gangs sometimes followed through with their promises of pain and death. George L. Stearns, the civilian commissioner for the organization of black troops in Tennessee, complained to secretary of war Edwin Stanton of the violence perpetrated by the soldiers on recruits. "On Sunday a large number were impressed" after the soldiers waited for the men to emerge from church services, related Stearns. "One was shot ... he died on Wednesday." Stearns feared that such actions would stymie his own recruiting efforts.[35] After reporting that a young boy of fifteen had been shot by soldiers as he tried to escape, Harriet Ware, the wife of a Northern planter in South Carolina, remembered that her cook's husband was shot and killed by Confederates when he resisted their impressment efforts. "How are they to understand the difference" between friend and foe, slavery and freedom, Ware wondered. Several of the men on her plantation decided to risk living among the "Secesh" on the mainland rather than stay on the Sea Islands and live in fear of impressment. "They openly say, some of them," wrote Ware, "that they wish the old times were back again."[36]

While it is important to note that planters like Ware and her husband competed with the army for labor, and therefore may have had ulterior motives for complaining to military officials about recruiters who deprived them of workers, the intense competition between civilians and the military in Union-occupied areas undoubtedly led both parties to sometimes disregard the wishes and plans of area blacks. The "recruiting" parties that scoured the coastal areas of South Carolina, Georgia, and Florida incited fear of slavery's return among blacks there. From the way they were treated, it was often impossible for fugitive slaves to tell the difference between their Union "liberators" and "Secesh." Blacks in Portsmouth, Virginia, accused white soldiers of the 99th New York of kidnapping men and selling them across the lines into slavery. Rousing them from their beds at night, the soldiers would entice them by saying, "The general has important work for your to do," only to betray their loyalty later. Portsmouth residents also reported how Union soldiers imprisoned, beat, and sometimes killed local blacks.[37]

It is no wonder, then, that the sight of armed men on horseback, regardless of the color of their uniforms, could send lowcountry people running for cover in nearby swamps and woods. Word of the recruiters' approach near the Ware plantation resulted in a standstill as laborers abandoned the fields. Another plantation superintendent on St. Helena Island told of a similar state of affairs. Only moments after a recruiting squad arrived, the superintendent went out to his fields only to find "where had been but a few moments before, field Hands at work, nothing but Horses and Ploughs, without Drivers, and idle Hoes." None of the remaining women or children admitted to knowing where the "able-bodied men" went, but one old man stated that they had "Smelt a very large Rat" and found it "very necessary to go to the woods to split Rails."

The fear among blacks in the occupied South became so great, according to yet another Northern planter in South Carolina, that the appearance of "a strange white face drives them from the field into the woods like so many quail." One white captain routinely told field hands that he had orders to shoot anyone who ran, which usually resulted in a frenzy on the plantations he visited. Field hands carried weapons to defend themselves against kidnapping, and press gangs that approached a cabin at night in search of recruits might well expect to be met with an unfriendly salute. The local army officer complained to Harriet Ware that the men on her plantation had taken to arming themselves against soldiers and shooting at them from their houses. Abolitionists like Edward Philbrick, who had gone south to minister the gospel of free labor to the slaves, also faced reports that shots were fired at black soldiers who visited one of his plantations near Beaufort. Recruiting soldiers chased two of his workers, named Sancho and Josh, into the marsh. Sancho, in possession of an Enfield rifle, fired at the soldiers. The ensuing shoot-out left Josh wounded in the leg and both men captured. Sancho insisted that he only wished to scare the soldiers away.[38]

Although army officials thought that black soldiers would have more luck appealing to the recruits' sense of community or obligation, this was hardly the case. The men on Harriet Ware's plantation were "very bitter that negroes should be sent against them." Not even Prince Rivers, the "Toussaint" of Sea Island blacks, had much luck persuading his neighbors to join the army. A soldier himself, Rivers traveled to Philadelphia to witness the recruiting drive there and testify to the ability of Southern blacks to become Union soldiers. However, he could not guarantee their desire. Back home, freedpeople listened to their revered elder more out of respect for him than for his message. The army began to employ black chaplains to appeal to the freedpeople's sense of Christian duty but to little avail. One such chaplain spent two full nights preaching near Edward Philbrick's Sea Island plantation but won no new recruits. Only the women came to hear his sermons. The men stayed away and "not one came near him, nor would they come near me when [the chaplain] was present," Philbrick reported. When recruiters attempted to use the church as a pulpit, they caused a "general stampede." Men jumped from the balcony and out of the windows to escape the recruiter's call.[39]

The impressed men looked to their plantation supervisors for reprieve, but none could be given. "Women and children gathered around the men to say 'farewell.' Fathers took the little children in their arms, while the Women gave way to the wildest expressions of grief," related one superintendent on St. Helena Island, bitter over his powerlessness to aid his employees. His attempts to comfort the grief-stricken women were unsuccessful. "One woman told me she had lost all her children and friends," he wrote, "and now her husband was taken, and she must die uncared for . . . all felt and believed this to be a final separation." Another woman wrote to President Lincoln asking to have her son released from the army. "He is all the subport I have now . . . his father is Dead and his brother that wase all the help that I had." Lincoln forwarded her letter to the Freedmen's Bureau, who informed the aging mother that "the interests of service will not permit that your request be granted." Thus, two scenes, the auction block and impressment, recall the fine line that existed between freedom and slavery for most Southern blacks, a line that they would cross, back and forth, many times over the coming decades.[40]

Once they were officially "free," Sea Island blacks harbored suspicion against the promises of emancipation due in no small part to the practice of impressment. A *New York Times* correspondent, attending an Emancipation Day celebration at Port Royal, noticed that at least one man looked very glum despite the joy of the occasion. When he asked this "very intelligent" freedman, named Sam, why he wasn't joining in the celebration, Sam responded that he had no appetite for food or drink. The correspondent pressed Sam for the source of his melancholy; after all, he was now free. Sam responded, "I ain't no fool massa. I know what dat means." Perplexed, the reporter asked Sam what he meant. Sam relented by taking the journalist into a small coatroom away from the crowd, and shouldering a broom as if it were a musket, he "slowly shook his head in a meaning way." Sam apparently dreaded the implications of a freedom that came on the tip of a bayonet. The plantation superintendent who had been so moved by the expressions of grief that the families of impressed soldiers displayed concluded that "this 'conscription' together with the manner of its execution has created a suspicion that the government has not the interest in the Negroes that it has professed."[41]

While some white officers were sensitive to charges that black troops were cannon fodder, others seemed more than willing to put them in harm's way to save white lives. Samuel Kirkwood, the governor of Iowa, informed General Henry W. Halleck that his "best colonel" hoped to see blacks die in place of whites. "When this war is over & we summed up the entire loss of life," the colonel wrote in a letter to Kirkwood, "I shall not have any regrets if it is found that a part of the dead are *niggers* and that *all* are not white men." The unnamed colonel echoed a sentiment that even one of the most ardent abolitionists in the Congress held. "If men are to be shot in the war," declared Radical Congressman Thaddeus

Stevens, "let it not be our cousins, relatives, and friends. Let it be the slaves of those traitors who have caused this war. I would to God that a hundred thousand of them had been at Richmond to receive the first fire of their villainous masters." Stevens worried that "the flower of our people are moldering the swamps of Virginia because we will not employ those who ought to be fighting this battle." Arming black men, he contended, would raise the morale of white troops who resented having to fight a war for the sake of slaves.[42] Stevens may have read the working-class rejoinder to "Father Abraham's" plea for more troops printed in *Frank Leslie's*, the leading Democratic pictorial and counterpart to *Harper's Weekly*. The verse mocked Douglass's pretensions of citizenship, making death the only reward for black soldiers:

So, Father Abraham, if you please, in this here game of chess,
You'd better take the black men against the white, I guess,
And if you work the niggers off before rebellion's slain,
Which surely ain't expectable—apply to us again.[43]

By denying that the death of black men on the battlefield held any redemptive promise, this verse reveals the racialized framework through which many white Americans, including some military officers like the Iowa colonel, viewed the citizen-soldier ideal. In this view, black soldiers were an expendable resource to be used up in place of white soldiers. In this view, soldiering represented the fulfillment of an obligation to white society, a way for blacks to earn their freedom, and as in the story of Quashi, to prove that they did not deserve enslavement. As the AFIC put it in their report to the secretary of war, "only through a baptism of blood" could black soldiers prove their manhood and secure their redemption in the eyes of the white nation. Freedom had an exorbitant price.[44]

Despite the hesitation blacks demonstrated in some Union-occupied areas where the free labor experiments on abandoned plantations gave them an attractive alternative to military labor, nearly 200,000 black men enlisted in the Union Army. Whether by force, desperation, or a desire to "strike a blow" for their freedom, both Northern and Southern black men became agents of a momentous political and social change. That they immediately recognized in this an opportunity for asserting their claims against the federal government is not surprising; however, the gendered quality of those claims laden with the violence of martial sacrifice set a tone for Reconstruction that, in the end, would diminish rather than enhance the African American struggle for citizenship.

A Higher Order of Citizen

The Civil War strengthened the relationship between voting, arms bearing, and citizenship. As one of the most potent ideologies in American political culture, the citizen-soldier ideal provided white men in early America with a powerful argument with which to advance their claims against the state, including their right to military pensions and to cast votes regardless of their personal wealth. Not so for antebellum black men. For them, the citizen-soldier ideal became "a vicious circle." Barred from militia duty, their lack of service became the justification for their disenfranchisement. Although some of the most radical abolitionists employed an argument for the "natural right" of suffrage, the idea that political rights belonged to every person regardless of race, class, or even sex was unpopular. The narrative power of martial manhood seemed to offer the strongest argument for black suffrage, especially once blacks began serving in large numbers during the Civil War. Despite the fear it inspired in whites about their propensity for violence, or maybe because of it, the discourse of martial manhood also provided black men with a sense of self-respect and personal as well as collective redemption that animated their push for civil and political rights.[45]

Black soldiers and veterans employed a discourse of "manhood rights" that rejected race-based limitations on their right to vote, own property, hold elective office, and serve on juries. Under the ostensibly equalizing rhetoric of martial manhood, black veterans argued that they had earned the same individual rights white men possessed. Across the nation in 1865 and 1866, black state and national conventions tied their claims to citizenship to the service of black Union soldiers. Focused almost exclusively on the elective franchise, these conventions argued that black soldiers' bravery and sacrifice had satisfied concerns whites might have had about black men's fitness to vote or hold public office. "I wonder," asked a black veteran in Wilmington, North Carolina, "as the Southern black man has got sense enough to fight for this country, if he ain't got sense enough to vote [?]" Others also pointed out the irony in giving black men bullets but not ballots. "The Government has asked the colored man to fight for its preservation and gladly he has done it," proclaimed a delegation of black men in Nashville. "It can afford to trust him with a vote as safely as it trusted him with a bayonet," they concluded. "We never inaugurated a servile insurrection," Georgia freedmen, some of them veterans, reminded their white neighbors.[46]

CHAPTER FOUR

Trust and loyalty were important issues for the black conventioners, and none embodied those qualities more than black soldiers who had risked their lives for their country. Black soldiers bravely faced "the savage barbarity, the uncivilized and fiendish cruelty" of "the nation's deadliest enemies." They pointed out that their allegiance and sacrifice came even when the nation's protection and gratitude did not. Conventioners in Arkansas recalled the peril black recruits faced in the South, where their patriotism was met with enslavement or death. They enlisted to fight for the Union even "when the Government could not, or did not, protect us from the halter of the Captor." Black veterans demanded the same consideration afforded treacherous white Southerners, whose political privileges President Johnson had restored in exchange for taking a meaningless test oath. "We will prove ourselves worthy of the elective franchise," proclaimed a colored convention in Norfolk, Virginia, "by never abusing it by voting the State out of the Union, and never using it for purposes of rebellion, treason, or oppression." Black veterans demanded recognition for their exceptional devotion to a country that, when all was said and done, did not deserve it. Yet it was *their* country, one "that none love so well as we."[47]

Images of unrequited suffering and sacrifice played an important role in the soldiers' claims to "this blood-bought right" of suffrage. At various moments, conventions invoked the specific memory of Ft. Pillow, where Confederates murdered black troops after they had surrendered, and a more general collective memory of wartime claims of rebel depredations against Union soldiers. "The freedman has no home, no oath, no rights, no vote," proclaimed William Forten at a meeting of the National Equal Rights League in October 1865. Instead, they were "left to the mercy of those who have made ornaments to decorate their persons from the bones of the sacred dead; cups to drink from their skulls, and candlesticks of their eye-sockets." A convention meeting in Boston remade this suffering into a sublime expression of national redemption, calling the black soldier a "Christ-like character," who had exchanged his life for "his enemy"—the white nation who had "abused and despised and ill-treated him." This powerful image of the black soldier as Redeemer reinforced the importance of redemptive suffering to postwar ideas of American nationalism and citizenship, as evidenced in Thomas Nast's engraving of a black war amputee at the side of Liberty who asks on his behalf, "And Not This Man?" as Congress considered the question of black suffrage (fig. 4.4).[48]

At other times, blacks' redemptive vision took a more apocalyptic tone. A controversy erupted at the Pennsylvania State Equal Rights' League convention in August 1865 over a resolution that proclaimed the

THE MILITARIZATION OF FREEDOM

FIGURE 4.4 "Franchise. And Not This Man?" Images of suffering played an important role in black soldiers' claims for political rights. *Harper's Weekly*, August 5, 1865.

"liveliest hope" that white Southerners "will go from bad to worse" and suffer as their slaves had done. The language of the resolution, which welcomed a "war of the races" to bring about democratic change in the South, including the right to vote for its former slaves, was violent—indeed, too violent for some members of the convention who urged the body to reconsider. The convention leaders refused, citing the need to use "the strongest language and all the means at our command to accomplish the end in view." Although few embraced the possibility of violence as openly as the Pennsylvania delegates did, other black conventions acknowledged whites' fear of black violence, as the Georgia freedmen did when they said they never instigated a "servile insurrection." These denials of fomenting violence against whites also could be read (as they surely were by many white observers) as veiled threats. The Georgia convention maintained, "It was in our power to rise, fire your houses, burn your barns . . . so much so, we could have swept the country like a fearful tornado." Abraham Galloway—a runaway slave, Union spy, and North Carolina state legislator—advised a mass meeting of freedmen "that their race would have not only their personal freedoms, but also political equality, and if this should be refused them at the ballot box they would have it at the cartridge box," reported a witness to the event. In Norfolk, blacks insisted that "among no other people could such a revolution have taken place without scenes of license and bloodshed," paying tribute to Southern blacks' forbearance. That forbearance, however, was not limitless, as the Colored Soldiers and Sailors convened at Philadelphia in 1867 pointed out. "We hope to avoid," they announced, "the stern necessity of placing ourselves in direct opposition to . . . law and order and the peaceful pursuit of happiness." The black soldiers and sailors did not need to spell it out any further. Their threat of revolutionary violence in the future rested upon the knowledge of the violence they had already performed in the United States military.[49]

That knowledge played no small part in white support for black suffrage. Calling blacks a "fierce and turbulent people," Rev. Henry Ward Beecher believed that denying them the right to vote might be dangerous. "If to give half a million men the vote is perilous," Beecher asked a crowd in Boston, "how will it be to have them lying at the bottom of society in a state of savagery, looking on laws as enemies, and the government as despotic, and bound to their fellows more by a sense of wrong than by common duties, interests, and ambitions?" However, he assured his apprehensive audience, "Make them citizens, and they are safe, and you are safe." Perhaps as a way to assuage white fears, General Clinton Fisk, commander of the Department of Tennessee, argued for the civilizing effect of suffrage when he referred to a "swarm of B's"—the Bible, bayonet, and ballot—that made slaves into citizens. Like military discipline and religious instruction, Fisk believed the ballot would uplift ex-slaves, a view not uncommon among white advocates of black suffrage. Likewise, Beecher understood the ballot as providing a kind of tutelage for the ignorant, saying, "You cannot educate a man for liberty in any way so well as by making him use it." Such condescending outlooks appear painfully naïve given what we now know about freedpeople's remarkably sophisticated political understanding and organizing skills. Nevertheless, it seemed prudent to Beecher, Fisk, and other white advocates of black voting to portray freedpeople as blank slates onto which they could write the South's and the nation's political future. By infantilizing former slaves, they downplayed the radicalism of their own agenda in the hopes of cementing a broader coalition of white support but at the cost of silencing black voices that did not recite the party line.[50]

Most veterans and their supporters chose to focus on black soldiers' fealty rather than their ferocity. With their loyalty, patriotism, and civic virtue demonstrated through black soldiers' performance of martial valor, the delegates to the black conventions reconstructed a vision of freedom and political subjectivity premised not on birthright or residency but upon the dutiful performance of martial manhood. A Tennessee convention enumerated the three "boxes" of American citizenship, declaring that possession of the cartridge box guaranteed acquisition of the other two: the ballot box and the jury box. Without equivocation, the postwar black conventions understood political rights as deriving from military service, not simply as a quid pro quo, but because the soldier embodied an ideal of manly independence that American citizenship required. Furthermore, black veterans believed their service had erased racial distinctions among men. As the Nashville delegation poignantly asked, "What higher order of citizen is there than the soldier?"[51]

Although black soldiers viewed martial manhood as a radical assertion of their political worth, the "higher order" they imagined nevertheless relied on traditional conceptions of patriarchal authority and male dominance that troubled the larger story of freedom they attempted to tell. By linking the individual rights of citizens to military service, the wartime discourse of martial manhood simultaneously opened up new pathways to political inclusion for black men and closed them off to women. This rhetoric enabled black men to dominate the postwar movement for civil rights. Despite reports of women's enthusiastic participation at less formal mass meetings and celebrations, the shift toward male leadership in this early civil rights movement is undeniable. Whereas black women abolitionists had demanded equal access to antislavery meetings before the war and played prominent and vocal roles in that movement, veterans and other male speakers dominated the podiums at the postwar state and national civil rights conventions. Although women may have endorsed men's formal leadership roles and even considered the ballot a collective possession, the presumption that black men's political identity as citizens subsumed black women's rested upon ideas of patriarchal authority and female dependency that belied the "collective ethos" often ascribed to freedpeople's social and political worldviews. Furthermore, by making voting, office holding, and jury service the paramount expressions of citizenship, the black state conventions avoided questions of economic citizenship, which further enabled planters to tighten their grip on black households.[52]

By replacing race with manhood in the calculus of American citizenship, postwar black spokesmen like John Mercer Langston believed the "imperishable glory" of black soldiers gave the lie to fantasies of white supremacy. In his efforts to secure African American men the right to vote, Langston argued that citizenship did not depend upon "the texture of a man's hair, the conformation of his countenance, or the color his skin," but rather that it was "a constituent element of manhood." Yet in their efforts to denaturalize racial qualifications for political citizenship, Mercer and others uncritically naturalized gender inequalities that would, in time, work to reinscribe racial ones. Having been long-denied authority over black women's bodies, freedmen endeavored to establish protective ownership of their wives and children. "All we ask of the white man is let our ladies alone," warned Henry McNeal Turner who believed that emancipation would now allow black men to claim the status of protector that slavery had denied them. With protection, however, came a certain level of domination, as Turner alluded to when he stated that "the difficulty has theretofore been, our ladies were not always at our own disposal." The patriarchal authority Turner claimed, however, failed to challenge the fundamental principles of racial hierarchy that he imagined it did. In her study of the importance of gender in rebuilding white supremacy in Reconstruction-era North Carolina, Laura Edwards argues that such claims to men's protective authority over women and their households "left key components of the antebellum power structure in place," which in time would enable white conservatives to restrict both African Americans' and women's access to the legal and political systems. Among those key components of antebellum power were the languages of dependency and manhood rights. Gendered distinctions, like the ones Langston and Turner drew, naturalized racial ones by making racial segregation, white domination, and black submission appear organic and necessary for good order and civilization.[53]

There were a few critics who challenged what they considered to be a myopic focus on voting, but their skepticism had nothing to do with gender. "Vote for whom?" asked one black veteran of the Massachusetts 55th. "The white man," he responded in answer to his own question. "What good do such rights ever do us—to be compelled always to be voting for the white man and never to be voted for?" Others questioned how voting would translate into economic security. Sgt. Major George S. Massey, a veteran of the 43rd United States Colored Infantry, urged fellow blacks to "remember that equality in this respect will do but comparatively little toward elevating our race or condition when we are wanting in every other respect." Massey believed freedmen would be better served by saving money and investing it in land and education. The "all powerful panacea" of suffrage, warned the *Christian Recorder*, might be a mixed blessing. "Of itself," the paper explained, "it can do nothing. It cannot make an ignorant man wise . . . It cannot make a poor man rich . . . it cannot even make a decent man respected." Writing in anticipation of the passage of the Fifteenth Amendment in 1869, the *Recorder* admonished its readers, "don't rely too much on the suffrage." Skeptics questioned whether black men would be able to exercise the franchise freely without economic independence, and whether it would bring about much-needed economic change for the impoverished mass of freedpeople. However, none of them questioned the assumptions of manhood or the martial justifications that underlay the campaign for black voting rights.[54]

The Price of Freedom

Black soldiers' deaths on Civil War battlefields represented the bitter irony of man-making in the age of emancipation. The quest for manhood resulted in no material gain for those lost to its exacting toll, and for those who remained alive, especially those who had not served in the military, their connections to the body politic remained tenuous. Even when men were not commanded at gunpoint, military service produced hardships and suffering for women and families who struggled to cope without husbands, fathers, and sons. Like the aged mother who implored President Lincoln to release her son from the service because "he is all the subport [*sic*] I have now," many women, especially the elderly and disabled, relied on young, military-age men for their daily existence. The men targeted for enlistment provided essential labor for their families and communities, but it was not simply that their labor and the fruits of it would be missed. As Jim Downs argues in his study

CHAPTER FOUR

of destitution and sickness among freedpeople in wartime contraband camps, "the employment of men by the military had unfortunate consequences for freedwomen and children," who were often denied shelter, rations, clothing, and other provisions reserved for "able-bodied men." With scarce resources to care for the thousands of black people fleeing to Union lines as the army advanced into the South, women and "dependents" unsurprisingly got the short end of the stick. Although the army eventually revised its policy toward freedwomen and children, the discourse of dependency that characterized those who could not or did not serve in a military capacity as burdens, not only to the army but also to the larger society, continued.[55]

William Wells Brown, the fugitive slave who had lived with the image of his mother whipped before him as a child imprinted on his memory, felt "anxious" to preserve the contributions of black soldiers to the war effort, but the enormity of the losses and the often cavalier expenditures of black life made his task difficult. "But had they accomplished anything more than the loss of many of their brave men?" he asked in the first historical treatment of black Union soldiers, *The Negro in the American Rebellion: His Heroism and Fidelity*.[56] In it, Brown told what has become the conventional story of black courage and manly achievement. However, at the same time Brown wrote his history of black Union troops, he also revised his acclaimed novel *Clotel* about the struggles of a mixed-race woman in and out of slavery first published in 1854. In the 1867 version, Brown introduces Clotel's husband Jerome, a black Union soldier who dies in an ill-planned assault mirroring the doomed Battle of Port Hudson, an episode Brown used to illustrate the ineptitude of white officers who played fast and loose with black lives in *The Negro in the American Rebellion*. Like its historical counterpoint, the battle that claims Jerome's life results from the murderous orders of a white officer unconcerned with protecting the lives of his troops. Ordered to retrieve the body of a fallen white officer under heavy fire, three times black men rush the field and are killed. In the final effort, Jerome succeeds in bringing the man's body back to Union lines, but at the last moment a cannon ball decapitates him. Brown's choice to have Jerome's head severed from the rest of his body portended the forced disengagement of African Americans from the body politic, a disengagement that by the late 1860s, when Brown added Jerome to Clotel's story, was already taking shape throughout the South. It also unsettled Brown's other attempts to glorify black military sacrifice as a means to citizenship and collective rebirth.[57]

Making men, it seems, was a violent business. For those who still seek to understand why Reconstruction was so violent as well as why military service ultimately proved to be such a weak hook on which to hang blacks' hopes for citizenship, the answer lies somewhere in the tangled relationship between freedom and violence that troubled W. E. B. DuBois when he wondered why "only murder makes men." Soldiering promised black men the redemption of their enslaved selves and their transformation into full citizens. However, many whites understood military service as a way to discipline instead of liberate the masses of black men crowding within Union lines. The debates about black recruitment centered on white fears of black violence and revenge, fears that made military service an unreliable marker of citizenship. The emancipationist vision of freedom as fighting fit quite comfortably into well-established traditions and practices that had defined the antebellum South as a militant and reactive society. It was a vision that played into deep-seated anxieties about emancipation and the form it would take.

Even radical abolitionist Gerritt Smith, who had backed John Brown's attempted slave insurrection at Harper's Ferry, feared the wholesale arming of black men. "God forbid that we should arm the slaves unless it be such of them as come into military organizations and under intelligent and merciful guidance," he wrote in 1861. Black men could act violently so long as white men directed the action, but they could not do so on their own. The ad hoc militias that freedpeople organized during Reconstruction violated this dictum, but to many the very act of taking up arms, whether under white leadership or not, seemed a violation of common sense and good order. Because freedom came through the "agonized violence" that Herman Melville wrote of and many others dreaded, it would be difficult to diffuse the postwar political culture that remained wedded to both the methods and ideology of martial manhood. As agents of that violence, black soldiers represented both the power of the victorious Union war machine and the loss and humiliation of the defeated. Just as Frederick Douglass had hoped, black men had become their own liberators, but it was not without a price. As a result of their wartime service, they had become potent symbols of the power of African Americans to affect the course of history as well as of the savage violence that had wracked the nation. There existed a fine line between respect and fear, a demarcation that the postwar political struggles in the South would erase.[58]

FIVE

Ballots and Bullets

"The liberties of our country, the freedom of our civil Constitution, are worth defending at all hazards; and it is our duty to defend them against all attacks. We have received them as a fair inheritance from our worthy ancestors: they purchased them for us with toil and danger and expense of treasure and blood, and transmitted them to us with care and diligence. It will bring an everlasting mark of infamy on the present generation, enlightened as it is, if we should suffer them to be wrested from us by violence without a struggle, or to be cheated out of them by the artifices of false and designing men." "CANDIDUS" (SAMUEL ADAMS), 1771

"It's got to be the ballot or the bullet . . . If you're afraid to use an expression like that, you should get on out of the country." MALCOLM X, 1964

The Atlantic hurricane season in 1868 was one of the quietest on record. Of the four documented storms that year, only one made landfall on the Florida panhandle, on October 4. As it moved up the gulf coast, the category 2 hurricane dumped torrents of rain on southeastern Louisiana, swelling the banks of Lake Pontchartrain and soaking New Orleans. The storm bid a soggy farewell to the Carolinas before disappearing out to sea. Having caused only $5,000 in damage, it was soon forgotten.[1]

During the peak months of the hurricane season, September and October, when the tropical depressions formed and then petered out without much notice, a different kind of storm was brewing in the South. It was election season. In November, the country faced its first presidential election since the end of the Civil War. The Republican candidate, General Ulysses S. Grant, ran under the motto "Let Us Have

FIGURE 5.1 Like father, like son. Frank Warmoth, son of onetime Louisiana governor Henry Clay Warmoth, poses with his all-black boy army in 1888. During Reconstruction, Warmoth made the racially integrated Metropolitan Police in New Orleans a branch of the state militia and used them as a kind of private army. Although he was not old enough to remember those "stormy days," as his father called them in his memoirs, Frank and his army embodied the spirit of martial manhood that once prevailed. Courtesy Southern Historical Collection, Wilson Library, University of North Carolina at Chapel Hill.

Peace," promising to quell the rancor and hostility that had come to dominate the nation's politics, both in Washington and at the local level in the former Confederacy. His opponent, Democrat Horatio Seymour, for the most part staked his bid for the presidency on his opposition to Radical Reconstruction and the expansion of the federal government. Yet, as important as the question of who would lead in Washington was, other issues captivated voters in the Southern hinterlands. Matters of local government, such as who would serve as judges, sheriffs, tax collectors, and state representatives, were also important. The men elected to these positions would largely control the course of Reconstruction by implementing (or not) congressional policies regarding the status of freed slaves. But that is not to say that the question of the presidency was superfluous. The choice of Seymour or Grant, of Democrats or Republicans, mattered immensely. To the American public, the choice was between "right and wrong . . . good and evil," according to the *Chicago Tribune*. It also was a choice between war and peace. Would tranquility be restored to the South, or would violence carry the day? The questions were clear. The answers, however, were not.[2]

At the eye of this storm sat the small town of Camilla, Georgia. The county seat of Mitchell County in the southwestern part of the state, Camilla lay twenty-four miles from Albany. Until emancipation, Mitchell County had been a white oasis nestled within the state's "black belt" of cotton plantations. There mostly non-slaveholding farmers grew a variety of agricultural products, including cotton. Once freedom came, however, so did the ex-slaves looking to escape the domination of the large planters of surrounding counties. According to one historian, the black population of Mitchell County doubled during Reconstruction. These new residents made their presence known, demanding fair wages, organizing political meetings, and electing the first black representatives to the Georgia General Assembly. Ironically, their success put them at increased risk. Once the Republican-led legislature had approved a new state constitution in the spring of 1868, Georgia was readmitted to the Union and federal troops were withdrawn, leaving Mitchell County blacks and their white allies vulnerable to increased intimidation, violence, and fraud. The resources and authority of the other major federal institution in the area, the Freedmen's Bureau, rapidly dwindled.[3]

As the election season heated up in late summer, Georgia Republicans lacked the federal support that had enabled them to make considerable inroads into state and county politics. Despite the vitriolic tirades against them from Democratic politicians who urged their constituents to "clean up their muskets, rifles, and shot guns" in preparation for the upcoming campaign, Republicans marched headfirst into the storm that awaited them. Driven by a political culture steeped in martial values, Georgia's Republicans, especially those in the Second Congressional District that contained Mitchell County, would not be cowed. Therefore, it is not surprising that when Sheriff Mumford S. Poore advised a parade of mostly black Republicans marching to a rally in Camilla on Saturday, September 19, to stack their arms before proceeding, they refused. William Pierce, the white Republican congressional candidate leading the procession, informed Poore that neither he nor Poore had the authority to order the people to give up their personal weapons. Pierce later admitted that found Poore's request to be "unreasonable and foolishly exacting." It had become "customary," according to one Freedmen's Bureau agent, for Republican candidates and freedpeople to carry firearms, and a rumor that the Young Men's Democratic Club in Camilla had placed a large order for rifles in advance of the rally made Sheriff Poore's advice seem foolish indeed. In fact, a drunken man named James Johns, notorious for his hatred of blacks and Republicans, had already accosted the group on the road to town with a loaded shotgun and threatened to shoot the drummer of a large "fife and drum band" that led the parade. He would soon make good on his threat. As the crowd entered town, they were met with hissing and jeers from whites gathered in anticipation of the event. In the midst of the jostling and confusion, Johns fired his gun at the band as it played, setting off a melee of shooting and panic. The marchers scattered in all directions, and many of those killed were hunted down in cold blood as they fled through the nearby fields and woods. The violence continued through the night and well into the next day as whites raided black homes and drove out their inhabitants. Although casualty reports conflicted, an estimated dozen freedpeople lost their lives and at least thirty others were wounded.[4]

The quintessential Reconstruction election riot, Camilla erupted into violence because of the longstanding and intimate relationship between ballots and bullets in the nineteenth century.[5] It was not the simple either-or relationship that Malcolm X described. Instead, it involved a complex and deeply problematic understanding about the requirements of manhood, republican citizenship, and democratic governance. Since the colonial period, military service and gun ownership helped erase class distinctions among white men and united them in a democratic brotherhood through narratives of manly self-defense, honor, and patriotism. These martial performances enabled non-elite white men to make larger claims against the state, namely the right to vote in the decades after the American Revolution. The expansion of the electorate in the early nineteenth century reflected the power of martial manhood to shape popular understandings of American identity; the explosion of political violence that accompanied the growth of white manhood suffrage was not coincidental. In fact, the storm had been brewing for decades.

Not only did soldiering provide one of the strongest justifications for voting rights, the political rituals surrounding nineteenth-century elections became increasingly warlike. From county courthouses and polling places to the halls of Congress, nineteenth-century Americans rioted, threatened, shot, whipped, burned, and killed each other in their struggles to win elections. The language of warfare as well as its instruments became commonplace in campaigns as the new political parties and constituencies emerged, vying for the right to speak for "the people." Similar to the way that early Americans shaped their sense of belonging through parades, holidays, oratory, print culture, and other less-violent forms of community building, riots also enabled Americans to define who they were as well as who they were not. Riots and mob violence spoke in a brutal dialectic of destruction and reconstruction, simultaneously tearing down and redrawing the boundaries of the body politic. As a result, nineteenth-century Americans experienced "a social climate with an extraordinary tolerance for riot."[6]

Camilla represented the climax of a violent, popular political tradition that linked freedom, manhood, and citizenship with guns and martial culture. This tradition was not entirely Southern made, but instead reflected a more collaborative effort shaped in Northern cities, where semi-private militias lent discipline and respectability to nineteenth-century "street theater," as well as on battlefields in the west and southwest as white men took up the mantle of Manifest Destiny. A militant defense of slavery among Southerners joined an equally militant expansion of American democracy in other regions to produce a culture of political violence that help make Camilla and other Reconstruction-era riots understandable not simply as means to and end for white supremacists but as a performance of citizenship with meaning for everyone involved. Crucial to this emerging popular understanding of American citizenship was a notion of manly self-defense that demanded violence, making it appear to be not only reasonable but also natural and inevitable.[7]

Despite their notoriety at the time and among historians today, Camilla and other Reconstruction riots cannot be fully understood without recognizing how the martial manhood engendered by radical abolitionism and the Civil War experiences of black soldiers shaped the political culture of the era. The equation of freedom with fighting created a vision of muscular democracy that intertwined questions of enfranchisement and arms bearing. "The hand that drops the musket cannot be denied the ballot," declared General William T. Sherman, who, despite his vocal criticism of Radical Reconstruction and black suffrage, found the powerful narrative of martial manhood irrefutable. Yet the problem of how to ensure that Southern blacks could freely exercise the right to vote demanded that the musket be kept close at hand. The troubling relationship between these twin political rituals—voting and bearing arms—plagued freedpeople and their white allies as they struggled to democratize the former Confederacy.[8]

War by Other Means

Nineteenth-century elections could be extremely violent. A typical election day might include not only a picnic or a pint of beer at the tavern, which likely doubled as a polling place, but also a street brawl or shooting if not an out-and-out riot. Due to the combative style of American party politics, election day became a test of manhood: if a man cast his ballot and made it home in one piece, then he had demonstrated his physical prowess as well as his dedication to the principles of popular democracy. On his way to cast a ballot in 1859, Baltimore Democrat George Kyle was knocked down from behind, shot in the arm, and hit by a brick before he eventually gave up and ran home. George was lucky; his brother, who had accompanied him, was killed. One historian estimates that in the 1840s and 1850s, at least eighty-nine people died as the result of election violence. Defeated candidates who challenged electoral results had to prove that a "man of ordinary courage" would have been intimidated, and results were rarely thrown out because of violence at the polls. In other words, real men understood that politics was a lot like war.[9]

The language of warfare infused nineteenth-century party politics. Candidates referred to their opponents as "enemies" and urged their "rank and file" followers "to do battle" and "man your guns." Militias and military-style marching companies rallied supporters and intimidated opponents. It was during the 1864 election, in the middle of the Civil War, that the efforts of each candidate to be elected became known as "campaigns," taking on the nomenclature of military conflict. Ballots were imagined as "paper bullets" and "bullets of war." Torchlight parades, popular both before and after the Civil War, exhibited torches "fashioned after gunstocks." This martial imagery further collapsed the boundaries between politics and war in ways typically associated with the antebellum South.[10]

Why did American elections evoke such hostility? Much of it had to do with the exalted status voting had achieved by the mid-nineteenth century. At the outbreak of the Civil War, voting had become "the defining act of American citizenship" and created what one contemporary observer believed was a new way of imagining what constituted the body politic: "votership." Votership effectively reduced citizenship to the act of casting a ballot. Although it did not yet appear in the Constitution as a hallowed right of citizens, voting nonetheless defined membership in the national as well as local political community. It created a community of men that transcended social, ethnic, and even religious differences.

That commonality was in no small part accentuated by the existence of those who could *not* vote, namely women, and in most places, black men. As the market revolution transformed the nature of work and families, and as women's suffrage and abolitionism challenged the presumption of "natural" hierarchies that previously sustained patriarchal authority, voting provided the basis for an emerging redefinition of white manhood in the mid-nineteenth century. Furthermore, elections were exciting and potentially dangerous events that provided entertaining public spectacles similar to other manly pastimes such as brawling.[11]

But voting was not merely mechanical. Elections were "more than just a means of choosing leaders," writes historian Jean Baker, who argues that voting's symbolic implications could be as important as its practical outcomes for parties and their candidates. The ceremonies that revolved around elections reproduced certain religious rituals, including the singing of patriotic "hymns" and political invocations or sermons. Indeed, elections could inspire moments of personal conversion, as they surely did for the Tennessee carpenter who chose to attend a political rally instead of a camp meeting, much to the dismay of his pious father, or the New York farmer who traded his Bible for a "Political Textbook." In a nation guided by an ideology of "civic millennialism," which understood republican government as a symbol of providence at work in the political system, voting became an expression of God's will. Not only could the outcomes of elections reveal the divine plan for America, they made individual voters agents of divinity. Even for the more secular-minded among the ever-expanding electorate, elections engaged men in a series of political ceremonies that resonated with the larger ritual culture of the nineteenth century.[12]

There was another reason for the warlike nature of American politics. Since the American Revolution, there had been a close association between the expansion of suffrage rights and military service. As one of the most potent ideologies in American political culture, the citizen-soldier ideal provided white men in early America with a powerful argument with which to advance their claims against the state, including their right to military pensions and to cast votes regardless of their personal wealth. Outraged by the idea that those who had fought for the nation's independence were denied a say in its governance, Revolutionary militiamen led attacks on franchise restrictions during the first decades of the Early Republic. Although the repeal of these restrictions came piecemeal, the veterans' efforts ignited a push to reward soldiering with political citizenship. "May all our citizens be soldiers, and all our soldiers be citizens," proclaimed one Revolutionary toast. "May only those Americans enjoy freedom who are ready to die for its defense," declared another. And kill for it.[13]

Giving soldiers the right to vote recognized a practical as well as moral dilemma. Militia duty often represented an onerous burden to the poor men called on the fill the ranks. Flowery appeals to duty or love of country could not put food on a family's table. Suffrage, however, provided men in the colonial period and Early Republic with a powerful incentive to enlist. As important as the period's high-toned idealism was, the new nation's vulnerability perpetuated the expansion of democracy in the late eighteenth and early nineteenth century. "Americans must be soldiers," declared John Adams, "they must war by land and by sea; they have no other security." By enfranchising military-age men, the nation secured their service.[14]

While not all voters were soldiers, the language of manly sacrifice and self-defense (both the individual's and the nation's) enabled all men to claim the right to cast a ballot even if they were not veterans, at least not yet. As John Adams noted, national defense required all white men (as codified in the 1792 federal militia law) to be at the ready. But their potential as warriors did not depend on the outbreak of hostilities with a foreign power. The broader context of arms bearing in the Early Republic included not only the collective duty to defend the state, but also the "natural right of resistance and self-preservation," according to the English jurist William Blackstone. This personal right of self-defense transformed all white men, including those who had not officially served in the armed forces, into the primary defenders of their homes, families, and dependents, including women and slaves. As national defense became linked to the defense of home and person, arms bearing lost many of its burdensome aspects. It became an inviolable right of manhood and citizenship that, like voting, constructed the body politic along racial and gender lines. The right of self-defense also demarcated the line between slavery and freedom. "He, who owns nothing and who himself belong to another, must be defended by him, whose property he is, and needs no arms," argued James Burgh, another English thinker who, along with John Locke, inspired the American revolutionaries. Nearly a century later, Chief Justice Roger Taney echoed this opinion when he concluded that Dred Scott was not a citizen of the United States because he possessed neither the right to vote nor the right to bear arms.[15]

Black men's postwar claims to suffrage reflected the importance of "votership." By the mid-nineteenth century, voting had become emblematic of American citizenship. As such, it represented more than a mere exercise of political choice. If voting had ever been merely mechanical, emancipation raised the stakes considerably, transforming the act of casting a ballot into the ultimate expression of a man's social and political status. As Alexander Keyssar points out, for blacks in post–Civil War America, voting was "a critical symbol and expression of their standing in American society." Thus, it is not surprising that the *Christian Recorder*, whose editors would later advise its readers not to rely on the ballot to solve all their problems, nonetheless viewed suffrage as a key to their larger struggle of elevating blacks' status. "Not to vote, in this country, is a disgrace," they declared. So, too, for white men, who had for decades in the first half of the nineteenth century enacted elaborate and often violent election rituals that were as important to their "democratic self-image" as the placing of a ballot in a box, perhaps even more so. The right to vote became something to be achieved and defended through both military and paramilitary means, by armies and militia companies, as well as by ward gangs and vigilance committees, united under a banner of manhood and self-defense. Voting, like soldiering, became a ritualized performance of manhood.[16]

The relationship between voting and arms bearing set the tone for popular politics in the nineteenth century. Not only did soldiers and veterans play important roles in political campaigns, the martial spirit that had become a "basic ingredient of American patriotism" often made politicking a warlike enterprise. "Seldom did an election go by without dirty tricks, nasty threats, and fighting," notes historian David Grimsted. Often the hostility boiled over into full-scale riots. As the nation's two-party system emerged in the early nineteenth century, one party seemed to court violence more deliberately than the other. Perhaps because it was the party of Jackson, a man known for his pugilistic style and combative spirit, the Democratic Party "cheerfully urged revolution" by employing bullies, toughs, and other strong-arm tactics to intimidate the opposition and exploit class, racial, and ethnic conflicts. Democrats' long-standing relationship with political violence would continue through the war years into Reconstruction. In 1863, then-Democratic governor of New York Horatio Seymour's vocal opposition to the Conscription Act and other Republican war policies, many critics argued, excused the draft riots that amounted to "a virtual racial pogram" against New York City's African American population. When Seymour became the Democratic Party's presidential nominee five years later, his reputation for courting violence would become a central feature of the Republican campaign, as would the Democrats' public embrace of Southern rebels, such as Nathan Bedford Forrest and John Brown Gordon, the reputed heads of the Ku Klux Klan in Tennessee and Georgia, respectively.[17]

Suffrage and Self-Defense

America's violent electoral history played a significant role in the movement to give African Americans the right to vote after the Civil War. As blacks continued to the be the targets of Democratic mobs and paramilitary organizations that backed the party, such as the Ku Klux Klan, the issue of black voting raised questions about the potential escalation of violence in the South. Moderate and conservative Republicans sought assurances that Radical plans to enfranchise black Southerners would not cause a "race war." This had been the standard conservative argument against Radical Reconstruction generally—putative policies against white Southerners, such as confiscation and disenfranchisement, along with military government and aid to the freedmen, would increase violence rather than diminish it. President Johnson had used the argument to rebuff a delegation of African Americans, which included Frederick Douglass, who met with him to press for the cause of black suffrage. Johnson claimed that "the hate that existed between the two races" in the South would lead to further strife if they were "thrown together at the ballotbox." Johnson refused to "commence a war of the races," saying that violence was the inevitable outcome "when you force it [black suffrage] upon a people without their consent." In what would become a familiar refrain among opponents to Radical Reconstruction, Johnson delegitimized the measures by portraying them as the products of force rather than consent of the people. Of course, Johnson's definition of the "the people," like so many others', did not include African Americans. But even freedpeople's self-proclaimed "friends" harbored anxieties about black enfranchisement. Recall Henry Ward Beecher's admonitions that denying those men who had been trained in the art of war a voice in the government could lead to violence. Beecher's assurances that allowing blacks to vote would protect the nation against a potential black uprising speaks to the ambivalence of many white Americans toward black political independence.[18]

For their part, African Americans and their white allies did their best to counter the "race war" argument. Early on in 1865, Carl Schurz defended black voting in the South as "the best permanent protection against classlegislation, as well as against individual persecution." The Republican *Cincinnati Daily Gazette* called universal manhood suffrage "the sovereign salve for the soreness of different classes, races, and interests." Black conventioners in Alexandria, Virginia, claimed the right to suffrage "because we can see no other safeguard for our protection." They explained that if they were "armed with the ballot," they would elect officials who would pass and enforce laws to protect their lives and property. Still maintaining the rhetorical link between war and suffrage, the delegates also argued that their votes would protect the nation from the "traitors" who had so recently sought to destroy it and would do so again if given the slightest chance. Other Southern conventions echoed the Virginia delegates' argument that the safety of both Southern blacks and the nation depended on black voting. Norfolk's Colored Citizens insisted that "the safety of all loyal men, black and white" in the South "requires that all loyal men, black and white, should have equal political and civil rights" as "a protection against the votes of secessionists and disloyal men." In Congress, the argument that black voting would protect rather than imperil the Union animated the supporters of black suffrage, such as Charles Sumner, who declared in 1866 that the freedman must be given the right to vote "(1) for his own protection, (2) for the protection of the white Unionist, and (3) for the peace of the country." This reasoning ultimately persuaded Congress, who in 1867 made black voting a requirement for Southern states' readmission to the Union.[19]

Yet the ballot alone would not provide Southern blacks and their white Republican allies with the protection they so desperately needed. Despite initial reports that claimed the Reconstruction Acts had soothed racial hostilities and stymied violence against freedpeople, it soon became apparent that these reports were mostly wishful thinking. Whites, both collectively and individually, continued to persecute former slaves as a means of controlling their labor as well as their growing political agency. Southern Democratic leaders' efforts to make nice with their new black constituents, by inviting them to barbeques and referring to them as "friends," did little to mask the ongoing intimidation, coercion, and outright brutality that accompanied freedpeople's entry into the arena of formal politics. Some Southern Democrats seemed open to the possibility that they might entice freedpeople to vote their ticket, but when blacks' response to their outreach efforts proved less than satisfactory, they fell back on more tried and true methods of control. In the politics of Reconstruction, sticks proved more reliable than carrots.[20]

In the face of that reality, it became apparent that Southern blacks required a more direct means of self-defense. Freedpeople's ability to freely exercise the franchise would continue to be tied to their arms bearing. Not only was their right to vote premised upon the military service of black veterans, their ability participate in the electoral process also depended upon their continued presence in state militias and other law enforcement bodies as well as their ability to possess arms as private citizens. The right to vote and the right to bear arms were inextricably linked in the minds of many Southern blacks, and with good reason. Freedpeople recognized that "the exercise of political power . . . demanded ready and effective access to the means of violence." Knowing firsthand the importance of paramilitary organizations, such as local militias and slave patrols, to the maintenance of slaveholders' hegemony, former slaves understood that those same institutions would play important roles in the reconstruction of Southern society.[21]

Not surprisingly, freedpeople viewed gun possession as a symbol of freedom and independence. Although legally barred as slaves from owning or carrying guns, many slaves had for decades carried weapons with permission from their masters to hunt or protect livestock from thieves. An especially trusted slave might even be allowed to keep a gun in his cabin for such purposes. Courts sometimes fined slave masters for selling guns to their slaves, but it remained "public policy" in many parts of the early South to arm slaves as in colonial militias and to protect isolated plantations. Even as slavery hardened into a more tightly controlled system of exploitation after the Revolution, the "private arming of slaves" continued. Thus, slaves came to freedom with some degree of personal knowledge of the practical and political benefits of having a gun, having used one himself, or if not, having been threatened with one or seen one used on other human beings.[22]

Northern observers found freedpeople's desire and appreciation for firearms remarkable. White Southerners, on the other hand, found it alarming, claiming that freedpeople were stockpiling weapons for a planned insurrection around Christmas. *Where were all the guns coming from?* they demanded to know. The answer did not ease their minds—many of the weapons that investigators found in freedmen's possession came from the army. A colonel sent to investigate planters' complaints that freedpeople near Chetaw, South Carolina, were amassing weapons, noted that he could find no one in the vicinity selling arms to the freedmen and that the guns came "principally from Genl. Sherman's army." Likewise, the Freedmen's Bureau superintendent on St. Helena Island informed Gen. Rufus Saxton that the arms freedpeople carried came from "Beaufort, Charleston, and Savannah," all Union Army camps, while others "were given to them in the early days of our occupation of these islands, as they might defend themselves against raids of the enemy." Similarly, army officials in Virginia reported, "There is no doubt but what a great many of the freedmen have U.S. muskets, in their possession." Some no doubt came from discharged black veterans who, upon leaving the service in the summer of 1865, were given the opportunity to purchase their "arms and accoutrements."[23]

Firearms accentuated the meaning of freedom for the newly free. Former slaves were "proud of owning a musket or fowling-piece," testified one Freedmen's Bureau agent. On her plantation in Liberty County, Georgia, near Savannah, Mary Jones wrote with much disgust that the freedmen used the money she now had to pay them to buy "either a musket, double-barreled gun, or revolver! They all bear arms of some sort in this county." Their pride in gun ownership often led to trouble for freedmen when they used their weapons to hunt on planters' land. One army captain reported "the new right to carry and use fowling pieces conflicts . . . with that other right which the planter has to object to shooting on his premises." South Carolina planters complained that freedmen were "hunting all day, depredating the stock of the country, killing cattle, sheep and hogs." They pleaded with army officials to disarm blacks, but one officer protested this move saying that to do so "would be to deprive some of them of the means of procuring game for subsistence." Although planters complained incessantly about blacks' use of firearms to hunt and cause mischief, government agents typically dismissed their complaints, especially their cries of insurrection. "No harm can result from the possession of arms, by the freedman," wrote one agent in Meridian, Mississippi, "if education can only keep pace with new found privileges." The agent advised his superiors to send some soldiers to instruct the freedman on the proper use and care of their weapons.[24]

Just as guns could aid freedmen in the procurement of food, they could also serve other important purposes. "Bring home your gun," wrote a black veteran to the *New Orleans Tribune*, urging his comrades to purchase their weapons when discharged. Many took his advice. A witness reported that freedpeople "procured great numbers of old army muskets and revolvers," and he was surprised to find how ready the freedmen were to use the "pistols, old muskets and shot-guns" in self-defense. When a boatload of planters arrived on James Island in December 1865, to take back their plantations, armed freedmen refused to allow them to disembark. In Tuskegee, Alabama, local freedmen asked their Bureau agent for arms to aid fellow workers who were being "very badly treated by the whites." The agent denied the freedmen's request, noting the "spirit of bitter retaliation" that accompanied it. Such denials did little to instill confidence in the freedpeople that Bureau agents were always on their side. Gabriel Manigault recalled with no little amusement that one of his former slaves brought "his old musket" with him to a meeting with a Freedmen's Bureau agent and "held it near him during the whole time that he listened to the talk." Manigault was uncertain if the musket was loaded but suspected that the freedman made a show of the weapon "so as to be prepared for any tricks that might be attempted against his freedom."[25]

Loaded or not, guns symbolized freedom in profound ways. On July 4, 1866, in Richmond, a "body of negroes mounted and armed with United States sabres and pistols, paraded through the streets" in a display of their own independence. Back on St. Helena Island, freedpeople used their government weapons to form a "Society" for mutual benefit and collective defense. The group had a distinctly "military character," according to the Freedmen's Bureau superintendent, and drilled regularly "in squads." The group raised funds "for emergencies" in addition to assuming police duties and sanitation work. "The education of the men has been in camps," explained the agent, noting the influence of military training and discipline, "and the rules in regard to cleaning their plantation streets are such as returned soldiers would make." Having been soldiers themselves, or having worked alongside and watched soldiers in nearby camps, the St. Helena freedmen found military organization useful for their postwar lives. Not only did such quasi-military companies give structure and organization to ex-slaves' daily lives, they also provided them with a means of collective self-defense and, at times, resistance to planters' coercive labor practices, especially in Louisiana's sugarcane fields. Yet the performance itself may have provided freedpeople with an even more important political tool. These "marching companies," Julie Saville argues, also "symbolically linked the power of a victorious national army to the individual bodies of workers," thereby allowing freedmen to collectively represent the power of the nation-state.[26]

Freedpeople's eargerness to perform the militarized rituals historically reserved for white men propelled a desperate effort to disarm them. Although one white Unionist was "amused at the vigor and audacity" freedpeople displayed in their arming practices, most white Southerners took the arming of blacks very seriously. Their "vague and terrible fears of black insurrection" led them to pass laws barring the sale of weapons to blacks and outlawing the possession of firearms by any person of color. White militias and the Klan raided black homes and confiscated or destroyed weapons they found. Just as freedpeople's use and display of firearms had symbolic as well as practical importance, so too did whites' seizure of their weapons. When the Klan attacked Charles Smith in his home in Walton County, Georgia, they took his gun and broke it into several pieces before throwing it into the fire. While the masked men could have taken Smith's gun for their own use, they chose instead to break it in front of him, a gesture aimed at Smith's independence and manhood. The Klan also used their own guns to beat or assault freedpeople. Pistol-whipping, in fact, occurred more frequently than shooting. Perhaps ammunition was scarce, but whipping also allowed white men to reclaim mastery over their former slaves. The Klan pelted Charles Smith with rocks and their pistols before finally whipping him with a hickory switch. They also repeatedly pushed the muzzles of their guns against his head, and one man forced his gun into Smith's mouth. In other attacks, the Klan used guns to demonstrate their mastery in other brutal ways. They used a pistol to rape Rhoda Ann Childs when they couldn't find her husband, a Union veteran.[27]

Southern blacks fought against whites' efforts to disarm them by claiming a right to bear arms as citizens of the United States. Delegates to the black state convention in Charleston, South Carolina, petitioned Congress to ensure the rights of citizenship for freedpeople, including the security of "life and property," schools, access to land, "equal suffrage," the right to sit on juries, and "the right to keep and bear arms" as guaranteed by the "Supreme law of the land." Citing the Second Amendment, the convention decried a recent law passed by the state legislature outlawing black gun ownership as a "plain violation of the Constitution" and "unjust to many of us . . . who have been soldiers, and purchased our muskets from the United States Government when we mustered out of service." Before claiming their right to bear arms, however, the convention appealed to the power of the United States, "the strong arm of the law and order," to protect them. By doing so, they acknowledged not only the authority of the federal government but also its duty to them. Yet their subsequent invocation of the Second Amendment recognized the limits of state authority if not its obligation, which still might be fulfilled by securing for blacks the right to "keep and bear arms." Likewise, the *Loyal Georgian*, a black newspaper published in Augusta, proclaimed the right to bear arms in self-defense a right of American citizenship to which blacks were now entitled. These petitions reveal that Southern blacks understood arms bearing and other citizenship rights, including voting, as mutually dependent; that is, without the ability to defend themselves against violence, then the other rights would be of little practical value.[28]

The wholesale disarming of Southern blacks provided Radical Republicans in Congress an important example of why legislation such as the 1866 Civil Rights Act and the Freedmen's Bureau Bill needed to be passed.

When Senator Lyman Trumbull introduced his civil rights bill in January 1866, he explained how Southern states had passed discriminatory laws against blacks, including prohibitions against "any negro or mulatto from having fire-arms." In Trumbull's estimation, arms bearing should be a protected civil right. Sen. Josiah Grinnell of Iowa included such prohibitions alongside laws that disallowed blacks the right to vote, give testimony in court, or sit on juries, as examples of "unconstitutional" discrimination. Alabama's law fining any black man $100 and up to three months in jail infuriated Senator Sidney Clark, who demanded that the state respect the Second Amendment in its local laws. Similarly, Representative Jacob Howard insisted that the right to bear arms constituted one of the "privileges and immunities" of citizenship. Kansan Samuel Pomeroy went further, elaborating on the three "indispensible safeguards of liberty": a "homestead," "the right to bear arms for the defense of himself and family and homestead," and "the ballot." The last one, like a gun, was a "weapon of defense and offense," according to Pomeroy, who also imagined that these three things combined would have a civilizing effect on freedpeople. "It will work out the regeneration of [their] race," Pomeroy argued, "secure their elevation, education, and full developed manhood." Reiterating the themes of martial manhood, Pomeroy viewed patriarchal authority, political rights, and self-defense as crucial to the Republican formula for citizenship. Pomeroy's colleague in the House of Representatives, New York Republican Henry Raymond repeated this calculus when he spoke of the "defined status" of the American citizen. Using the male pronoun uncritically but not unintentionally, Raymond located the moral center of Republican arguments for black civil rights in a domesticated image of protective male violence. "He," Raymond explained, "has a country and a home; a right to defend himself and his wife and children; a right to bear arms" as well as vote and sit on juries.[29]

As lawmakers quarreled over the course Southern Reconstruction should take, the issue of black arms-bearing highlighted the dangerous ideological terrain on which Republicans tread. By making the right to bear arms central to their program for civil rights, Radicals heightened the volatility of an already militarized political culture that prized displays of martial prowess as evidence of one's fitness for freedom and citizenship. Paramilitary culture played important symbolic and practical roles in freedpeople's postemancipation political rituals. Whites, too, relied on militias, patrols, and other paramilitary organizations to police and control former slaves. Federal authorities struggled to deal with the burgeoning crisis in public safety. The army prohibited the sale of pistols and knives in Charleston after "several outrages [were] committed by whites upon Blacks and the reverse." In St. James, South Carolina, men and women of all races were prohibited from carrying "guns, pistols, or other weapons of War." Eventually, the Department of the South issued a regional order outlawing any "organizations of white or colored persons bearing arms, or intended to be armed, not belonging to the military or naval forces of the United States." Although his order declared that "the constitutional rights of all loyal and well-disposed inhabitants to bear arms will not be infringed" as a remedy to white South Carolinians' rampant disarming of freedpeople, General Daniel Sickles also warned that this policy "shall not be construed to sanction the unlawful practice of carrying concealed weapons, nor to authorize any person to enter with arms on the premises of another against his consent." However, not everyone agreed with Sickles's insistence that army officials could regulate private arms-bearing. William Sinclair, the assistant commissioner of the Freedmen's Bureau at Matagorda, Texas, admonished his field agent in the town of Millican for disarming local blacks at a July 4 celebration. He informed the agent that he should not disarm blacks if he did not disarm whites, too. "As long as the whites of all classes are allowed to carry arms, the freedpeople must be allowed the same privileges," he concluded. Perhaps Sinclair's egalitarianism should be commended, but why not advise his agent to disarm both races if he felt that their behavior threatened the public celebration? Almost as if he anticipated that question, Sinclair provided the answer in his letter. In short, he found such a proposition ridiculous. He asked rhetorically, "Who ever heard of a white man in Texas being arraigned for carrying concealed weapons?" Not only in Texas but also throughout much of the South, arms bearing had become a customary right of white men, and now that custom was becoming codified as a constitutional right. Rather than challenge that transformation based upon its negative impact on public safety, Sinclair accepted it as absolute—but at what cost?[30]

The proliferation of guns in the South became a growing problem for Republicans. Pennsylvania Congressman William D. Kelley worried about the reports of "swiftly recurring invoices" for "great numbers of Winchester rifles, and a particular species of revolving pistol" through the port at Charleston. Kelly believed the Confederates were reinvigorating their cause among the war-torn South's destitute population. He warned that "poor men, without visible means of support, whose clothes are ragged and whose lives are almost or absolutely those of vagrants, are thus armed with new and costly rifles, and wear in their belts a brace of expensive pistols."[31]

If Radicals ignored the implications of making the right to bear arms a federally protected civil right, their opposition did not. Tennessee Democrat Washington Whittorne posed a troubling question. Whitthorne worried that the Civil Rights Act, if interpreted to include an individual's constitutional right to bear arms, would make it impossible for state forces to control crime and violence. He wondered whether a police officer in any Northern or Southern city who disarmed a drunken man could be sued for breach of the man's civil rights. Whitthorne suspected so, concerned that the CRA would make unconstitutional a common duty performed on behalf of public safety—and one very necessary in the Reconstruction South. Whitthorne signaled a potentially dangerous dilemma that Republicans failed to anticipate. Would their own legitimacy—as well as freedpeople's safety—be compromised if an expansive interpretation of the Second Amendment became popular? Could the emphasis on the right to bear arms impede their project of initiating biracial democracy in the South? Would the language of manly self-defense fan the flames of Southern violence?[32]

Once again, the specter of black violence played an important role in the postwar imagination. Nevada Senator James Nye recognized the growing dilemma of public safety, but in his eyes, the risk came not from white paramilitaries but from blacks who had been trained as soldiers. "We have gone on . . . wisely or unwisely, converting the colored population into being of power through military discipline," he explained. "We have taught one hundred and sixty thousand of them in the art of killing . . . As citizens of the United States they have [an] equal right to protection and to keep and bear arms for self-defense . . . It must be a poor observer of human nature who does not realize that the colored people South can be goaded into desperation." To Nye, there was no turning back. Endorsing Radical Reconstruction was the only way to avoid a "race war." Curiously, the challenge, as Nye put it, was not to impede whites in their violent attacks on freedpeople but to pacify blacks' growing anger. Once again, this placed the responsibility for violence, if and when it occurred, squarely on blacks' shoulders.[33]

"The sight of a few dead men will calm their excited feelings more effectually than many words . . . "

The violence that defined the 1868 election season had roots deep in the nation's political history. As such, it was not entirely new. Yet the war and emancipation had initiated some startling changes that exacerbated the tensions already present in American electoral politics. For one, the war necessitated an increased production in arms, as well as the introduction of thousands of men to the art of war. The language of martial manhood militarized Americans' understandings of freedom and citizenship, giving rise to claims for political rights based upon their performance of state-sponsored violence during the war and the continued need for manly self-defense. As a result, the thin line that separated war from politics, which German military theorist Carl von Clausewitz had observed during the Napoleonic Wars decades earlier, became even thinner. In the South during the election of 1868, it was virtually erased. Riots like the one at Camilla became their own kind of political statement. From her plantation near Augusta, Georgia, Gertrude Thomas observed the power of violence to communicate certain political commitments as well as silence and disorient the opposition. "The sight of a few dead men," she believed, "will calm their [freedpeople's] excited feelings more effectually than many words."[34]

Violence defined the 1868 election not just in the South but across the nation. Politicians and newspapers informed voters that, in choosing a president, they were also choosing between war and peace. Democrats scoffed at Grant's motto, "Let Us Have Peace," arguing that the general who had been responsible for thousands of deaths on the battlefields of 1864, during the war's stalemate, and in Southern prison camps when he refused to exchange prisoners, was not fit to reunite the nation or bring peace to the South—and could do so only at the point of a bayonet. Republicans likewise chided Democratic candidates Horatio Seymour and Frank Blair for their violent pasts. In 1863 Seymour had courted the draft rioters, who had murdered African Americans and destroyed thousands of dollars in property. They also criticized Blair's advice to Southern whites to actively resist the Reconstruction Acts and his very public friendship with the notorious rebel cavalryman Nathan Bedford Forrest, the butcher of Fort Pillow and reputed Grand Wizard of the Ku Klux Klan. In fact, Forrest and other Southern commanders, including Generals Wade Hampton and John Brown Gordon, had attended the Democratic National Convention in New York City that July as delegates. All three enthusiastically endorsed Seymour and Blair, with Hampton going so far as to give the ticket the blessing of all Southern soldiers. Not coincidentally, the Republican press pointed out, the Democrats adopted an "ultra-conservative" platform that declared the Reconstruction Acts, specifically black voting, unconstitutional and illegitimate to appease the Southerners. This amounted to a war cry for Southern vigilantes like the Klan, Republicans argued. Carl Schurz recalled that it "stopped but little short of advocating violence in its denunciations of Reconstruction and black suffrage. Democrats responded by dismissing the Klan as a ludicrous attempt to stir up Northern voters. Instead, they posited that the real sources of violence in the South were the coercive Union Leagues—led by carpetbagging radicals who deluded freedpeople with false promises and goaded them into violence—and the strong-arm tactics of the federal government against law-abiding white citizens.[35]

Violent spectacles seasoned an already fiery campaign. Campaign rallies and parades across the country featured martial performances from veterans, who played a prominent role on both sides. The "Boys in Blue" marched in torchlight parades for their beloved Grant, and according to the *New York Times* "awakened an unprecedented lively interest in political affairs" as evidenced by the crowds that gathered to watch them. In Indiana, the "White Boys in Blue," a veterans group devoted to the Democratic platform of white supremacy, marched for Seymour, "firing off their pistols at random . . . hooting and yelling" and knocking down "everyone they met." Political parades frequently turned violent. A teenage "lad" threw stones at a Republican procession in Newark, instigating a riot in early September. In Pittsburgh, a gang of "roughs" attacked another Republican torchlight parade, wounding the mayor. Similar outbreaks happened in Astoria and Baltimore, while in San Francisco the "Grant Invincibles" met the "Seymour Club" for a gun-and-knife fight just two days before the election. These violent outbreaks in northern and western cities accompanied more notorious incidents that summer and fall in the South.[36]

The year 1868 marked a turning point in Southern violence. Not only did white attacks against freedpeople and Republicans become more organized and directed at the heart of their political organizations, the rationale for violence became more coherent. Growing out of earlier complaints that freedpeople were "insolent" and difficult to control, a discourse of black predation emerged in the wake of the Reconstruction Acts and the Fourteenth Amendment to delegitimize Republican control of the South as well as black citizenship. In particular, white Democrats in the South took aim at black voting and arms bearing. In the weeks leading up to the Camilla Riot in September 1868, local newspapers printed story after story of black crime, particularly armed assaults against whites. On July 23, the *Savannah Morning News* ran a story about a "radical Negro" who drew a pistol on a well-known white Democrat after proclaiming, "every G_d_d one of them should be killed." Another story about "High Handed Negroes" informed readers that a gang of armed blacks patrolled the main road between Savannah and Augusta and attempted to collect "tolls" from whites in order let them pass. Armed blacks reportedly ambushed and robbed a one-armed Confederate veteran, telling him that he should "go and work for some more" if that was all he had. A posse of white men pursued the "highwaymen" and shot two of them, but they escaped, leaving the community to worry about these armed bandits on the loose. Columns simply entitled "Crime" routinely listed the numerous assaults blacks allegedly committed not only in Georgia but also throughout the South. Tales of rape, murder, and robbery in South Carolina, Kentucky, Tennessee, and Texas let readers know they were not suffering alone.[37]

If such stories were not horrifying enough to white readers, the reports of black militias working to carry the election for Grant alerted whites to the impending "race war." The *Atlanta Constitution* reported that Republican governor Rufus Bullock had obtained "new army weapons" and was using them to train and drill "colored troops." The *Macon Telegraph* denounced these "war preparations." Black militias in Americus, not far from Camilla, were "sowing the dragon's teeth of distrust, hatred, and strife, reckless of the fearful consequences that must result sooner or later to both races." Reports from neighboring South Carolina also carried the message of "lawless armed bands of negroes" preparing to overawe the whites and ensure a Republican victory. Such stories amounted to more than simple fearmongering, however. They laid the foundation for a Democratic challenge to a Republican victory that most Democrats, north and south, expected despite their repeated insistences to the contrary. Party officials in Washington said as much in their private conversations, and their Southern foot soldiers saw the writing on the wall. On election night, Gertrude Thomas confided in her diary that she expected Grant to be elected despite white Georgians' best efforts to have Seymour in the White House. Disappointment aside, the narrative of an election won by black arms set the stage for later movements against Republicans.[38]

That's not to say that many white Southerners did not take stories of race war seriously. Gertrude Thomas was shocked to see her husband emerge from under the floor of their house, covered in cobwebs, where he had been hiding in order to hear their servants talk about their alleged plans to murder whites on election day. Mr. Thomas spent several days in his clandestine operations, crawling under freedpeople's cabins in order to stay one step ahead. Their neighbors made plans to move their families off the plantations and into nearby Augusta in anticipation of the "approaching crisis" and rumors that local blacks were vying with each other for which houses they got to burn. Although Thomas thought her husband's "watching out" a bit extreme, she felt as if she were "standing upon the mouth of a volcano, expecting every moment an eruption." She informed two of her former slaves, a couple named Bob and Patsey, who were also worried about an outbreak of violence, "The white people were anxious to avoid a difficulty but that if forced to it they would fight and fight well." Mr. Thomas spent election day cleaning and loading his guns, one of which he gave to his wife to take to bed with her that night.[39]

Ironically, the image of Thomas defending his wife and children mirrored the justifications Republicans had given for extending black men the right to vote and bear arms. Demonstrating how the narrative of citizenship as self-defense could be used to deconstruct black claims for equality, white Southerners offered a competing vision of white self-defense. When a group of armed freedmen came to the defense of a young boy who had been whipped by his employer, the *Savannah Morning News* applauded the white planter, Jonathan Collins, who "rallied an equal force to protect his castle." A few weeks later, the editors called on other white men to follow Collins's lead. "If in these disordered and revolutionary times there is no law to protect the people from political and social incendiarism," they reminded readers, "there is still a law recognized by civilized and uncivilized men the world over—the law of self-preservation." In the aftermath of Camilla, the *Atlanta Constitutionalist* warned critics that white Georgians "are not obliged to meekly submit to armed invasions of our cities and villages." Similarly, Democrat Benjamin H. Hill, who had counseled cooperation with Republicans, saw a lesson in the violence. The riot "will exhibit to the Northern people more clearly than a thousand speeches could," Hill wrote to the *New York Times*, "the exact reason why the southern whites are, at present, unwilling to extend universal, indiscriminate suffrage to the Negroes."[40]

Leading Democrats in Georgia spun white fears of black violence into a complex ideological justification for political violence. Pairing black voting and arms bearing as the twin pillars of Republican misgovernment, Georgia Democrats issued their own call to arms for white men to defend their families and their state. At a large rally in Atlanta on the Fourth of July, former congressman, Speaker of the House, and Confederate general Howell Cobb electrified the crowd by calling on the "Georgia's Sons" to "come and unite in this great and glorious work" of taking back their state government. "When she was a white man's government," said Cobb, "she was proud, honored, and prosperous. Come, and at this altar, unite with me, and, by the grace of Heaven, let us once more make Georgia a white man's government." While Cobb's gendered vision of the state as a woman was not unique—the American nation had often been imagined in female terms—it did emphasize the centrality of both race and manhood to Democrats' critique of Reconstruction. It also revealed the renewed importance of men's "private" identities as fathers and husbands to their "public" identities as voters. This reasoning had played an important role in the politics of secession in 1860-61, and it continued to serve as a rallying cry for Southern Democrats' in 1868. The sensational tales of marauding blacks, armed and violent, preparing to pillage and murder served as proof that secessionists had been right: anarchy, violence, and "negro supremacy" had followed Republican political ascendency.[41]

Howell Cobb and other Democrats used the language of victimization to create a white counternarrative to Republican images of black suffering and Southern depravity. In a letter to the chairman of a Washington, DC, Democratic committee who had invited him to an event there in January 1868, Cobb wrote of his growing despair. "The people of the South, conquered, ruined, impoverished, and oppressed, bear up with patient fortitude under the heavy weight of their burdens," Cobb explained, but their patience was wearing thin. "Disarmed and reduced to poverty," Cobb proclaimed, "they are powerless to protect themselves against wrong and injustice." Cobb's lamentations grew in part from those earlier worries about Southern desolation that informed many of the postwar travel narratives and the activities of the Southern Relief Commission. The main difference consisted of Cobb's attack on Reconstruction as the source of Southern woe. "They have deprived us of the protection afforded by our state constitutions and laws, and put life, liberty, and property at the disposal of absolute military power," Cobb said of the Reconstruction Acts. Reconstruction—not the war—had made the South into "a pandemonium and a howling wilderness" by engendering "a spirit of bitter antagonism on the part of our negro population towards the white people." This was to become a fundamental tenet of the emerging "Lost Cause" movement. Edward Pollard, that movement's official author and historian, explained how Southern suffering might be expected and even endured as the outcome of a military loss; their sense of honor demanded it. However, the suffering endured from Reconstruction made the war itself pale in comparison. "The Negro was first armed," Pollard recalled in his 1868 call to arms *The Lost Cause Regained*, "then forcibly emancipated; then used as a partisan instrument; then made a political master . . . then and now held up as a standing threat, not only of insurrection in the South, but of a war of races, the most terrible exhibition that could possibly be made in the living age." In this outrage and suffering, Pollard found the hope for the South's future, a way to regain its lost cause. More was at stake than the election. "We are living not in the excitement of party," Pollard surmised, "but in the solemnity of Revolution." Through suffering, the white South was being reborn.[42]

By 1868 the time for suffering was coming to an end, although the shared memory of the Reconstruction as a time of horrific oppression would continue to inform much of the white South's outlook for the next century. The time for action had arrived. Elite white Southerners began to abandon the strategy of "masterly inactivity" that had characterized their behavior with regard to formal politics since the end of the war.[43] Despite their hesitation to endorse a party that many of them felt had abandoned them during the war, men like Howell Cobb, Robert Toombs, Alexander Hamilton Stephens, and Wade Hampton embraced the Seymour ticket and actively campaigned in their home states. They also encouraged other white men to come back into the fold. At the same time, white Southerners began to target the nucleus of black political life. Planters colluded against their workers, vowing not to hire anyone who voted the Republican ticket. Laborers who refused to vote as their employers wanted were driven from their farms, losing their homes and wages. Yet economic intimidation was not enough. Although many of the South's "best men" publicly renounced the Klan's terrorism, most turned a blind eye if they did not actively participate in night riding. Charles Smith's wife, Caroline, testified that their employer promised to protect them from the Klan if they stayed with him and helped get the crop laid by. Just days after the harvest, however, the Klan raided the Smiths, forcing them to abandon their farm and the wages they were owed. Although the planter told Caroline that he had no knowledge of the Klan's attack, she doubted it, and told him so. "I said, 'Mr. Moore, Mr. Willis Gilbert is a man who owned a heap of darkies in slavery times, and he has lots on his plantation, and he says no Ku-Klux can come on his premises without he says so,'" Caroline told congressional investigators. Moore's silent response confirmed her suspicion that he was involved: "Mr. Moore did not say anything more to me." With at least the tacit approval of many planters, the night riders targeted black veterans, black voters, and black political organizations, including churches and schools, as well as the Union Leagues. They disarmed those with weapons, thereby denying black men the practical and symbolic power ballots and guns had come to represent. In Georgia, they effectively destroyed grassroots black political organizing. For Charles Smith, it simply wasn't worth the risk. "I never voted but once in my life," he admitted, and then only because his white employer forcibly took him to the polls and made him vote the Democratic ticket. After his brutal beating from the Klan, who also whipped Caroline and her sister, Smith decided never to vote again. All he wanted to do was "live in the country and make cotton and corn; I love to do that," he explained, but it had become impossible for him to do what he loved.[44]

Southerners' justifications for their violent opposition to Republicans that year reflected many of the arguments made by their Northern counterparts in the Democratic Party. As such, their attacks on black voting and arms bearing was part of a much larger conversation between Northern and Southern Democrats about race and Reconstruction. The national Democratic Party actively engaged in a discourse of white supremacy in order to stir "the great reactionary spirit of the masses." The party's platform laid out the three key issues of the election: "opposition to Congressional usurpation, opposition to negro supremacy," and "immediate restoration to the unity and peace of the nation." In order to prepare candidates and stump speakers for the canvass, *The Democratic Speaker's Handbook* contained partisan news reports on Republican governor William G. Brownlow's use of the militia to combat the Klan in Tennessee, a vindication of Nathan Bedford Forrest's actions at Fort Pillow, a lengthy indictment of the Freedmen's Bureau for corruption and promoting "social amalgamation," and numerous accounts of "negro outrages" throughout the South. One leading Democrat believed that "the most effective campaign document that can possibly be circulated" was "the series of portraits of the negroes who now govern Louisiana." Although they sometimes published "unpredictable" images of freedpeople as respectable, hard-working citizens, the Democratic press routinely referred to Southern blacks as "barbarians" and reported stories of alleged rapes and murders committed by freedpeople. "The Red String League," an engraving appearing in *Frank Leslie's*, allowed readers to visualize the popular white rationale for violence against blacks. Showing Southern blacks in a macabre euphoria, with knives raised to the sky in unanimity of purpose, this scene evoked the image of native Africans enacting exotic rituals or preparing to make a pagan sacrifice. It also raised troubling questions in the minds of *Leslie's* white Northern audience. Was the "Red String League," the local variation of the Union League in North Carolina, working to bring about Republican electoral victories or start a race war? How far were they prepared to go in ensuring blacks cast votes? Were they the guarantors of liberty as their proponents claimed or menacing insurgents bent on the subjugation of Southern whites? Democratic victory, according to the party's candidate for governor in Ohio, was the only way to avoid "the most cruel, merciless, and devastating of all wars."[45]

Not all Democrats were united on the issue of violence. Samuel Tilden expressed his concerns that violent rhetoric and extreme racial intolerance would diminish the party's chances among more moderate voters and urged "the greatest moderation, prudence, and forbearance" by candidates and speakers. The Northern Democratic press also criticized Wade Hampton for waving the bloody shirt of the Lost Cause in a series of speeches he gave in South Carolina. The rabidly Democratic *New York World* called them "silly," while even the *Charleston Mercury* and *Richmond Whig* cautioned against "showing our hand too soon." Moreover, a few white Southerners questioned the efficacy if not the values that underlay the growing violence. Herschel V. Johnson, former governor of Georgia, warned that "Blood & Thunder" would do more harm than good. After reading his vitriolic speech to the Atlanta Democratic rally, a "Friend to the Cause" from New York wrote to Howell Cobb advising him against taking such a hostile tone, especially his invocation of the Confederacy. "You can well imagine how a wrong construction may be placed on your intentions and motives," the anonymous writer stated. The writer then informed Cobb that he had met "a common mechanic" on a streetcar and asked how he thought the election would go. The mechanic replied, "If we could only get the Southern politicians to keep silent there would be a chance for our ticket, but they will ruin everything with their speeches." "Friend" asked Cobb to "stay at home" and "keep quiet."[46]

Perhaps Cobb's "Friend" was right. In the end, Grant soundly defeated Seymour, in no small part due to the growing violence in the South and the way in which the Democratic Party appeared to encourage it. One historian argues that the Klan spectacle, the Camilla riot, and other instances of political violence "had created a unity among Republicans that had not existed even during the war." That unity, however, was problematic. Initially, the Republican press condemned the violence at Camilla as a renewal of the rebellion encouraged by none other than Horatio Seymour and Frank Blair. Horace Greeley's *New York Tribune* denounced the "rebel version" of events put forth by the Associated Press that accepted whites' explanation that they were putting down an "armed invasion" of their town. The AP report applauded Sheriff Poore's attempt to peacefully disarm the black "mob." In its denunciation of such apologies for the violence, the *Tribune* took up the mantle of arms bearing as a fundamental right of *all* citizens. "Shall the late Rebels be the only class in the Southern communities suffered to hold political meetings and bear arms?" the paper asked. Believing this to be the "essential question," the *Tribune* denied that the sheriff or even the Republican governor Rufus Bullock—who had issued a proclamation days prior to the riot that disallowed any armed organizations from drilling except the US Army—had any right to ask

African Americans to lay down their arms if whites were allowed to keep theirs. In fact, Bullock's proclamation, although intended to help local authorities avoid the kind of violence that erupted at Camilla, did not authorize those authorities to disarm any individual. The proclamation reaffirmed section 14 of the Georgia Constitution, which took verbatim the Second Amendment of the US Constitution: "The right of the people to keep and bear arms shall not be infringed." The *Tribune* took this as a prohibition against disarming the marchers at Camilla since they were carrying their arms for self-protection, a common practice in Georgia. Further, the marchers "would have been laughed at as fools [and] sneered at as cowards" if they had stacked their arms and gone home. Democrats then would have hailed "the admirable harmony" in Georgia politics, but it would have been to the detriment not only of the Republican Party but also American democracy. In short, the *Tribune* welcomed the violence at Camilla as a demonstration of Republican fortitude and freedpeople's commitment to democratic principles.[47]

Reconstruction violence proved to be useful political propaganda for Republicans in 1868, but soon rifts began to appear within the party on the issue. With the presidential contest decided, the meanings Republicans assigned to political violence in the South began to change, and its unifying message weakened. In her analysis of how the media responded to the Ku Klux Klan in the late 1860s and early 1870s, Elaine Parsons demonstrates that the organization's mystical performances and comical appearance often led observers to discount Republican claims that it was part of a larger political conspiracy to undo Reconstruction. Even Republican stalwarts, such as the *New York Times* and *New York Tribune*, began to grow wary of the spectacular stories continually emerging from the South. The papers claimed that sources of Klan stories, primarily freedpeople and white Republicans, were unreliable, and that the Republican Party used the "Ku Klux Bugbear" to fire up Northern minds against Democrats. The *Tribune*'s editor, Horace Greeley, sympathized with Southerners who had been painted with the Ku Klux brush and, after a series of investigations into the Klan, concluded New York City had more of a problem with lawless thugs than anywhere in the South. As a result, public interest in the Klan waned.[48]

It became increasingly common after 1868 to portray Southern Republicans and freedpeople as weak, ineffectual, and unmanly due to their perpetual complaints of being terrorized by the Klan. The fact that Seymour won both Georgia and Louisiana, two states where political violence and fraud had demolished the Republican campaign, signaled to some observers that black voters were unreliable. Instead of concluding that the Klan was, in fact, the dangerous conspiracy Southern Republicans had said it was all along, leading Republicans in the North chose to see the outcomes in those two states as evidence that black voters lacked the requisite independence needed to perform the duties of citizenship. Of planters' efforts to starve blacks into the Democratic Party, the *National Republican* commented that freedpeople were like "dumb, driven cattle" who followed their employers' lead. Long fearful that blacks would fall under the spell of "demagoguery," Republicans wondered if freedpeople were too ignorant and too poor to be useful citizens. Massachusetts representative George Boutwell worried that freedpeople were too "timid, careworn, and broken down in spirit" to participate in "political struggles." How could they compete with the "cunning, skill, knowledge, and influence of the ex-rebels," asked Minnesota's Ignatius Donnelly? In the debates over the Reconstruction Acts and later the Fifteenth Amendment, Republicans recognized freedpeople's vulnerability but did little to counter it.[49]

Republicans were also concerned about the effects of freedpeople's political mobilization on the South's economic recovery. In short, they feared that politics distracted freedpeople from their agricultural labors. In the fall of 1868, John W. DeForest, the former Freedmen's Bureau agent who detested the begging freedmen on ration day, published two short essays in the *Atlantic Monthly* entitled "The Man and Brother," an ironic play on the old abolitionist motto, "Aren't I a Man and a Brother?" These essays would become the basis of DeForest's longer memoir of his time with the Bureau in South Carolina. DeForest scoffed at freedpeople's primary "amusement": politics. He recounted how he often had to "discourage the zeal of the freedmen for political gatherings" because they neglected the crops. A writer to the *New York Times* echoed these claims, saying that corn and cotton were rotting in the fields in Georgia because "the negro was absent, tending to speeches and elections." Once a staunch advocate of black suffrage, the *Nation* also turned sour on the subject in the 1870s, comparing the ballot to "the discovery of a parcel of diamonds" that demoralized the man who possessed it. Politics "turn[ed] his mind away from steady industry" and therefore portended not the freedman's elevation but his destruction. In another article written in response to the passage of the Fifteenth Amendment, the *Nation* warned "very litle good will come to [freepeople] from laws or constitutional amendments unless . . . the Negro will work and earn money, if he will put it away in banks and not squander it on riotous living, if he learns to make as sharp a bargain as his white neighbor, then the ballot will be some use to him, but not otherwise." In other words, the ballot could not give blacks the respectability that many whites believed they lacked.

CHAPTER FIVE

Ironically, this echoed the *Christian Recorder*'s warning to its readers that the ballot was not a panacea for all their ills. Suffrage failed to endow blacks with the esteem and status they desired, at least in the eyes of whites. And given the lack of sustained state or federal protection to secure their safety in voting, it put them at risk for increased intimidation and violence from whites. In a cruel twist to the meaning of citizenship in postemancipation America, it now seemed that their onetime "friends" who had encouraged their political activities when it suited them now viewed freedpeople's enthusiastic embrace of politics and votership as evidence of their unfitness for self-governance.[50]

By the mid-1870s, the belief that enfranchising Southern blacks had been a mistake took hold among moderate Republicans and even some reconstructed Radicals. In 1871, James S. Pike, a Maine-born journalist who had been the chief Washington correspondent for Greeley's *New York Tribune*, penned an "eye-witness" account of the state of affairs in South Carolina under "negro rule." Although Pike wrote most of *The Prostrate State* before he ever set foot in South Carolina, the book was marketed and received as an authentic, nonpartisan account of the effects of black voting on state government. The book received much acclaim in the North, especially among Democrats, and became the leading textbook on Republican misrule in the South. That Pike skewed his presentation of "evidence" to paint South Carolina blacks in the most negative light possible has been well established; however, it is important for our present discussion of the Northern perception of Southern violence to note how the crusading reporter depicted the subject. Aside from calling the state's black legislators "ignorant, thievish, immoral, stupid, and degraded," Pike noted that their favorite topics of discussion were the "Ku Klux" and "then the business of arming and drilling the black militia." While Pike's description of the raucous legislature bordered on the comical at times, he ensured that readers did not come away thinking South Carolina blacks were merely ridiculous. Reprinting testimony from white South Carolinians given during the Ku Ku Klan investigations, Pike allowed his readers to believe that whites were the primary victims of black violence instead of the other way around. One judge testified that blacks routinely beheaded and disemboweled their victims and criticized the Republican governor, Robert K. Scott, for pardoning black criminals so that he could fill the ranks of his militia.[51]

Aside from Pike's main theme of black venality, he also spent a great deal of time sympathizing with Southern whites. Southern desolation and suffering also played a key role in Pike's narrative of a state brought to its knees. He recounted tales of Sherman's depravity in 1865 as images of burned-out mansions and lost fortunes littered the pages of his book. White Southerners had endured "famine... and suffering beyond computation, the story of which has never been told," Pike claimed. As he grieved for a people reduced to eating "cornbread and cow-peas," he argued that Reconstruction had continued the cruelty Sherman began, and it was time to stop. Pike adopted the term becoming popular among Southern whites for imagining Reconstruction's end: redemption. "The Redemption of the State [is] possible," he wrote, if white men could organize to reestablish their supremacy. Articulating what would soon become the guiding principle of Redemption, Pike acknowledged the convergence of manhood, race, and violence in the Southern attack on Reconstruction. "It would be a violent presumption against the manliness, the courage, and the energy of South Carolina white men, to allow the State to remain in the permanent keeping of her present rulers," he concluded.[52]

The image of black violence presented in *The Prostrate State* seemed to be at odds with the notion circulating among Northern Republicans that Southern blacks were too weak and dependent. This narrative of black victimization became a common theme used throughout the Ku Klux Klan hearings, which were convened by Republicans to investigate the rising tide of assault, murder, and voter intimidation by masked groups of "night riders," and subsequent Congressional investigations into other incidents of Southern violence in the 1870s. This narrative enabled Republicans to counter white Southerners' claims that the Klan and other vigilante movements were organized to defend against the "Loyal Leagues" and black militias who terrorized local whites and corrupted the democratic process. By painting freedpeople as "unoffending," Republicans downplayed instances of black resistance to white aggression, making them seem to be passive and meek in order to play upon the sympathy of Northern white audiences who were ambivalent, at best, to displays of black self-determination. As had been the case during the war when abolitionists and Republicans pushed for black recruitment in the Union Army, black violence had to be tightly controlled by white authorities and channeled into discrete expressions on the battlefield. Black men were expected to maintain a nearly impossible balance between martial valor and discipline, which tilted considerably if not entirely toward discipline during Reconstruction.[53]

That double-bind plagued black Southerners and their white allies as they struggled to respond to the increasing violence directed against them in the mid-1870s. Their continual pleas for federal intervention were beginning to annoy those in Washington inclined to be believe that Congress helped those who helped themselves. In November 1875, after white supremacist violence had rocked Mississippi and resulted in a contested election with both parties claiming victory, Massachusetts congressman Benjamin Butler, once a "Beast" to Southerners when he oversaw Union-occupied New Orleans, became an unwitting ally in their struggle for Redemption. When a delegation of African Americans asked Butler, who was also the father-in-law of besieged Republican governor Adelbert Ames of Mississippi, for a contribution to purchase arms to send to their Southern brethren, Butler flatly refused. Instead he proposed to give them "twenty-five cents for a package of Lucifer matches" so that they could burn down the plantations of their persecutors. Why Southern blacks did not do so confounded him. "If you cannot take care of yourselves," Butler told them, "you are not worthy to be freeman." Butler repeated his disappointment with what he understood as black submissiveness when he wrote to a friend in Louisiana, "So long as they will submit to be killed by every marauding white man who will do so, so long there will be no help; nor do I believe there is any aid to be looked for from the United States . . . I should take to killing equally if I were a colored man." This was hardly the first time the pugnacious little politician had shown such a cavalier attitude toward the value of black lives. He had issued the first order making runaway slaves "contrabands of war" in 1861. Once again, he placed on their shoulders the burdens of freedom as a challenge to demonstrate their worthiness to the cause.[54]

What are we to make of these two conflicting narratives of Reconstruction violence? Had freedpeople met the demands of citizenship too well or not well enough? According to most white Southerners, and some Northern observers like James Pike, they had proved too proficient in wielding the ballot *and* the bullet. Although they decried the corruption and violence that resulted from black enfranchisement, their claims of "negro supremacy" spoke to the many successes of black political mobilization in the South. Whites had not been able to control black votes in most places, especially in South Carolina where the governor's militia had been able to ensure black voting. Black men's voting and arms bearing symbolized Republican illegitimacy and mobilized Southern men to become more organized in their efforts to end Reconstruction. That narrative coexisted with the other view, growing in popularity in the North, that Southern blacks needed to defend themselves instead of relying on the government to do it for them. In some respects, this view replicated the ambivalence that defined the abolitionist understanding of slavery and the benefits of black military service. Whites had long been torn between the image of black men's docility and their rebellious potential.

They employed both of these images at various times depending on their particular needs. However, that ambivalence left Republicans in a lurch in the 1870s as white violence became more focused, concentrated, and self-consciously revolutionary. Having made voting and arms bearing central to their conceptions of citizenship, Republicans faced a monster partially of their own making. They could either fight it out, or let Southern blacks bear the responsibility for being either too violent or not violent enough. Either way, they had constructed blacks as being clearly unfit for citizenship.

At the center of these conflicting narratives about the political violence that erupted in 1868 were questions about race and manhood. Was bearing arms necessary for a man's political identity? What was the relationship between freedom and manly self-defense? Did the political independence of one race require the violent suppression of the other? Did ballots depend on bullets? The Republican victory at the polls did little to settle these issues, and as a new decade dawned, they would become the guiding questions in a new movement to redeem the South and Southern manhood.

SIX

The Violent Bear It Away

"And from the days of John the Baptist until now, the kingdom of heaven suffereth violence, and the violent bear it away." MATTHEW 11:12[1]

"The qualities which in a white man would win the applause of the world in a negro be taken as the marks of savagery." CHARLES CHESNUTT, 1905[2]

Between 1868 and 1873, Southern whites struggled to find an appropriate response to Grant's election and his promise to bring peace to the warring region by protecting black voters. Dejected by their defeat at the polls in 1868 and again in 1872, many leading Democrats looked for ways to rejuvenate their party and get their foot in the door, so to speak, of Southern state and local governments. They worried that as long as the hard-liners among them, men like Howell Cobb who preached violent resistance, were seen as the face of the party, Northern voters would continue to support Republican candidates. Echoing President Grant's calls for peace, many new departurists turned away from party politics and looked to the region's economic modernization under the banner "Let Us Have Cotton Factories." According to Eric Foner, "Southern Democrats suffered their own legitimacy crisis" that raised important questions about what they as a party represented. Were they a party of reactionary violence and extremism or of moderation and conservatism? Should they accept the reality of black voting and seek compromise with Republicans? Could they form biracial coalitions of moderates in both parties to offset the more radical aspects of Reconstruction? Or should cooperationism be resisted in all forms and by any means necessary?[3]

These questions revealed more than just a rift over political strategy. The quarrels over the Democratic Party's "new departure" in the South revealed tensions over the meaning of manhood among whites, for whom the arena of politics became a battleground not simply for control of governments but for control over their own subjectivity. Confederate defeat and slave emancipation crippled white Southern men, both literally and figuratively. Even those who made it home in one piece from the war found it difficult to reassert their authority over their households, manage the confusing new system of free labor, and accept the terms of their military surrender and political neutering. The enlistment of black soldiers in the Union Army and the mobilization of "black militias" by Republican officials in the South exacerbated these feelings of racial emasculation. Often overcome by fear and panic, once-proud men like James Thomas took to crawling on hands and knees under their homes and the homes of their former bondsmen in desperate attempt to regain control over their lives. The cobwebs that covered Thomas when he emerged from underneath the floor represented how the past could sully both a man's body and his spirit by making him stoop, bend, and crawl in places he never thought he would go.[4]

To many white men in the South, the "new departure" seemed like an acceptance of this fate, a second surrender. For all their talk of leaving behind the antagonistic racial politics of 1868, the "new departure" retained many aspects of the old racism that previously defined the Democratic Party. For instance, Taxpayer's Conventions in several Southern states, most notably Mississippi and South Carolina, turned their attention to the Republican administration's financial mismanagement of the state, but they still called for "intelligent property owners" to seek office. A coded language meaning elite white men, their appeals to intelligence and property "implicitly denied blacks [and poor whites] any role in the South's public affairs except to cast votes for their social betters." The "new departure" had not traveled too far after all. Still, even their begrudging acknowledgement of Southern powerlessness in the face of Republican dominance on both the national and local scenes left a sour taste in the mouths of many Southern whites who viewed cooperation as weak, ineffectual, and dishonest.[5]

Perhaps even more troubling than this dissension among the South's native political elite were the calls for "reform" made by poorer whites who had grown increasingly restless from years of war, poverty, and upheaval. The war and Reconstruction in many ways leveled the Old South's social hierarchy, and landless white men neither felt beholden to the planter elite nor viewed their economic and political fates as

CHAPTER SIX

inextricably tied together as they once had. As C. Vann Woodward put it in, "no love was lost between Black-Belt gentry and hillbilly commoners—then or now." Universal manhood suffrage, as well as other Republican policies, such as the creation and funding of a public school system and the Homestead Act, appealed to men whose livelihoods had been strangled by the planters' death grip on land and capital in the region. Republicans spoke a new language of opportunity that, in certain moments and in certain places like East Tennessee and upcountry Georgia, threatened to drown out the shrill cries of "black Republicanism" coming from same men who some yeomen felt had goaded them into war and then failed to deliver the independence they had promised.[6]

The struggle to unify Southern whites propelled the region into full-out armed rebellion in the mid-1870s. Beginning in Louisiana in 1873, then spreading north into Mississippi in 1874 and 1875, and culminating in a spectacular orgy of violence in South Carolina in the year of the nation's centennial, the self-proclaimed "white liners" and "straight-outs" repudiated not only Republican control of their local and state governments but also the cooperationists' calls for moderation and restraint. "We, having grown weary of tame submission to this most desolating war of the negro upon us, propose to take a bold state to assert the dignity of our manhood, to say in tones of thunder and with the voice of angry elements STOP! THUS FAR SHALT THOU GO, AND NO FURTHER!" proclaimed the *Caucasian*, a white supremacist newspaper published in Alexandria, Louisiana, by former Confederate officers. Claiming to give voice to white men across the South, the paper made violent resistance the litmus test of white manhood. Despite the fact that so much of their anger was directed at the federal government, the white liners' formulation of violent manhood was also an appeal to Northern whites' sense of self. In their excesses, which included the slaughter of innumerable freedmen and armed coup d'etats, the straight-outs redeemed their own manhood and, ironically, laid the foundations for sectional reconciliation.[7]

Redemption was not a movement solely for the South's political deliverance. It was also a highly gendered movement that spoke to the underlying dilemma regarding manhood, violence, and citizenship, a dilemma ignited by emancipation and exacerbated by Radical Reconstruction. Historians have begun to tease out the importance of manhood to white Southerners' political worldviews in the postwar period, but it remains to be seen exactly how the violence unleashed in the mid-1870s helped shape the meaning of white masculinity not just for Southerners but for the entire nation. This chapter begins to answer that question. While the tensions between restraint and unbridled aggression that typified earlier eras remained a cause for concern for postemancipation men, Redemption offered a momentary respite from the pretensions of gentlemanly self-discipline. It also helped usher in an era of "militaristic patriotism" that reunited Northern and Southern white men so recently divided by civil war and slave emancipation. A close examination of the white supremacist insurgencies in the Deep South reveals the importance violence played not only in the unification of Southern whites against Reconstruction but also in a broader Americanization of Southern violence based upon the nation's revolutionary principles. The fact that some of the bloodiest and most self-consciously revolutionary battles for white supremacy occurred around the nation's centennial celebration was no coincidence. In 1876, the nation celebrated violent white manhood and confronted its own investment in Southern deliverance.[8]

Waking Lazarus

For all its power as a religious metaphor, Redemption was an uneven and contentious political project for white Southerners. Lacking the clarity of purpose and unanimity of support that the term belied, those men who claimed the mantle of "Redeemers" were, in fact, a motley crew. Members of the prewar plantation elite stood alongside "New South" industrialists and the emerging middle class of merchants, all claiming leadership in the movement to restore "Home Rule" by ridding their states of Yankee and negro domination, yet divided on how to achieve it as well as how to proceed once it happened. A town-country divide accentuated the planter-industrialist divide, as the growth of urban centers such as Atlanta and Louisville and the railroad lines that followed them left oncevital towns and villages literally in the dust. Although these factions may have eventually found compromise in the post-Reconstruction years, the early to mid-1870s were a time of profound conflict and indecision over the future of the white South.[9]

Nowhere was this more true than in the Deep South states of Louisiana, Mississippi, and South Carolina, where large black populations, combined with turmoil among white Democrats, enabled Republicans to maintain control long after other states had been "redeemed." Even before Democrats' pitiful performance in the election of 1872 in which the national party endorsed Liberal Republican candidates instead of running their own, some white Southerners had concluded that the party was "deader than Lazarus" in Mississippi. Likewise in Louisiana, a struggle to organize white men ensued; here failed attempts at "fusion" and "unification" had alienated downstate political elites, who had allied themselves with Republicans and New Orleans creoles, from whites in the rural parishes. In South Carolina, where there was "no Democratic organization worthy of the name" since the fall of 1868, a black-controlled state legislature benefitted from the strong party organization of Republican governor and Union army veteran Robert K. Scott, who employed his mostly black state militia to great effect during elections so as to ensure that white violence and intimidation, which were considerable, failed to overawe black voters. Federal prosecution of local Klans in these states, although limited, disabled the vigilante movement and prolonged Republican control in the Deep South. Such a demonstration of federal support no doubt contributed to whites' indecision and lack of focus.[10]

The growing frustration and sense of alienation among the mass of native white men from their political leaders fertilized the seeds of white supremacy in the early 1870s. Opponents of the "new departure" and other cooperationist strategies gave voice to this growing dissatisfaction through a gendered ideology of redemption that called for the violent defense of native white manhood. A founder of the white league movement in Louisiana, Alexandre DeClouet, a sugar planter and former Confederate congressman from St. Martin Parish, paid homage to the hardships of poor whites in the rural areas and used that unrest to galvanize them to his cause. In a speech "to the White Citizens of St. Martin," DeClouet recognized how economic hard times and political corruption had left them with little choice but to take extreme measures. DeClouet blamed the cotton worm, yellow fever epidemics, the financial panic of 1873, and Republican malfeasance for the "gloom of abject poverty, of despair, and of mortal agony over our downtrodden community." The answer, DeClouet informed his audience, was to form a white league and "reclaim their rights and their government." Praising the recent albeit short-lived armed takeover of the city of New Orleans by white leaguers, DeClouet promised eventual victory despite the setback they had suffered when federal troops moved in to restore order. The more immediate effects of organization and action would be to rejuvenate a sense of involvement and duty among white men who DeClouet believed had neglected their commitment to the race. Although their apathy and inattention was perhaps understandable given the trying economic times, DeClouet announced that the time had come to rededicate themselves to the cause of white manhood.[11]

DeClouet's message echoed throughout the Deep South. In the summer and fall of 1874, in advance of the elections that November, whites in both Louisiana and Mississippi struggled to unite on a statewide level against the "fusionists" who symbolized the prospects, however lopsided in favor of whites, of biracial democracy. "Let us have no fornicating with the Radical Party, under the idea of begetting a 'new South,'" declared one Mississippi newspaper, "but let us nail our colors to the mast, and stand by them like men. Nothing else will save us." The *People's Vindicator*, a white league newspaper published in Natchitoches, Louisiana, called on the "men of manhood" to rescue "your suffering State." The paper welcomed violent confrontations, either with blacks or the federal government, and declared, "Better that we should occupy unnumbered graves than to live as recreant cowards." The Opelousas White League in St. Landry Parish issued a resolution around the same time denouncing "a renewal of any further attempts at compromise" because "a temporizing policy" was "destructive to our self-respect and manhood." Only "the banner of the White League," they declared, "can rescue us from dissention and defeat." The *Shreveport Times* called on the state's white men to exercise their "manly qualities," specifically their ability to intimidate blacks. The *Catholic Messenger* took a slightly different tack and derided white men for their weakness. "They have shown no courage, no spirit of sacrifice, no public spirit whatever," only "the most accommodating submissiveness," declared the official organ of the New Orleans Archdiocese. Likewise, another mainstream Democratic paper, the *Picayune*, scoffed at the possibility that a white uprising might be put down by federal troops: "The most abject spectacle we can imagine is that of a regiment of able-bodied human beings crouching and whimpering before the effigy of the United States Army." By appealing to their injured manhood, the growing white league movement created a salve for Southern men.[12]

The white leagues' paramilitary roots ran deep. They shared an organizational structure and protofascist methodology reminiscent of the "vigilance committees" formed during the secession crisis of 1861. Like those earlier paramilitary groups, the white leagues had two overlapping functions: to mobilize popular support, particularly among the yeoman and poorer classes, and to suppress dissent among whites. Although they proclaimed the natural affinity of white people for each other and their unquestioned opposition to Republicanism, the unity that the white leagues presumed to represent was itself the product of intimidation and violence.[13]

The white leagues' more recent roots lay in the various "Democratic clubs" that proliferated during the 1868 election season, and included veterans from the Ku Klux Klan, Knights of the White Camellia, and other loosely organized vigilante groups that terrorized freedpeople and Republicans until the federal roundups in 1871 and 1872. With their

CHAPTER SIX

disguises outlawed by the Enforcement Acts, the white leagues chose a more open, self-conscious style of political warfare. While the Klans had maintained an element of the carnivalesque, creating a self-mocking inversion of racial and gender norms that allowed white men to sometimes wear women's clothes and blacken their faces, the white leagues produced a unabashedly hypermasculine ethos that glorified violence as the father of political change. When it came to the question of manhood, white leaguers did not equivocate, mask, or otherwise obscure who they were or what they stood for. Indeed, newspapers like the *Caucasian* proudly published the full names of men elected to head local white leagues in northern Louisiana as well as the statewide White Man's Party, which pushed Democrats to adopt a no-compromise approach to the fall elections. Unafraid to publicly challenge not only Republicans but also Democrats who resisted falling into line, leaguers made openness central to their movement. The white leagues had "nothing to conceal, nothing to say or do what we will not publish to the world," they declared in response to criticisms of their violent rhetoric. "Let our actions be such that everybody will know what we want," advised white leaguers in DeSoto Parish. Their mission was not simply to rid the South of Republicans, or even to embarrass or terrify blacks (which they did to great effect), but to redeem white men's roles as warriors and patriarchs.[14]

Thus, it was no coincidence that most white league officers were also Confederate veterans. Men like Christopher Columbus Nash in Louisiana, James Z. George in Mississippi, and Matthew C. Butler and Martin W. Gary in South Carolina transformed an amorphous yet energetic movement into well-disciplined paramilitary units, a veritable "white league army" that would provide the muscle needed to turn words into actions.[15] Witnesses from across the Deep South reported with great alarm the warlike preparations the leagues were making. White leaguers in Yazoo, Mississippi, rode out to the fairgrounds at least once a week for target practice. South Carolinians formed "rifle clubs" under the pretense that they were social groups for gun aficionados but whose meetings gave white men an excellent opportunity to hone the skills that would make them a formidable fighting force: riding and shooting. The club members also pooled their money to buy new weapons, including the latest Remington and Winchester rifles. The Washington Artillery, named after a prewar Charleston militia unit, even purchased two cannons. These clubs made no efforts to hide their drilling maneuvers, and when Republican governor Daniel Chamberlain outlawed private armed organizations in the fall of 1876 during the bitter, blood-soaked campaign to retain his seat, the clubs simply changed their names. Only their new names—the

Allendale Mounted Baseball Club, First Baptist Church Sewing Circle, and Mother's Little Helpers—were ironic. In urban areas like Charleston and New Orleans, white paramilitaries acted as private police forces, patrolling the streets and sometimes aiding city or federal officials in keeping order.[16]

The Leagues' militarization precipitated an arms race in the Deep South. Hard economic times, however, forced them to be thrifty. In St. Martin's Parish, Louisiana, white leaguers repaired broken artillery left over at a nearby foundry, including an "iron gun with a four-inch bore" and two Napoleon guns raised from Bayou Teche. Martin Gary, the architect of the "straight-out" movement in the Palmetto State, informed the captains of the rifle clubs that they should ensure each man in their unit was "well armed and provided with at least thirty rounds of ammunition" as well as three days' rations. Many white leagues required that members supply their own weapons, while others, like the Carolina rifle clubs, which were more centrally organized than most, purchased arms collectively. But good weapons were expensive. A local dealer informed members of the Colleton Mounted Rifle Club that he could obtain their preferred Enfield rifles at $3 apiece and a thousand rounds of ammunition for $15. The club collected $116—enough to buy 38 rifles or 23 boxes of bullets, not including shipping costs. The St. Martin's White League used their foundry to cast their own ammunition. Reports from Mississippi stated that "many Winchester rifles, with proper supplies of ammunition" flooded places like Vicksburg, where the white liners were amassing their forces in the summer of 1874. By September, men "armed with all sorts of weapons"—Winchesters, needle-guns (the common name for the new Springfield breech-loaders), shotguns, and pistols—marched almost daily upon the streets. These were new models of "the most improved patents." Some of those weapons had been purchased by the state of Mississippi for the militia, but sympathetic city officials in Vicksburg distributed them to the white leagues instead. As a result, the state forces suffered a severe shortage of arms. "Not more than two hundred men can be armed," the captain of the state militia in Jackson informed the state adjutant general. Witnesses reported that the arms that blacks possessed individually were decidedly inferior to those owned by the white leagues. According to one Republican official, the freedpeople near Yazoo "were wholly without arms except now and then an old pistol or squirrel-gun." Overall, most white leagues managed to accumulate impressive arsenals second only to the United States Army and routinely outgunned their opponents, including the New Orleans Metropolitan Police and various units of state militia in northern Louisiana and Mississippi.[17]

In addition to providing an effective means of waging war against Republicans and freedpeople, guns had become important emblems of manhood. According to a Charleston journalist embedded with the South Carolina rifle clubs as they embarked on the 1876 campaign, "a thirty-eight was the very smallest caliber tolerated in respectable society. The really well-dressed man wore a forty-four." Embarrassed by his comparatively tiny twenty-eight caliber six shooter, the writer soon learned the importance of displaying a properly sized sidearm. "By the end of that year," he recalled, "the most conservative and well mannered young gentleman making evening calls took his artillery from his hip pocket and laid it on the mantel as casually as he hung his hat on the rack in the hallway." In other words, the size of a man's personal weapon reflected his standing in society. Like a hat or piece of jewelry, guns had become fashionable accoutrements of respectability. Yet they were more than mere decoration. The journalist noted, "A man without a revolver felt undressed and embarrassed, as a man would now walking the public streets at noon lacking his trousers." An unarmed man was exposed, vulnerable, and weak. This was a lesson Albert Morgan learned the hard way. Shortly after arriving in Yazoo, Mississippi, the "carpetbagger" received a brutal beating from a gang of white toughs. A federal army officer who witnessed the assault advised Morgan to "never be seen in public without a weapon of some sort—that *they* carried them and had taken pains to let the fact be known—that I would not have been attacked had it been known that I was armed."[18]

Being part of an armed paramilitary group inspired martial fantasies of battlefield glory that many white Southern men longed for. Men like Nash, George, and Gary used their Confederate reputations to rally men to their cause. Such leadership caused the Natchitoches White League to boast, "The white men of this State are no mere beginners in the arts of peace and war." When white league organizer William Hardy spoke to a crowd in Meridian, Mississippi, in 1875, he invoked the memory of Stonewall Jackson, who had supposedly called out on his deathbed, "Prepare for action!" Some chose to make more of their Confederate heritage than others. The Carolina clubs, in particular, understood themselves as reincarnations of Confederate units. Both the Carolina Rifle Club (CRC) and Washington Artillery displayed their old regimental banners. In 1874, Charlestonians presented the CRC with the "old secession flag" that had flown on the "Liberty pole" at the corner of Hayne and Meeting streets after the secession ordinance passed on December 20, 1860. Several of the clubs also held "anniversary suppers" on that date every year. Even in states with little or no white paramilitary activity, such as Virginia, martial reputations became the focus of the political struggles between white men for control of the state legislature well into the 1880s.[19]

Yet the white leagues' martial fantasies transcended their recent Confederate history. Participants and observers alike cast the leagues as modern incarnations of great armies from the past. They invoked heroic episodes, such as the battles of Trafalgar and Balaklava, to imagine themselves as sharing in a glorious military history where individual deaths were redeemed through manly sacrifice and heroism. Like Admiral Nelson and the Light Brigade, white Southern men would ride "into the jaws of death and into the mouth of Hell." They also compared their leaders to Oliver Cromwell, Henry of Navarre (France's first Protestant king), and George Washington. South Carolina's Red Shirts, according to one source, took their uniform from Guiseppe Garibaldi's Italian renegades who wore blazing scarlet blouses as they battled to establish their country's independence. A white league unit near Vicksburg called themselves the "Modocs," in honor of the California Indians who had frustrated the US Army for years and had recently assassinated Lt. General Edward Canby. Sometimes these fantasies exceeded reality. Despite being armed with only a pistol and half a brick in his pocket, George Holmes imagined he was a member of a "crack" squad in Charleston.[20]

Perhaps these non-Confederate examples of military greatness helped speak to those young men who had come of age since the war and could only associate the rebel army with defeat. Not only did white league leaders often call upon men they had commanded during the war, men who felt connections to their old leaders through the war experience, they also needed to engage a new generation of soldiers who lacked those bonds. Presenting themselves as elder statesmen and battle-hardened warriors, these veterans urged young ones who had not yet experienced the thrill of battle to "prove their mettle." A young man in his late teens or early twenties might join a league or rifle club in order to ease "the vague feeling that the fates had cheated him out of his own, in that he had not the opportunity to be a soldier," recalled one young boy who longed to join the legions of mounted men he watched on parades demonstrating their military skills. James Gibson was only fifteen when he joined the Vicksburg "Modocs," in part to live up to the sacrifice of his older brother who had been a prisoner of war for two years at Ft. Delaware. He joined along with his friend Tobe Whitaker, whose uncle had been wounded at Gettysburg. Both boys modeled themselves after their warrior kin. "Many boys nearing manhood donned red shirts and proudly rode away, determined to be as vociferous . . . as were their fathers and older brothers," according to one historian. The white leagues also provided the opportunity for young men who had been children during the war to fraternize with men who represented not simply the "Lost Cause" of Confederate nationhood but also the lost male relatives—fathers, older brothers, uncles, and cousins—who had never returned home. White league membership and participation in the paramilitary conflicts of the 1870s became a rite of passage for many in the postwar generation, a means to gain acceptance in a community of men for whom martial valor was crucial but whose recent military defeat remained an open and painful wound. The militarization of local politics reminded all those who participated "of what white men could do when they stood together and of being on the winning side once more."[21]

For those who did not succumb to the lure of military comradeship, the white leagues offered other temptations that few men could resist: food, liquor, and women. Like antebellum militias, the leagues often hosted barbeques where local people could eat, mingle, and "compare notes" with white leaguers from neighboring parishes. In the rural districts, these kinds of events offered a welcome opportunity to congregate and socialize, and during the lean years of the mid-1870s, their edible offerings demonstrated the beneficence of local elites. William Ball, an eleven-year-old in Laurens, South Carolina, recalled how his father plied local "ruffians" with a seemingly endless supply of whiskey, allowing the inebriated young men to stay at the family's home, much to the dismay of Ball's mother, where they "sang and shouted" through the night. Food attracted some freedpeople to these gatherings as well. Frank Adamson, who joined South Carolina Red Shirts in their 1876 campaign, appreciated the biscuits, fried chicken, and "heap of brandy" whites showered on the men during a procession in Columbia. "If a nigger gets hungry, all he have to do is go to de white folks house, beg for a red shirt, and explain hisself a democrat," recalled Ed Barber, who had a hard time making ends meet before he took up the cause of white supremacy. No doubt the same was true for many poor whites who also struggled to feed themselves and their families. Although some hard-liners wished to avoid "the ordinary tactics of elections," including barbeques and other public gatherings, presumably for fear that Republicans might gain too much knowledge about their plans, such events proved exceedingly useful for rallying public support and disseminating information among each other.[22]

Another attractive perk for young white league recruits were the throngs of adoring females who attended the picnics, "speakings," and parades held in their honor. "We were delighted at the sight of many beautiful ladies," wrote the correspondent for the Pickens *Sentinel* after a mass meeting in Anderson, South Carolina. "Our hearts were thrilled with the sound of sweet, joyous welcome from these blessed ladies." In addition to their vocal encouragements, white women made uniforms, banners, floral arrangements, and food for the men at these mass gatherings. One participant from South Carolina praised the "unyielding and defiant" women of his state who encouraged the men and with whom he credited "redemption from radical rule." White women played prominent roles in the pageantry of Redemption in South Carolina, often posing as the "Prostrate State" personified in "dramatic tableaux" at Democratic political rallies where a gallant white man would strike her chains and deliver her from the clutches of Republicanism. As recruiters for the cause of white supremacy, a woman's expectations of a male relative's or potential beau's service to the league could go a long way in filling the ranks. Albert Morgan, the "carpetbagger" sheriff of Yazoo, Missisipppi, noted the commanding influence women had over white league men. More so than even the area's Confederate veterans, white women "were foremost in the work of recruiting for these companies," according to Morgan. Women's influence could be felt in more indirect ways as well. Fifteen year-old James Gibson became a white leaguer shortly after his mother died. Injured in a carriage accident, Mrs. Gibson made James promise to look after his younger sisters while on her deathbed. The white leagues gave James an opportunity to fulfill his mother's dying wish. Dosia Williams Moore, who was only a teenager at the time her "sweetheart" and other men from Grant Parish, Louisiana, raided and murdered more than one hundred freedmen in the town of Colfax in April 1873, became an adoring witness to the men's preparedness and commitment to white supremacy. Women like Moore added another level of romance to the white league movement, acting as an audience for the men to woo and impress. It worked—for Moore at least, who wondered, "What is sweeter than romance in the face of death?"[23]

The belief that they were acting to protect women and children compelled many rank-and-file white leaguers to commit acts of violence they might not have otherwise. As Stephanie McCurry points out, the "trope of protecting women" was not empty rhetoric; Southern men took their roles as protectors very seriously. The white league propaganda machines—racist news rags like the *Caucasian* and *People's Vindicator*—drummed up stories of black crime in order to rally popular support for their hard-line agenda. The *Caucasian* admitted that there was no "direct testimony" to support the reports that the Republican governor was arming blacks; however, the paper defended its credibility by alleging, "There is little possibility of such evidence leaking out." Just as they had during the heated election season of 1868, "reports" of black militias drilling in preparation for a mass slaughter of whites became a staple of the white league movement. Stories of the rapes of white women at the hands of black men also became more prevalent during Redemption, spurring men to take up arms in defense of female honor and virtue. Playing on long-standing white fears about emancipation, these narratives of black predation and white victimization, particularly female victimization, made the risky venture of armed resistance to state and federal authority seem worthwhile. And although the white league fearmongers possessed little in the way of solid evidence to prove that blacks were, indeed, rising against whites, the narrative of white self-defense was too compelling to require proof, as Albert Morgan found out when his deputy interrogated local whites in Yazoo as to why they had organized a military company. The men told the deputy that they had formed to defend their homes against "ruthless bands of armed men," but when the deputy pushed them to say who was involved in such illegal activity, promising that he would go immediately to arrest them, the whites could not produce any names. The deputy warned them against listening to the agitations of newspaper editors intent on stirring up trouble, one of whom, after being arrested, had admitted to spreading rumors in order to deflect attention away from his own misdeeds. The deputy reported that the men "appeared to be ashamed of themselves" and went home. Unfortunately, few others could be persuaded that their fears were unjustified.[24]

Protectionist rhetoric gave the burgeoning white league movement a powerful rationale for its own existence. Before the emergence of the "escapist dream fantasy" of the Old South's paradise lost, white Southern men created martial fantasies that redeemed not only their military defeat in 1865, but also their ideological defeat with regard to slavery.[25] The white leagues' paramilitary structure provided the social apparatus for mobilizing large numbers of white men while its martial ethos naturalized violence as an inevitable outcome of blacks' freedom and political enfranchisement. Republicans' efforts to reform freedpeople and Southern society, white paramilitaries claimed, were the root causes of Southern violence. White violence, in return, was not only a logical but also a desirable response. In typical white league fashion, the Forest (Mississippi) *Register* asked,

"Does any sane man believe the negro capable of comprehending the Ten Commandments? The miraculous conception of the birth of our Savior? The high moral precepts taught from the temple on the mount? Every effort to inculcate these great truths but tends to bestialize his nature and by obfuscating his little brain unfits him for the duties assigned him as a hewer of wood and drawer of water. The effort makes him a demon of wild, fanatical destruction, and consigns him to the fatal shot of the white man."[26]

By blaming Republicans and freedpeople for the violence that, in most cases, they instigated themselves, white paramilitaries mounted an audacious repudiation of emancipation. White league spokesmen often contradicted themselves by arguing that freedpeople were essentially peaceful dupes to nefarious white demagogues who incited them to violent acts as well as uncivilized beasts bent on revenge and domination, but such inconsistencies mattered little. Both messages appealed to different segments of the white population—those who still romanticized the antebellum master-slave relationship and those whose racial hatred lacked the slightest hint of paternalism. Either way, the white leagues offered "proof" that Reconstruction violence had demonstrated the inability of freedpeople to govern themselves.

An important corollary to black culpability in the white leagues' ideology was the valorization of white violence as a response to the problem of freedom. As praise mounted for "the aggressive instincts of the white people" in their displays of "pluck" and resistance, the brutal suppression of black political independence became naturalized. White liners in Mississippi declared their "intimidation" of blacks to be "not only lawful, but eminently proper and essentially necessary for the protection of public or private rights." "A White man in a White man's place. A black man in a black man's place. Each according to the 'Eternal fitness of things,'" ran one headline on the eve of the white leagues' ousting of the Mississippi's Republican governor, Adelbert Ames. In Yazoo, just weeks before Sheriff Albert Morgan would be forced to flee under cover of darkness despite having learned to carry a gun and use it, the county paper declared, "Mississippi is a white man's country, and by the Eternal God, we'll rule it." To the white leagues, their violence appeared ordained by Nature and/or God, evidence of their own superiority over the "stolid, inert, and illiterate" freedmen. Martin Gary's plan for the 1876 Red Shirt campaign in South Carolina stressed the importance of physical intimidation as a performance of white supremacy. "In speeches to negroes you must remember that <u>argument</u> has not effect upon them!" he explained to his followers. "Do not attempt to flatter and persuade them," he ordered. Instead, he recommended, "treat them so as to show them you are the superior race, and that their natural position is that of subordination to the white man."[27]

White leaguers routinely mocked Republicans as weak, cowardly, and inept. When Governor Ames issued a proclamation commanding private military bodies to disband, the Jackson *Clarion*, a paper that had once been a "new departure" organ, ridiculed Ames's presumption of power: "Ha! Ha! Ha!!! 'Command.' 'Disband.' That's good." South Carolina Red Shirts, who interrupted Republican meetings by loudly cocking their pistols or shouting candidates off the stage, gloried in the fact that their intimidation made Republican governor Daniel Chamberlain too fearful to openly campaign for his own reelection. At times the disparagements of Republican manhood bordered on the comedic. Not only did Chamberlain cower in the governor's house in Columbia, he "bore the pallor of the indoors man." Compared with the proclaimed physical prowess of Democratic candidate and Civil War hero Wade Hampton III, "a big, powerful, athletic man" who it was said held a record for killing eighty black bears in the Mississippi swamps with only a hunting knife, the "crudely smart" Yankee could not compete in terms of manliness. Humiliation played an important role in the campaign's assault on Republican manhood. A black Red Shirt recalled helping to put croton oil, a strong purgative, into liquor bottles that were then given to attendees at a Republican rally at the courthouse in Winnsboro, South Carolina. After locking the Republicans inside, the Red Shirts waited for the oil to take effect. Within a few minutes, the men inside were pounding on the doors to be let out. Outside the Red Shirts had a good laugh as the Republicans were forced to defecate on themselves, turning the courthouse into an outhouse.[28]

But there was nothing funny about the murderous rage that the white leagues unleashed on the Deep South. Although the martial displays, parades, and picnics provided a certain entertainment value, perhaps even a sense of fun for Southern whites, those spectacles served more serious purposes. Not only were they designed to intimidate and terrorize blacks with ostentatious displays of white martial power, they were also intended to impress upon whites the need for unity. Militant white supremacy was neither an automatic nor easy solution to the problem of white political discombobulation. While the promise of the vindication of white manhood provided the impetus to unite, and the martial culture and paramilitary institutions gave white men the vehicles through which to organize a new collective identity, the political culture of white supremacy required additional elaboration—proof that it could reorder Southern society and bring about its redemption.

The Spectacle of White Supremacy

Although the white leagues and rifle clubs eschewed the mystical costumes and incantations associated with the Ku Klux Klan, they nonetheless maintained their own sense of pageantry and spectacle. In stylized demonstrations of martial organization, paramilitaries performed their redemption of Southern manhood and demonstrated the unity of Southern whites. Some were more elaborate than others. In rural northwest Louisiana, the birthplace of the white league movement, armed bodies seized government offices in no fewer than six parishes and forced Republican officials to resign. Whites in Natchitoches initiated these "forced retirements" beginning on the anniversary of American independence—July 4, 1874—when they broke up a meeting of black Republicans gathered to celebrate the holiday. The meeting included several members of the parish police jury, a judge, and the tax collector. Although reports of the incident did not mention the use of any weapons, the whites were undoubtedly armed. Most attendees at the meeting "fled immediately," and the parish officials were forced to resign their positions "unconditionally." Those who did not were driven from the parish. Their resignations signaled to the white league press the extent of Republican corruption and inspired similar demonstrations throughout the state. Although crude, these spectacles allowed whites to perform a kind of purification ritual, placing them in the role of an aggrieved citizenry while demonstrating the weakness and illegitimacy of Republican officials. After the Natchitoches resignations, the *Louisiana Democrat* declared that the parish was "cleansed and her recuperation is begun." These white "mass meetings" followed by a demand for Republican officials to resign often became a prelude to violence in both Louisiana and Mississippi. By embodying "the people" and claiming to represent popular will, these public spectacles legitimated the violence that followed when Republicans resisted. Such demonstrations also enacted white unity where there was none.[29]

The South Carolina rifle clubs adopted an even more elaborate performative aspect. As other historians have noted, the Red Shirt campaign of 1876 incorporated spectacular military parades, theatrical performances, and pageantry that demonstrated not only the sophistication of the paramilitary groups but also the extent of their efforts to appeal to the masses of South Carolina whites. The "Hampton Days" celebrations, which featured Confederate general and Democratic gubernatorial candidate Wade Hampton III, allowed everyday South Carolinians to meet the famed warrior as he made his tour through the state, often arriving in a chariot flanked by mounted guards. Processions, often several miles in length, featured hundreds of mounted men as well as regiments of foot soldiers. The "everlasting thud of horses' hoofs" left a lasting impression on those who came to witness it. The spectacle of a cavalry procession filled spectators with immense pride, adoration, and awe. Consider its effect on Walt

CHAPTER SIX

Whitman, who, in July 1863, upon seeing federal troops marching out of Washington declared, "How inspiriting always the cavalry regiments! . . . The noise and the movement and the tramp of many horses' hoofs has a curious effect on one." Similarly, this war show allowed white spectators to reclaim the South's proud martial tradition. "I remember that they were the first company of even semi-military men that I had ever seen, except 'Yankees,'" recalled William Ball, who was only a boy when he witnessed the parade near Laurens. "In fact," Ball noted, "until then I rather supposed the words 'Yankee' and 'soldier' [were] synonymous." The sight of hundreds and sometimes thousands of men wearing blood-red shirts dramatized Redemption in a singular way. Although closer inspection might reveal imperfectly hand-dyed calico instead of the best silk, the red shirts not only symbolized the blood sacrifice of the state's Confederate dead but also of the countless freedpeople who had died and were yet to die in the efforts to redeem South Carolina.[30]

Of course, the martial spectacle was not just for show. The white leagues' armed assaults on local governments demonstrated the extent of their military capabilities. Nowhere was this more apparent than in New Orleans, where a series of "street battles" between the Crescent City White League (CCWL) and the city's racially integrated Metropolitan Police demonstrated the white paramilitary's discipline, organization, and overall military prowess. On September 14, 1874, the CCWL routed the Metropolitans in what would be remembered as the "Battle of Liberty Place." The Metropolitans were no ragtag bunch; they were a well-trained, well-armed force that doubled as a regiment of the state militia. Their primary task, in addition to providing routine law enforcement in the city, was to protect the governor. Former Republican governor Henry Clay Warmoth, in making the Metropolitans a unit of the state militia, had created his own private army and spared no expense in their training and equipment, much to the chagrin of the city's white Democrats. Warmoth's successor, Republican Henry Pitt Kellogg, also employed the services of the Metropolitan Police, and he needed their services more than ever since a rival Democratic administration contested his legitimacy by claiming that the 1872 election had been rigged. Although President Grant recognized Kellogg as Louisiana's rightful governor, the state, in effect, had dual governments. In the summer of 1874, as the white league movement spread from northwest Louisiana down to the state capital in New Orleans, the Metropolitans focused on seizing weapons that the CCWL had imported into the city that Kellogg suspected would be used to disrupt the elections that November and push him out once and for all. In early September, the Metropolitans made three large "busts," including the confiscation of six crates of Springfield rifles on the steamship *City of Dallas*, and on the night of September 13th, just one day prior to the battle, they occupied the steamer *Mississippi*, making it impossible for the CCWL to obtain the cache of weapons the ship held.[31]

The events of the next day began in typical white league fashion. CCWL leaders called a "mass meeting" to express the outrage of the "people of Louisiana" and demand that Kellogg and other Republican officials admit their "usurpation" by resigning their posts. The rally, however, was a diversion. While several thousand white New Orleanians gathered that hot Monday morning on Canal Street, at the base of the Henry Clay Statue, the CCWL set up barricades from the Mississippi River to the St. Louis Hotel, which at the time was used as the State House, near Jackson Square. The barricades isolated the Metropolitans in the French Quarter. In addition, the CCWL cut telegraph lines so that Kellogg, when he realized what was happening, could not send for help. They also enlisted the aid of sympathetic railroad agents to slow or stop incoming trains carrying any troops that might be dispatched to aid Republicans should word of the coup get out.[32]

Several Metropolitan units who had gathered on Canal Street to observe the "mass meeting" scheduled for two p.m. were left exposed and vulnerable, nearly surrounded by CCWL on three sides and the Mississippi River on the other. The ensuing battle, which lasted only about an hour, left the Metropolitan commander, A. S. Badger, seriously wounded in his leg, which eventually would be amputated. General James Longstreet, who commanded the state militia, was thrown from his horse and re-injured the arm that he nearly lost at the Battle of the Wilderness in 1864. When the fighting broke out, Governor Kellogg sought refuge on federal property in the US Customs House. With their military leadership wounded, the remaining Metropolitans and state militia, along with a few Republican officials, holed up in the abandoned State House, until they finally surrendered to the CCWL in the early hours of Tuesday morning.[33]

Although federal troops reinstalled Kellogg and the rest of the Republican officials three days later, the CCWL claimed victory. They had, in fact, executed an impressive military coup, due in no small part to their Confederate leadership whose strategic planning gave the CCWL the element of surprise. The CCWL demonstrated a level of organization and military discipline that inspired whites throughout Louisiana and the rest of the South as well. In Taugipahoa Parish, whites passed resolutions endorsing the actions of the CCWL and formed themselves into militia companies in the hopes of enacting a similar outcome. A planter in

CHAPTER SIX

St. John Parish suggested that "some competent person" write a history of "our brilliant coup d'etat" in order to raise funds for the widows and orphans of the twenty-one white league men killed in the battle and give readers "North and West" the "correct views" of the situation in Louisiana. The CCWL's commander, Frank Nash Ogden, received telegrams from Texas, Mississippi, North Carolina, and Kentucky, all congratulating him on his accomplishments. The chief of police in Louisville offered "five hundred men at your service at any moment." Likewise, former Confederate General Braxton Bragg wrote from Galveston, "Texans send you greeting & wish you speedy deliverance." Striking a more opprobrious note, Sarah Chilton of Jackson, Mississippi, advised Ogden that he had not gone far enough and refused to commend his "prudence." Accordingly, the CCWL could feel vindicated and see their removal from power as only a temporary setback. "The events of the 14th of September cannot be rolled back on the march of time," declared the Morehouse *Clarion*, calling the battle "the first step in the progress of [a] mighty revolution." It was as if white league violence had become transcendent. As one participant mused, "No battle for freedom, won or lost, is ever in vain. The fight itself is victory."[34]

If the "Battle of Liberty Place" represented the ability of the white leagues to organize and command the power of white disaffection and rage, then other episodes of violence demonstrated its excessive potential. Exemplifying what Primo Levi termed *violenza inutile*, or "useless violence," the massacre of at least fifty-nine freedmen at Colfax, Louisiana, on Easter Sunday 1873 exhibited a level of white rage that far exceeded the perpetrators' stated purpose: disbanding a local black militia unit and installing Democratic candidates into the parish offices occupied by Republicans. But as Levi pointed out in his ruminations about the torture of Jews imprisoned in Nazi camps during World War II, "useless violence" was not really useless. It became "an end in itself, with the sole purpose of inflicting pain." Stripping prisoners naked, refusing them facilities for bathing or relieving themselves, tattooing them with numbers that replaced their names, forcing the sick and nearly dead on thousand-mile journeys in fetid railway cars only to shoot them upon arrival—these gratuitous acts of cruelty dehumanized the victims, giving some perpetrators a sadistic sense of pleasure and accomplishment. More importantly, Levi argues, the humiliation and degradation forced Jewish prisoners to perform their own inferiority, allowing Germans to feel justified in the Final Solution. "Before dying," Levi writes, "the victim must be degraded, so that the murderer will be less burdened by guilt." This, he believed, was the "sole usefulness of useless violence."[35]

Although Reconstruction violence did not come close to the genocide of Nazi Germany, there were moments when white Southerners exhibited their own "genocidal fantasies" as a response to the upheavals of emancipation. Joseph Higgenbottom, "a rampant rebel," according to the Provost Marshall at Fernandina, Florida, who knew him well, repeatedly declared, "before his Niggars would be free he would poison every damned one of them." Higgenbottom made good on his promise, having his wife mix strychnine in his laborers' food. Fortunately, they detected the poison and did not eat it. But Higgenbottom was not alone. Unable to cope with the loss of authority, North Carolina plantation mistress Ann Pope declared, "I want the power of annihilation." When one congressional examiner expressed his belief that the more educated and refined class of Southerners would not countenance such violence and hostility, John C. Underwood, a new US district court judge in Virginia, explained how he believed the different classes felt toward blacks. The educated men, Underwood reasoned, would say that they "would prefer their total annihilation" than to see their former slaves achieve legal and political equality. In contrast, the "vulgar and uneducated man" said that he "would kill a nigger as soon as he could see him." The difference was one of language, not sentiment.[36]

For many ex-slaveholders, emancipation signaled freedpeople's violent end. Whether wishing they had "the power to blow their brains out" or fantasizing about blacks' demise from disease or starvation, whites like Mary Jones, the wife of the planter and Presbyterian minister Rev. Dr. Charles Colcock Jones of Savannah, believed that "with their emancipation must come their extermination."[37] In their minds, freedom and life for Southern blacks were simply incompatible. Such sadistic expressions contradicted the laws of reason and self-interest that the most skeptical interlocutors believed would stay Southern hands even if the impulse to strike remained. Why would landowners harm freedpeople when they needed their labor, a congressional committee asked George Smith, to which he threw up his hands. It was "human depravity," he guessed, and the fact that "a man's passions go beyond his interests."[38]

The mutilation of victims spoke to the power of violence to mark the inferiority of blackness. "They amuse themselves by cutting off the ears, noses, or lips of their former slaves," wrote a journalist who reported seeing five men in Montgomery, Alabama, "with ears cut off and in an almost nude state. Others came in with throats cut, while others appeared terribly marked over their bodies with blows from sticks and stones." Acts such as these possessed a performative aspect that belied simple functionalist explanations. In her study of the Memphis Riot and how the rape of black women served to reestablish racial boundaries after emancipation, Hannah Rosen argues that Southern violence after the war became "a complex rhetoric of power and a stage for the formation and contestation of racial and gender meanings, identities, and hierarchies." That is to say violence, particularly the brutal assaults upon freedpeople in their homes as opposed to public, political rallies, and the often sexualized nature of those attacks, far exceeded the force necessary for achieving the political goals of white supremacy. The forms Southern violence took—cutting, maiming, raping—seemed excessive and incongruent to their supposed function. However, they symbolized the assailants' vision for a reconstructed Southern society; these brutal scenes, in Rosen's words, "righted a world turned upside down."[39]

In much the same way that the degradation of Jewish prisoners represented a performance of Nazi racial ideology, Southern violence after emancipation often communicated meanings about race and citizenship in post–Civil War America. In particular, the violence at Colfax functioned as a kind of racial discourse that simultaneously spoke of white supremacy and black inferiority. In his study of racial violence in colonial Africa, Jonathan Glassman argues that riots and other forms of collective violence constituted "discursive acts" that communicated a variety of messages about perpetrators and victims alike. The wounds mobs inflicted signified the victim's debasement and inferiority. Extreme head wounds and facial disfigurements erased the victim's individuality and humanity, often making it difficult to distinguish between a human corpse and animal remains. Disembowelments likewise signified the animal-like status of the victim. Sexual assaults alienated victims from their families and attacked the targeted group's ability to reproduce. At Colfax, whites cut the throats of dead bodies in a final silencing of black opposition and dissent. The corpses were "badly shot to pieces" and received "numerous wounds to the head," leading US attorney J. R. Beckwith, who prosecuted the case, to declare the murders genocidal, an attempt to wipe out the black population of the area. There was "a wantonness of killing uncalled for by anything except that motive," Beckwith remarked. The whites at Colfax indeed refused to recognize the humanity of their victims. Referring to the dead men as "beeves," the perpetrators left the bodies strewn about the settlement to be fed upon by carrion birds and vermin, denying them the dignity of a proper burial and leaving a reminder to the living of the price of political independence.[40]

As was the case in many previous white assaults on freedpeople, rumor played an important role in compelling whites to commit preemptive violence at Colfax. In the days leading up the massacre, as whites lay siege to the town, a rumor that some of the black men in Colfax had robbed a local white man, disinterred the body of his dead child, and desecrated the remains, whipped the whites into a frenzy. This rumor, along with another one that "the negroes intended to burn houses [and] ravish the women," reinforced the view of blacks as inhuman and savage, thereby allowing whites to disregard any qualms they might have about attacking otherwise unoffending people. By creating an alternative "moral framework" for committing acts of brutal, unprovoked violence, rumors of black crime and the degradation inflicted upon the victims suggest the depth of conviction whites held regarding the necessity of their acts.[41]

For Louisiana whites, the Colfax killings formed the basis of an emerging violent subjectivity that shaped their understanding of themselves as white people. Neither Colfax nor the daylight murders of white Republican officials at Coushatta in August 1874 were seen as the work of "ruffians" from other states or even regrettable lapses in control of otherwise good men. Rather, they represented important lessons about the nature of politics and the problem of black freedom.[42] Emboldened by the March 1874 acquittal of one of the men charged with the murders at Colfax and a mistrial of another eight, white leaguers openly praised the massacre as a "wholesome lesson" to blacks who dared defy white authority.[43] Despite the brutality exhibited that day, the white league press declared it was the work of "cool, determined, and just men, who knew just how far to go." Louisiana needed more men like them, "bold and resolute," who were not "afraid of a little blood-letting." Violent spectacles like Colfax were powerful demonstrations of white superiority to be applauded and glorified. As the *Shreveport Times* proudly concluded, "whenever the Anglo-Saxon and African have met in arms, the result has not been a battle but a butchery." Albert Morgan read the repeated calls to kill freedpeople and their white allies in Mississippi as evidence of a belief in "force as the true race solvent."[44]

Violent demonstrations such as these were not only lessons for unruly blacks. They also spoke to white men who hesitated to fully endorse the white leagues. From the beginning, there had been men opposed to the formation of a White Man's Party in Louisiana, pushing instead for a "People's Party" that welcomed black support. Those who supported "Fusion" tickets, however, became the enemies of the white leagues, who viewed them as far more dangerous than "deluded negroes" whose ignorance could be understood. Even a man who wanted to avoid politics altogether was "a traitor to his race and to his country, and false to his wife and children, and deserves to be ruled forever by negroes." According to the white leagues, white men must actively support their cause or risk the

Leagues' wrath. "Words of sympathy will not do," warned the *People's Vindicator*. "When a war of the races is imminent . . . [whites] should be found but on one side with the Caucasian race." Predicting a racial apocalypse, the *Vindicator* informed skeptical whites, "they have yet time to redeem themselves." The white leagues declared war on whites as well as blacks, encouraging members to ostracize those who refused to join the movement. The Franklin *Enterprise* advocated keeping a "book of remembrance" of those who refused to join the Leagues so that their progeny would be "forever cast out from all association with the Caucasian race." The white leagues in northwest Louisiana purported to keep a hit list of targets of white men who had hesitated to join their movement. John R. Lynch, a black congressman from Natchez, Mississippi, recalled how local blacks tried in vain to keep their white allies from deserting them. They were informed that "no white man can live in the South in the future and act with any other than the Democratic Party unless he is willing and prepared to live a life of social isolation and political oblivion." Unwilling to become a "martyr," one prominent white planter who had been a staunch Republican put it coldly to his black friends: "I am compelled to choose between you, on one side, and my family and my personal interests, on the other."[45]

Threats of ostracization, however vitriolic they were, paled in comparison to the threat of physical harm or death that hung over whites who failed to hoist the banner of white supremacy high enough. "The white men who ally themselves with negroes in this conflict need not expect any better fate than they—fact is, they will be the first to suffer," warned the Forest (Mississippi) *Register*. Similarly, the Yazoo *Democrat* called for a "stout rope and a short shrift," for any white who opposed the "Mississippi Plan" of violent redemption. When a Northern observer traveling through Mississippi in 1875 asked a white-liner he met how he expected to steer all the white people "with all their diverging views" into the movement, the white-liner simply replied, "We'll make it too damn hot for them to stay out." In the aftermath of the Colfax massacre, one witness from northwest Louisiana surmised that "one half of the white population took to the woods" in fear of their lives. "The effect of the Colfax murder and the murders near Coushatta," he explained, "with the use made of them by keeping them constantly before the minds of the people" was not only a landslide Democratic victory that fall (in some parishes not a single Republican vote was cast) but also the coalescence of white supremacy. Although it had to be forced into existence with excessive brutality, white unity nonetheless emerged from those violent assaults on freedpeople and their white allies.[46]

White supremacy did not precede these violent expressions of racial superiority. The Colfax massacre inaugurated the white league movement in Louisiana, which then spread to Mississippi and South Carolina. Colfax mobilized white Southerners by giving tangibility to their cause—not a "lost cause" but a very present and winnable one. When the Colfax defendants were released after their first trial in 1874, whites in Grant and neighboring parishes hailed the men heroes and gave them a fitting welcome home. "Their cause was our cause," declared the Shreveport *Times*, "their release was our release." The trial, which initiated the telling and retelling of the events and memories of Colfax, remade a very localized occurrence into a communal experience that encompassed people who were not directly involved. In effect, the entire state, and eventually whites in other parts of the South, became witnesses to the chilling display of unity that the violence purported to show. That this unity was to a certain extent compelled instead of spontaneous or organic, as the white league press insisted it was, highlights the importance violence played in creating a convincing image of white supremacy and black inferiority.[47]

It is difficult to exaggerate the riskiness of displaying open hostility to state and federal officials when only recently the Grant administration had demonstrated its willingness to use military force in support of Republicans. Not only did Grant send troops to reinstall Governor Kellogg in the fall of 1874, public outcries in the North after Colfax, Coushatta, and Hamburg signaled to the white leagues that they walked on shaky ground. Such bald demonstrations of violence risked alienating them from perhaps their most important audience: the Northern public. With that in mind, some mainstream Democrats publicly disavowed attempts to form a White Man's Party in both Louisiana and Mississippi, calling it a "suicidal policy" that invited federal intervention. The state Democratic committee attempted to change the name to the People's Party in Louisiana, a move replicated with success later in Mississippi. Lucius Q. C. Lamar, the Democratic leader in Mississippi, worried that vitriolic denunciations of Republicans and an attempt to exclude blacks would alienate Southern Democrats from their Northern counterparts and make them targets of unwelcome scrutiny. At the state's Democratic convention in the summer of 1875, Lamar succeeded in getting a statement affirming "the civil and political equality of all men" and inviting blacks to join the Democratic Party added to the party platform, much to the chagrin of white liners. When one wrote to chastise him for being "inclined to temporize too much," Lamar responded that being too extreme would play into Radicals' hands and invite federal intervention in the upcoming election. "A few inflammatory speeches from our side would do their work for them," Lamar informed the disgruntled constituent. Lamar, like his counterparts in Louisiana, believed the party needed the help of "any voter who may wish to act with us," including blacks. This belief led Wade Hampton, South Carolina's Democratic gubernatorial candidate, to actively court the black vote despite the opposition of elements within his own party who viewed black enfranchisement as the root of all evil. Hampton even welcomed black Democrats into his Red Shirt brigades. In order to deflect criticism from Republicans both north and south that they incited violence and ran roughshod over the constitutional rights of blacks, Democratic figureheads had to maintain some semblance of ideological distance from those who advocated racist violence. Despite their reliance on the extremist tactics of paramilitary units like the rifle clubs, the need to appear respectable forced men like Lamar and Hampton to walk a very fine line.[48]

Although their motto became "peaceably if we can, forcibly if we must," hard-liners in the Deep South understood violence as the key to political and social change. They presented the impending political contests in the mid-1870s as well as the very nature of their society using the language and imagery of war. War served to justify their violent redemption of the South and the reestablishment of "home rule," but it also situated white paramilitaries squarely within an American revolutionary tradition. As effective as the spectacle of violence had been within the South for uniting white people politically, it remained to be seen if their movement could translate to non-Southerners. "Is there no language strong enough to awake the people of the North to a sense of the danger which threatens to forever bury their liberties?" wondered a white man from Taugipahoa Parish when Grant reinstalled Governor Kellogg after the 1874 coup in New Orleans. That man recognized how white Southerners were acting not just on a regional stage but a national one. In order for the Democratic Party to succeed, a majority of white Northern voters would have to come to feel, as white Louisianans had about the Colfax murderers, "their cause was our cause . . . their release was our release."[49]

The Spirit of '76

1876 marked a pivotal year in the history of the United States. Not only did the nation celebrate its centennial, it was also a presidential election year, and although few, if any, realized it at the time, it would become the final act of the South's Redemption. Those three events—the centennial, the presidential election, and Redemption—became intertwined that summer and fall; in fact, one might argue that they became concurrent scenes in a great pageant of American nationalism produced by the spirit of martial manhood that percolated wildly throughout the country that year.

Despite the uncertainty of the nation's financial and political future in the mid-1870s, Americans found many reasons to celebrate their country's birthday. Among the more notable celebrations, which included a grandiose centennial exhibition in Philadelphia, was the participation of Charleston's Washington Light Infantry in Boston's Bunker Hill memorial extravaganza in 1875. Organized in 1807, the unit had seen action in most of the major military involvements of the nineteenth century. During the Civil War, its primary function was the defense of Charleston, but some regiments saw action in Virginia, most notably at the Battle of Petersburg. Reorganized as part of the South Carolina rifle club movement, the Washington Light Infantry helped pave the way for white paramilitarism in the state.[50]

Not knowing the role they would play the next year in his administration's unraveling, Governor Daniel Chamberlain, a Massachusetts native, heartily endorsed the unit and its mission of brotherly goodwill as they departed for Boston on June 12, 1875. As they left Charleston Harbor, the US troops stationed there bid them farewell with the thirty-seven-gun salute. Newspapers charted their northward journey and the warm reception the ex-Confederates received from Northern audiences. In New York City, dignitaries feted them at the famed Delmonico's restaurant after a parade with the city's Civil War regiments. Upon their arrival in Boston, which the *Post* claimed was "the first appearance on Northern streets of a military unit which had fought for the Confederacy," crowds infused with both curiosity and patriotism turned out to welcome the unit. Local leaders made speeches at various rally points praising the renewal of bonds based in the two states' shared military history. "We are strangers and aliens no longer," declared one member of the Charleston unit in a speech at Harvard University, "but brothers and fellow-citizens of one common country." Boston's mayor echoed these sentiments, calling on "good men" to recognize that America's revolutionary heritage remained strong despite more recent hostilities. As if part of a family who had endured a short but painful falling-out, he urged Americans to rejoice in the common goal of opposing despotism and tyranny. General Fitzhugh Lee, nephew of the great Robert E., attended the celebration with the other invited Southern regiment—the Norfolk Light Artillery Blues—and summed up the feelings of all involved: "When I reflect that

CHAPTER SIX

I am an American citizen, and that I too am a descendant of those men who fought at Bunker Hill, and that I too have a right to be here and celebrate their splendid victory, I take courage."[51]

Lee was right to be encouraged by the warm reception the Norfolk and Charleston units received in Boston. Not only were they greeted as brothers in arms instead of enemies, Northern speakers at the celebration decried the "mire of corruption and degradation" that had beset South Carolina in the wake of emancipation and black enfranchisement. General Charles Devens, Jr., the former national leader of the Grand Army of the Republic, declared, "All true men are with the South in demanding for her peace, order, honest and good government, and encouraging her the work of rebuilding all that has been made desolate." In a particularly symbolic gesture, the commander of the Washington Light Infantry presented the Massachusetts governor with a palmetto cane engraved with the coats of arms of both states. Did anyone attending the event see the irony in such a presentation? One chronicler of the event noted, "If the presentation recalled the treatment of Charles Sumner by Preston Brooks, no mention was made of the early use of a South Carolina cane." There were other omissions as well. Nowhere in the accounts of the celebration appear the famed Massachusetts 54th, whose gallantry in South Carolina had so recently been the pride of the Bay State. One wonders how those veterans along with the rest of Boston's black community marked the nation's centennial.[52]

The gift of the palmetto cane symbolized more than the growing amnesia surrounding slavery and the Civil War. It also represented the shared history of revolutionary violence that united white Americans. Instead of dividing them, this history brought white men together as soldiers in the common cause of "good government," which by 1875 had become the code word for white supremacy. The memory of the American Revolution paved the way for sectional reunification after the Civil War by allowing former enemies to see themselves as the torchbearers of revolutionary violence against corrupting elements that sought to destroy the nation's exceptional mission. White paramilitaries in Louisiana invoked the memory of 1776 numerous times in their violent struggles against Republicans. "We complain of grievances a thousand times more monstrous than Boston port bills or paltry taxes upon tea and stamped paper," proclaimed the *People's Vindicator*. Invoking Patrick Henry's ultimatum to his fellow colonists, the paper declared, "If we wish to be free . . . we must fight!" During and after the Battle of Liberty Place in September 1874, members of the CCWL referred to themselves as new "minutemen" charged with protecting the rights of white Americans, namely the right to bear arms. By appropriating the legacy of the American Revolution, white paramilitaries legitimized their armed assaults on democratically elected state governments in the Deep South.[53]

The military displays that marked the centennial demonstrated the cultural power of martial manhood as well as its instability. For black veterans, the world in 1875 was very different from the one in 1865, when their service inspired the nation's lawmakers to begin to formally recognize black citizenship. At the centennial fair in Philadelphia, representations of African Americans were limited to "a band of old-time plantation 'darkies'" who sang "quaint melodies" for white patrons at a Southern-themed concession stand and a single bronze statue of a freed slave stretching for his broken manacles, which inspired something less than admiration. One visitor described it as "a most offensively Frenchy negro, who has broken his chain, and spreading both his arms and legs abroad is rioting in a declamation of something (I should say) from Victor Hugo; one longs to clap him back into hopeless bondage." Like the Philadelphia fair, the Bunker Hill celebration excluded black men from the band of brothers who had secured and maintained American independence. These stylized performances of race and nation signaled the reunification of the country around a concept of aggressive masculinity that Northern audiences could identify with and applaud in their white Southern counterparts but disdained in black men.[54]

Although one correspondent wondered if "Bunker Hill brain fever" might be a fleeting and empty display of mass delirium, evidence of "a renewal of that fraternal love that shone so brightly one hundred years ago" abounded. Boston and New York regiments traveled to Charleston to march alongside the South Carolina units to celebrate Washington's birthday in February 1876, as well as to participate in the Fort Moultrie celebration later that summer. The Fort Moultrie celebration came in June just as the election season kicked off. That year, Confederate war hero Wade Hampton III challenged Republican incumbent Daniel Chamberlain, and with the help of his Red Shirts, which included those same Charleston militia units gathered at Fort Moultrie to commemorate the battle to save the city in 1776, Hampton terrorized and defrauded his way into office. So it was with great irony once again that Chamberlain praised the "citizen soldiery" that would drive him out of office within a few weeks.[55]

Not coincidentally, the beginning of the end of Reconstruction in South Carolina came on the Fourth of July. In celebration of that day in the little town of Hamburg near the Georgia border, the local black militia unit drilled and paraded their usual route up and down Market

Street. Led by a man named Doc Adams, the militia drilled weekly, to the chagrin of local whites, who found their martial activities a sign of "impudence." Adams was careful to avoid a confrontation and required that his men drill with unloaded weapons. He even checked their pockets for hidden ammunition. His conscientiousness, however, did little to allay the concerns of whites in Aiken County who knew that the militia was an obstacle to their political success. Upon taking over the militia a few months earlier, Adams had increased their drilling from once a month to once or twice a week in preparation for the election season. In Aiken County, as in other counties throughout the state, Adams's militia would guard the polls on Election Day and escort black voters to and from the ballot box. Therefore, when Adams's militia marched on Market Street on the anniversary of American independence, they embodied an idealized citizenship that the white men who sat watching them on the other side of the street could not tolerate.[56]

The white men, who just happened to the be the son and son-in-law of one of Aiken County's most prominent men, attorney R. J. Butler, took their wagon down a side a street and turned back up Market Street below where the militia marched. Although the street was wide enough for the men to pass the militia on either side, they headed straight for the middle intent on making the unit disperse to let them through. When Adams asked that they show him and his men some respect, the white men cursed him and demanded that he move his men. Not wanting to start a fight, Adams relented and ordered his unit to let the men pass. Some members of the militia grumbled, perhaps even cursing the white men as they passed through. According to the white men, one of the militiamen made a gesture as if he was loading or cocking his weapon. Whatever unpleasant words may have been exchanged, the white men carried on home and Adams thought the matter was over.[57]

The chain of events that unfolded over the next four days repeated similar patterns leading up to previous instances of large-scale white violence, most notably the Colfax Massacre. The Butler men filed a complaint with the town justice claiming that Adams and his men had threatened them. There was a hearing, but when the black justice did not order the unit disbanded, the white men proceeded to implement their own plans for disarming Hamburg's black militia. Along with Martin Gary, who was at the time emerging as the spokesmen for the "straight-out" contingent of the Democratic Party, the Butlers organized white men from the surrounding area, including neighboring Georgia. Some witnesses later testified that men bragged about coming from as far away as Texas. By July 8, several hundred well-armed white men surrounded the tiny village and closed in on Adams and his militia, who had holed up in Adams's home. The group's leader, General M. C. Butler, who had lost an arm in the Civil War and eventually would become South Carolina's US senator after Redemption was complete, informed Adams that if he did not surrender the militia's weapons to him, the militia would be fired upon. Adams refused, stating that he had no authority to hand over state arms to a private citizen. After Adams's refusal to surrender, firing commenced, and in the end, seven black men were dead along with one white agitator. Compared to the many hundreds who attacked them, there were only thirty-eight men with Adams, not all of whom were armed. In all, Adams estimated that his men fired only about six rounds.[58] The black men had been shot, one by one, after having surrendered to their captors in a field outside of town. The rest of the militia, including Adams, fled the area. The Hamburg militia was no more.[59]

Like the Colfax Massacre, Hamburg galvanized the white supremacist movement in its efforts to control the Democratic Party. "By God! We will carry South Carolina now!" "This is the beginning of the redemption of South Carolina." Doc Adams heard these declarations as whites rampaged through Hamburg. The leaders of the white paramilitaries, who would soon become known as the Red Shirts, understood the power of collective violence to not only terrorize their opponents but also demonstrate their determination to reluctant whites. Up until then, it appeared that the Democratic Party would not run a candidate to oppose Governor Chamberlain, so certain they were of defeat. The "cooperationists" found no worthwhile reason not to throw their support to the Republican. Their "watch and wait" policy infuriated Gary and Butler. In the aftermath of the massacre, Francis Warrington Dawson, a leading cooperationists and editor of the *Charleston News and Courier*, saw the writing on the wall. "I think the unhappy affair at Hamburg will be made such use of in the canvas that no alternative would probably have been left us than to 'take it straight,'" he wrote, acknowledging the persuasiveness of the straight-outs' violent logic. At the state Democratic Convention in August, the "coldly furious men from Edgefield," Gary and Butler, won a small majority, putting Hampton on the ticket and inaugurating a campaign of terror and intimidation.[60]

Although some feared federal retaliation for the killings and sought to distance themselves from Gary and the Butlers, Northern reaction to the Hamburg Massacre was predictably shrill but essentially toothless. The Republican press used Hamburg to impugn the candidacy of Samuel Tilden and the Democratic Party in general (fig. 6.1), but no federal action backed up the outrage. Thomas Nast recognized the irony of these

CHAPTER SIX

FIGURE 6.1 "The 'Bloody Shirt' Reformed." Nast used the Hamburg Massacre as an object lesson in the dangers of Democratic victory in the 1876 presidential election. *Harper's Weekly*, August 12, 1876.

murders occurring in the midst of the country's centennial celebrations when he created "Is This a Republican Form of Government?" (fig. 6.2), which showed a devastated black man amid the ruin of a desolated town surrounded by the bodies of dead African Americans, including women and babies. No women or children were killed at Hamburg, but Nast's depiction of black suffering once again replicated sentimental conventions meant to pull at the heartstrings of Northern whites who would not be moved by the killing of black men alone, much less militiamen. A few weeks later, Nast did depict black armed resistance in an image entitled "He Wants a Change Too" (fig. 6.3), a play on the Democratic promise of "reform." In this cartoon, a shirtless black man clutching a rifle stares angrily at the reader. With his teeth bared in defiance and desperation, the black man represents a kind of bloody atonement that Nast feared white America would one day be forced to pay. Although Nast intended to indict white Southerners for their violence against this man and their justifications of it based upon "American" principles, the image recalls the perpetual fear of "race war" that haunted Reconstruction from its inception. This image might well have inspired support for the white paramilitaries instead of condemnation.

Despite Nash's pointed critiques of white paramilitaries' patriotic posturing, these activities nonetheless lent them an air of respectability they needed. During the campaign, the Red Shirts hoisted banners that read "1776–1876" and "What we did in 1776 we will do in 1876." Inspired by the colonialists' boycotts, South Carolina ladies patronized only Democratic-owned businesses. Wade Hampton entered Charleston

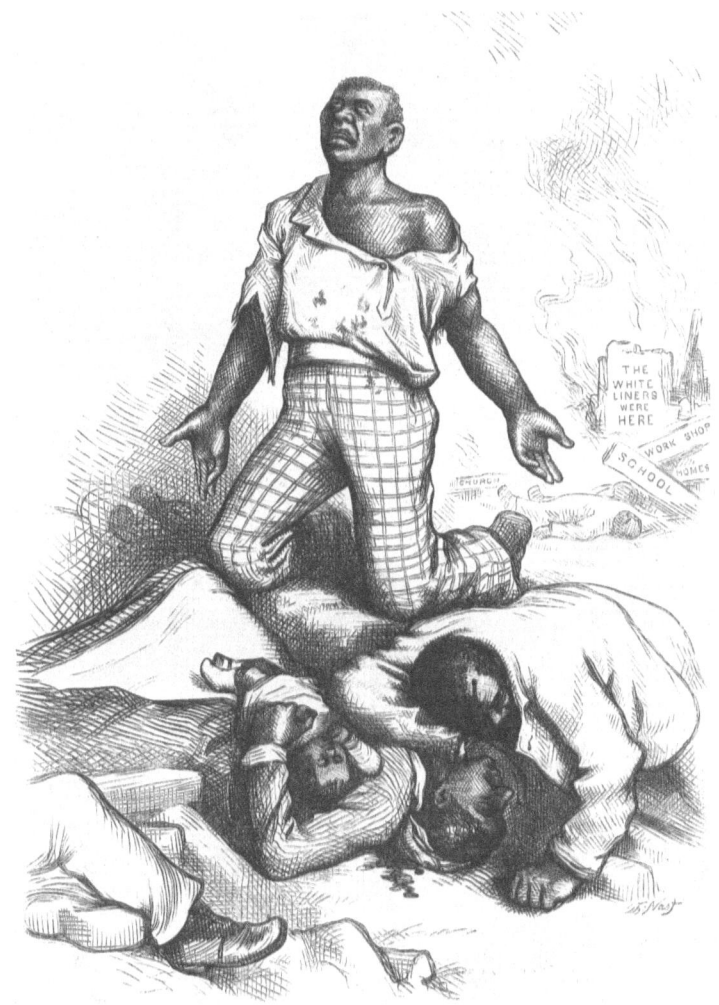

FIGURE 6.2 "Is *This* a Republican Form of Government? Is *This* protecting Life, Liberty, or Property? Is *This* the equal protection of the law?" The freedman pleads for protection. *Harper's Weekly*, September 2, 1876.

FIGURE 6.3 "He Wants *Change* Too." Nast invokes the specter of black violence as the atonement for Northern inaction against white violence in the South. *Harper's Weekly*, Oct. 28, 1876.

flanked by thirteen little girls dressed in white, representing the original thirteen colonies. A few people even objected to the Red Shirts' uniforms because red was the "Tory color." That fall, South Carolinians succeeded in remaking the Southern cause into a national one. Through their use of patriotic rhetoric and imagery, the straight-outs performed political alchemy, creating a precious and potent ideology that linked Southern violence to both the past and future of the nation. America's second revolution was complete.[61]

Violent spectacles like the ones at Colfax, Liberty Place, Vicksburg, and Hamburg rallied Southern whites to the cause of white supremacy. Whether or not the unbreakable unity such events purported to represent was illusory or not is beside the point. At a critical moment in their history, these martial performances of Southern manhood and the brutalization of black bodies enabled whites to envision their supremacy on a grand scale. Although risky, such spectacles demonstrated the inferiority of blacks, the impotency of Republican government, and the insecurity of anyone who got in the way. Surely not everyone agreed with the violent course of action Deep South Redeemers chose, but in the face of such impressive if imperfect displays, who could say so publicly?

And at the same time, white paramilitaries cloaked their unrivaled brutality in the shroud of American nationalism. This, perhaps, marks the most underappreciated aspect of Redemption. White paramilitaries went to great lengths to portray themselves not as the brigands and ruffians Republicans claimed but as progenitors of America's revolutionary heritage, the new minutemen. Their unabashed embrace of armed resistance lent their movement a kind of romantic gravitas that, by 1876, spoke to the nation's nostalgia for its revolutionary past. While crowds gathered to welcome the Washington Light Infantry to Boston and New York in celebration of the nation's centennial, paramilitary units ran roughshod over elected officials in New Orleans and Vicksburg. This convergence begs an important question: did the Northern public simply grow tired of these by now routine "autumnal outbreaks," or did they realize a deeper investment in Southern deliverance?

The outcry against General Philip Sheridan's attempt to delegitimize the Louisiana White League suggests a growing sympathy among Northerners for white Southerners' struggle against "tyranny." Despite federal intervention that effectively circumvented their "September rebellion," by January 1875 white leaguers had once again taken over the state legislature, only this time without force. After Grant sent his dependable right-hand to New Orleans to deal with the second crisis in five months, Fighting Phil, as he was known among his men during the war, sent a telegram to the secretary of war asking that he be allowed to treat the white leagues as "banditti."[62] The term stripped the white leagues of their presumed legitimacy, casting them not as patriotic revolutionaries but as common criminals. The reaction in Louisiana was predictable. Crowds hissed and booed Sheridan when he ventured outside his hotel room. His windows were shot out, and he was burned in effigy. A meeting of the city's clergymen, including the archbishop, a rabbi, and a passel of Protestant church leaders, passed a resolution appealing to the whole American people to see "that these charges are unmerited, unfounded, and erroneous, and can have no other effect than of serving the interests of corrupt politicians."[63] Their appeal seemed to have the intended effect. The fair-mindedness Sheridan had hoped for when he issued his report outlining the sufferings of "bleeding negroes" did not pour forth from the Northern press.[64] The banditti telegram took the North by surprise, which is itself surprising given the state of affairs in Louisiana in the fall of 1874. "We have never published such a document before," wrote a shocked *New York Times*, "and we must say that nothing like it has ever been seen in a country under a constitutional government." Taking a cue from the New Orleans press, the *Times* compared Sheridan to a notorious historical figure—Oliver Cromwell. "It almost induces one to believe that the world has gone back, two or three hundred years in the theory and practice of government," the paper declared, reminding readers that "Cromwell did, indeed, serve Ireland pretty much as Gen. Sheridan proposes to treat Louisiana."[65]

The Northern press, like their Southern counterparts, contested the "facts" Sheridan presented in his reports. Joseph Hawley's *Hartford Daily Courant*, which had suffered the backlash of earlier controversy over exaggerated claims of Southern violence, now called Sheridan's telegram an "egregious blunder" because "not all the facts in the case are known."[66] Hesitant to risk supporting the "outrage mill" again, Hawley, who also had served the Republican Party in Congress, retreated from his earlier support of Southern intervention. He reasoned that "it is of course among the possibilities that the charges made by the democratic press are true, that a deliberate design existed to use the United States troops to perpetrate a gross fraud upon the people of the state of Louisiana." Sheridan's estimate that more than 1,200 people had been killed or wounded since 1868 and the testimony he presented of terrified local officials made little or no impact on the press. "Such dispatches as that which Gen. Sheridan sent to the Secretary of War . . . is not warranted by any facts known to the public," and furthermore, according to the *Times*, "could scarcely be warranted under any conceivable circumstances. The "indignation meetings" convened in Northern cities including Springfield, Boston, Indianapolis, and Columbus echoed these sentiments.[67]

The nationwide reaction to Sheridan's telegram and Grant's general acceptance of it was so hostile that several of the president's supporters began to fear for his life. Rufus Bullock, the former Republican governor of Georgia, wrote to Grant's close friend and advisor Orville Babcock, "I am not an alarmist, but the time has arrived when the President is in danger of assassination, and extraordinary caution should be exercised." Bullock noted that a "dangerous hot headed zealot" from Atlanta who had named his son in honor of John Wilkes Booth and had been seen "loafing around Washington" was "just the character who would seize an opportunity to win the applause of the 'Banditti' in that same infamous role." Hot-headed zealots abounded, and they notified the president of their existence. A man who signed his letter "Conservative" from Norfolk cautioned Grant, "You had better mend your course towards the Sothern States [sic] . . . if you do not you will not be a living man Two months from to day." "Deadshot" from New Orleans warned Grant "PREPARE FOR, THE NEXT, WORLD!!!" More historically minded, "A Texan" informed the president, "Ceaser [sic] had his 'Brutus' Charles the 1st his 'Cromwell' & Abe Lincoln his 'Booth!' You will have your name attached to History With them as Sure as God Made Moses." The threats came from the Northern section as well. "An American Citizen" from Philadelphia who claimed to be a member of the "Ku Klux, of the North" predicted that "the *'Booth'* who will give the *'Drunken' 'Blackguard,' 'Ignorant' 'Imbecile' 'Dirty,' 'contempible,' Smoking 'son of a bitch,'* who now is Executive officer of this once great nation his quietus, does not reside more than a thousand miles from here, and a greatful people will revere his memory by raising a monument to his patriotism [sic]." These threats reveal the extent to which the banditti controversy signaled a near breaking point in American democratic culture.[68]

Many Northern Republicans publicly disavowed Sheridan's statements in an attempt to distance themselves from the brouhaha and its worsening political implications. Both the Pennsylvania and Ohio legislatures denounced both the telegram and Grant's refusal to condemn it and immediately withdraw Sheridan from Louisiana.[69] Carl Schurz, who in 1865 had urged President Johnson to pursue a tough course of action against Southern rebels, now found Sheridan's proposition "so appalling that every American citizen who loves his liberty stands aghast." He had introduced Abraham Lincoln at the same venue in 1860, but in 1875 William Cullen Bryant denounced Sheridan at Cooper Union, saying the general should "tear off his epaulets and break his sword and fling the fragments into the Potomac rather than go upon so imperious an errand." Quick to disassociate the party with Sheridan, the *New York Times* declared, "We are sorry to find the *Evening Post* identifying the Republican Party with this reckless dispatch." Even while they acknowledged the "rascality" of Louisiana Democrats, the editors of the *Chicago Tribune* admitted that their rhetorical ingenuity "very seriously complicated the Louisiana question." As a result there emerged a "dissatisfied and uneasy feeling among their constituents" that made it difficult for Republicans in Congress to "look with any gratification upon the spectacle of a State Legislature organized under the protection of Federal bayonets." The "broader view of Southern matters" that the *Tribune* encouraged Republican leaders to take reflected a growing consensus in the North that the federal government was no longer the protector of its citizens, as Republicans had claimed in 1865. Now it was what citizens—white citizens, that is—needed protection from. Sheridan himself sensed the political tide was changing. Writing in early 1875 at the height of the Louisiana fiasco, he predicted, "the next rebellion was to be fought under the stars and stripes and in the North as well as the South." Sheridan believed Southerners had learned an important lesson from the war. "The mistake [Confederates made] in 1861," he wrote, "was to have had their own flag."[70]

In 1876, as Americans celebrated a century of independence, the country seemed to teeter on the precipice of another revolution. South Carolina's warlike Redemption inspired Democrats nationwide to make preparations for the fall's presidential contest. Reports of rifle clubs being organized across the North worried Republican officials to the extent that Grant issued a stern warning to anyone who planned to disrupt Rutherford B. Hayes's upcoming inauguration. That contested election spurred "indignation" conventions across the North where Democrats called for armed resistance to Hayes. The sergeant-at-arms of the House proposed to "deputize" 100,000 men to enforce Tilden's election. Drunk with revolutionary imagery, Joseph Pulitzer, editor of the *New York World*, declared his readiness to "bare his breast to the bullet of the tyrant and rush headlong upon his glittering steel." In a staggering political conversion, former abolitionist George Julian, the congressman from Indiana who had supported Radical Reconstruction, the Civil Rights Act, as well as suffrage for African Americans *and* women, had become a Tildenite. At a Democratic rally in Indianapolis, Julian fired up his audience with invocations of both 1776 and 1861, reminding the crowd that "[a] century ago, our fathers took up arms in defense of their right to a voice in the Government . . . We assert that right now," he proclaimed, "when we ask that the will of the people be registered as the supreme law, and that whoever may defy it by overt acts shall receive the same treatment which the nation awarded to the men who appealed from the ballot to the bayonet in 1861." Furthermore, Julian promised that "millions of men would be found ready to offer their lives as hostages to the sacredness of the ballot as the palladiums of our liberty." To a modern reader, these statements may read like hyperbole of the worst sort, but the crowds in Indianapolis, Columbus, and elsewhere, by all reports, lapped it up. Grant and Hayes prepared for an onslaught that never came but the threat of which remained real nonetheless. The South's Redemption had tapped into strains of revolutionary romanticism and disillusionment with the federal government that coalesced in the centennial year to highlight the centrality of violence to American national identity. Americans were a people at war—with Indians, with the labor movement, with immigrants and racial "others," and with a growing host of enemies within, but Southerners were no longer among them. Ironically, as George Julian pointed out, war had reconciled the nation at last.[71]

Epilogue

"Jesus, the South is fine, isn't it. It's better than the theater, isn't it. It's better than Ben Hur, isn't it." SHREVE MCCANNON TO QUENTIN COMPSON IN WILLIAM FAULKNER'S *ABSALOM, ABSALOM!*

"Alabama's got me so upset, Tennessee made me lose my rest, and everybody knows about Mississippi Goddam." NINA SIMONE, "MISSISSIPPI GODDAM"

After President Rutherford B. Hayes recognized Democrat William McEnery as Louisiana's governor in exchange for the party's support of his own contested election, a lone black man "carrying a large placard elevated on a long pole" positioned himself on the corner of St. Louis and Royal Streets in front of the Louisiana State House in New Orleans. His placard bore the inscription REMEMBER SEPTEMBER 14TH, 1874. White leaguers soon surrounded the man and destroyed his sign. The white press denounced this "pre-concerted attempt to create a riot," and Democratic governor William McEnery quickly prohibited any assemblies near the state house. The man's silent protest echoed in the emptiness left by the federal government's abandonment of Southern Republicans. The protester reminded New Orleans's blacks that their political defeat had been assured three years earlier when the Crescent City White League mounted their armed attack on the city's integrated police force; Hayes's deliverance of the governor's seat to McEnery was but the final acknowledgement of that fact. In his invocation of the memory of armed conflict, it is also possible that the man hoped to inspire black New Orleanians to respond to

Hayes's betrayal in the same revolutionary manner that white leaguers had to Kellogg's "misrule" in 1874. Whatever his intentions, this solitary protester armed only with his placard revealed both the defiance and the disillusionment of a community disarmed and without recourse to call on the state for protection in the nineteenth-century South.[1]

However, the story does not end there even if this book must. It would be a tremendous disservice to the vibrant historiography of African American life in the late nineteenth and early twentieth centuries not to point out some ways that Southern blacks continued their struggles against white violence. New work on black grassroots politics in places like Natchez, Mississippi, stresses the resiliency of black political networks, which continued well into the 1880s despite the intense white backlash in surrounding areas. This new scholarship suggests that black resistance to white violence was both much more prevalent and more successful than historians have assumed. Such persistence signals some of the limits of the "Mississippi Plan" and of whites' ultimate commitment to violence. While white paramilitary forces managed to gain momentum in the mid-1870s when their movement coalesced around a particular set of ideological principles that placed them conveniently within the bounds of legitimate action, what the white unity Redeemers claimed to represent was hardly solidified after 1876. Although the pageantry of white league and Red Shirt performances of white martial masculinity might have appeared irrefutable, Democratic victories in 1876 still relied on stuffed ballot boxes and protracted negotiations in Washington to secure the South's political redemption. On the local level, those political struggles continued well into the 1880s.[2]

The redemption of white manhood, too, seemed to still need work. Even as Southern legislatures began enacting disenfranchisement laws and segregating public spaces in the 1880s and 1890s, white violence did not subside. Instead, it metastasized into a brutality of shocking proportions. The excessive, ritualized performances of white dominance and black degradation that characterized lynching had their roots in Reconstruction, in places like Camilla and Colfax, as well as the countless public whippings, shootings, and rapes that entailed a complex internal logic of their own. The utility of such violence often transcended the outcomes of elections, the control of labor, and decisions made in courts of law. There existed a collective ethos that linked the Regulators, Klan, white leagues, and Red Shirts with the Jim Crow lynch mobs who deployed terror both as an instrument of political power and as a meditation on the rights (and rites) of whiteness, manhood, and citizenship.[3]

EPILOGUE

Such spectacles of racial violence should be read as evidence of the tenuousness of white racial identity rather than its cohesiveness. Although the narrative of Redemption that emerged during and after 1876 was powerful, it required repeated affirmation. Efforts to memorialize the violent actions of white Southern men during Reconstruction hint at the continuing need to justify their Pyrrhic victory. At a Red Shirt reunion in 1909, Ben "Pitchfork" Tillman, by then South Carolina's representative in the US Senate, labored against the efforts of his political rivals to make his role in the Hamburg massacre a political liability. "My old enemies have been 'raising Cain,'" he told the crowd gathered at Anderson on a hot August afternoon. "Certain editors resent these invitations [to speak at Red Shirt memorials] being sent and are also disgruntled because I have accepted them," he explained. Tillman then proceeded with a long diatribe into the necessity of violence in 1876, the villainy of local blacks, and the manly sacrifice of himself and other white men. Put on the defensive by his opponents, who portrayed him as a vestige of a violent and disorderly past, Tillman insisted that his role in Redemption represented the most essential characteristics of American patriotism. "The spirit of 1776 which made Moultrie," he declared, "pulsated in the bosom of every brave Carolinian, when they learned that a body of seventy-five poorly armed whites had dared to attack a legally organized militia company, capture its armory, and then put to death some of it members." Irked by the memorials to Wade Hampton, who had strategically disassociated himself from the violence perpetrated by Tillman and the others, Tillman insisted that "Butler and Gary [the architects of the "straight-out" plan] are entitled to equal, if not more credit for the victory in 1876." Tillman's effort to remind the crowd of the crucial role violence played in the state's Redemption revealed his worry that white South Carolinians had forgotten the sacrifices he and his compatriots had made for them.[4]

Tillman was not alone in his efforts to redeem Redemption. In New Orleans, veterans of Liberty Place staged reunions, and in 1891 erected a monument on Canal Street in honor of the white men who died in the struggle against the Metropolitan Police. The monument came at a crucial moment for elite whites in the Crescent City, who were "self-conscious about their baptism by fire" and invoked the memory of September 14 to create a "civic ritual that extolled racial solidarity and upper-class civic reform" in an era when those prerogatives were increasingly under attack. Tangible monuments like the Liberty Place obelisk as well as reenactments of the event helped realign the city's serious class and political divisions in favor of future generations of elite white men.[5]

EPILOGUE

Perhaps the biggest monument to the violence of Redemption came in an altogether new form. D. W. Griffith's 1915 film *Birth of a Nation* demonstrates that the work of memorialization was not a strictly regional phenomenon. The outcry over the film from the NAACP and other African American organizations also points to the contestation over Reconstruction's memory in the United States in the early twentieth century. Furthermore, not all whites applauded Griffith's cinematic portrayal of Klan heroism. In a curious response to the film, a white moviegoer from Tennessee living in Canada called the idea that white men sought protection in disguises and darkness "absurd and idiotic." Accusing Griffith of suffering from "negrophobia," the Tennessean called the premise of the film and its literary inspiration, Thomas Dixon's novel *The Clansman*, a "falsehood" that was designed to incite "pernicious" race hatred and ought not to be shown publicly. "We have censored the exhibition of prize fights," he argued, "which are not half so immoral and brutal as the exhibition of which I am speaking." However, the basis of the viewer's dismissal of film as "disgusting" was really that white men would wear hoods and sneak around at night in order to protect their women, not that they would turn to violence. In fact, the viewer claimed there was "not a neighborhood in the South, and never has been, where Lynch would not have been shot down like a dog, as he ought to have been, if he had made an attempt as reported in the picture, to force a white girl to marry him." To him, the Klan was a ridiculous farce that symbolized white fear and self-loathing instead of the high-minded manliness he believed Southern white men to possess. Presumably, this viewer would have found little to contest in the Red Shirts' "straight-out" campaign.[6]

As the contested popularity of novels like *The Clansman* and films like *Birth of a Nation* show, Reconstruction violence became a hallmark of American culture by the twentieth century. This study's attention to the ways that violence created meaning within the nation's broader political culture reexamines the legacy of Reconstruction. Efforts to democratize the former Confederacy, to bring wage labor to the slave South, and to replace the lash with the law, were stymied by recalcitrant whites and their relentless attacks against freedpeople and their white Republican allies, but those liberal policies aimed at limiting violence and injustice often relied upon coercion and violence as well. Although it would take nearly a century for Southern blacks to obtain the rights of citizenship promised to them during Reconstruction, they long reaped the bitter fruits of the racialized understandings of violence and suffering that guided the transformation from slavery to freedom and back again. As Leigh

Raiford demonstrates in her recent study of photography in the long civil rights movement, African Americans struggled to control representations of their own suffering and construct a meaningful and politically potent response to it. Raiford and other civil rights scholars underscore the precariousness of white sympathy for black suffering and whites' tendency to narrate the history of violence through a lens of victimization, dependency, and objectification. These ongoing struggles speak to yet another aspect of Reconstruction's "unfinished revolution"—the legacy of violence, both in slavery and beyond, for African Americans as well as for the entire nation.[7]

The most vocal critics of Redemption were African Americans who repeatedly demonstrated that Southern violence was neither natural nor inevitable and was, in some ways, an outgrowth of American nationalism. In the aftermath of the Colfax Massacre, the *Christian Recorder* denounced white Northerners for failing to condemn the perpetrators of Southern violence, explaining that the nation itself was implicated in an ever-expanding system of racial subjugation and violence in the West. Although over one hundred freedmen had been killed and mutilated in northwest Louisiana in the spring of 1873, the paper reasoned, "in the eyes of the nation, this massacre is no more than a ripple in the stream of its life." Citing the wholesale slaughter of Native Americans by white settlers and US troops, the *Recorder* observed that it was not altogether surprising that Colfax did not elicit much outrage among whites. "It is astonishing how placid the national countenance has continued in the very presence of this bloody scene. It has shown neither pity nor wrath toward the slain, wrath toward the slayers. But how to expect it, when it itself is engaged in enacting a scene of blood not altogether unlike the one in Louisiana?" they asked. By implicating all whites in the system of racial oppression that produced both the killing of freedpeople and Native Americans, the paper connected Southern violence to American expansionism, which was fast becoming the country's raison d'etre in the last decades of the nineteenth century.[8]

The relationship between the "national crime" of racial violence and US imperialism troubled black writers and activists who struggled to find an appropriate response to the problem.[9] In Charles Chesnutt's 1901 novel about the Wilmington Race Riot three years earlier, *The Marrow of Tradition*, the character who orchestrates white violence is a mysterious stranger named General Belmont. Bedecked in a Panama hat, "the dapper little gentleman" has spent time in Central America, as his attire suggests. According to the general himself, the lessons he learned "down in the American tropics" were useful for white men in the South looking to redeem their local governments from "inferior races." General Belmont explained,

Down in the American tropics they have a way of doing things. I was in Nicaragua ten years ago, when Paterno's revolution drove out Igorroto's government. It was as easy as falling off a log. Paterno had the arms and the best men. Igorroto was not looking for trouble, and the guns were at his breast before he knew it. We have the guns. The negroes are not expecting trouble, and are easy to manage compared with the fiery mixture that flourishes in the tropics.[10]

Chesnutt uses this fictitious coup d'etat to demonstrate two important aspects of Southern racial violence. First, it reveals how local whites manipulated and planned the event. Like many of the other "riots" that came before it, Wilmington was hardly the spontaneous outburst that whites claimed it to be; nor was it the result of black aggression. Despite the pretense of black crime that propelled Wilmington's white men to lash out in defense of their homes and families, the riot was, in fact, a concerted effort of the city's business and political elite to unseat democratically elected officials and displace middle-class African Americans, such as the novel's protagonist, Dr. William Miller. Second, the character of General Belmont and his involvement in Latin America suggests that the riot was part of a much larger system of global politics and oppression. The general's Nicaraguan revolution had its counterparts throughout Latin American in the 1890s, when the United States intervened in numerous instances to protect American interests in Argentina, Chile, Nicaragua, Panama, Puerto Rico, and most notably, Cuba and the Philippines. Those imperialist endeavors abroad informed how Americans read the political scene at home. Not only did Wilmington whites mimic the kind of violent subterfuge that characterized General Belmont's Latin American coup d'etat, Northern imperialists looked "to Southern racial policy for national guidance in the new problems of imperialism." Lawmakers wondering how to organize and discipline populations of "inferior" peoples found solutions in the Jim Crow South. Soon, according to C. Vann Woodward, "the Mississippi Plan had become the American Way." At the anniversary of the battle of Antietam in 1899, President William McKinley, himself a Union veteran, marveled at the ability of empire to reconcile the once-warring sections and reestablish the brotherhood of white men. "The followers of Confederate generals with followers of the Federal generals fought side by side in Cuba, in Porto Rico [sic], and in the Philippines," he crowed, "and together in those far-off islands are standing together fighting and dying for the flag they love, the flag that represents more than any other banner in the world the best hopes and aspirations of mankind." By expanding the context within which his readers understood Southern violence, Chesnutt implicitly questioned how effectively African Americans could counter it within the context of the rise of global white supremacy.[11]

This question haunted Frederick Douglass, who, in his waning years, struggled to keep his redemptive narrative of emancipation alive. Writing in the *North American Review* in 1884, Douglass pondered the "fate of the negro" and concluded that American blacks must find a way to cement their relationship to the nation. Although Reconstruction had failed to secure the level of political citizenship that Douglass had once envisioned, he implored his audience not to become discouraged. In particular, he argued against the impulse to emigrate, an option that more and more Southern blacks were entertaining in the post-Reconstruction years. However, he used the example of the American Indian to "show what may happen to the Negro" if he did not stand his ground. "The thought of setting apart a State or Territory and confining the Negro within its borders is a delusion," he argued. "If the North and South could not live separately in peace and without bloody and barbarous border wars," he explained, "the white and black cannot. If the Negro could be bottled up, who could or would bottle up the irrepressible white man?" Accepting what to him appeared to be the undeniable logic of imperial conquest, Douglass concluded that the only way to avoid "the fate of the Indian" was to secure a place on the other side of the reservation fence. Douglass ended his essay by striking a familiar chord that again linked white men and black men together in a common destiny. "Manly self-assertion and eternal vigilance are essential to Negro liberty," he wrote, "not less than to that of the white man." Because of the intimate relationship between imperialism and manhood, Douglass and many other middle-class proponents of racial uplift in the coming decades found redemption in the language of conquest and civilization.[12]

Douglass's embrace of the colonizing impulse brings up the question of African Americans' role in the creation of Reconstruction's violent political culture. According to Ida B. Wells, who charted the progression of white violence against Southern blacks from emancipation to the end of the century, Reconstruction represented "a long, gory campaign" with "countless massacres of defenseless Negroes, whose only crime was the attempt to exercise the right to vote." But were they merely victims of white aggression, or did African Americans also help to create a martial culture that linked freedom, independence, and citizenship with fighting and manly self-defense? As the *Colored Tribune* (Savannah) defiantly acknowledged in 1876, as Southern blacks faced abandonment by their national party, violence "is a game both sides can play." And both sides played it well, albeit not to the same degree or the same ends. Black abolitionists and Union veterans articulated the militarized vision of freedom that emerged during the war and exploited it during Reconstruction to reap substantial political rewards, most notably the right to vote. Freedpeople's militancy secured a place for the Republican Party in the South, and as Kidada Williams suggests, the scale of white violence might be read as a testament to black unwillingness to bow and scrape to their former masters in matters of labor, politics, or personal relationships. Yet some also became willing agents in America's colonial projects in the West and elsewhere in the late nineteenth century as a way of claiming their place as citizens within the nation. The quest to redeem black manhood converged with the burgeoning discourse of martial manhood that guided American imperialism at the turn of the century. After Reconstruction, the importance of manhood for black political struggles grew despite the searing rebuke it received at the hands of the Redeemers.[13]

These critiques ask us to reconsider the South's place within the nation and the world. In the past, narratives of Southern violence have enabled the construction of what James Cobb identifies as "the utopianized, liberal idea of America itself." Instances of this dialectic in contemporary America abound. Not only is it visible in the civil rights atonement trials like Edgar Ray Killen's, it appeared in 1986 when Ed Koch, then mayor of New York City, responded to the beating death of a young African American man named Michael Griffith by whites in Queens by saying that one would "expect this kind of thing to happen in the Deep South." The image of the "violent South" was again invoked twelve years later when white police officers in Riverside, California, shot to death an African American woman, Tyisha Miller, as she sat in her disabled car waiting for help to fix a flat tire. A local minister called Miller's death a lynching and concluded, "This might as well be Mississippi." The message was clear: such acts of racist brutality are only supposed to happen in the South, and their occurrence outside of that designated violent space signified the South's corruption of the nation.[14]

The South occupies a special place in America's "moral geography," as sociologist Larry Griffin noted in his analysis of how the idea of the South continues to function as kind of landfill for dumping the nation's sins, especially when it comes to matters of racial violence. The construction of racial violence as a regional problem obscures the institutionalized structure of racism throughout the country and makes it seem that such events are the result of individual pathology, extremists and other such "bad seeds," who do no represent the norm of American society. While the "violent South" holds a special place in this moral geography, it is not the only South that Americans use to mark their paths. There are many Souths, not all of them bad. Yet those more celebrated aspects of the country's "Dixiefication"—barbecue joints, stock car racing, blues, bluegrass, and country music—often sit uncomfortably next to embarrassing anti-American characteristics of extremism, violence, poverty, and all-around backwardness. Despite the popularization of many Southern cultural forms, the "benighted South" remains a touchstone for Americans as they seek to distinguish themselves, their nation, and its history as exceptional.[15]

My position should by no means be read as an apologia for the South and its violent past. I concur with Griffin, who writes, "The white South exhaled such toxicity for so long on the nation, and more particularly on its own people of color, that if the very word 'South'—or Mississippi—has indeed become a metaphor, a symbol for evil, so be it." Yet if there remains any hope of understanding and perhaps changing the South's historical association with violence, especially racial violence, then it behooves scholars to think critically about the ways that violence structures not just Southern culture but American culture.[16]

The roots of Reconstruction violence lay deep within American political culture and history. Elements of that culture, present since the revolutionary era—the ideal of martial manhood and the militarized vision of freedom—became more pronounced during the Civil War. More importantly, their violent implications grew as slavery crumbled and new opportunities for black mobilization opened up. Ironically, these elements justified the struggle for black citizenship as well as the South's white counterrevolution of white supremacy. Although Republicans tended to blame Southern violence on slavery and its corrupting effects on white morality, the fact is, they often used the same ideological playbook as their enemies. In some ways, the narratives of redemption that guided both Radical Reconstruction and Redemption were strikingly similar. Both rested on conceptions of masculinity and martial valor as the keys to collective rejuvenation. A belief in redemptive suffering also linked them together as well as an essential ambivalence regarding violence itself. For much of their history, Americans have embraced revolutionary violence for whites but not for blacks. They have celebrated black martyrdom in the greater cause of Union but not black self defense in the cause of racial justice. Today, we disavow acts of individual violence committed by unrepentant racists like Edgar Ray Killen but find questions of institutional racism and violence harder to address, much less resolve.[17]

The alluring trope of redemptive suffering continues to shape our understanding of race in American society. On August 22, 2011, in Washington, DC, the memorial to Martin Luther King, Jr., was unveiled. The memorial consists of a thirty-foot high statue of the fallen civil rights leader carved out of a mountain of stone, inspired by King's "I Have A Dream" speech, which he delivered nearby at the Lincoln Memorial in 1963. In that speech, King spoke of carving a "stone of hope" from "a mountain of despair." Visitors to the site literally have to pass through the mountain of despair in order to view King's stone of hope. Like King's prophetic message, the memorial's arrangement of public space invokes a sense of redemption and overcoming. By walking through it, we all become "the veterans of creative suffering" that King praised.[18]

At the same moment the public was meeting the new King memorial, an ugly reminder that racial violence continues unfolded—where else?—in Mississippi. In June, a group of white teenagers beat, robbed, and then ran over a black man named James Craig Anderson in a motel parking lot in Jackson. The young man who drove the truck has since been charged not only with capital murder but with a hate crime. Witnesses told police that the teenagers yelled "white power" and other racial slurs as they attacked Anderson, but this has not been enough to convince everyone that race was a primary motivation in the attack. After all, Mississippi "has struggled mightily to move beyond its past," compelling a *New York Times* correspondent to ask, "Was the killing of Mr. Anderson premeditated racial violence" or "an act indicative of a deep cultural divide?"[19]

To juxtapose race and culture as if they were different things is perplexing, but it serves an important purpose. By blaming "the Southern-boy country thing," a culture of "country music, Bible verses, Bud Light and pickup trucks," for producing the men who murdered Mr. Anderson, those who do not participate in that culture are absolved. Racism, the local psychologist interviewed in the article points out, "is not unique to the Deep South," and neither is the "redneck" culture that he blames for the violence. Nonetheless, it helps to draw the line between those who have passed through the mountain of despair and the others who have yet to do so. The writer also points out that the number-one movie in Jackson during the previous weekend was *The Help*, a film criticized for its simplistic depiction of white redemption and racial reconciliation.[20]

The Help also makes whites the protagonists in the story of black redemption. This has hardly been the case. If anything, whites more often have been the antagonists in black Americans' efforts to overcome the pain and suffering of slavery, and following that the terror and violence of Reconstruction and Jim Crow. Sometimes they inflicted the pain directly with their own hands; other times, their attempts to author freedpeople's redemption resulted in even more suffering.

Ben Chaney's dissatisfaction with Edgar Ray Killen's trial and conviction for killing Chaney's brother and the other two civil rights workers in 1964 stemmed from the knowledge that the atonement white Mississippians proclaimed came too easily. Their efforts to reduce one episode within centuries of institutionalized racism and brutality to a matter of individual criminality ignored the systematic injustices that plagued black Americans, including but not limited to outrageous acts of violence like the Freedom Summer murders. White atonement, however that may be defined, did not equal black redemption, at least not in the way Chaney or many ex-slaves had imagined it. For freedpeople emerging from the trauma of slavery, a vision of home moved them toward the future. Home meant more than just the land on which they lived. It included the people that lived on it, for those people performed work that was in many respects more valuable than the wages or shares that they earned. The work of family helped ease the burdens of the past and present, soothed old pains as well as new ones, and made redemption possible. Even when blood kin were no longer present, the memories of them and the hope for their return, however remote, functioned in the same way. Recall Clara Allen's beautiful hand-knit blanket that the WPA interviewer so admired and suggested she sell. "Naw'm I wouldn't part wid dat. I knit dat at de old place an those what show me is dead an' gone," she explained. "Dats all I got lef uf um." Allen found a kind of redemption in that bedspread, painstakingly stitched together over time. To see redemption in that piece of fabric requires that we think of it as an ongoing process, never complete, always imperfect, and certainly not easy. "Then," as James Baldwin hoped, "history becomes a garment we can wear; and share, and not a cloak in which to hide; and time becomes a friend."[21]

Acknowledgments

I have accrued enormous debts—financial, intellectual, and emotional—in writing this book. First, the financial ones. I received funding for research and travel from a number of institutions, including Northwestern University, where this project began as a dissertation. In particular, I would like to thank the history department at Northwestern, the Frankel Foundation, and the Alice Berline Kaplan Center for the Humanities for research support. Duke University, the North Caroliniana Society, the Deep South Regional Humanities Institute at Tulane University, the American Historical Association, and the Huntington Library also provided generous support. A predoctoral fellowship from the Smithsonian at the National Museum of American History allowed me the precious time to think and write. For their help in making a book out of a dissertation, I am thankful to the Baldy Center for Law and Social Policy at the University at Buffalo, a Mellon Research Fellowship from the Virginia Historical Society, and a visiting scholar grant from the Southern Historical Collection at the University of North Carolina–Chapel Hill. A faculty fellowship from the Buffalo Humanities Institute and a semester leave from Dr. Nuala McCann Drescher Leave Program for junior faculty allowed me to complete the manuscript. The archival staffs at the aforementioned institutions, as well as the South Caroliniana Library, and the state archives in South Carolina, Mississippi, Alabama, and Texas, and the Inter-library Loan Department at the University at Buffalo all deserve my thanks.

The intellectual and emotional debts I owe are staggering, but I cherish them. From the beginning, my dissertation committee saw the value in this project. For their tireless efforts in helping me through that stage of the process, I am forever grateful to Steven Hahn, Stephanie McCurry, Dylan Penningroth, Josef Barton, and Susan Pearson. As his other students can attest, Steve remains a steady source of advice and encouragement, as well as a model of the very best historical scholarship. A cadre of former Hahn and McCurry students has become a second family. Aaron Astor, Justin Behrend, Greg Downs, and Susan O'Donovan, in particular, have given me much support and intellectual camaraderie.

Along the way, I have met many scholars who have read drafts of chapters and conference papers, and shared their own work. At the Smithsonian, Pete Daniel became an invaluable mentor, ally, and friend. In North Carolina, Montgomery Wolf and Barbara Hahn opened their homes to this nomadic researcher and made the lonely work of archival research much more enjoyable. I met Amy Wood while interviewing for a position in her department, and although I did not get the job, I made a great friend whose insights helped shape this book at a crucial moment in its writing. Likewise, William Blair's unflagging support represents everything that is good about working in this profession. As editor of the *Journal of the Civil War Era*, Bill and the anonymous reviewers provided helpful suggestions for an essay that grew out of this manuscript. I would also like to thank the University of North Carolina Press for permission to republish portions of that essay here in chapter 4. Nancy Bercaw, Fitz Brundage, Jane Dailey, Jim Downs, Laura Edwards, Steve Kantrowitz, Kate Masur, Elaine Parsons, Kimberly Phillips, Larry Powell, Hannah Rosen, Michael Ross, and Margaret Storey shared ideas and their time. At Wesleyan University, where I spent a wonderful year as a visiting assistant professor, I had the good fortune to work with Renee Romano, Kehaulani Kauanui, Claire Potter, and Patricia Hill, all of whom offered friendship and intellectual companionship. In particular, Renee read most of this manuscript, and it was her work on the redemptive narrative of the civil rights "atonement trials" like Killen's that first alerted me to the prevalence of this theme throughout Southern history.

I was also fortunate to end up in a department steeped in collegiality and support for its junior members. To my fellow historians in the department of history at UB, especially my cohort of Americanists, I owe a large debt of gratitude. Susan Cahn, David Herzberg, Jason Young, and Erik Seeman have all read drafts and revisions and offered their unconditional support. Tamara Thornton, Gail Radford, Claire Schen, and Ramya Sreenivasen offered professional advice, encouragement, and friendship. It is a department rich in creativity and dedication if not in resources. I could not have ended up in a better place; in fact, I suspect that had I ended up anywhere else, this book might never have been written. William Pritchard and Sarah Handley-Cousins, my PhD students, provided additional research assistance, and Mark Boonshoft copyedited an early version of the manuscript. I look forward to reading their contributions to the study of American history.

Special thanks are also reserved for Robert Devens, my editor at the University of Chicago Press, who shepherded this project through the befuddling review and publication process. He and his assistant, Russ Damian, patiently answered innumerable questions about pretty much everything. I am proud to be a part of the American Beginnings series and thank Stephen Mihm, the series editor, along with Ed Gray and Mark Peterson, for initially contacting me about it. I would also like to thank Thavolia Glymph and an anonymous reader, whose comments helped make this book far better than I could have managed on my own.

"My friends are my estate"—if Emily Dickinson was right, then I am rich beyond compare. From my graduate school days, Karen O'Brien has remained a confidant and collaborator in all aspects of my life. In addition to her friendship, Rachel Unruh gave me the greatest gift one can give to a writer—a copy of Anne Lamott's *Bird by Bird*. Shirley Wajda and I have followed each other around a lot, from the Smithsonian to Wesleyan, and I have enjoyed every minute of it! Now that the book is finished, hopefully we can make it back to that mecca of knitting and fiber arts, the New York State Sheep and Wool Festival, once again. At UB, Theresa Runstedtler, Theresa McCarthy, Cindy Wu, and LaKisha Simmons have been sources of "raucous validation" and laughter.

Above all else, my best friend and husband, Darrell Stevens, has given me love, support, and companionship that I cannot imagine living without. Although he did not realize that in marrying me he was also marrying my book, he has borne the trial with stoicism and good humor, as only an Englishman could. It is to him and my parents that I dedicate this book. Although at some level I cringe to dedicate a book about the horrible things people do to one another to people who have only ever shown me love and kindness; without them I could not have faced another report of wickedness. An avid reader, my mother opened my eyes at an early age to the power and beauty of the written word and encouraged me to dream. I am sad my father did not live to see this book published, but I will always think of him and remember what hard work really means. He was a railroad man who rose before dawn for nearly forty years to feed and clothe my brothers and I before it literally broke his back. Although writing is hard, it is not that kind of hard, and I know he was glad of that.

Notes

INTRODUCTION

1. "Mississippi Jury Convicts Ex-Klansman in 1964 Killings," *New York Times*, June 22, 2005.
2. Chaney quoted in "Freedom Summer's Agony Revisited," June 12, 2005, http://www.msnbc.msn.com/id/7209834/ns/us_news-race_and_ethnicity/page/2/.
3. Renee Romano examines how narratives of racial redemption informed the recent "atonement trials" like Killen's in "Narratives of Redemption: The Birmingham Church Bombing Trials and the Construction of Civil Rights Memory," in *The Civil Rights Movement in American Memory*, ed. Renee Romano and Leigh Raiford (Athens: University of Georgia Press, 2006), 96–134. For a good example of how one writer used the Killen trial as a redemptive moment, see Howard Ball, *Justice in Mississippi: The Trial of Edgar Ray Killen* (Lawrence: University of Kansas, 2006).
4. On regeneration narratives, see Richard Slotkin's classic study, *Regeneration through Violence: The Mythology of the American Frontier, 1600–1800* (Norman: University of Oklahoma Press, 1973); and, more recently, Jackson Lears, *Rebirth of a Nation: The Making of Modern America, 1877–1920* (New York: Harper, 2009). David Blight also discusses rebirth metaphors as a means through which Americans struggled over the meaning of the Civil War and its legacy in *Race and Reunion: The Civil War in American Memory* (Cambridge, MA: Belknap Press, 2002), 31–63. On the rhetorical power of redemption, see George Shulman, *American Prophecy: Race and Redemption in American Political Culture* (Minneapolis: University of Minnesota Press, 2008), x. On the blending of secular and religious ideology in American history, see Nathan

Hatch, *The Sacred Cause of Liberty: Republican Thought and the Millennium in Revolutionary New England* (New Haven, CT: Yale University Press, 1977). Hatch argues that the conflation of Christian theology and republicanism during the American Revolution resulted in the creation of a "civic millennialism" that advanced the colonists' dissolution with Great Britain as "the cause of God." Foreshadowing how Southern Redeemers would justify their armed revolt against Republicans in the 1870s, the colonists justified their violent overthrow of authority by invoking images from the book of Revelation—the violent confrontation between good and evil.

5. Orlando Patterson, *Rituals of Blood: Consequences of Slavery in Two American Centuries* (Washington, DC: Counterpoint, 1998), 210.

6. Religious scholars note the dualistic meanings of redemption within Christianity. See among others Timothy Gorringe, *God's Just Vengeance: Crime, Violence, and the Rhetoric of Salvation* (New York: Cambridge University Press, 1996).

7. George Rable discusses the theme of atonement within the religious views of Civil War–era Americans in *God's Almost Chosen Peoples: A Religious History of the Civil War* (Chapel Hill: University of North Carolina Press, 2010). On the role of religion in white supremacist violence, see Daniel Stowell, "Why 'Redemption'?: Religion and the End of Reconstruction, 1869–1877"; and W. Scott Poole, "Confederate Apocalypse: Theology and Violence in the White Reconstruction South"; both in *Vale of Tears: New Essays on Religion and Reconstruction*, ed. Edward J. Blum and W. Scott Poole (Macon, GA: Mercer University Press, 2005), 133–46 and 36–52, respectively. See also Charles Reagan Wilson, *Baptized in Blood: The Religion of the Lost Cause, 1865–1920* (Athens: University of Georgia Press, 1980); and Paul Harvey, *Redeeming the South: Religious Cultures and Racial Identities among Southern Baptists, 1865–1925* (Chapel Hill: University of North Carolina Press, 1995). The relationship between white violence and religion has been a question of debate among scholars of lynching. See Joel Williamson, *The Crucible of Race: Black/White Relations in the South Since Emancipation* (New York: Oxford University Press, 1994); Donald J. Mathews, "The Southern Rite of Human Sacrifice," *Journal of Southern Religion* 3 (2000), http://jsr.fsu.edu/mathews.htm; Trudier Harris, *Exorcising Blackness: Historical and Literary Lynching and Burning Rituals* (Bloomington: Indiana University Press, 1984); Patterson, *Rituals of Blood*; and most recently, Amy Louise Wood, *Lynching and Spectacle: Witnessing Racial Violence in America, 1890–1940* (Chapel Hill: University of North Carolina Press, 2009), 45–70.

8. For an exploration of the power of redemption in colonial New England, see John Demos, *The Unredeemed Captive: A Family Story from Early America* (New York: Knopf, 1994). See also Slotkin, *Regeneration through Violence* and *The Fatal Environment: The Myth of the Frontier in the Age of Industrialization, 1800–1890* (New York: Athenaeum, 1985); and more recently, Richard Bailey, *Race and Redemption in Puritan New England* (New York: Oxford

University Press, 2011). On evangelical reform, see Douglas M. Strong, *Perfectionist Politics: Abolitionism and the Religious Tensions of American Democracy* (Syracuse, NY: Syracuse University Press, 1999). On slave religion, see Albert J. Raboteau, *Slave Religion: The "Invisible" Institution in the Antebellum South* (New York: Oxford, 1978). Candace Vogler and Patchen Markell discuss the paradoxical relationship between liberalism and redemption in "Introduction: Violence, Redemption, and the Liberal Imagination," special issue, *Public Culture* 15, no. 1 (Winter 2003): 1–10. Arguing that "violence haunts the liberal imagination," Vogler and Markell relate how although social contract theory aims to provide citizens protection from the state of nature, the state's legitimacy rests upon the continued threat of violence as well as its own monopoly of coercion and violent force. Thus, the liberal state's redemptive promise hinges upon a fearful vision of the individual as dangerous, and furthermore, because its own authority derives from this fear, the promise can never be fulfilled. On this point see also Judith Shklar, "The Liberalism of Fear," in *Liberalism and the Moral Life*, ed. Nancy L. Rosenblum (Cambridge, MA: Harvard University Press, 1989), 21–38.
9. Charles Royster, *The Destructive War: William Tecumseh Sherman, Stonewall Jackson, and the Americans* (New York: Vintage, 1991), 256.
10. Herman Melville, "Supplement," in *Battle-Pieces and Aspects of the War: Civil War Poems* (Amherst, NY: Prometheus, [1866] 2001); Stowell, "Why 'Redemption'?."
11. Drew Faust, *This Republic of Suffering: Death and the American Civil War* (New York: Knopf, 2008), xiii. On the role of the "suffering slave" in antislavery politics, see Elizabeth Clark, "'The Sacred Rights of the Weak,' Pain, Suffering, and the Culture of Individual Rights in Antebellum America," *Journal of American History* 82, no. 2 (September 1995), 463–93. My analysis of the politics of suffering in the postwar period draws heavily from the work of literary scholars whose critiques of these images and their implications for the creation of black political subjectivities question the celebratory narrative that Clark endeavors to tell. See Elizabeth Spelman, *Fruits of Sorrow: Framing Our Attention to Suffering* (Boston: Beacon Press, 1997); Marcus Wood, *Blind Memory: Visual Representations of Slavery in England and America, 1780–1865* (New York: Routledge, 2000); Saidiya Hartman, *Scenes of Subjection: Terror, Slavery, and Self-Making in Nineteenth-Century America* (New York: Oxford, 1997).
12. On the efforts of Southern planters to control freedpeople's labor, see Steven Hahn, *A Nation under Our Feet: Black Political Struggles in the Rural South from Slavery to the Great Migration* (Cambridge, MA: Belknap Press, 2005); Julie Saville, *The Work of Reconstruction: From Slave to Wage Laborer in South Carolina, 1860–1870* (New York: Cambridge University Press, 1994); John Rodrigue, *Reconstruction in the Cane Fields: From Slavery to Wage Labor in Louisiana's Sugar Parishes, 1862–1920* (Baton Rouge: LSU Press, 2001); Tera Hunter, *To 'Joy My Freedom: Black Women's Lives and Labors After the Civil*

War (Cambridge, MA: Harvard University Press, 1998); Leslie Schwalm, *A Hard Fight for We: Women's Transition from Slavery to Freedom in South Carolina* (Urbana: University of Illinois Press, 1997); Eric Foner, *Reconstruction: America's Unfinished Revolution, 1863–1877* (New York: Harper & Row, 1988); Leon Litwack, *Been in the Storm So Long: The Aftermath of Slavery* (New York: Knopf, 1979); John Hope Franklin, *Reconstruction after the Civil War* (Chicago: University of Chicago Press, 1961); and W. E. B. DuBois, *Black Reconstruction* (New York: Harcourt, Brace, and Co., 1935).

13. John Trowbridge, *The Desolate South, 1865–1866* (New York: Duell, Sloan, and Pearce, 1956 [1866]), 435–36. Historians of postwar labor and the Republican Party have stressed the importance of the "labor question" to Reconstruction, arguing that fears of working-class agitation, race, and cycling economic crises in the North severely compromised Radical Republicans' mission to expand civil rights protection for freedpeople. See David Montgomery, *The Fall of the House of Labor: The Workplace, the State, and American Labor Activism, 1865–1925* (New York: Cambridge University Press, 1987); Heather Cox Richardson, *The Death of Reconstruction: Race, Labor, and Politics in the Post–Civil War North, 1865–1901* (Cambridge, MA: Harvard University Press, 2001); Nancy Cohen, *The Reconstruction of American Liberalism, 1865–1914* (Chapel Hill: University of North Carolina Press, 2002); and Amy Dru Stanley, *From Bondage to Contract: Wage Labor, Marriage and the Market in the Age of Slave Emancipation* (New York: Cambridge University Press, 1998). Scholars of emancipation in the Caribbean also note the importance of labor control and discipline to planters and government officials on the islands. See Thomas Holt, *The Problem of Freedom: Race, Labor, and Politics in Jamaica and Britain, 1832–1928* (Baltimore: Johns Hopkins University Press, 1992); Demetrius Eudell, *The Political Languages of Emancipation in the British Caribbean and the U.S. South* (Chapel Hill: University of North Carolina Press, 2002); Diana Paton, *No Bond but the Law: Punishment, Race, and Gender in Jamaican State Formation, 1780–1870* (Durham, NC: Duke University Press, 2004); Rebecca Scott, *Degrees of Freedom: Louisiana and Cuba after Slavery* (Cambridge: Belknap Press, 2005); and Gale Kenny, *Contentious Liberties: American Abolitionists in Post-emancipation Jamaica, 1834–1866* (Athens: University of Georgia Press, 2010).

14. Hartman, *Scenes of Subjection*, 3. Hannah Rosen discusses the struggles of freedwomen to testify to their experiences of rape in *Terror in the Heart of Freedom: Citizenship, Sexual Violence, and the Meaning of Race in the Postemancipation South* (Cambridge, MA: Harvard University Press, 2009). Freedpeople's testimony of violence is the central focus of Kidada Williams's study *They Left Great Marks on Me: African American Testimonies of Racial Violence from Emancipation to World War I* (New York: New York University Press, 2012). Williams stresses the importance testifying about violence played in establishing a legacy of injustice that grounded the long civil rights movement.

15. On the politics of writing about slaves' agency, see Walter Johnson, "On Agency," *Journal of Social History* 37, no. 1 (Fall 2003): 113–24. See also Nell Painter, "Soul Murder and Slavery: Toward a Fully Loaded Cost Accounting," in *Southern History across the Color Line* (Chapel Hill: University of North Carolina Press, 2002), 15–39. Jennifer Morgan considers the limitations of the archive and the creativity of historical writing in *Laboring Women: Reproduction and Gender in New World Slavery* (Philadelphia: University of Pennsylvania Press, 2004), 196–201. On "trauma studies," see generally Didier Fassin, *The Empire of Trauma: An Inquiry into the Condition of Victimhood* (Princeton, NJ: Princeton University Press, 2009); Veena Das, *Life and Words: Violence and the Descent into the Ordinary* (Berkeley: University of California Press, 2006); Veena Das et. al., eds., *Violence and Subjectivity* (Berkeley: University of California Press, 2000); Ron Eyerman, *Cultural Trauma: Slavery and the Formation of African American Identity* (New York: Cambridge University Press, 2001); and Arthur Kleinman et. al., eds., *Social Suffering* (Berkeley: University of California Press, 1997). See also Williams, *They Left Great Marks on Me*.
16. Ned Blackhawk, *Violence over the Land: Indians and Empires in the Early American West* (Cambridge, MA: Harvard University Press, 2006): 6. In addition to Blackhawk's groundbreaking work, other recent scholarship has begun to explore the formative role violence has played both in the military conquest of the American nation as well as the ideology of American nationalism. See Carroll Smith-Rosenberg, *This Violent Empire: The Birth of an American National Identity* (Chapel Hill: University of North Carolina Press, 2010); Peter Silver, *Our Savage Neighbors: How Indian War Transformed Early America* (New York: W. W. Norton, 2008); Karl Jacoby, *Shadows at Dawn: An Apache Massacre and the Violence of History* (New York: Penguin, 2008); Amy Greenberg, *Manifest Manhood and the Antebellum American Empire* (New York: Cambridge University Press, 2005); Joann Freeman, *Affairs of Honor: National Politics in the New Republic* (New Haven, CT: Yale, 2002); and Cecelia O'Leary, *To Die For: The Paradox of American Patriotism* (Princeton, NJ: Princeton University Press, 1999).
17. Homi K. Bhabba, "DissemiNation: Time, Narrative, and the Margins of the Modern Nation," in *Nation and Narration* (New York: Routledge, 1990), 310.
18. On this point, see Franklin, *Reconstruction after the Civil War*; Dickson D. Bruce, Jr., *Violence and Culture in the Antebellum South* (Austin: University of Texas Press, 1979); Bertram Wyatt-Brown, *Southern Honor* and *The Shaping of Southern Culture: Honor, Grace, and War, 1760s–1880s* (Chapel Hill: University of North Carolina Press, 2001); Douglas Blackmon, *Slavery by Another Name: The Reenslavement of Black Americans from the Civil War to World War II* (New York: Random House, 2008); Michelle Alexander, *The New Jim Crow: Mass Incarceration in the Age of Colorblindness* (New York: The New Press, 2010).
19. Foner, *Reconstruction*, 346. Historians have documented that many federal institutions of this period, most notably the Freedmen's Bureau, lacked the manpower and funding necessary to function as the protectors freedpeople

expected them to be, arguing that these institutions' authority both on the state and national level was too weak for Reconstruction to succeed. As I have argued elsewhere, federal officials seemed curiously naïve about the importance that displays of power could have on a people's willingness to recognize their authority. See Carole Emberton, "Reconstructing Loyalty: Love, Fear, and Power in the Postwar South," in *The Great Task Remaining Before Us: Reconstruction as America's Continuing Civil War*, ed. Paul A. Cimbala and Randall M. Miller (New York: Fordham University Press, 2010), 173–182. Greg Downs also makes the case for state weakness in *Declarations of Dependence: The Long Reconstruction of Popular Politics in the South, 1861–1908* (Chapel Hill: University of North Carolina Press, 2011). While the state's structural weakness is an undeniable factor in assessing Reconstruction's limitations, it is important not to overlook the ideological dilemmas that circumscribed the transition from slavery to freedom, including what Downs describes as an "an enduring queasiness around dependence" (9).

20. Richard Yarborough, "Race, Violence, and Manhood: The Masculine Ideal in Frederick Douglass's 'The Heroic Slave,'" in *Haunted Bodies: Gender and Southern Texts*, ed. Anne Goodwyn Jones and Susan V. Donaldson (Charlottesville: University Press of Virginia, 1997), 161.

21. The term "martial manhood" comes from Amy Greenberg, who posits that the Civil War resulted in a pacification of American manhood that continued until the end of the nineteenth century. See Greenberg, *Manifest Manhood*, 17. On the emergence of "primitive masculinity" in the late nineteenth century, see also Clifford Putney, *Muscular Christianity: Manhood and Sports in Protestant America, 1880–1920* (Cambridge, MA: Harvard University Press, 2001); Dana D. Nelson, *National Manhood: Capitalist Citizenship and the Imagined Fraternity of White Men* (Durham: Duke University Press, 1998); Gail Bederman, *Manliness and Civilization: A Cultural History of Race and Gender in the United States, 1880–1920* (Chicago: University of Chicago Press, 1996); Michael Kammen, *Manhood in America: A Cultural History* (New York: Free Press, 1996); and E. Anthony Rotundo, *American Manhood: Transformations in Masculinity from the Revolution to the Modern Era* (New York: Basic Books, 1993). The history of black manhood will be discussed in more detail in chapter 4. On the "right to brutality" as a function of postemancipation politics, see Diana Paton, *No Bond but the Law*.

CHAPTER ONE

1. Melville, "Shiloh: A Requiem," in *Battle-Pieces*, 63.
2. *New York Times*, 8 July 1865. See also Elizabeth D. Leonard, *Lincoln's Avengers: Justice, Revenge, and Reunion after the Civil War* (New York: W. W. Norton, 2004).

3. David DeWitt, *The Judicial Murder of Mary E. Surratt* (1895; repr., St. Clair Shores, MI: Scholarly Press, 1970), 15; John Weis, "War and Literature," *Atlantic Monthly* (June 1862), 681.
4. See Melinda Lawson, *Patriot Fires: Forging a New American Nationalism in the Civil War North* (Lawrence: University of Kansas Press, 2002), 11.
5. For example, see C. Vann Woodward, *Reunion and Reaction: The Compromise of 1877 and the End of Reconstruction* (New York: Oxford, 1966); Foner, *Reconstruction*; Nicholas Lemann, *Redemption: The Last Battle of the Civil War* (New York: Farrar, Straus & Giroux, 2006).
6. Orville Vernon Burton, *The Age of Lincoln* (New York: Hill & Wang, 2007), 299.
7. Richard Carwadine discusses Lincoln's apotheosis in *Lincoln: A Life of Purpose and Power* (New York: Knopf, 2006), 316. On postwar nationalism as a civic religion, see Michael Kammen, *Mystic Chords of Memory: The Transformation of Tradition in American Culture* (New York: Knopf, 1991). See also Allen C. Guelzo, *Abraham Lincoln: Redeemer President* (Grand Rapids: William B. Eerdmans, 1999).
8. *New York Daily Tribune*, April 4, 1865. For an in-depth discussion of African American freedom celebrations, including the Charleston parade, see Kathleen Clark, *Defining Moments: African-American Commemoration and Political Culture in the South, 1863–1913* (Chapel Hill: University of North Carolina Press, 2009).
9. Rev. Robert F. Sample, *The Curtained Throne, A Sermon, Suggested by the Death of President Lincoln, Preached in the Presbyterian Church of Bedford, Pa., April 23, 1865, and repeated April 30, 1865* (Philadelphia: J. S. Claxton, 1865), 12; A. G. Thomas, *Our National Unity Perfected by the Martyrdom of the President* (Philadelphia: Smith, English & Co., 1865), 5; R. Jeffery, *The Mission of Abraham Lincoln* (Philadelphia: Bryson & Son, 1865), 25; Gilbert Haven, *The Uniter and Liberator of America: A Memorial Discourse on the Character and Career of Abraham Lincoln, Delivered in the North Russell Street M. E. Church, Boston, Sunday, April 23, 1865* (Boston: J. P. Magee, 1865), 27, 22.
10. Henry Champion Deming, *Eulogy of Abraham Lincoln* (Hartford: A. N. Clark & Co., 1865), 47; Rev. Frank L. Robbins, *A Discourse on the Death of Abraham Lincoln* (Philadelphia: H. B. Ashmead, 1865), 9; Haven, *The Uniter and Liberator of America*, 32. Melinda Lawson discusses how Lincoln came to embody the promise of the new national state after his death in *Patriot Fires*, 160–78; as does Eric Foner in *Fiery Trial: Abraham Lincoln and American Slavery* (New York: W. W. Norton, 2010).
11. On this tension between Garrisonians and political abolitionists, see Douglas M. Strong, *Perfectionist Politics: Abolitionism and the Religious Tensions of American Democracy* (Syracuse, NY: Syracuse University Press, 1999).
12. Foner, *Fiery Trial*, 326.
13. Massachusetts Constitution, pt. 1, art. 10 (1780). On the idea of protection in the classical legal tradition, see Steven J. Heyman, "The First Duty of

Government: Protection, Liberty, and the Fourteenth Amendment," *Duke Law Journal* 41 (1991): 507-71.
14. James Madison, *The Federalist No. 10*, in *The Essential Federalist and Anti-Federalist Papers*, ed. David Wooten (Indianapolis: Hackett, 2003), 168-69; US Constitution, art. 4, sec. 4.
15. William J. Novak, *The People's Welfare: Law and Regulation in Nineteenth-Century America* (Chapel Hill: University of North Carolina Press, 1996), 51-82, 191-233.
16. Howard K. Beale, ed., *The Diary of Edward Bates, 1859-1866* (Washington, DC: Government Printing Office, 1933), 312; Michael Vorenberg, *Final Freedom: The Civil War, the Abolition of Slavery, and the Thirteenth Amendment* (New York: Cambridge University Press, 2001), 69.
17. Speech of Isaac Arnold, Cong. Globe, 38th Cong., 1st Sess., (June 15, 1864), p. 2989; George Julian, *Political Recollections*, 1840-1872 (Miami: Mnemosyne Pub. Co., 1969), 251; Vorenberg, *Final Freedom*, 208, 51; *Liberator*, February 10, 1865, p. 2.
18. *Christian Recorder*, November 18, 1865.
19. Cong. Globe, 39th Cong., 2d Sess. 39 (29 January 1866), 474.
20. Cong. Globe, 39th Cong., 1st Sess. (4 April 1866), 1757. On the understanding of citizenship as a "discrete right," see Christopher R. Green, "The Original Sense of the (Equal) Protection Clause," *George Mason University Civil Rights Law Journal* 19 (Spring 2009): 1-76.
21. Civil Rights Act (1866), Sec. 2; Cong. Globe, 39th Cong., 1st Sess. (30 January 1866), 504.
22. Daniel Stowell, *Rebuilding Zion: The Religious Reconstruction of the South, 1863-1877* (New York: Oxford, 1998), 42; Earl Schenck Miers, ed., *When the World Ended* (New York: Oxford, 1957), 95. On Lost Cause theology see Charles Reagan Wilson, *Baptized in Blood: The Religion of the Lost Cause, 1865-1920* (Athens: University of Georgia Press, 1980); and Paul Harvey, *Redeeming the South: Religious Cultures and Racial Identities among Southern Baptists, 1865-1920* (Chapel Hill: University of North Carolina Press, 1997). On memorialization of the Lost Cause and Confederate dead, see Blight, *Race and Reunion*; Karen Cox, *Dixie's Daughters: The United Daughters of the Confederacy and the Preservation of Confederate Culture* (Gainesville: University of Florida, 2003); William Blair, *Cities of the Dead: Contesting the Memory of the Civil War in the South, 1865-1914* (Chapel Hill: University of North Carolina Press, 2004); John Neff, *Honoring the Civil War Dead: Commemoration and the Problem of Reconciliation* (Lawrence: University of Kansas, 2004); and Gaines M. Foster, *Ghosts of the Confederacy: Defeat, the Lost Cause, and the Emergence of the New South, 1865-1913* (New York: Oxford, 1987).
23. "John Brown's Body" became a favorite of the antislavery vanguard after Brown's execution in 1859 and inspired Julia Ward Howe to compose the "Battle Hymn of the Republic" in 1863.
24. *New York Daily Tribune*, April 4, 1865.

25. Daniel Aaron, *The Unwritten War: American Writers and the Civil War* (New York: Knopf, 1973), xiv; *Confederate Baptist*, quoted in Faust, *This Republic of Suffering*, 33; Anne C. Rose, *Victorian America and the Civil War* (New York: Cambridge University Press, 1992), 1. See also Wilson, *Patriotic Gore: Studies in the Literature of the American Civil War* (repr., New York: Norton, 1994); George M. Fredrickson, *The Inner Civil War* (Urbana: University of Illinois Press, 1965); Harry S. Stout, *Upon the Altar of the Nation: A Moral History of the Civil War* (New York: Viking, 2006); and Mark Schantz, *Awaiting the Heavenly Country: The Civil War and American's Culture of Death* (Ithaca, NY: Cornell University Press, 2008).
26. On crime and sensationalism in the nineteenth century, see Patricia Cline Cohen, *The Murder of Helen Jewett* (New York: Vintage, 1999); Karen Halttunen, *Murder Most Foul: The Killer and the American Gothic Imagination* (Cambridge, MA: Harvard University Press, 2000); Michael Ayers Trotti, *The Body in the Reservoir: Murder and Sensationalism in the South* (Chapel Hill: University of North Carolina Press, 2008). More generally, see Marcus Daniel, *Scandal and Civility: Journalism and the Birth of American Democracy* (New York: Oxford, 2009).
27. *Lynchburg Virginian*, June 22, 1867; *Milwaukee Sentinel*, May 21, 1881; *Twenty-first Annual Report of the Prison Association* (New York, 1866), 173; *New York World*, *Lynchburg Virginian*, May 2, 1867.
28. See Roger Lane, *Violent Death in the City: Suicide, Accident, and Murder in Nineteenth-Century Philadelphia* (Cambridge, MA: Harvard University Press, 1979), 53.
29. *Appleton's Journal* (New York) 3, no. 47, February 19, 1870, 211–12; *Christian Recorder* (Philadelphia), January 23, 1869; *Lynchburg Virginian*, June 22, 1867.
30. Eric H. Monkkonen, *Murder in New York City* (Berkeley: University of California Press, 2001). See also Monkkonen, "Estimating the Accuracy of Historic Homicide Rates: New York City and Los Angeles," *Social Science History* 25, no. 1 (2001), 53–66; Richard Lane, *Murder in America* (Columbus: Ohio State University Press, 1997); Ted R. Gurr, "Historical Trends in Violent Crimes: A Critical Review of the Evidence," in *Crime and Justice: An Annual Review of Research* 3, ed. Michael Tony and Norval Morris (Chicago: University of Chicago Press, 1981), 296–353. See also Randolph Roth, *American Homicide* (Cambridge, MA: Belknap, 2009).
31. On Civil War reporting, see J. Cutler Andrews, *The North Reports the Civil War* and *The South Reports the Civil War*; Lewis M. Starr, *Bohemian Brigade: Civil War Newsmen in Action* (New York: Knopf, 1954); Emmett Crozier, *Yankee Reporters, 1861–1865* (New York: Oxford University Press, 1956); Donald E. Reynolds, *Editors Make War: Southern Newspapers in the Secession Crisis* (Nashville: Vanderbilt University Press, 1970); Donald Lewis Shaw, "At the Crossroads: Change and Continuity in American Press News 1820–1860," *Journalism History* 8, no. 2 (Summer 1981), 38–50; Fermer Douglas,

James Gordon Bennett and the New York Herald: A Study of Editorial Opinion in the Civil War Era 1854–1867 (New York: St. Martin's Press, 1986); Richard A. Schwarzlose, *The Nation's Newsbrokers: The Formative Years: From Pretelegraph to 1865* (Evanston, IL: Northwestern University Press, 1990); David Sachsman, ed., *The Civil War and the Press* (New Brunswick, NJ: Transaction Publishers, 2000). Studies focusing on sensationalism and the popular press include John D. Stevens, *Sensationalism and the New York Press*; William E. Huntzicker and William David Sloan, eds., *The Popular Press, 1833–1865*; James L. Crouthamel, *Bennett's New York Herald and the Rise of the Popular Press*; Dan Schiller, *Objectivity and the News: The Public and the Rise of Commercial Journalism*; Mark Wahlgren Summers, *The Press Gang: Newspapers and Politics, 1865–1878*; Richard L. Kaplan, *Politics and the American Press: The Rise of Objectivity, 1865–1920*; and Joshua Brown, *Beyond the Lines: Pictorial Reporting, Everyday Life, and the Crisis of Gilded Age America* (Berekeley: University of California Press, 2002). On the telegraph, see Daniel Walker Howe, *What Hath God Wrought: The Transformation of America, 1815–1848* (New York: Oxford University Press, 2007), 658–700; Menahem Blondheim, *News over the Wires: The Telegraph and the Flow of Public Information in America, 1844–1897* (Cambridge, MA: Harvard University Press, 1994).

32. On the advent of hard war, see especially Charles Royster, *The Destructive War*; Mark Grimsley, *The Hard Hand of War*; and Michael Fellman, "At the Nihilist Edge: Reflections on Guerilla Warfare during the American Civil War."

33. *Second Annual Report of the Massachusetts Board of State Charities* (1866), 213; *Report on the Prisons of the United States*, Senate Document no. 74, 38th Congress (1865); *North American Review*, October 1866, p. 409; Edith Abbott, "Civil War and the Crime Wave of 1865–70," *Social Service Review* 1, no. 2 (1927): 212–34.

34. Nathaniel Hawthorne, "Chiefly about War Matters: By a Peaceable Man," *Atlantic Monthly* (July 1862); repr. in *The American Civil War*, ed. Ian Frederick Linseth, 390–410. This reprint contains material omitted in the original publication. John Stauffer also discusses Hawthorne's discomfort with martial culture in "Embattled Manhood and New England Writers," in *Battle Scars: Gender and Sexuality in the American Civil War*, ed. Catherine Clinton and Nina Silber (New York: Oxford University Press, 2006), 124–25.

35. John G. Nicolay and John Hay quoted in Abbott, "Civil War and the Crime Wave of 1865–70," 223; *Report on the Prisons of the United States*, 91.

36. "The Woman Question," *Catholic World* 9, no. 50 (May 1869): 145–47; *Appleton's Journal* 3, no. 47 (February 19, 1870): 211–12; *Appleton's Journal* 2, no. 29 (October 16, 1869): 280–81; *Nation*, June 5, 1866.

37. Harriet Beecher Stowe, "The Chimney Corner," *Atlantic Monthly* (January 1865), 109–115. See also Patricia Hill, "Writing out the War: Harriet Beecher Stowe's Averted Gaze," in *Divided Houses: Gender and the Civil War*, ed. Catherine Clinton and Nina Silber, 260–78; and Blight, *Race and Reunion*, 38–39.

NOTES TO PAGES 31–33

38. T. Carrington et al. to the Chief of the Freedmen's Bureau for Virginia, September 1865, reprinted in *Freedom: A Documentary History of Emanciaption, 1861–1867*, ser. 3, vol. 1, *Land and Labor, 1865*, ed. Steven Hahn (Chapel Hill: University of North Carolina Press, 2008), 286–87. Hereafter cited as *Land & Labor*.
39. "W. Storer How to the Assistant Freedmen's Bureau Assistant Commissioner, Enclosing a Proposed Circular," 14 July 1865, in *Land and Labor*, 136–37.
40. Slavery's role in the development of American political ideology, and its particular importance to ideas of wage labor, contract theory, and the rights of citizens, is discussed in Amy Dru Stanley, *From Bondage to Contract*, chapter 1. Both David Roediger and J. Mills Thornton have argued that workers in the antebellum period, both urban industrial workers and farm workers, respectively, defined themselves as "freemen" in opposition to enslaved blacks. Roediger and Thornton argue that antebellum workers recognized the actual existence of slaves as a threat to their existence and prosperity. See Roediger, *Wages of Whiteness: Race and the Making of the American Working Class* (New York: Verso, 1991), 31–36, 55–56; and Thornton, *Politics and Power in Slave Society: Alabama, 1800–1860* (Baton Rouge: LSU Press, 1978). Other scholars examine the more metaphorical uses of "slavery" versus "tyranny." See Stephanie McCurry, *Masters of Small Worlds: Yeomen Households, Gender Relations, and the Political Culture of the South Carolina Low Country* (New York: Oxford, 1995); Edmund S. Morgan, *American Slavery, American Freedom: The Ordeal of Colonial Virginia* (New York: Norton, 1975), 376; Hahn, *Roots of Southern Populism: Yeomen Farmers and the Transformation of the Georgia Upcountry, 1850–1890* (New York: Oxford, 1983), 89–90.
41. "Justice to the Negro," *DeBow's Review* 2, no. 1 (July 1866): 91–92. See also "The Negro Imbroglio," *DeBow's Review* 3, no. 6 (June 1867): 518–522; "Thoughts on Slavery," *Southern Literary Messenger* 4, no. 12 (December 1838): 737–47; *Lynchburg Virginian*, June 22, 1867. Two representative defenses of slavery as providing social cohesion, order, and peace are Augustus Baldwin Longstreet, *A Voice from the South: Comprising Letters from Georgia to Massachusetts, and to the Southern States* (Baltimore: S. E. Smith, 1848), and J. D. B. DeBow, *Statistical View of the United States* (Washington: B. Tucker, 1854). On the antebellum South's criminal justice system, see Edward L. Ayers, *Vengeance and Justice: Crime and Punishment in the Nineteenth-Century American South* (New York: Oxford University Press, 1984). Sally Hadden discusses the organization and function of the slave patrol in *Slave Patrols: Law and Violence in Virginia and the Carolinas* (Cambridge, MA: Harvard University Press, 2001).
42. On Helper's declining mental state, see Brown, *Southern Outcast*. Kate Masur discusses how images of contrabands portrayed Southern blacks as social threats or criminals in "'A Rare Phenomenon of Philological Vegetation':

The Word 'Contraband' and the Meanings of Emancipation in the United States," *Journal of American History* 93, no. 4 (March 2007): 1050-84. See also V. Jacque Voegeli, "A Rejected Alternative: Union Policy and the Relocation of Southern 'Contrabands' at the Dawn of Emancipation," *Journal of Southern History* 69, no. 4 (2003): 765-90.

43. On the events at Morant Bay, see Thomas Holt, *The Problem of Freedom: Race, Labor, and Politics in Jamaica and Britain, 1832-1938* (Baltimore: Johns Hopkins University Press, 1992), 263-306. For more on American reactions to the rebellion, see Nichola Clayton, "Managing the Transition to a Free Labor Society: American Interpretations of the British West Indies during the Civil War and Reconstruction," *American Nineteenth Century History* 7, no. 1 (March 2006): 89-108.

44. Cong. Globe, 39th Congress, 1st Sess., p. 657; Richard Henry Dana, *Speeches in Stirring Times, and Letters to a Son* (New York: Houghton Mifflin, 1910), 251; *New York Times*, December 8, 1865; *Nation*, December 7, 1865. Edward Rugemer discusses some of the American reactions to the Morant Bay Rebellion in *The Problem of Emancipation: The Caribbean Roots of the American Civil War* (Baton Rouge: LSU Press, 2008), 291-301.

45. Carl Schurz, *Report on the Condition of the South* (New York: Arno Press, 1969), 39.

46. On the perpetual fears of slave rebellion, see Scot French, *The Rebellious Slave: Nat Turner in American Memory* (Boston: Houghton Mifflin, 2004).

CHAPTER TWO

1. Edmund Burke, *A Philosophical Enquiry into the Origin of Our Ideas of the Sublime and Beautiful* (New York: Oxford University Press, 1990), 36-37.
2. O. O. Howard, *Autobiography*, vol. 2 (New York: Baker and Taylor, 1907), 248.
3. Cong. Globe, 39th Cong., 1st Sess., (January 1866), 341.
4. Louisa May Alcott, "My Contraband," in *Short Stories*. For other discussions of "My Contraband" and Alcott's problematic views on race, see *Louisa May Alcott on Race, Sex, and Slavery*, ed. Sarah Elbert (Boston: Northeastern University Press, 1997); Joy James, *A Freedom Bought with Blood: African American War Literature from the Civil War to World War II* (Chapel Hill: University of North Carolina Press, 2007); and Elizabeth Young, *Disarming the Nation: Women's Writing and the American Civil War* (Chicago: University of Chicago Press, 1999).
5. Masur, "'A Rare Phenomenon of Philological Vegetation,'" 1050-84.
6. Frederick Douglass, "West Indies Emancipation," in *The Life and Times of Frederick Douglass* (1892; repr., New York: Collier, 1962), 493-508; Laura Wexler, *Tender Violence: Domestic Visions in an Age of U.S. Imperialism* (Chapel Hill: University of North Carolina Press, 2000); Eudell, *Political Languages of Emancipation*. On the disciplining impulse of postwar capital-

ism, see also Nancy Cohen, *The Reconstruction of American Liberalism, 1865–1914* (Chapel Hill: University of North Carolina Press Press, 2001). Pierre Bourdieu coined the term "misrecognition" to describe how systems of power and violence, such as gender domination, often become unrecognizable as such. Through the practice of symbolic violence, Bourdieu argues, domination appears natural and just because actual violence is no longer employed to compel submission. The term, I believe, is equally useful in describing how "free labor" came to be viewed as the antithesis of slavery's violent and coercive practices even though it, too, relied upon methods of compulsion entrenched in racial, gender, and class hierarchy. Those methods employed not only symbolic violence in the sense that Bourdieu understood the work of culture, but also direct physical violence that free laborites nonetheless justified as essentially peaceful and protection. See Bourdieu, *The Logic of Practice* (Stanford, CA: Stanford University Press, 1980).

7. On Civil War suffering, see Faust, *This Republic of Suffering*; Mark Shantz, *Awaiting the Heavenly Country: The Civil War and America's Culture of Death* (Ithaca, NY: Cornell University Press, 2008); and Stout, *Upon the Altar of the Nation*.

8. Elizabeth Spelman, *Fruits of Sorrow: Framing Our Attention to Suffering* (New York: Beacon Press, 1998), 47; Hartman, *Scenes of Subjection*, 4–5. See also Wood, *Blind Memory*. See also Anna Mae Duane, *Suffering Childhood in Early America: Violence, Race, and the Making of the Child Victim* (Athens: University of Georgia Press, 2010); and Susan J. Pearson, *The Rights of the Defenseless: Protecting Animals and Children in Gilded Age America* (Chicago: University of Chicago Press, 2011). Both Duane and Pearson explore the ambivalence inherent within discourses of suffering.

9. Clark, "'Sacred Rights of the Weak,'" 471, 474.

10. For an overview of the political sympathies of *Harper's*, and its publication during the 1860s and 1870s, see Joshua Brown, *Beyond the Lines: Pictorial Reporting, Everyday Life, and the Crisis of Gilded Age America* (Berkeley: University of California Press, 2002), 120–26.

11. "Past and Future," *Franklin Repository* (Chambersburg, PA), 27 November 1867.

12. Testimony of Josiah Millard in Report of the Joint Committee on Reconstruction, Part 2, 39th Cong., 2nd Sess. (Washington, DC: Government Printing Office, 1866), 28. Hereafter cited as JCR.

13. Summary Report of Col. E. L. Whittlesey, JCR, Part 2, 198; *Acts and Resolutions Adopted by the General Assembly of Florida* (Tallahassee: Office of the Floridian, 1866), 18–26; *Acts and Joint Resolutions of the General Assembly of the State of South Carolina, Passed at the Sessions of 1864–65* (Columbia: J. A. Selby, 1866), 274; William Blair on "Whippings by consent"; Theodore Wilson, *The Black Codes of the South* (Tuscaloosa: University of Alabama Press, 1965).

14. Wilson, *The Black Codes of the South*, 72, 89; William L. Tidball to James A. Bates, 31 August 1866, BRFAL-VA, M1048, roll 65; "The Whipping and Selling of American Citizens," *Harper's Weekly*, 12 January 1867. On lynching spectacles and the function of spectators, see Wood, *Lynching and Spectacle*.
15. Wood, *Blind Memory*, 260; Cong. Globe, 31st Cong., 2nd Sess., 13 December 1850, 2058; Cong. Globe, 32nd Cong., 1st Sess., 7 January 1852, 219. For an overview of antebellum efforts to abolish whipping, see Myra Glenn, *Campaigns against Corporal Punishment: Prisoners, Sailors, Women, and Children in Antebellum America* (Albany: SUNY Press, 1984).
16. See Roediger, *The Wages of Whiteness*.
17. Glenn, *Campaigns against Corporal Punishment*, 60; New York State Senate, *Annual Report of the Inspectors of the Mt Pleasant State Prison*, Sen. doc. no. 20, vol. 1, 67th Sess., 12 January 1844, 29.
18. "Murder of Union Soldiers," Senate Rep. no. 23, 39th Cong., 2nd Sess., March 2, 1867; Summary Report of Col. E. L. Whittlesey, JCR, Part 2, 196–97; Testimony of Dexter Clapp, JCR, Part 2, 209; Testimony of Maj. Gen. Thomas, JCR, Part 1, 111.
19. *Nation*, May 7, May 15, and August 16, 1866. See also the *Chicago Tribune*, May 4, May 5, and August 1, 1866. For a complete account of the New Orleans riot, see James G. Hollandsworth, *An Absolute Massacre: The New Orleans Race Riot of July 30, 1866* (Baton Rouge: LSU Press, 2001); MR&M, 5, 7, 9.
20. Wood, *Blind Memory*, 218.
21. On the objectification of black bodies in early photography, see Molly Rogers, *Delia's Tears: Race, Science, and Photography in Nineteenth-Century America* (New Haven, CT: Yale University Press, 2010). See also Wood, *Blind Memory*, and more recently, *The Horrible Gift of Freedom: Atlantic Slavery and the Representation of Emancipation* (Athens: University of Georgia Press, 2010). In a similar vein, Leigh Raiford explores the instability of lynching photographs and their complex meanings for the civil rights movement in the twentieth century in *Imprisoned in a Luminous Glare: Photography and the African American Freedom Struggle* (Chapel Hill: University of North Carolina Press, 2011).
22. Rosen, *Terror in the Heart of Freedom*, 222–41. On black testimony before the JCR, see Carole Emberton, "Testimony Before the Joint Committee on Reconstruction on Atrocities in the South Against Blacks," *Milestone Documents in African American History*, vol. 2: 1853–1900 (Dallas: Shlager Group, 2010), 633–49.
23. Wood, *Blind Memory*, 262. On the pornographic elements of antislavery literature, see also Saidiya Hartman, *Scenes of Subjection*. On the sexualized context of Reconstruction violence see Rosen, *Terror in the Heart of Freedom*; Lisa Cardyn, "Sexualized Racism/Gendered Violence: Trauma and the Body Politic in the Reconstruction South" (PhD diss., Yale University, 2003); Martha Hodes, "The Sexualization of Reconstruction Politics: White

Women and Black Men in the South After the Civil War," *Journal of the History of Sexuality* 3 (January 1993): 402–17.
24. U. S. Grant to US Atty. Gen. Edwards Pierrepont, September 13, 1875, in *The Papers of Ulysses S. Grant, Vol. 26: 1875*, ed. John Y. Simon (Carbondale: Southern Illinois University Press, 2003), 312–13.
25. Kathleen Brown, *Foul Bodies: Cleanliness in Early America* (New Haven, CT: Yale, 2009), 11, 348.
26. Charles E. Kerwin to Tom Ellis, February 29, 1872, in E. John, Thomas C. W. Ellis and Family Papers, Louisiana and Lower Mississippi Valley Collections, Hill Memorial Library, LSU. Megan Kate Nelson discusses the valorization of white soldiers' war wounds in *Ruin Nation: Destruction and the American Civil War* (Athens: University of Georgia Press), 160–227.
27. "To the Freed People of Orangeburg," enclosed within letter from Charles Soule to O. O. Howard, 12 June 1855, Letters Rec'd, Washington Headquarters, BRFAL, M752, roll 17.
28. Soule to Howard, 12 June, 1865, BRFAL, M752, roll 17.
29. On the problem of "class legislation" and efforts to provide social welfare for blacks, see Nancy Cohen, *The Reconstruction of American Liberalism*, 74–75; Chad Alan Goldberg, *Citizens and Paupers: Relief, Rights, and Race from the Freedmen's Bureau to Workfare* (Chicago: University of Chicago Press, 2007).
30. Circular No. 2, 19 May 1865, and Circular No. 11, 22 August 1865, both in Select Series of Record Issued by the Commissioner, BRFAL, M742, roll 7; Eudell, *Political Languages of Emancipation*, 153–55.
31. Report of Edward O'Brien, 5 September 1866, and Report of J. E. Cornelius, 23 October 1866, both in Records of the Asst. Commissioner for the State of South Carolina, BRFAL, M869, Roll 34. The Bureau's ration reports are an untapped source for understanding the function of the Freedmen's Bureau. The ration reports for South Carolina are found in the Records of the Field Offices, M 1910; Charlotte Lewis's case appears on roll 21 and is dated December 11, 1865. For more on the Bureau's medical activities, see Alan Raphael, "Health and Social Welfare of Kentucky Black People, 1865–1870," *Societas* 2 (Spring 1972): 143–57; Marshall Scott Legan, "Disease and the Freedmen in Mississippi during Reconstruction," *Journal of the History of Medicine and Allied Sciences* 28 (July 1973); Jude Thomas May, "A Nineteenth Century Medical Care Program for Blacks: The Case of the Freedmen's Bureau," *Anthropological Quarterly* 56 (July 1973): 160–71; Gail Hasson, "Health and Welfare of Freedmen in Reconstruction Alabama," *Alabama Review* 35 (April 1982): 94–110; Randy Finley, "In War's Wake: Health Care and Arkansas Freedmen, 1863–1868," *Arkansas Historical Quarterly* 51 (Summer 1992): 135–62; Todd L. Savitt, "Politics in Medicine: The Georgia Freedmen's Bureau and the Organization of Health Care, 1865–1866," *Civil War History* 28 (1982): 45–64; and Reggie L. Pearson, "'There Are Many Sick, Feeble, and Suffering Freedmen': The Freedmen's Bureau

Health-Care Activities during Reconstruction in North Carolina, 1865–1868," *North Carolina Historical Review* 79, no. 2 (April 2002): 141–81. No book-length study of the Freedmen's Bureau medical activities exists except for Jim Downs, *Sick from Freedom: The Deadly Consequences of Emancipation* (New York: Oxford University Press, 2012). In it, Downs recounts the ravaging effects of smallpox on the freed population as well as the inability, and at times unwillingness, of the government to deal with such crises. See also Downs's essay "The Continuation of Slavery: The Experience of Disabled Slaves during Emancipation," *Disability Studies Quarterly* 28, no. 3 (Summer 2008).

32. Report of Edward F. O'Brien, 5 September 1866 and 1 October 1866; Report of J. E. Cornelius, 23 October 1866; Report of G. A. Williams, 24 October 1866; Report of F. W. Liedtke, 1 November 1866, all in BRFAL-SC, M869, roll 34.
33. Report of Edward F. O'Brien, 5 September 1866 and Report of J. D. Greene, 30 October 1866, both in M869, roll 34; De Forest, *A Union Officer in the Reconstruction* (Baton Rouge: LSU Press, 1997), 61.
34. De Forest, *A Union Officer*, 77.
35. Goldberg, *Citizens and Paupers*, 3; De Forest, *A Union Officer*, 60.
36. Circular No. 9, Office of the Asst. Commissioner, State of Mississippi; Circular Letter of Orlando Brown; O. O. Howard, Circular No. 11, all reprinted in "Freedmen's Bureau," Ex. Doc. No. 70, 39th Cong., 1st Sess. (1866), 158, 120, 105. See also Circular No. 25, State of Louisiana, 28–29.
37. "Freedmen's Bureau," 62–63.
38. James Barrett Steedman, *The Freedmen's Bureau: Reports of Generals Steedman and Fullerton on the Condition of the Freedmen's Bureau in the Southern States* (1866), 5–6. Critics of this report include Karin L. Zipf, *Labor of Innocents: Forced Apprenticeship in North Carolina, 1715–1919* (Baton Rouge: LSU Press, 2005). In his autobiography, O. O. Howard described Fitz as "personally guiltless" of the charges made against him, alluding to the possibility that someone else might, in fact, be guilty of ordering Fitz to commit some of his misdeeds. See Howard, *Autobiography*, 299.
39. Steedman, *The Freedmen's Bureau*, 6–7; *New York Times*, 23 July 1866; Howard, *Autobiography*, 217, 299.
40. Hawley to Thomas, 4 July 1865; *Land & Labor*, 122; Bvt. Maj. Gen. Jon. E. Smith to Maj. Gen. O. O. Howard, 22 June 1865, S-27, Letters Rec'd, ser. 15, Washington HQ, RG 105; reprinted in *Land & Labor*, 99–100.
41. John T. Trowbridge, *The Desolate South*, 435–6; David M. Oshinsky, *Worse Than Slavery: Parchman Farm and the Ordeal of Jim Crow Justice* (New York: Free Press, 1996), 29, 36. On convict leasing, see also Alex Lichetenstein, *Twice the Work of Free Labor: The Political Economy of Convict Labor in the New South* (London: Verso, 1996); and Mary Ellen Curtin, *Black Prisoners and Their World: Alabama, 1865–1900* (Charlottesville: University of Virginia Press, 2000). On the "crisis in legitimacy," see Foner, *Reconstruction*, 412.

42. George Fitzhugh, "Camp Lee and the Freedmen's Bureau," *DeBow's Review*, ser. 2, vol. 2 (1866): 347.
43. Fitzhugh, "Camp Lee and the Freedmen's Bureau," 347–48.
44. Louis Agassiz to Samuel Gridley Howe, 9, 10, 11 August 1863, Agassiz Papers. Houghton Library. Harvard University. For more on the popularization of Darwinian theory, particularly the work of Herbert Spencer, and its effects on American public policy after the Civil War, see Richard Hofstadter, *Social Darwinism in American Thought* (1944; repr., Boston: Beacon Press, 1992). Although some scholars have criticized Hofstadter's work as an oversimplification of Spencer's ideas, I believe that Hofstadter's general argument about the popularization and reception of Spencer's work, particularly the political implications of phrases like "survival of the fittest," which Spencer coined, remain important for understanding the intellectual climate that contributed to the end of Reconstruction. On Spencer see, among others, Mark Francis, *Herbert Spencer and the Invention of Modern Life* (Ithaca: Cornell University Press, 2007). See also George Fredrickson, *The Black Image in the White Mind: The Debate on Afro-American Character and Destiny, 1817–1914* (New York: Harper and Row, 1971), 161.
45. N. S. Shaler, "An Ex-Southerner in South Carolina," *Atlantic Monthly* (July 1870): 53–61. On Shaler's life and career, see Shaler, *The Autobiography of Nathaniel Southgate Shaler* (New York: Houghton Mifflin, 1909).
46. E. L. Godkin, "The Race Question," *The Nation*, 21 July 1870, 39.
47. Shaler, "An Ex-Southerner in South Carolina," 58.
48. Cong. Globe, 39th Cong., 1st Sess. (January 16, 1866), 252.
49. Frederick Douglass, "What Shall Be Done With the Slaves?" in *Life and Writings* 3: 188–191; "The Unholy Alliance of Negro Hate and Antislavery," in *Life and Writings* 2: 385–387.
50. Octavius Brooks Frothingham, *Theodore Parker: A Biography* (Boston: James R. Osgood and Co., 1874), 466–467, 472–473. See also Fredrickson, *Black Image in the White Mind*, 157.
51. Rev. J. M. Sturtevant, "The Destiny of the African Race in the United States," *Continental Monthly*, Vol. 3, Issue 5 (May 1863): 603–605.

CHAPTER THREE

1. "We Shall Overcome," adapted from a number of black spirituals at the Highlander Folk School in eastern Tennessee. Eileen Southern, *The Music of Black Americans: A History*, 2nd ed. (New York: Norton, 1971), 546–47, 159–60.
2. Marcus Wood, *The Horrible Gift of Freedom: Atlantic Slavery and the Representation of Emancipation* (Athens: University of Georgia Press, 2010), 5.
3. Steven Hahn argues that the Edisto Islanders sought "to protect and consecrate their own project of community building by placing it under the jurisdiction of an early sovereign power that they themselves had helped

to sustain," in *A Nation Under Our Feet*, 144. On the importance of land to black aspirations, see also Saville, *The Work of Reconstruction*; John Rodrique, *Reconstruction in the Cane Fields* (Baton Rouge: LSU Press, 2001); Dylan Penningroth, *The Claims of Kinfolk: African American Property and Community in the Nineteenth-Century South* (Chapel Hill: University of North Carolina Press, 2002); Susan O'Donovan, *Becoming Free in the Cotton South* (Cambridge, MA: Harvard University Press, 2007).

4. Committee of Freedmen on Edisto Island, South Carolina, to Major General O. O. Howard, 20 or 21 October 1865, Letters Received, ser. 15, Washington Headquarters, Bureau of Refugees, Freedmen, and Abandoned Lands, RG 105 (hereafter cited as RG 105), National Archives. Italics in original.

5. Maj. Gen. O. O. Howard to the Committee of Colored People of Edisto Island, 22 October 1865, vol. 64, 415–16, Letters Sent, ser. 2, Washington Headquarters, RG 105; Henry Bram et. al. to the President of These United States, 28 October 1865, filed as P-27 1865, Letters Received, ser. 15, Washington Headquarters, RG 105.

6. On the role of everyday forms of violence, see Thavolia Glymph's discussion of it in *Out of the House of Bondage: The Transformation of the Plantation Household* (New York: Cambridge University Press: 2008).

7. Hendrik Hartog, "The Constitution of Aspiration and 'The Rights That Belong to Us All,'" *Journal of American History* 74, no. 3 (December 1987): 1019. Greg Downs discusses a corollary to this tradition in what he terms "patronalism," a political style stressing a person's dependence that emerged during the Civil War in *Declarations of Dependence: The Long Reconstruction of Popular Politics in the South, 1861–1907* (Chapel Hill: University of North Carolina Press, 2011). Unlike Hartog, however, Downs sees the language of dependence as contrary to ideas of autonomy and citizenship rights. Either way, the long-standing concern with physical vulnerability can be understood as a central if unacknowledged tenet of liberal politics, what Judith Shklar denotes as the "liberalism of fear" that constituted the flip side of the liberalism of rights. See Shklar, "The Liberalism of Fear," in *Liberalism and the Moral Life*, ed. Nancy L. Rosenblum (Cambridge, MA: Harvard University Press, 1989), 21–38. See also Williams, *They Left Great Marks on Me*.

8. The thrust of most revisionist histories of Reconstruction, beginning with W. E. B. DuBois's *Black Reconstruction*, and continuing with Foner's *Reconstruction* to Hahn's *A Nation Under Our Feet*, to name a few of the most influential, large-scale studies of the period, seek a reassessment of black political life and freedpeople's contributions to the both the national and grassroots struggles for freedom after emancipation. These larger works along with innumerable local studies, have resulted in a vast, complex, and nuanced understanding of the experience of Southern blacks during Reconstruction. Central to them all is a rightful admiration and appreciation for freedpeople's perseverance and determination in the face of at

NOTES TO PAGES 76-79

times unimaginable violence and hostility, both from Southern whites and the federal government. My aim is not to detract from this appreciation or to cast doubt on the veracity of those interpretations but rather to imagine other possible emotional reactions to violence that existed alongside the ones we are more familiar with, to consider how the struggle to overcome was always plagued by the possibility of not overcoming. For a more pointed critique of what he calls "history writing as a mode of redress," see Walter Johnson, "On Agency," *Journal of Social History* 37, no. 1 (Fall 2003): 113-24.

9. Elaine Scarry, *The Body In Pain: The Making and Unmaking of the World* (New York: Oxford, 1985); Karl Jacoby, *Shadows at Dawn: An Apache Massacre and the Violence of the History* (New York: Penguin, 2008), 7. On the dissolution of language through violence, see also Veena Das, *Life and Words: Violence and the Descent into the Ordinary* (Berkeley: University of California Press, 2007). See also Darlene Clark Hine, "Rape and the Inner Lives of Black Women and the Middle West: Preliminary Thoughts on the Culture of Dissemblance," *Signs* 14, 4 (Summer 1989): 912-20; Nell Painter, "Soul Murder and Slavery: Toward a Fully Loaded Cost Accounting," in Southern History Across the Color Line (Chapel Hill: University of North Carolina Press, 2002), 15-39; and Paul Gilroy, *The Black Atlantic: Modernity and Double Consciousness* (Cambridge, MA: Harvard University Press, 1993), 187-223.

10. Julie Saville discusses the importance of home in *The Work of Reconstruction: From Slave to Wage Labor in South Carolina, 1860-1870* (New York: Cambridge University Press, 1996), 18; Committee of Freedmen on Edisto Island, October 28, October 20 or 21, 1865. On the importance of land, see also Rodrique, *Reconstruction in the Cane Fields*; and Steven Hahn et. al., eds., *Freedom: A Documentary History of Emancipation, 1861-1867, Series 3: Volume I, Land & Labor, 1865* (Chapel Hill: University of North Carolina Press, 2008). Hereafter cited as *Land & Labor*.

11. O'Donovan, *Becoming Free in the Cotton South*, 143-207; Interview with Delicia Patterson, Missouri Narratives, *Born in Slavery*: http://memory.loc.gov/cgi-bin/ampage?collId=mesn&fileName=100/mesn100.db&recNum=275&itemLink=S?ammem/mesnbib:@field%28AUTHOR+@od1%28Patterson,+Delicia%29%29. See also Penningroth, *The Claims of Kinfolk*.

12. Gen. Sherman tells of his meeting with the Savannah ministers in *Memoirs of General William T. Sherman, Written by Himself* (New York, 1891), 2: 245-52. See also Vincent Harding, *There is a River: The Black Struggle for Freedom in America* (New York: Harcourt, 1981), 261-65; and "Colloquy with Colored Ministers," *Journal of Negro History* 16 (January 1931), 88-94.

13. Brevet Maj. Gen. Jno. E. Smith to Maj. Gen. O. O. Howard, 22 June 1865, reprinted in Hahn et. al., *Land & Labor, 1865*, 99-100.

14. Foner, *Reconstruction*, 70-71.

15. Testimony of Henry M. Turner and Abram Colby, *Condition of Affairs: Georgia, Vol. 1* (Washington, DC: Government Printing Office, 1872), 1040

and 700, respectively. The testimony, which documented the activities of the Ku Klux Klan in the South, is replete with similar explanations of rural blacks' migration to cities and towns. See also the testimony of Thomas Allen, 610: Anthony Martin, 692; Jasper Carter, 477; Hannah Flournoy, 532; Alexander Hinton; 694–95; Daniel Lane, 653; William C. Morrell, 1088; Alfred Richardson, 9; Caroline Smith, 402; and H. D. D. Twiggs, 1045–46.

16. On the rise in black urban residents after the war, see among others Howard Rabinowitz, *Race Relations in the Urban South, 1865–1890*. New Ed. (Athens: University of Georgia Press, 1996); Tera Hunter, *'To Joy My Freedom: Southern Black Women's Lives and Labors after the Civil War* (Cambridge, MA: Harvard University Press, 1997); and Michael Fitzgerald, *Urban Emancipation: Popular Politics in Reconstruction Mobile, 1860–1890* (Baton Rouge: LSU Press, 2002). Stephanie Camp coined the phrase "rival geography" to describe slaves' appropriation of social space on the plantation in *Closer to Freedom: Enslaved Women and Everyday Resistance in the Plantation South* (Chapel Hill: University of North Carolina Press, 2004), 7.

17. On this, see Glymph, *Out of the House of Bondage*.

18. "Report of Outrages, July 1867," BRFAL-SC, M869, roll 34; Testimony of Sidney Andrews, *JCR*, Part III, 175.

19. *Charlotte Revis v. Adam Revis*, July 4, 1866; *Hester Ann Burwell v. Celia Franklin*, July 14, 1866; *Martha Cosby v. Charles Lewis*, July 11, 1866, all on Roll 67, Vol. 131; Lt. Andrew Mahoney to Headquarters of the Military Commissioner in Pittsylvania County, August 26, 1867, Roll 72; and *Caroline Jenkins v. James Hawkins*, Roll 192; all BRFAL-VA, Records for the Field Offices of the State of Virginia, M1913. Although Catherine Clinton argued that "most freedwomen resisted bringing [Freedmen's Bureau] agents into domestic matters," the evidence unearthed by Laura Edwards, Nancy Bercaw, and Susan O'Donovan suggests otherwise. See Clinton, "Bloody Terrain: Freedwomen, Sexuality, and Violence during Reconstruction," in *Half Sisters of History: Southern Women and the American Past*, ed. Catherine Clinton (Durham, NC: Duke University Press, 1994), 135–53; Laura Edwards, *Gendered Strife and Confusion*; Nancy Bercaw, *Gendered Freedoms*, 117–34; O'Donovan, *Becoming Free in the Cotton South*, 195–200. While a fuller discussion of domestic and intra-racial violence among former slaves is beyond the scope of this project, it nonetheless calls into question the tendency to focus on white violence against the "unoffending freedman," a political strategy devised by Republicans to combat the growing intransigency of white Southerners during Radical Reconstruction and reproduced by revisionist historians seeking to overturn the "tragic era" of the Dunning School. I take up this strategical deployment of white-on-black violence later in chapter 5.

20. Capt. James H. Mathews to Maj. George D. Reynolds, 27 November 1865, reprinted in *Land & Labor*, 850–52; Emancipation Proclamation, 1 January 1863; Capt. W. Storer How to Col. Orlando Brown, 14 July 1865, reprinted in *Land & Labor*, 136–37. Italics in original.

NOTES TO PAGES 82-87

21. J. S. Fullerton to Maj. Gen. O. O. Howard, 28 July 1865, reprinted in *Land & Labor*, 148-49; Oliver O. Howard, *Autobiography*, 1901, vol. 2, 253; Foner, *Reconstruction*, 143; Donald Nieman, *To Set the Law in Motion*, 9. On the Freedmen's Bureau as arbiters of the law, see also Barry Crouch, *Freedmen's Bureau and Black Texans*; Paul Cimbala, *Under the Guardianship of the Nation*; Wayne K. Durrill, "Political Legitimacy and Local Courts: 'Politicks at Such a Rage' in a Southern Community during Reconstruction," *Journal of Southern History*, 70, 3 (2004): 577-617.
22. Address of the Equal Rights League of Wilmington, NC, AMAA, North Carolina series, roll 2 (doc. # 100288); Proceedings of Mass Meeting at Norfolk, VA, 6 December 1865, reprinted in *Land & Labor*, 455-59.
23. Committee of Freedmen on Edisto Island, South Carolina, to Major General O. O. Howard, 20 or 21 October 1865.
24. Cong. Globe, 39th Cong., 1st Sess., (1866), 474; *New York Tribune*, June 17, 1865.
25. Rev Lewis Bright et al. to General Clinton B. Fisk, 27 July 1865, B-36 1865, Registered Letters Received, ser. 3379, TN Assistant Commissioner, RG 105; reprinted in *Land & Labor*, 252-264.
26. William, Toney Golden et al. to Col. H. F. Sickles, 28 November 1865, Unregistered Letters Rec'd, ser. 1013, Savannah GA Subassistant Commissioner, RG 105; James Rawl, et. al. to W. W. Holton, August 20, 1866, in Misc. Records Relating to Complaints (ser. 3167), Columbia, South Carolina. Records of the Acting Asst. Commissioner, RG 105. On the Black Codes, see Theodore B. Wilson, *The Black Codes of the South*; Leon Litwack, *Been in the Storm So Long*, 366-71; Eric Foner, *Reconstruction*, 199-201; and Christopher Waldrep, "Substituting the Law for the Lash: Emancipation and Legal Formalism in a Mississippi County Court," *Journal of American History* 82, no. 4 (March 1996): 1425-51.
27. On reciprocity and customary rights of slavery, see Eugene Genovese, *Roll, Jordan, Roll: The World the Slaves Made* (New York: Vintage, 1972).
28. Capt. W. Storer to Col. O. Brown, 14 July 1865, published in *Land & Labor*, 136-37; O. O. Howard to the Committee of the Colored People of Edisto Island, 22 October 1865.
29. On notions of embodiment and citizenship in the American liberal tradition, see Bernard Bailyn, *Ideological Origins of the American Revolution* (Cambridge: Belknap Press, 1967); Gordon Wood, *Radicalism of the American Revolution* (New York: Knopf, 1991); Joyce Appleby, *Liberalism and Republicanism in the Historical Imagination* (Cambridge, MA: Harvard University Press, 1992); Bruce Burgett, *Sentimental Bodies: Sex, Gender, and Citizenship in the Early Republic* (Princeton, NJ: Princeton University Press, 1998). Other scholars have focused on the persistence of ascriptive, physical limitations placed on citizenship, most notably Rogers Smith, *Civic Ideals: Conflicting Visions of Citizenship in U.S. History* (New Haven, CT: Yale University Press, 1997). On the American Equal Rights Association, see Paula Baker,

"The Domestication of Politics: Women and American Political Society, 1780–1920," *American Historical Review* 89, no. 3 (June 1984): 620–47; Ellen DuBois, *Feminism and Suffrage: The Emergence of an Independent Women's Movement in America, 1848–1869* (Ithaca: Cornell University Press, 1978); and Smith, *Civic Ideals*, 311. The term "badges and incidents of slavery" is taken from Justice Harlan's dissent the 1885 Civil Rights Cases and is discussed in William M. Carter, Jr., "Race, Rights, and the Thirteenth Amendment," *UC Davis Law Review* 40, no. 4 (April 2007): 1311–79.

30. Emily Russell, *Reading Embodied Citizenship: Disability, Narrative, and the Body Politic* (New Brunswick: Rutgers University Press, 2011), 4. On the history of the Disability Rights Movement and its construction of citizenship, see also Michale Bérubé, "Citizenship and Disability," *Dissent* (Spr. 2005): 52–55; Simi Linton, *Claiming Disability: Knowledge and Identity* (New York: NYU Press, 1998); Rosemarie Garland-Thomson, *Extraordinary Bodies: Figuring Physical Disability in American Culture and Literature* (New York: Columbia University Press, 1997). Douglas Baynton discusses the centrality of race to notions of disability and debates over citizenship in the nineteenth and twentieth centuries in "Disability and the Justification of Inequality in American History," in *The New Disability History: American Perspectives*, ed. Paul K. Longmore and Lauri Umansky (New York: NYU Press, 2001), 33–57. See also Christopher M. Bell, ed., *Blackness and Disability: Critical Examinations and Cultural Interventions* (Ann Arbor: University of Michigan Press, 2011).

31. Kathleen Clark, *Defining Moments*, 50.

32. Edward Bell, et. Al. to Col. J. W. Sprague, 3 May 1866, J-33 (1866), Letters Rec'd (ser. 1691), Dept. of Florida, United States Army Continental Command (RG 393) [Freedmen and Southern Society Project, University of Maryland, College Park, MD, C-317]; Lt. Col. H. B. Clitz to Lt. J. M. Johnson, 9 October 1867, J-68 (1867), Letters Rec'd (ser. 4111), 2nd Military District, USACC (RG 393) [FSSP SS-81]; William Blake to Gen. Pope, 14 June 1867, A-642 (1867), Letters Rec'd (ser. 5782), 3ᵈ Military District, USACC Pt. 1 (RG 393) [FSSP SS-620]; H. L. Benford to Bvt. Brig. Gen. E. R. S. Canby, 11 June 1868, Letters Rec'd (ser. 4111), 2d Military District, USACC Pt. 1 (RG 393) [FSSP SS-120]; Gen. O. O. Howard to E. M. Stanton, 14 May 1866, H-171 (1866), Letters Rec'd (ser. 15), Records of the Commissioner, BRFAL (RG 105) [FSSP A-9716]; Thomas Pennamore, et. Al. to Bvt. Maj. Crofton, August 1868, T(D) 67 (1866), Headquarters of the Army (ser. 22, RG 108); Colored Men of Richmond to Gov. Francis H. Pierpont, 6 August 1866, Francis H. Pierpont Executive Papers; Maj. Gen. Lorenzo Thomas to Gen. Ulysses S. Grant, 29 May 1867, Letters Rec'd (ser. 12), Records of the Adjutant General's Office (RG 94) [FSSP K-107].

33. Lt. J. B. Johnson to Capt. E. C. Woodruff, 15 January 1867, Letter's Rec'd (ser. 1691), Dept. of FL, RG 393 [FSSP C-353]; Capt. E. W. H. Read to Bvt. Maj. E. L. Deane, 5 January 1867, vol. 156 DS p. 127, Letters sent (ser. 2389), Post of Georgetown SC, RG 393, Pt. 2, No. 142 [FSSP C-1619]; Anonymous

Freedmen to Freedmen's Bureau Agent, 23 May 1867, A-272 (1867), Letters Rec'd (ser. 15), Records of the Commissioner, RG 105 [FSSP A-2973].

34. Julie Saville, *The Work of Reconstruction: From Slave to Wage Laborer in South Carolina, 1860–1870* (New York: Cambridge University Press, 1996); Burton, *In My Father's House*; Penningroth, *Claims of Kinfolk*; Hahn, *A Nation Under Our Feet*; Otis Singletary, *Negro Militia and Reconstruction* (Austin: University of Texas Press, 1959); Elsa Barkley Brown notes the importance of militias for black public life after emancipation in "Negotiating and Transforming the Black Public Sphere." According to Brown, both freedmen and women participated in militia activities. Jeffery R. Kerr-Ritchie makes a case for the importance of antebellum black militias in "Rehearsal for War: Black Militias in the Atlantic World."

35. Lt. S. J. Clark to Joseph Dickenson and Timothy Harrison, 11 June 1866, repr., Ira Berlin et al., eds., *Freedom: A Documentary History of Emancipation, 1861–1867*, series 2, The Black Military Experience (Cambridge: Cambridge University Press, 1982), 763. Hereafter cited as *BME*. Erasmus Booman to Edward M. Stanton, 14 May 1865, reprinted in *BME*, 666–67; Capt. Edwin O. Latimer to Lt. Col. A. G. Chamberlain, 27 June 1865, reprinted in *BME*, 738–39; Sgt. E. S. Robison to Maj. Gen. Q. A. Gilmore, 7 August 1865, reprinted in *BME*, 742; Rodrique, *Reconstruction in the Cane Fields*.

36. On paramilitary politics in the Reconstruction South, see Hahn, *A Nation Under Our Feet*, 265–316.

37. Ann Malone, "Matthew Gaines: Reconstruction Politics," in *Black Leaders: Texans for Their Time*, ed. Alwyn Barr and Robert Calvert (Austin: Texas State Historical Association, 1981).

38. Speech of Matt Gaines, June 7, 1870, in *Debates and Proceedings of the Twelfth Legislature of the State of Texas* (Austin: Tracy, Siemering and Co., 1870).

39. Quoted in Merlin Pitre, *Through Many Dangers, Toils, and Snares: The Black Leadership of Texas, 1868–1900* (Austin: Eakin Press, 1985), 162.

40. "D. F. Davis to Gov. Davis, January 1870." Davis Papers, Texas State Library and Archives Center, Austin, TX.

41. Edmund S. Morgan, *Inventing the People: The Rise of Popular Sovereignty in England and American* (New York: W. W. Norton, 1988), 13. On the tension between force and consent in Reconstruction politics, see my earlier essay "Reconstructing Loyalty: Love, Fear, and Power in the Postwar South," in Paul Cimbala and Randall Miller, eds. *The Great Task Remaining Before Us: Reconstruction as America's Continuing Civil War* (New York: Fordham University Press, 2010), 173–82.

42. Saidiya Hartman, *Lose Your Mother: A Journey Along the Atlantic Slave Route* (New York: Farrar, Straus, and Giroux, 2007), 14–15. On history and its "burden" for Southerners, see C. Vann Woodward, *The Burden of Southern History*, 3rd ed. (Baton Rouge: LSU Press, 1993).

43. Henry McNeal Turner, "On the Anniversary of Emancipation," reprinted in Redkey, ed., *Respect Black: The Writings and Speeches of Henry McNeal Turner*

(New York: Arno Press, 1971), 5–7; James Lynch, *Mission of the United States Republic: An Oration* (Augusta: Steam Power Press Chronicle and Sentinel Office, 1865), 6–7. For more on the divisions among African Americans regarding slavery's memory, see Kathleen Clark, *Defining Moments*, 46–50.

44. Hawkins Wilson to his sister Jane, 11 May 1867, Records for the Field Offices for the State of Virginia, M1913, roll 58, RG 105.
45. David A. Gerber, "Acts of Deceiving and Withholding in Immigrant Letters: Personal Identity and Self-Presentation in Personal Correspondence," *Journal of Social History* 39, 2 (Winter 2005): 315–30; 320–21.
46. Interview with Clara Allen, in Charles L. Perdue, et. al. eds, *Weevils in Wheat: Interviews with Virginia Ex-Slaves* (Charlottesville: University of Virginia Press, 1976), 6; Interview with Sarah Debro, North Carolina Narratives, *Born in Slavery*: http://memory.loc.gov/cgi-bin/query/S?ammem/mesnbib:@field%28AUTHOR+@od1%28Debro,+Sarah%29%29.
47. Interview with Minnie Folkes, Arthur Greene, Clara Allen, and Charles Crawley, *Weevils in the Wheat*, 92, 124, 6, 78–79, respectively. On the coded language of ex-slaves and "the slipperiness and elusiveness of slavery's archive," see Hartman, *Lose Your Mother*, 16–17.
48. As other historians have pointed out, the WPA slave narratives are a problematic set of archives. Questions pertaining to the relationship between the interviewer and respondent, the writers' use of dialect when transcribing the interviews, and the overall racial politics of the project have made some historians hesitant to use them. Others are doubtful of the reliability of the interviewees' recollections about slavery, given their advanced age; many of them were in their eighties or nineties at the time they were interviewed. But as Thavolia Glymph points out, the interviews were a unique opportunity for former slaves to speak out about their experiences, to express their feelings, and reflect on their lives since emancipation. That their responses sometimes seem overly sentimental, or fail to express the kinds of emotions we might expect or hope to see from ex-slaves, should not cause us to dismiss their testimony out of hand. In fact, it is precisely the fragmentary and conflicting nature of the memories that I wish to consider. See Glymph, *Out of the House of Bondage*, 15–16.
49. Interviews with Beverly Jones and Elizabeth Sparks, *Weevils in the Wheat*, 181 and 273–77, respectively.
50. Interview with Minne Folkes, *Weevils in the Wheat*, 96.
51. Interview with Robert Ellett, *Weevils in the Wheat*, 84–85.
52. Interview with Arthur Greene, Katie Blackwell Johnson, and Henrietta King, *Weevils in the Wheat*, 122, 162, and 191, respectively.
53. Interview with Ellaine Wright, Missouri Narratives, *Born in Slavery*: http://memory.loc.gov/cgi-bin/query/S?ammem/mesnbib:@field%28AUTHOR+@od1%28Wright,+Ellaine%29%29.
54. Interviews with Clara Allen and Charles Crawley, *Weevils in the Wheat*, 8 and 78, respectively.

55. Clark, *Defining Moments*, 44; Interview of Charlie Moses, Mississippi Narratives, *Born in Slavery*: http://memory.loc.gov/cgi-bin/query/S?ammem /mesnbib:@field%28AUTHOR+@od1%28Moses,+Charlie%29%29.
56. Interview with Thomas Hall, North Carolina Narratives, *Born in Slavery*: http://memory.loc.gov/cgi-bin/ampage?collId=mesn&fileName=111/mesn111 .db&recNum=364&itemLink=S?ammem/mesnbib:@field%28AUTHOR+@ od1%28Hall,+Thomas%29%29.
57. W. E. B. DuBois, *The Souls Of Black Folk* (New York: Penguin, 1996 [1903]), 106.
58. On black cultural production and the legacy of slavery, see among others Paul Gilroy, *The Black Atlantic*; Darieck Scott, *Extravagant Abjection: Blackness, Power, and Sexuality in the African American Literary Imagination* (New York: NYU Press, 2010); Sandra Gunning, *Rape, Race, and Lynching: The Red Record of American Literature, 1890–1912* (New York: Oxford, 1996); Adam Gussow, *Seems Like Murder Here: Southern Violence and the Blues Tradition* (Chicago: University of Chicago Press, 2002); Tricia Rose, *Black Noise: Rape Music and Black Culture in Contemporary America* (Middletown, CT: Wesleyan University Press, 1994); Raiford, *Imprisoned in a Luminous Glare*; and Korita Mitchell, *Living with Lynching: African American Lynching Plays, Performance, and Citizenship, 1890–1930* (Urbana: University of Illinois Press, 2011).

CHAPTER FOUR

1. *Harper's Weekly*, July 4, 1863.
2. The backstory of the photograph is discussed in the *New York Times*, September 30, 2009 (see letters to the editor). Marcus Wood discussed the transatlantic uses of the image in *Blind Memory*, 268–70. See also Mary Mitchell's discussion of the photographs of freedchildren, which told a similar tale of redemption, in *Raising Freedom's Child: Black Children and Visions of the Future after Slavery* (New York: New York University Press, 2008).
3. Richard Yarborough, "Race, Violence, and Manhood: The Masculine Ideal in Frederick Douglass's 'The Heroic Slave,'" in *Haunted Bodies: Gender and Southern Texts*, ed. Anne Goodwyn Jones and Susan V. Donaldson (Charlottesville: University Press of Virginia, 1997), 161; *BME*, 34. Other works that praise the efforts and accomplishments of black soldiers include William Wells Brown, *The Negro in the American Rebellion: His Heroism and Fidelity*; Carter G. Woodson, *The Negro in Our History* (Washington, DC: Associated Publishers, 1922), 233–38; Woodson, "Black History Week," *Journal of Negro History*, vol. 11, no. 2 (April 1926): 240; James McPherson, *The Negro's Civil War: How American Negroes Felt and Acted during the War for the Union* (New York: Pantheon, 1965); Joseph T. Wilson, *The Black Phalanx* (New York: Arno, 1968); Benjamin Quarles, *The Negro in the Civil War* (Boston: Little, Brown, 1969); Joseph Glathaar, *Forged in Battle: The Civil War Alliance of Black Soldiers and White Officers* (New York: Free Press, 1990);

Edwin S. Redkey, *A Grand Army of Black Men* (New York: Cambridge University Press, 1992); James G. Hollandsworth, *The Louisiana Native Guards* (Baton Rouge: LSU Press, 1995); John David Smith, ed., *Black Soldiers in Blue* (Chapel Hill: University of North Carolina Press, 2002); Noah Andre Trudeau, *Like Men of War* (Boston: Little, Brown, 1998); Keith P. Wilson, *Campfires of Freedom* (Kent: Kent State University Press, 2002); Martin H. Blatt et al., eds., *Hope and Glory: Essays on the Legacy of the Fifty-Fourth Massachusetts Regiment* (Amherst: University of Massachusetts Press, 2001); Richard M. Reid, *Freedom for Themselves: North Carolina's Black Soldiers in the Civil War* (Chapel Hill: University of North Carolina Press, 2008); Margaret Humphreys, *Intensely Human: The Health of the Black Soldier in the Civil War* (Baltimore: Johns Hopkins, 2008); Chandra Manning, *What This Cruel War Was Over: Soldiers, Slavery, and the Civil War* (New York: Knopf, 2007) and Christian G. Samito, *Becoming American Under Fire: Irish Americans, African Americans, and the Politics of Citizenship during the Civil War* (Ithaca: Cornell, 2009). The importance of military service for the coming of freedom also plays a central role in Kate Masur, *An Example for All the Land: Emancipation and the Struggle Over Equality in Washington, D.C.* (Chapel Hill: University of North Carolina Press, 2010); Eric Foner, *Fiery Trial: Abraham Lincoln and American Slavery* (New York: W. W. Norton, 2010); and Gary Gallagher, *The Union War* (Cambridge, MA: Harvard University Press, 2011).

4. For more on the contradictory and often "restrictive" meanings of citizenship in American political culture, see Rogers Smith, *Civic Ideals: Conflicting Visions of Citizenship in U.S. History* (New Haven, CT: Yale, 1997); Mary Frances Berry, *Military Necessity and Civil Rights Policy: Black Citizenship and the Constitution, 1861–1868* (Port Washington, NY: Kennikat Press, 1977). Kimberly Phillips takes a critical stance toward the military and its impact on the civil rights movement in the twentieth century in *War! What Is It Good For? Black Freedom Struggles and the U.S. Military from World War II to Iraq* (Chapel Hill: University of North Carolina Press, 2012). For a more literary approach that considers the ambivalence among black writers regarding the sacrifices of military service, see Jennifer James, *A Freedom Bought with Blood: African American War Literature from the Civil War to World War II* (Chapel Hill: University of North Carolina Press, 2007).

5. This ambivalence regarding black men's capacity for violence characterized both black and white representations of slaves and slavery. It proved especially difficult for black abolitionist writers seeking to demonstrate their own agency and fitness for freedom while not reproducing negative stereotypes prevalent among whites. See Richard Yarborough, "Race, Violence, and Manhood," as well as Karen Taylor, "Reconstructing Men in Savannah, Georgia, 1865–1876," in *Southern Masculinity: Perspectives on Manhood in the South Since the Civil War*, ed. Craig Thompson Friend (Athens: University of

Georgia Press, 2009), 1–24; and Lisa A. Long, *Rehabilitating Bodies: Health, History, and the American Civil War* (Philadelphia: University of Pennsylvania Press, 2004), 211–37. The complexities and contradictions within notions of black masculinity have become the focus of a number of important recent studies, including Martin Summers, *Manliness and Its Discontents: The Black Middle Class and the Transformation of Masculinity, 1900–1930* (Chapel Hill: University of North Carolina Press, 2004); Charise Cheney, *Brothers Gonna Work it Out: Sexual Politics in the Golden Age of Rap Nationalism* (New York: NYU Press, 2005); and Riché Richardson, *Black Masculinity and the U.S. South: From Uncle Tom to Gangsta* (Athens: University of Georgia Press, 2007).

6. Francois Furstenberg, "Beyond Freedom and Slavery: Autonomy, Virtue, and Resistance in Early American Political Discourse," *Journal of American History* 89, 4 (March 2003): 1295–1330; 1304, 1295, 1314–15; 1318–19.

7. Douglass tells the story of his battle with Covey each of his three autobiographical works, first in his *Narrative* in chapter 10, and in chapters entitled "The Last Flogging" in both *My Bondage and My Freedom* and *Life and Times*. As his time in freedom progressed along with the nation's conflict over slavery, Douglass singled out the story and gave it a more pronounced importance within his narrative of liberation. On Douglass's work as an army recruiter, see James H. Cook, "Fighting with Breath, Not Blows: Frederick Douglass and Antislavery Violence," in John R. McKivigan and Stanely Harrold, eds. *Antislavery Violence: Sectional, Racial, and Cultural Conflict in Antebellum America* (Knoxville: University of Tennessee Press, 1999), 128–64.

8. John Blassingame, ed., The Frederick Douglass Papers, Series One: Speeches, Debates, and Interviews, vol. 3 (New Haven, CT: Yale University Press, 1986), 550, 552. Hereafter cited as *FDP*. For more on Douglass's millennial vision of the Civil War, see David W. Blight, *Frederick Douglass's Civil War: Keeping Faith in Jubilee* (Baton Rouge: LSU Press, 1989).

9. William Cooper Nell, *The Colored Patriots of the American Revolution* (repr., NY: Arno, 1968). On the Dred Scott case, see Fehrenbacher, *The Dred Scott Case*.

10. *FDP*, 596, 592. Kantrowitz also discusses the importance of respectability in "Fighting Like Men: Civil War Dilemmas of Abolitionist Manhood," in Clinton and Silber, *Battle Scars*, 19–40.

11. Bruce Dorsey, *Reforming Men and Women* (Ithaca: Cornell, 2002), 147; William Wells Brown, *Narrative of William W. Brown, A Slave. Written by Himself*, Electronic Edition (Chapel Hill: University of North Carolina Press, 1996), http://docsouth.unc.edu/fpn/brownw/brown.html: 16; Harriet Jacobs, *Incidents in the Life of a Slave Girl*.

12. Theodore Parker, "A Sermon on Slavery"; Theodore Tilton, *The Negro: A Speech at the Cooper Institute, May 12, 1863* (New York: American Anti-Slavery Society, 1863), 11–12. See also James Oliver Horton, "Defending the Manhood of the Race," in Blatt, et. al., eds., *Hope and Glory*, 13–15.

13. On black women abolitionists and the politics of womanhood, see Shirley J. Yee, *Black Women Abolitionists: A Study in Activism, 1828–1860* (Knoxville: University of Tennessee, 1992) and Martha S. Jones, *All Bound Up Together: The Woman Question in African American Public Culture, 1830–1900* (Chapel Hill: University of North Carolina Press, 2007). Henry Highland Garnet, "An Address to the Slaves of the United States of America," in *A Documentary History of the Negro People in the United States*, ed. Herbert Aptheker (New York: Citadel Press, 1951). John Stauffer argues that fantasies of rebellion drew white and black radical abolitionist men closer together in *The Black Hearts of Men: Radical Abolitionists and the Transformation of Race* (Cambridge, MA: Harvard University Press, 2004). See also James Oliver Horton and Lois E. Horton, "Violence, Protest, and Identity" in Darlene Clark Hine and Earnestine Jenkins, eds. *A Question of Manhood*, 382–98.
14. Maria W. Steward, "An Address Delivered at the African Masonic Hall, Boston, February 27, 1833," in *Maria W. Stewart, America's First Black Woman Political Writer*, ed. Marilyn Richardson (Bloomington: Indiana University Press, 1987), 56–64. See also Horton and Horton, "Violence, Protest, and Identity," 387. See also Kantrowitz, "Fighting Like Men."
15. Thomas Wentworth Higginson, "The Ordeal by Battle," *Atlantic Monthly* (July 1861), 94.
16. Cong. Globe, 37th Congress, 2d Session (July 1862), 3124, 3204–3206; Douglass quoted in Eric Foner, ed., *Nat Turner* (Englewood Cliffs, NJ: Prentice-Hall, 1971), 139.
17. Cong. Globe, 37th Congress, 3d Session (1862), 85, 3200. See also the speech of H. B. Wright of Pennsylvania, 75–76. Italics mine.
18. Thomas Wentworth Higginson, *Army Life in a Black Regiment* (New York: Collier, 1969), 66–67, 70; Saxton quoted in "Negroes as Soldiers," *Harper's Weekly*, 14 March 1963.
19. Gerritt Smith, "More About the War for the Union," *Boston Journal*, June 1, 1862; Keith Wilson, "In the Shadow of John Brown: The Military Service of Colonels Thomas Higginson, James Montgomery and Robert Shaw in the Department of the South," in *Black Soldiers in Blue: African Americans Troops in the Civil War Era* (Chapel Hill: Univ. of North Carolina Press, 2002), 317.
20. Keith Wilson, "In the Shadow of John Brown," 317, 320, 322–23; Russell Duncan, ed., *Blue-Eyed Child of Fortune: The Civil War Letters of Colonel Robert Gould Shaw* (Athens: University of Georgia Press, 1999), 342–44.
21. Alcott, *My Contraband*, 80–82. Charles Russell Lowell to Josephine Shaw, June 20, 1863, in Edward W. Emerson, *Life and Letters of Charles Russell Lowell* (Boston: Houghton Mifflin, 1907), 261. For an additional discussion of the behavior of black troops and charges that they transgressed the limits of "civilized warfare," see Richard M. Reid, *Freedom For Themselves: North Carolina's Black Soldiers in the Civil War Era* (Chapel Hill: University of North Carolina Press, 2008), 111–152.
22. The records of the AFIC, including both their preliminary and final reports

as well as testimony taken, can be found in Letters Received by the Office of the Adjutant General, 1861-90, NARA, M619, Rolls 199-201. Hereafter cited as AFIC Papers. Eaton's report is located on Roll 200, file no. 6, 24-5.
23. *Preliminary Report of the American Freedman's Inquiry Commission*, June 30, 1863, AFIC Papers, Roll 199, 5-9.
24. *AFIC Preliminary Report*, 16-17. See also See Dudley Taylor Cornish, "The Union Army as a School for Negroes," *Journal of Negro History* 37 (October 1952): 368-82; "Negro Emancipation," *Harper's Weekly*, 10 January 1863.
25. Peter Hunt, "Arming Slaves and Helots in Classical Greece," in Christopher Leslie Brown and Philip D. Morgan, eds. *Arming Slaves: From Classical Times to the Modern Age* (New Haven, CT: Yale University Press, 2006), 30-32.
26. Allen Isaccman and Derek Peterson, "Making the Chikunda: Military Slavery and Ethnicity in Southern Africa, 1750-1900," in Brown and Morgan, *Arming Slaves: From Classical Times to the Modern Age* (New Haven, CT: Yale University Press, 2006), 95-119.
27. On the French Revolution and subsequent revolutions in the French Caribbean, see Laurent Dubois, *Colony of Citizens: Revolution and Slave Emancipation in the French Caribbean, 1787-1804* (Chapel Hill: University of North Carolina Press Press, 2006). See also Bruce Levine, *Confederate Emancipation: Southern Plans to Free and Arm Slaves during the Civil War* (New York: Oxford, 2005) and Stephanie McCurry, *Confederate Reckoning: Power and Politics in the Civil War South* (Cambridge, MA: Harvard University Press, 2010) for discussions of how Confederates planned to arm slaves and nominally free them while maintaining their legal, economic, and political inferiority.
28. Edward Bates, *Opinion of Attorney General Bates on Citizenship* (Washington: Government Printing Office, 1862), 3-5. On the limited definition of citizenship during the Civil War, see also Herman Belz, "Military Service and National Citizenship," in *A New Birth of Freedom: The Republican Party and Freedmen's Rights, 1861-1866* (Westport, CT: Greenwood Press, 1976), 17-34. On obligation, see Linda Kerber, *No Constitutional Right to be Ladies: Women and the Obligations of Citizenship* (New York: Hill and Wang, 1998).
29. Edwards, "Status without Rights: African Americans and the Tangled History of Law and Governance in the Nineteenth-Century U.S. South," *American Historical Review* 112, no. 2 (April 2007): 392.
30. BME, 153-57.
31. Higginson, *Army Life in a Black Regiment*, 69-70.
32. Frank Rollin, *Life and Public Services of Martin R. Delany* (Boston: Lee and Shepard, 1868), 148.
33. BME, 94; FDP, 590.
34. BME, 55-6, 422, 424; 139-40; Bell Irvin Wiley, *Southern Negroes, 1861-1865* (New Haven, CT: Yale University Press, 1965), 108.
35. BME, 140.
36. Elizabeth Ware Pearson, ed., *Letters from Port Royal, 1863-1868* (New York: Arno Press, 1969), 186.

37. Henry L. Swint, *Dear Ones at Home* (Nashville: Vanderbilt, 1966), 165–69. On the competition between civilians and federal authorities, see Willie Lee Rose, *Rehearsal for Reconstruction*.
38. Pearson, *Letters from Port Royal*, 186–89, 185–86; *BME*, 49–50; Wiley, *Southern Negroes*, 309.
39. Pearson, *Letters from Port Royal*, 102–3, 186, 188–89; Gerald Robbins, "The Recruiting and Arming of Negroes in the South Carolina Sea Islands, 1862–1865," *Negro History Bulletin* 28 (April 1965): 165; Higginson, *Army Life in a Black Regiment*, 57–58. Leslie Schwalm notes some resistance to recruitment efforts among blacks in the Midwest as well in *Emancipation's Diaspora: Race and Reconstruction in the Upper Midwest* (Chapel Hill: University of North Carolina Press, 2009), 114.
40. *BME*, 49–50; 664–65.
41. *BME*, 49–50.
42. *BME*, 85–86; Cong. Globe, 37th Congress, 2d Session (1862), 3125–27.
43. "To Abraham Lincoln, On His Demand for Three Hundred Thousand Men," *Frank Leslie's Illustrated Newspaper*, 20 September 1862.
44. AFIC *Preliminary Report*, 20.
45. Berg, "Soldiers and Citizens," 190. See also Masur, *An Example for All the Land*.
46. J. H. Payne, 27th USCI to the *Christian Recorder*, August 19, 1865; "Petition of the Colored Citizens of Nashville," January 9, 1865, reprinted in Berlin, et. al. eds., *BME*, 811–816; Foner and Walker, eds., *Proceedings*, 233.
47. Foner and Walker, eds., *Proceedings*, 139, 192, 90, 61.
48. Foner and Walker, eds., *Proceeedings*, 175, 64, 62, 205.
49. Foner and Walker, eds., *Proceedings*, 233, 87, 292–93; David S. Cecelski, "Abraham Galloway," 47.
50. Henry Ward Beecher, *Universal Suffrage: An Argument* (Boston: Rand and Avery, 1865), 5–7; Fisk quoted in Foner and Walker, eds., *Proceedings*, 122. On the depth and sophistication of slaves' and freedpeople's political worldviews, see Hahn, *A Nation Under Our Feet*, especially part 1.
51. Foner and Walker, eds., *Proceedings*, 116; "Petition of the Colored Citizens of Nashville," January 9, 1865, reprinted in *BME*, 811–816.
52. In her study of black political mobilization in postwar Richmond, Elsa Barkley Brown finds freedwomen taking action alongside their men by attending mass meetings, parades, and other forms of direct action. However, men claimed official roles among these delegations as spokespersons of the race. See Brown, "Negotiating and Transforming the Public Sphere: African American Political Life in the Transformation from Slavery to Freedom," *Public Culture* 7, no. 1 (1994): 107–146. See also Leslie Schwalm's discussion of the gendered dimensions of African Americans' postwar political struggles, which she sees as complimentary rather than antagonistic, in *Emancipation's Diaspora: Race and Reconstruction in the Upper Midwest* (Chapel Hill: University of North Carolina Press, 2009), 175–218. Evelyn Brooks

Higginbotham also notes the struggles etween men and women within the black church in *Righteous Discontent: The Women's Movement in the Black Baptist Church, 1880–1920* (Cambridge, MA: Harvard University Press, 1993).

53. John Mercer Langston, "Citizenship and the Ballot," reprinted in Langston, *Freedom and Citizenship: Selected Lectures and Addresses* (Coral Gables, FL; Mnemosyne Publishing, 1969), 110, 116–17; Turner, "On the Anniversary of Emancipation," in Edwin S. Redkey, ed., *Respect Black*, 10; Laura Edwards, *Gendered Strife and Confusion: The Political Culture of Reconstruction* (Urbana: University of Illinois Press, 1997), 185. See also Clark, *Defining Moments*. My understanding of the intersection of race and gender in the postbellum South owes much to Edwards work as well as Stephanie McCurry's discussion of the family metaphor in proslavery ideology and the "organic" nature of both gender and racial hierarchy, which she explores in *Masters of Small Worlds* as well Barbara Young Welke, who argues that "segregation by sex provided a natural analogy for segregation by race" in her essay "When all the Women Were White, and All the Blacks Were Men: Gender, Class, Race, and the Road to Plessy, 1855–1914," *Law and History Review*, 13, 2 (August 1995): 298. See also Welke's longer work, *Recasting American Liberty: Gender, Race, Law and the Railroad Revolution, 1865–1920* (New York: Cambridge University Press, 2001).
54. *Christian Recorder*, June 11, 1864; Redkey, *A Grand Army of Black Men*, 220; *Christian Recorder*, September 11, 1869.
55. Jim Downs, "Destitution, Disease, and Dependency among Freedwomen and Their Children during and after the Civil War," in Clinton and Silber, *Battle Scars*, 78–79. See also Amy Dru Stanley, "Instead of Waiting for the Thirteenth Amendment: The War Power, Slave Marriage and Inviolate Human Rights" *American Historical Review* 115, no. 3 (June 2010): 732–65.
56. William Wells Brown, *The Negro in the American Rebellion*, xliii, 99.
57. William Wells Brown, *Clotelle; or, The Colored Heroine*. Brown published four editions of *Clotel* from 1854 to 1867. The final version reflects the change in spelling as well as an alteration in the title (orig. entitled *Clotel; or the President's Daughter*) and the introduction of Jerome. Jerome's death scene takes place in Chapter 3. Jennifer James discusses Brown's ambivalence toward battlefield sacrifice as depicted in Jerome's decapitation in *A Freedom Bought with Blood*, 34–35.
58. Gerritt Smith, "More About the War for the Union," *Boston Journal*, 1 June 1862; Herman Melville, "Supplement," in *Battle-Pieces*, 257–72.

CHAPTER FIVE

1. J. F. Partagas and H. F. Diaz, *A Reconstruction of Historical Tropical Cyclone Frequency in the Atlantic from Documentary and Other Historical Sources: 1851–1880, Part I: 1851–1870* (Boulder, CO: Climate Diagnosis Center, 1995), 45–49.

2. *Chicago Tribune*, March 14, 1868.
3. Lee W. Formwalt, "The Camilla Massacre of 1868: Racial Violence as Political Propaganda," *GHQ* 21 (Fall 1987): 403. On the Georgia Freedmen's Bureau, see Paul A. Cimbala, *Under the Guardianship of the Nation: The Freedmen's Bureau and the Reconstruction of Georgia, 1865–1870* (Athens: University of Georgia Press, 2003). For other accounts of the Camilla Riot, see Melinda Meek Hennessy, "To Live and Die in Dixie: Reconstruction Race Riots in the South," PhD Dissertation, Kent State University (1978), 123–31; Drago, *Black Politicians and Reconstruction in Georgia: A Splendid Failure* (Athens: University of Georgia Press, 1992), 51–53; Lewis N. Wynne and Milly St. Julien, "The Camilla Race Riot and the Failure of Reconstruction in Georgia," *JSWGH* 5 (Fall 1987): 15–37; Susan O'Donovan, "Philip Joiner: Southwest Georgia Black Republican," *JSWGH* 4 (Fall 1986): 57–62; Hahn, *A Nation Under Our Feet*, 287–89.
4. Affidavit of William P. Pierce, September 26, 1868 and Christian Raushenberg to Maj. Gen. O. O. Howard, September 28, 1868, both in RG 105, M798, Roll 22.
5. Other election riots shared many similarities with Camilla, namely an outbreak of violence between armed companies or groups at campaign rallies or polling places. See Hennessy, "To Live and Die in Dixie"; Carolyn E. DeLatte, "The St. Landry Riot: A Forgotten Incident of Reconstruction Violence," *La. History* 17, no. 1 (Winter 1976): 41–49; Rable, *But There Was No Peace*; Hahn, *A Nation Under Our Feet*, 265–31. More recently, Aaron Astor explores the relationship between voting and racial violence in "No Gun, No Vote: Violence and the Fifteenth Amendment in Kentucky," unpublished paper presented at the 2009 Southern Historical Association Meeting, Louisiville, KY. See also Astor's longer work, *Rebels on the Border: Civil War, Emancipation, and the Reconstruction of Kentucky and Missouri* (Baton Rouge: Louisiana State University Pres, 2012).
6. David Grimsted, "Rioting in Its Jacksonian Setting," *AHR* 77, no. 2 (April 1972), 373. On the violence of nineteenth-century elections, see Richard Bensel, *The American Ballot Box in the Nineteenth Century* New York: Cambridge University Press, 2004); Jean Baker, *Affairs of Party: The Political Culture of Northern Democrats in the mid-Nineteenth Century* (New York: Fordham University Press, 1998): 287–89; and more recently Jill Lepore, "Rock, Paper, Scissors: How We Used to Vote," *New Yorker*, October 13, 2008. On antebellum rioting generally see also, Carl E. Prince, "The Great 'Riot Year': Jacksonian Democracy and Patterns of Violence in 1834," *JER* 5, 1 (Spr. 1985): 1–19; Michael Feldberg, *The Turbulent Era: Riot and Disorder in Jacksonian America* (New York: Oxford, 1980); Paul Gilje, *Rioting in America* (Bloomington: Indiana University Press, 1996); David Grimsted, *American Mobbing, 1828–1861: Toward Civil War* (New York: Oxford, 1998); and Mary Ryan, *Civic War: Democracy and Public Life in the American City during the Nineteenth Century (*Berkeley: University of California Press, 1997). On

the formation of community and national identity generally, see Benedict Anderson, *Imagined Communities: Reflections on the Origin and Spread of Nationalism* (New York: Verso, 1991). In the American context, see Susan Davis, *Parades and Power: Street Theater in Nineteenth-Century Philadelphia* (Philadelphia: Temple University Press, 1986); Michael Warner, *Letters of the Republic: Publication and the Public Sphere in Eighteenth-Century America* (Cambridge, MA: Harvard University Press, 1990); Jay Fliegelman, *Declaring Independence: Jefferson, Natural Language, and the Culture of Performance* (Stanford: Stanford University Press, 1993); David Waldstricher, *In the Midst of Perpetual Fetes: The Making of American Nationalism, 1776–1820* (Chapel Hill: University of North Carolina Press, 1997); Sandra M. Gustafson, *Eloquence is Power: Oratory and Performance in Early America* (Chapel Hill: University of North Carolina Press, 2000); and Trish Loughran, *The Republic in Print: Print Culture in the Age of U.S. Nation-Building, 1770–1870* (New York: Columbia University Press, 2007).

7. On northern militias and public culture, see Davis, *Parades and Power*. While historians have studied these seemingly disparate events and movements, they've often done so in regional isolation, thereby failing to notice broader themes taking shape around issues of violence, race, gender, and citizenship. Amy Greenberg explores the gendered discourse of conquest and the frontier in *Manifest Manhood*. See also Paul Foos, *A Short, Offhand, Killing Affair: Soldiers and Social Conflict during the Mexican-American War* (Chapel Hill: University of North Carolina Press, 2001). On Southern militancy, see John Hope Franklin's classic study *The Militant South, 1800–1861* (Cambridge, MA: Harvard University Press, 1956) among others.

8. Keyssar, *The Right to Vote: The Contested History of Democracy in the United States* New York: Basic, 2000), 88. Several late nineteenth-century figures, including Pres. Rutherford B. Hayes, attributed this pithy quotation to Sherman, although evidence suggests his exact words were less of an endorsement of black suffrage. In an 1864 letter to Sec. of War Edwin Stanton regarding the prospects for black enlistment, Sherman advised against it because doing so would then require the nation to extend voting rights to them: "Those who hold the swords and muskets at the end of this war . . . will have something to say. If negroes are to fight, they, too, will not be content with sliding back into the status of slave or free negro." Despite his opposition both to black enlistment and suffrage, Sherman nonetheless highlighted an important link between military service and political rights that informed the postwar struggles in the South. See Charles Richard Williams and William Henry Smith, *The Life of President Rutherford B. Hayes* (Boston: Houghton Mifflin, 1914), 316; Maj. Gen. William T. Sherman to Edwin Stanton, 26 October 1864, reprinted in *Sherman's Civil War*, ed. Brooks D. Simpson (Chapel Hill: University of North Carolina Press, 1999), 740–41.

9. Jill Lepore, "Rock, Paper, Scissors," 1–2. See also Richard Bensel, *The American Ballot Box*.

10. Jean Baker, *Affairs of Party*, 287–89. See also Marcus Cunliffe, *Soldiers and Civilians: The Martial Spirit in America, 1775–1865* (New York: Simon and Schuster, 1973), 96; Michael E. McGerr, *The Decline of Popular Politics: The American North, 1865–1928* (New York: Oxford, 1986), 3–41; and Kristin L. Hoganson, *Fighting for American Manhood: How Gender Politics Provoked the Spanish-American and Phillipine-American Wars* (New Haven, CT: Yale, 1998). On the South's martial tradition and its influence on electoral politics, see John Hope Franklin, *The Militant South*; Rhys Issac, *The Transformation of Virginia, 1740–1790* (Chapel Hill: University of North Carolina Press, 1982), 104–114; Stephanie McCurry, *Masters of Small Worlds*, 265–271; Sally Hadden, *Slave Patrols: Law and Violence in Virginia and the Carolinas* (Cambridge, MA: Harvard University Press, 2001).
11. Lepore, Rock, Paper, Scissors," 1; Caleb Cushing, "Speech Delivered in Faneuil Hall, October 27, 1857," 7; Jean Baker, *Affairs of Party*, 267; Paula Baker, "The Domestication of Politics," 628–29; Bensel, *The American Ballot Box*, x–xi; David Grimsted categorizes voting as a "manly sport" that created "an arena of culture where the traits deemed peculiarly and even dangerously male had especially free reign, sanctified by their integration to patriotic duty," in *American Mobbing*, 183.
12. J. Baker, *Affairs of Party*, 270–72. On "civic millennialism," see Nathan Hatch, *The Sacred Cause of Liberty*. On rituals, see Mark C. Carnes, *Secret Ritual and Manhood in Victorian America* (New Haven, CT: Yale, 1989) and Ami Plufgrad-Jackish, *Brothers of a Vow: Secret Fraternal Orders and the Transformation of White Male Culture in Antebellum Virginia* (Athens: University of Georgia Press, 2010).
13. Kerber, *No Constitutional Right to be Ladies*, 236, 240. On the relationship between the Revolutionary War and the expansion of the franchise, see also Alexander Keyssar, *The Right to Vote*, 14–19; Manfred Berg, "Soldiers and Citizens," in David K. Adams and Cornelius van Minnen, eds. Reflections on American Exceptionalism (Staffordshire, UK: 1994), 191–92; and Cunliffe, *Soldiers and Civilians*, 65–68.
14. Cunliffe, *Soldiers and Civilians*, 68. See also Keyssar, *The Right to Vote*, 14–15.
15. Blackstone quoted in Kerber, *No Constitutional Right*, 240, 243. See also Joyce Lee Malcolm, *To Keep and Bear Arms: The Origins of an Anglo-American Right* (Cambridge, MA: Harvard University Press, 1996), 130. On the Taney opinion, see Donald E. Fehrenbacher, *The Dred Scott Case: Its Significance in American Law and Politics* (New York: Oxford, 2001), 335–365.
16. Keyssar, *The Right to Vote*, 88, xvi; *CR*, November 9, 1867.
17. Cunliffe, *Soldiers and Civilians*, 66; David Grimsted, *American Mobbing*, 205, 199–217; Eric Foner, *Reconstruction*, 32. On the draft riots, see also Iver Bernstein, *The New York City Draft Riots: Their Significance for American Society and Politics in the Age of the Civil War* (New York: Oxford, 1990). Both Forrest and Gordon were invited to attend the 1868 Democratic National

Convention, where Forrest walked arm in arm with soon-to-be vice presidential nominee, Frank Blair. Both Forrest and Gordon, and many other former Confederates, became active in Democratic politics at both the state and national level. See Charles Coleman, *The Election of 1868*, 310–31; Jack Hurst, *Nathan Bedford Forrest*, 297–302; Court Carney, "The Contested Image of Nathan Bedford Forrest," *JSH* 67, no. 3(August 2001): 601–30; John B. Gordon, *Reminiscences of the Civil War* (New York: Charles Scribner's and Sons, 1904). On the Democratic Party's internal struggles with the legacy of violence, see Joel H. Silbey, *A Respectable Minority*. Curiously, Silbey doesn't explore Forrest's and Gordon's contributions to the 1868 campaign.
18. Foner and Walker, eds., *Proceedings*, 216. Beecher is discussed in chapter 4.
19. Schurz, "Report," 43; *Cincinnati Daily Gazette*, April 25, 1867, quoted in Richardson, *The Death of Reconstruction*, 43; Foner and Walker, eds., *Proceedings*, Vol. II, 262, 271; Foner and Walker, eds., *Proceedings*, 90; Edward Lillie Pierce, ed., *Memoir and Letters of Charles Sumner*, 275. On Republican support for black suffrage as "self protection," see also William Gillette, *The Right To Vote*; Xi Wang, *The Trial of Democracy: Black Suffrage and Northern Republicans, 1860–1910* (Athens: University of Georgia Press, 1997); and Richard Abbott, *The Republican Party in the South*.
20. On the violent response of Southern whites to black political mobilizations, see Franklin, *Reconstruction*; Trelease, *White Terror: The Ku Klux Klan Conspiracy and Southern Reconstruction* (Westport, CT: Greenwood Press, 1979); Rable, *But There Was No Peace*; Foner, *Reconstruction*, 412–459; Fitzgerald, *The Union League Movement in the Deep South: Politics and Agricultural Change during Reconstruction* (Baton Rouge: LSU Press, 2000); Hahn, *A Nation Under Our Feet*.
21. Hahn, *A Nation Under Our Feet*, 266.
22. Peter H. Wood, *Black Majority: Negroes in Colonial South Carolina from 1670 Through the Stono Rebellion* (New York: Alfred A. Knopf, 1974), 124; Philip Morgan, *Slave Counterpoint: Black Culture in the Eighteenth-Century Chesapeake and Lowcountry* (Chapel Hill: University of North Carolina Press, 1998), 390–91.
23. *Land & Labor*, 381, 157, 846n; 887n. General Grant rescinded the policy allowing black soldiers to purchase their weapons after being advised by Maj. Gen. Philip Sheridan, then commander of the Louisiana and Florida, that allowing black men to keep their weapons as civilians "will create some uneasiness in this section of the country." See Maj. Gen. Philip H. Sheridan to Brig. Gen. John A. Rawlins, 24 October 1865 and Brig. Gen. John A. Rawlins to Maj. Gen. Philip Sheridan, 26 October 1865, both in John Y. Simon, ed., *The Papers of Ulysses S. Grant*, Vol. 16 (Carbondale: SIU Press, 2008), 447.
24. Mary Jones to Mrs. Mary s. Mallard, 15 March 1867 in Myers, ed., *Children of Pride* (New Haven, CT: Yale, 1987), 1376; "Testimony of J. W. Alvord," in *JCR*, 242; *Land & Labor*, 97, 591n, 551.

25. *New Orleans Tribune*, August 31, 1865; "Benjamin C. Truman to Andrew Johnson, April 9, 1866," in *Papers of Andrew Johnson, Vol. 10*, ed. Paul H. Bergeron (Knoxville: University of Tennessee Press, 1989), 384; Gabriel Edward Manigault, "Reminiscences," n.d., SCHS.
26. Adjutant Gen. William Richardson to Gov. Francis H. Pierpont, 12 July 1866, in Francis H. Pierpont Executive Papers, Library of Virginia; *Land & Labor*, 157; Julie Saville, "Rites and Power: Reflections on Slavery, Freedom, and Political Ritual," *Slavery and Abolition* 20, no. 1 (April 1999): 89. See also her longer study of South Carolina freedpeople, *The Work of Reconstruction*. Other historians have also studied the importance of marching companies and militias to freedpeople's notions of freedom. See Rebecca Scott, "'Stubborn and Disposed to Stand Their Ground': Black Militia, Sugar Workers, and the Dynamics of Collective Action in the Louisiana Sugar Bowl, 1863–87," Slavery and Abolition 20, no. 1 (April 1999): 103–26; John Rodrique, *Reconstruction in the Cane Fields*; Hahn, *A Nation Under Our Feet*; Jeffrey Kerr-Ritchie, "Rehearsal for War," *Slavery and Abolition* 6 (2005): 1–34; and Kate Masur, *An Example for All the Land*.
27. "Benjamin C. Truman to Andrew Johnson, April 9, 1866," in *Papers of Andrew Johnson, Vol. 10*, ed. Paul H. Bergeron (Knoxville: University of Tennessee Press, 1989), 384; Testimony of Charles Smith in *Condition of Affairs*: Georgia, vol. 2, 597–601; *BME*, 800. Freedpeople repeated stories similar to Smith's to the investigating committees in the South during the Klan investigation, which are compiled in the *Condition of Affairs*. Klan violence frequently involved sexualized attacks, such as castration, whipping of the genitals, and rape. Freedwomen like Childs often suffered sexual assaults during the Klan attacks or were stripped naked and whipped in front of their husbands and children. See Lisa Cardyn, "Sexual Terror in the Reconstruction South" in Clinton and Silber, *Battle Scars*, 140–67; and Rosen, *Terror in the Heart of Freedom*.
28. Foner and Walker, *Proceedings*, vol. 2, 302; *Loyal Georgian*, February 3, 1855.
29. Cong. Globe, 39th Cong., 1st Sess., (1866), 474, 651, 654, 1621, 1838, 2765, 1182, 1266. Legal scholars such as Akhil Amar have noted how the Reconstruction civil rights debates transformed the legal meaning of the Second Amendment. See Amar, *The Bill of Rights: Creation and Reconstruction* (New Haven, CT: Yale, 2000), 259–265; Stephen Halbrook, *Freedmen, the Fourteenth Amendment, and the Right to Bear Arms, 1866–1876* (Westport, CT: Praeger, 1998); Clayton Cramer, *For Defense of Themselves and the State: The Original Intent and Judicial Interpretation of the Right to Bear Arms* (Westport, CT: Praeger, 1994). Halbrook and Cramer, it should be noted, are part of a very vocal community of scholars who support modern-day gun rights and have a tendency to overstate their case that the framers of the Fourteenth Amendment intended citizens to have unrestricted access to firearms. On this point, see among others Saul Cornell, *A Well Regulated Militia: The Founding Fathers and the Origins of Gun Control in America* (New

York: Oxford University Press, 2006). The best general treatment of the Fourteenth Amendment and the debates over its meaning, whether or not it incorporated the Bill of Rights, and its application to the individual states is Michael Kent Curtis, *No State Shall Abridge: The Fourteenth Amendment and the Bill of Rights* (Durham, NC: Duke University Press, 1986).

30. "Order of General Sickles, January 17, 1866," in *The Political History of the United States during Reconstruction*, 2nd ed., ed. Edward McPherson (New York: Negro Universities Press, 1969), 35–36; Bvt. Brig. Gen. W. Bennet to Capt. Rice, February 27, 1866, Letters and Reports Received Relating to Freedmen and Civil Affairs, RG 393; William Sinclair to Sub. Asst. Comm. at Matagorda, July 25, 1866, Records of the Asst. Comm. for the State of Texas, Letters Sent, 1865–69, RG 105, M821, roll 8.
31. Cong. Globe, 42nd Cong., 1st Sess. (1871), 339.
32. Cong. Globe, 42nd Cong., 1st Session (1871), 337.
33. Cong. Globe, 39th Cong., 1st Sess. (1866), 1073.
34. Carl von Clauswitz, *On War*; Virginia Ingrahm Burr ed., *The Secret Eye: The Journal of Ella Gertrude Clanton Thomas, 1848–1889* (Chapel Hill: University of North Carolina Press, 1990), 298. On the impact of the Civil War on American arms production, see Michael Bellesiles, *Arming America: The Origins of a National Gun Culture* (New York: Soft Skull Press, 2003), 406–429.
35. On the campaign of 1868, see Charles Hubert Coleman, *The Election of 1868:The Democratic Effort to Regain Control* (New York: Columbia University Press, 1933); Joel H. Silbey, *A Respectable Minority: The Democratic Party in the Civil War Era, 1860–1868* (New York: Norton, 1977), 177–236; Richard H. Abbott, *The Republican Party and the South, 1855–1877* (Chapel Hill: University of North Carolina Press, 1986), 173–203; George Rable, *But There Was No Peace: The Role of Violence in the Politics of Reconstruction* (Athens: University of Georgia Press, 1984), 68–80. See also Willima S. McFeeley, *Grant: A Biography* (New York: Norton, 1982); Brooks D. Simpson, *Let Us Have Peace: Ulysses S. Grant and the Politics of War and Reconstruction, 1861–1868* (Chapel Hill: University of North Carolina Press, 1991); and Joan Waugh, *U.S. Grant: American Hero, American Myth* (Chapel Hill: University of North Carolina Press, 2009); Carl Schurz, *Reminiscences*, vol. 3 (New York: McClure, 1907), 286.
36. *New York Times*, October 5, October 12, September 9, October 8, September 27, October 15, October 30, 1868.
37. Rable discusses the changing nature of Southern violence around 1868 in *But There Was No Peace*, 69. *Savannah Morning News*, July 23, September 1, August 4.
38. Reprinted in *Savannah Morning News*, August 17, August 15, August 13. On Democratic expectations, see Coleman, *The Election of 1868*; Silbey, *A Respectable Minority*; Burr, *The Secret Eye*, 298.
39. Burr, *The Secret Eye*, 293–98.
40. *Savannah Morning News*, August 15, September 3; *Atlanta Constitutionalist*,

quoted in Rable, *But There Was No Peace*, 74; *New York Times*, September 25, 1868. On Hill's political career, see E. Merton Coulter, "Alexander H. Stephens Challenges Benjamin H. Hill to a Duel," *GHQ* 56 (Summer 1972): 175–92; and "The New South: Benjamin H. Hill's Speech Before the Alumni of the University of Georgia, 1871," *GHQ* 57 (Summer 1973): 179–99; William W. Freehling and Craig M. Simpson, eds., *Secession Debated: Georgia's Showdown in 1860* (New York: Oxford, 1992); Haywood J. Pearce, Jr., *Benjamin H. Hill, Secession and Reconstruction* (Chicago: University of Chicago Press, 1928).

41. *Savannah Morning News*, August 11. On the role of gender in secession, see McCurry, *Masters of Small Worlds*.
42. Howell Cobb to J. D. Hoover, January 4, 1868, reprinted in *The Correspondence of Robert Toombs, Alexander H. Stephens, and Howell Cobb*, ed. Ulrich B. Phillips (Washington, DC: Government Printing Office, 1913), 691; Edward Pollard, *The Lost Cause Regained*, 58, 15. On Southern "purification" and rebirth, see Rable, *But There Was No Peace*, 63; Wilson, *Baptized in Blood*; Harvey, *Redeeming the South*, 17–44; Foster, *Ghosts of the Confederacy*; Stowell, *Rebuilding Zion*; Blight, *Race and Reunion*, 37–38; Poole, *Never Surrender*.
43. On the memory of Reconstruction, see Bruce Baker, *What Reconstruction Meant: Historical Memory in the American South* (Charlottesville: University of Virginia Press, 2007). On "masterly inactivity" as the white Southerner's early response to Reconstruction prior to 1868, see Perman, *Reunion Without Compromise: The South and Reconstruction, 1865–1868* (New York: Cambridge University Press, 1973), 229–266; Carter, *When the War Was Over: The Failure of Self-Reconstruction in the South, 1865–1867* (Baton Rouge: LSU Press, 1985); Foner, *Reconstruction*, 176–227.
44. Testimony of Caroline Smith, *Condition of Affairs: Georgia*, Part I, 400–402; Testimony of Charles Smith, 600. On the destruction of freedpeople's grassroots organizing in Georgia, see O'Donovan, *Becoming Free in the Cotton South*, 257–63.
45. Silbey, *A Respectable Minority*, 202–203; *New York World*, April 14, 1868; *The Democratic Speaker's Handbook*, 202–7, 213, 187–88, 154–56; Silbey, 209, 191. See also Kirk H. Porter and Donald Johnson, *National Party Platforms* (Urbana: University of Illinois Press, 1956). On the popular press and representations of Southern Reconstruction, see Brown, *Beyond the Lines*. Brown argues that *Frank Leslie's* published contradictory images of Southern blacks, some of which portrayed them in a positive light. However, he also concedes that these images were rare, and moreover, that they often contained elements of racist depictions even when the image in its entirety might be read in a positive light. See *Beyond the Lines*, 112–30.
46. Silbey, *A Respectable Minority*, 313; *The Nation*, August 6, 1868; An Anonymous Writer to Howell Cobb, August 3, 1868 in *The Correspondence of Toombs, Stephens and Cobb*, 702.

47. Rable, *But There Was No Peace*, 59; *New York Tribune*, September 22, 23, 24, 1868.
48. Elaine Parsons, "Klan Skepticism and Denial in Reconstruction-Era Public Discourse," *Journal of Southern History* 7, vol. 1 (February 2011): 64–66.
49. *National Republican* August 15, 1868; Cong. Globe, 39th Cong., 1st Sess., 1209–10, 1316, 1323. Richard Abbott discusses Republican fears that black votes could be trusted in *The Republican Party and the South*, 77–79. See also Richardson, *The Death of Reconstruction*, 63–64.
50. J. W. DeForest, "The Man and Brother," 342; *New York Times*, January 16 and February 2, 1868; *The Nation*, May 19, 1870, February 16, 1869; *Christian Recorder*, September 11, 1869. Heather Cox Richardson explores the growing skepticism among Republicans about the effects of politics on black labor and the links they made between the South's "labor problem" and unrest amongnorthern workers in *The Death of Reconstruction*, 62–64. See also Nancy Cohen and her discussion of the "respectability" issue in *The Reconstruction of American Liberalism*, 72–79.
51. James S. Pike, *The Prostrate State: South Carolina Under Negro Government* (New York: Loring and Mussey, 1935), 47, 17, 225. On Pike and the reception of his work, see Robert Durden, *James Shepherd Pike: Republicanism and the American Negro, 1850–1882* (Durham, NC: Duke University Press, 1957).
52. Pike, *The Prostrate State*, 85, 89.
53. For Republican depictions of "unoffending freedmen," see for example the "Report of the Joint Select Committee to Inquire into the Condition of Affairs in the Late Insurrectionary States," 42nd Cong., 2nd Sess., Sen. Rep. 41 (1872), 21; and *Mississippi in 1875* (also known as the Boutwell Report) (Washington, DC: Government Printing Office, 1876), xv. Historian Kidada E. Williams critiques the tendency to portray black Southerners as passive victims of white violence in "Resolving the Paradox of Our Lynching Fixation: Reconsidering Racialized Violence in the American South after Slavery," *American Nineteenth-Century History* 6, no. 3 (September 2005): 323–50.
54. Richard West, Jr., *Lincoln's Scapegoat General: A Life of Benjamin F. Butler, 1818–1893* (Boston: Houghton Mifflin, 1965), 363.

CHAPTER SIX

1. This is the translation from the Douay-Rheims Catholic Bible as used by Flannery O'Connor in her novel, *The Violent Bear It Away* (New York: Farrar, Straus and Giroux, 1960).
2. Charlest Chestnut, *The Marrow of Tradition* (1905; rpt. 1990); 719.
3. Perman, *Road to Redemption: Southern Politics, 1869–1879*, 2nd ed. (Chapel Hill: University of North Carolina Press, 1985), 69; Foner, *Reconstruction*, 412. See also Peter S. Carmichael, *The Last Generation: Young Virginians in Peace, War, and Reunion* (Chapel Hill: University of North Carolina Press,

2005), 213–36. Carmichael argues that elite Virginians readily embraced the "New South" ethos of economic advancement and modernization while repudiating the "Cavalier" mythology as emblematic of aristocratic indolence and unmanly violence.

4. Burr, *The Secret Eye*, 293–94. On the emasculation of Southern men after the war, see Nina Silber, *The Romance of Reunion: Northerners and the South, 1865–1900* (Chapel Hill: University of North Carolina Press, 1993); LeeAnn Whites, *The Civil War as a Crisis in Gender: Augusta, Georgia, 1860–1890* (Athens: University of Georgia Press, 1995); Bertram Wyatt-Brown, *The Shaping of Southern Culture: Honor, Grace, and War, 1760s–1880s* (Chapel Hill: University of North Carolina Press, 2001); and Nancy Bercaw, *Gendered Freedom: Race, Rights, and the Politics of Household in the Delta, 1861–1875* (Gainesville: University of Florida Press, 2003), 75–93.

5. Foner, *Reconstruction*, 416.

6. C. Vann Woodward, *Origins of the New South, 1877–1913* (Baton Rouge: LSU Press, 1951), 75. On class conflict among Southern whites and the appeal of the Republican Party to yeoman, see also Gordon McKinney, *Southern Mountain Republicans, 1865–1900* (Chapel Hill: University of North Carolina Press Press, 1978); Steven Hahn, *The Roots of Southern Populism: Yeoman Farmers and the Transformation of the Georgia Upcountry* (New York: Oxford, 1983). Nelson, *Iron Confederacies: Southern Railways, Klan Violence, and Reconstruction* (Chapel Hill: University of North Carolina Press, 1999); Dailey, *Before Jim Crow: The Politics of Race in Postemancipation Virginia* (Chapel Hill: University of North Carolina Press, 2000); and Stephen Kantrowitz, *Ben Tillman and the Reconstruction of White Supremacy* (Chapel Hill: University of North Carolina Press, 2000).

7. *Caucasian* [Alexandria, LA], March 28, 1874.

8. Steven Kantrowitz describes Redemption as a struggle over the meaning of white manhood in *Ben Tillman*. Likewise, Scott Poole notices the importance of gendered imagery in South Carolina's Red Shirt campaigns in *Never Surrender: Confederate Memory and Conservatism in the South Carolina Upcountry* (Athens: University of Georgia Press, 2004). See also Jane Dailey's discussion of the gendered opposition to the Readjuster's public school programs in *Before Jim Crow*. My argument also draws upon Bertram Wyatt-Brown's general observations about the psychological effects of defeat on Southern men's honor, which he explores in *The Shaping of Southern Culture: Honor, Grace, and War, 1760s–1880s* (Chapel Hill: University of North Carolina Press, 2001). Cecelia O'Leary coined the term "militaristic patriotism" in her study of post–Civil War patriotic culture, *To Die For*, 8. On the Early Republic and antebellum periods, see Lorri Glover, *Southern Sons: Becoming Men in the New Nation* (Baltimore: Johns Hopkins, 2007); John Mayfield, *Counterfeit Gentlemen: Manhood and Humor in the Old South* (Gainesville: University of Florida Press, 2009); Thomas A Foster, ed., *New Men: Manliness in Early America* (New York: NYU, 2011).

9. Woodward most notably downplays the divisions within the Redeemer elite, emphasizing their middle-class priorities and business/industrial ties. See *Origins*, 1–22. More recently, historians have noted the importance of these divisions and the struggle over leadership among whites. One example is Virginia's Readjuster Party, as chronicled by Dailey in *Before Jim Crow*. See also Kantrowitz, *Ben Tillman*; Cresswell, *Rednecks, Redeemers, and Race: Mississippi After Reconstruction, 1877–1917* (Oxford: University of Mississippi Press, 2006); Perman, *Road to Redemption*.
10. Jackson *Weekly Pilot*, August 8, 1870; Francis Simkins and Robert H. Woody, *South Carolina During Reconstruction* (Chapel Hill: University of North Carolina Press, 1932), 480. On political turmoil among Democrats in Mississippi, see William C. Harris, *The Day of the Carpetbagger: Republican Reconstruction in Mississippi* (Baton Rouge: LSU Press, 1979); Richard N. Current, *Those Terrible Carpetbaggers* (New York: Oxford, 1988); Foner, *Reconstruction*, 558–63; Hahn, *A Nation Under Our Feet*, 297–302. Democratic strife in Louisiana is discussed by Joe Gray Taylor, *Louisiana Reconstructed, 1863–1877* (Baton Rouge: LSU Press, 1974); Current, *Those Terrible Carpetbaggers*; Hahn, *A Nation Under Our Feet*, 292–96; Nystrom, *New Orleans after the Civil War: Race, Politics, and a New Birth of Freedom* (Baltimore: Johns Hopkins, 2010). On Robert Scott and South Carolina, see Singletary, *Black Militia*; Holt, *Black Over White: Negro Political Leadership in South Carolina During Reconstruction* (Urbana: University of Illinois Press, 1979); Current, *Those Terrible Carpetbaggers*; Richard Zuczek, *State of Rebellion: Reconstruction in South Carolina* (Columbia: University of South Carolina Press, 1996).
11. "Address to the White Citizens of St. Martin," [1874] Alexandre DeClouet Papers. Hill Memorial Library, Louisiana State University (LSU).
12. Meridian *Mercury* quoted in Hodding Carter, *Their Words Were Bullets* (1969), 43–44; Natchitoches *People's Vindicator*, July 1874, quoted in 43rd Cong. 2nd Sess., House Rep. 261, pt. 3, "Louisiana Affairs," 760; *Caucasian*, May 2, 1874; *Shreveport Times*, July 29, 1874; *Morning Star & Catholic Messenger*, June 14, 1874; and New Orleans *Picayune*, August 27, 1874, all quoted in "Louisiana Affairs," 765, 770–71. On the Louisiana White Leagues, see also Joel Gray Taylor, *Louisiana Reconstructed*, 279–86; Oscar Lestage, "The White League in Louisiana and Its Participation in Reconstruction Riots," *La. Hist. Q.* 18 (1935): 617–95.
13. On the uses of paramilitary enforcers by the Fire-eaters in 1860–61, see McCurry, *Confederate Reckoning*, 47–49.
14. *The Caucasian*, August 1, September 5, 1874; *Mansfield Reporter*, July 4, 1874, quoted in "Louisiana Affairs," 772. Oscar Lestage discusses the White League's predecessors, such as ward clubs, in "The White League in Louisiana," 628. See also Nystrom, *New Orleans After the Civil War*. On the Klans' carnivalesque attributes, see Elaine Franz Parsons, "Midnight Rangers: Costume and Performance in the Reconstruction-Era Ku Klux Klan," *JAH* (December 2005): 811–36. Even in places like Virginia, where

white paramilitarism never took hold, the problem of white manhood still infused Reconstruction-era politics. For instance, opponents of the bi-racial Readjuster movement labeled them "political hermaphrodites." See Dailey, *Before Jim Crow*, 141–46.
15. Franklin [La.] *Enterprise*, quoted in "Louisiana Affairs," 757.
16. Morgan, *Yazoo; Or, On the Picket Line of Freedom in the South* (rpt. Columbia: University of South Carolina Press, 2000), 454. The Carolina Rifle Club based in Charleston listed its official mission as "the promotion of social intercourse an the enjoyment of the members by means of target shooting and such other amusements as they may see fit to determine." Records of the Carolina Rifle Club, South Carolina Historical Society (SCHS). See also Louisa McCord Smith Recollections, in A. T. Smythe Papers, Rene Jervey, "A History of the South Carolina Rifle Club and Carolian Rifle Batallion," and South Carolina Rifle Club Minutes, SCHS; George S. Homes to Mary L. Burckmyer, Aug, 9, 1876, in Homes Family Papers, SCHS; and "Constitution and Rules of the Richland Rifle Club," SCL. On the policing activities of urban paramilitaries see George S. Holmes to Mary L. Burckmyer, September 2 and 28, 1876, in Holmes Family Papers, SCHS; "Recollections of Louisa Rebecca Hayne McCord," South Carolina Library (SCL); Simkins and Woody, *South Carolina During Reconstruction*, 509.
17. "Louisiana Affairs," 778; "Plan of the Campaign," Gary Papers, SCL; C. J. C. Huston Papers, SCHS; "Vicksburgh Troubles," 42nd Congress, 2nd Session, H. Rep. no. 265 (1875), iii, vii, 19, 21, 52, 74, 377; Capt. Arthur W. Allyn to Maj. Edward R. Platt, December 5, 1874, in in John Y. Simon, ed., *The Papers of Ulysses S. Grant*, vol. 25: 1874 (Carbondale: SIU Press, 2003), 307; Morgan, *Yazoo*, 461.
18. Williams, *Hampton and His Red Shirts: South Carolina's Deliverance in 1876* (Charleston: Walker, Evans and Cogswell, 1935), 64–65; Morgan, *Yazoo*, 101.
19. W. H. Hardy, "Recollections of Reconstruction in East and Southeast Mississippi," *Publications of the Mississippi Historical Society* 7 (1903), 207; Jervey, "A History of the Carolina Rifle Club." On the Confederate leadership of the White Leagues, see James Hogue, "The 1873 Battle of Colfax: Paramilitarism and Counterrevolution in Louisiana," available online at http://warhistorian.org/hogue-colfax.pdf, as well as his longer study *Uncivil War: Five New Orleans Street Battles and the Rise and Fall of Radical Reconstruction* (Baton Rouge: LSU Press, 2006). See also Scott Poole, *Never Surrender*. In Virginia, controversies over politicians' Confederate war records characterized the struggle between the Funders and Readjusters in the late 1870s and 1880s. On this see Jane Dailey, *Before Jim Crow*; and Amy Feely Morsman, *The Big House After Slavery: Virginia Plantation Families and Their Postbellum Domestic Experiment* (Charlottesville: UVA, 2010), 138–39; and Kevin Levin, "William Mahone, the Lost Cause, and Civil War History," *Va. Mag. of Hist. & Bio.* 113, no. 4 (2005): 378–412.

20. Williams, *Hampton and His Red Shirts*, 38, 310; Roberty Lowry and W. H. McCardle, *A History of Mississippi* (New York: AMS Press, 1974 [1891]), 391; John R. Abney to Eugene B. Gary, December 17, 1923, in Gary Papers, SCL; J. M. Gibson, *Memoirs of J. M. Gibson: Terrors of the Civil War and Reconstruction Days* (1966), 71; George S. Holmes to Mary L. Burckmyer, September 2, 1876, in Holmes Family Papers, SCHS.
21. *People's Vindicator*, quoted in "Louisiana Affairs," 758–59; W. W. Ball, *A Boy's Recollections of the Red Shirt Campaign of 1876 in South Carolina* (Columbia: The State Co., 1911), 21; Henry Tazewell Thompson, *Ousting the Carpetbagger from South Carolina* (New York: Negro Universities Press, 1969), 116; Gibson, *Memoirs*, 75; Williams, *Hampton and His Red Shirts*, 174.
22. *Caucasian*, May 23, 1874; Ball, *A Boy's Recollections*, 10–11; Edmund Drago, *Hurrah for Hampton! Black Red Shirts in South Carolina During Reconstruction* (Fayetteville: University of Arkansas Press, 1998), 97, 103; Francis Butler Simkins and Robert H. Woody, *South Carolina During Reconstruction* (Chapel Hill: University of North Carolina Press, 1932), 498.
23. Pickens *Sentinel*, September 14, 1876; John A. Leland, A Voice from South Carolina (Charleston: Walker, Evans and Cogswell, 1879), 163; Henry T. Thompson, *Ousting the Carpetbagger from South Carolina* (New York: Negro University Press, 1969), 116–17; Simkins and Woody, *South Carolina During Reconstruction*, 497; Poole, *Never Surrender*, 135; Morgan, *Yazoo*, 454; Gibson, *Memoirs*, 73; Carol Wells, ed., *War, Reconstruction, and Redemption on Red River: The Memoirs of Dosia Williams Moore* (Ruston, LA: Louisiana Tech, 1990), 70–71.
24. McCurry, *Confederate Reckoning*, 94–95. Jane Dailey also stresses the "rhetorical link between black suffrage and interracial sex" that tied political rights to manhood and the protection of women in *Before Jim Crow*, 87–107; *Caucasian*, July 11, 1874; Morgan, *Yazoo*, 437–40. See also Wharton, *The Negro in Mississippi*, 190. On the ways that narratives of black crime functioned in Reconstruction politics, see Rosen, *Terror in the Heart of Freedom*, 40–44 and Martha Hodes, "The Sexualization of Reconstruction Politics." For a non-American comparison, Jonathan Glassman discusses the importance of rumor, specifically crime rumors, in the process of inciting mass racial violence in *War of Words, War of Stones: Racial Thought and Violence in Colonial Zanzibar* (Bloomington: Indiana University Press, 2011), 179–229.
25. Wolfgang Shivelbush, *The Culture of Defeat: On National Trauma, Mourning, and Recovery* (New York: Henry Holt and Co., 2001), 97.
26. *Forest Register*, September 15, 1875, quoted in Wharton, *The Negro in Mississippi*, 184.
27. *Jackson Times*, June 8, 1875, quoted in Harris, *Day of the Carpetbagger*, 650–51; Edward Mayes, ed., *Lucius Q. C. Lamar: His Life and Speeches, 1825–93*, 2nd ed. (Nashville: Methodist Episcopal Church, 1896), 258–59; "Intimidation," n.d., clipping in Gary Papers, SCL. Wharton, *The Negro in Mississippi*, 184; "Plan of the Campaign," Gary Papers, SCL.

28. *Jackson Clarion*, quoted in Wharton, The Negro in Mississippi, 193; Williams, *Hampton and His Red Shirts*, 90–91; Drago, *Hurrah for Hampton!*, 113–14.
29. Taylor, *Louisiana Reconstructed*, 285–86; Lestage, "The White League in Louisiana," 653–56. James Hogue discussed the White League's claims to "spontaneity" and representations of popular will in *Uncivil War*, 133. These forced resignations also fit patterns in Mississippi, as discussed in Morgan, *Yazoo*, 467–88; Wharton, *The Negro in Mississippi*, 181–98; Harris, *Day of the Carpetbagger*, 650–90. See also "Vicksburgh Troubles," 42nd Cong., 2nd Sess., H. Rep. 265, 1875. My reading here of the spectacular and theatrical aspects of Reconstruction violence draws heavily on Amy Louise Wood's insights into the production of lynching spectacles in the later decades of the nineteenth century. While Wood sees these highly ritualized events that made witnessing an active form of participation, drawing in large portions of the white community into the violence, as exemplary of late nineteenth and early twentieth century anxieties, I see many similarities with Reconstruction-era violence. See Wood, *Lynching and Spectacle*.
30. Scott Poole discusses the pageantry and the importance of the Lost Cause to the Red Shirts in *Never Surrender*, 116–35. See also Drago, *Hurrah for Hampton*; Simkins and Woody, *South Carolina During Reconstruction*, 496–97; Williams, *Hampton and His Red Shirts*; Ball, *A Boy's Recollections*, 9–11; Walt Whitman, "The Most Inspiriting of All War's Shows," in *Specimen Days*, reprinted in *Whitman: Poetry and Prose* (New York: Library of America, 1982), 728.
31. The best accounts of the Battle of Liberty Place include James Hogue, *Uncivil War*, 116–43; Lawrence N. Powell, "Reinventing Tradition: Liberty Place, Historical Memory, and Silk-stocking Vigilantism in New Orleans Politics," *Slavery and Abolition* 20, no. 1 (1999): 127–49; Taylor, *Louisiana Reconstructed*, 291–96. See also Justin Nystrom, *New Orleans After the Civil War*. Several other accounts written in the twentieth century by writers sympathetic to the CCWL include Frank L. Richardson, "My Recollections of the Battle of the Fourteenth of September, 1874," *La. His. Q.* 3 (1920): 498–501; W. O. Hart, "History of Events Leading Up to the Battle of Liberty Place," *La. His. Q.* 7 (1924): 571–95; Walter Prichard, "Origin and Activities of the 'White League' in New Orleans," *La. His. Q.* (Spring 1940): 525–43; Stuart Omar Landry, The Battle of Liberty Place: The Overthrow of Carpetbag Rule in New Orleans, September 14, 1874 (New Orleans: Pelican, 1955).
32. Hogue, *Uncivil War*, 132–33.
33. Ibid., 136–38.
34. "Meeting of the Citizens of the 7th Ward, Parish of Taugipahoa . . . September 17, 1874," in E. John, Thomas C. W. Ellis and Family Papers, LSU; Frederick Nash Ogden Scrapbook, Folder 14, Howard-Tilton Memorial Library, Tulane University; New Orleans *Picayune*, September 20, 1874, quoted in Landry, *The Battle of Liberty Place*; Morehouse Clarion quoted in "Louisiana Affairs," 765–66; "Address of Dr. J. Dickson Bruns," Ogden Scrapbook.

35. Primo Levi, *The Drowned and the Saved* (New York: Vintage, 1989), 106, 126. The best treatments of the Colfax Massacre are Taylor, *Louisiana Reconstructed*; Hahn, *A Nation Under Our Feet*; LeeAnna Keith, *The Colfax Massacre: The Untold Story of Black Power, White Terror, and the Death of Reconstruction* (New York: Oxford University Press, 2008); and Charles Lane, *The Day Freedom Died: The Colfax Massacre, the Supreme Court, and the Betrayal of Reconstruction* (New York: Henry Holt and Company, 2008).
36. Provost Marshall R. C. Loveridge to the Headquarters of the Post at Fernandina, Florida," 2 June 1865 reprinted in *Freedom: A Documentary History of Emancipation, 1861–1867. Series 3: Volume I, Land and Labor, 1865* (Chapel Hill: University of North Carolina Press, 2008), 89 (Hereafter cited as *Land and Labor*); Ann Pope to Rosa Biddle, 1865, Samuel Simpson Biddle Papers, DU; Testimony of Judge John C. Underwood, *JCR*, Part II, 14. "Genocidal fantasies" is a common term used by scholars in Holocaust Studies, as well as Indigenous and Post-colonial Studies, to describe the effects of white racial ideology and its exterminationist tendencies, both physical and cultural, toward nonwhite peoples across the world. Thavolia Glymph also uses the term in the context of American emancipation in *Out of the House of Bondage*, 166.
37. Mary Jones in her journal, January 11, 1865; reprinted in *The Children of Pride: A True Story of Georgia and the Civil War*, vol. 2, ed. Robert Manson Myers (New York: Popular Library, 1972), 1244. Jones attributes the desire to "blow their brains out" to "the Yankees" whom she believes hold as much if not more contempt for blacks as their former masters.
38. Testimony of George S. Smith, *JCR*, Part II, p. 16.
39. *National Anti-Slavery Standard*, June 3 and 17, 1865. See also issues for the month of July for additional reports of Southern atrocities. Rosen, *Terror in the Heart of Freedom*, 181, 189. Thavolia Glymph also theorizes white violence as an emotional response to emancipation that defies "rationalist" explanations. See Glymph, *Out of the House of Bondage*, 44. See also Amy Louise Wood, *Lynching and Spectacle*.
40. Jonathan Glassman, *War of Words, War of Stones: Racial Thought and Violence in Colonial Zanzibar* (Bloomington: Indiana University Press, 2011), 256; "Louisiana Affairs," 4, 415, 417. See also Lane, *The Day Freedom Died*.
41. "Louisiana Affairs," 414; Glassman, *War of Words, War of Stones*, 233.
42. The Coushatta Massacre is chronicled in Ted Tunnel, *Edge of the Sword: The Ordeal of Carpetbagger Marshall H. Twitchell in the Civil War and Reconstruction* (Baton Rouge: LSU Press, 2001).
43. The case would eventually make it to the Supreme Court, which stripped the federal governments of its enforcement powers with regard to civil rights. See *United States v. Cruikshank*, 92 U.S. 542 (1876).
44. "Louisiana Affairs," 771–72; Morgan, *Yazoo*, 448. On how violence creates collective subjectivities, see Glassman, *War of Words, War of Stones*, 234.

45. "Louisiana Affairs," 763, 760, 758, 761, 772, 765, 764, 382, 314; John R. Lynch, *The Facts of Reconstruction* (New York: Arno, 1968), 119–22.
46. *Yazoo Democrat*, September 28, 1875; *Forest Register*, September 28, 1875, quoted in Warren A. Ellem, "The Overthrow of Reconstruction in Mississippi," *J. of Miss. His.* 54, no 2 (1992); Charles Nordhoff, *The Cotton South in the Spring and Summer of 1875*, 77; 175–201; "Louisiana Affairs," 312, 314.
47. "Louisiana Affairs," 772.
48. Wharton, *The Negro in Mississippi*, 184–85; Edward Mayes, ed., *Lucius Q. C. Lamar: His Life, Times, and Speeches, 1825–1893* (Nashville: Methodist Episcopal Church South, 1896), 211–12; *The Caucasian*, July 4, 1874. One the difficulties white Democrats like Lamar and Hampton had in managing violence and spinning northern perceptions of it, see Kantrowitz, *Ben Tillman*, 91–98; Rod Andrew, Jr., *Wade Hampton: Confederate Warrior to Southern Redeemer* (Chapel Hill: University of North Carolina Press, 2008); E. Culpepper Clark, *Frances Warrington Dawson and the Politics of Restoration: South Carolina, 1874–1889* (Tuscaloosa: University of Alabama Press, 1980), 53–70; Rable, *But There Was No Peace*, 150–55. On the black Red Shirts see Drago, *Hurrah for Hampton!*
49. [Signature unreadable] to Tom C. W. Ellis, September 18, 1874, in Ellis Family Papers, LSU; *Caucasian*, July 4, 1874.
50. On the history of the unit, see Newton B. Jones, "The Washington Light Infantry at the Bunker Hill Centennial," *South Carolina Historical Magazine* 65 (October 1964): 195–204.
51. *Charleston News and Courier*, June 12, 14, 18, 19, 1875; *Boston Post*, June 17, 1875; Jones, "The Washington Light Infantry," 197–99.
52. *Boston Post*, June 18, 19, 1875; Jones, "The Washington Light Infantry," 200–201.
53. "Louisiana Affairs," 759; Emberton, "The Limits of Incorporation."
54. On the erasure of black veterans from Civil War memorials, see Savage, *Standing Soldiers, Kneeling Slaves*. Cynthia O'Leary discusses the role of patriotism in sectional reunification in *To Die For*. On the Philadelphia Centennial Fair, see Robert W. Rydell, *All the World's A Fair* (Chicago: University of Chicago Press, 1984), 28–29.
55. *Charleston News and Courier*, June 22, 1875; Thompson, *Ousting the Carpetbagger*, 70.
56. Testimony of Doc Adams in "South Carolina in 1876," 44th Cong., 2nd Sess. (1876), 34–35.
57. Adams testimony, 35–37.
58. Adams testimony, *South Carolina in 1876*, 63.
59. Adams testimony, 63.
60. Testimony of Doc Adams, 47; Simkins and Woody, *South Carolina during Reconstruction*, 480–83, 488–89; *Charleston News and Courier*, July 28, 1876.
61. Williams, *Hampton and His Red Shirts*, 63, 172, 3400, 134.
62. Philip Sheridan to Secretary of War Belknap, January 4, 1875. Philip H.

Sheridan Papers. Library of Congress. Washington, DC (Hereafter cited as Sheridan Papers).

63. Printed in the *Chicago Tribune*, January 2, 1875. On local reaction to the telegram, see also Ella Lonn, *Reconstruction in Louisiana after 1868* (New York: Putnam, 1918), 298–301; and Joel Gray Taylor, *Louisiana Reconstructed*, 306–7.
64. Sheridan dismissed the attempts to discredit him by saying "there have been too many bleeding negroes and white citizens for their statement to be believed by fair-minded people." Sheridan to Belknap, January 7, 1875. Sheridan Papers.
65. *New York Times*, January 7, 1875.
66. *Hartford Daily Courant*, January 7, 9, 1875. In 1874, the *Courant* published a letter from Alabama Republican congressman Charles Hays describing a number of political assassinations in his district, which ignited a controversy over the veracity of his claims. Alabama Democrats denied the charges, citing Hays's inability to produce any evidence of those murders. They claimed that Hays and Republican papers like the *Courant* fabricated an "outrage mill" to discredit their political opponents and invite federal intervention in order to assure their power in local offices. See William Warren Rogers, "Reconstruction Journalism: The *Hays-Hawley Letter*," *American Journalism* 6 (Fall 1989): 235–44.
67. Reports of these meetings of prominent clergymen, politicians, and business leaders featured prominently in northern newspapers as evidence of the inappropriateness of Sheridan's dispatch and the North's unwillingness to support federal military intervention in the South any longer. See for instance the *New York Times*, January 6, 7, 9, 10, 1875; *Chicago Tribune*, January 5, 6, 9, 1875.
68. Simon, ed., *Grant Papers*, vol. 26: 19–20.
69. See *Grant Papers*, vol. 26: 22, 25.
70. Shurz and Bryant quoted in Paul Andrew Hutton, *Phil Sheridan and His Army* (Lincoln: University of Nebraska Press, 1985), 268; *New York Times*, January 7, 1875; *Chicago Tribune*, January 9, 1875. Philip Sheridan to Orville Babcock, January 24, 1875. Philip Sheridan Papers, Library of Congress.
71. C. Vann Woodward, *Reunion and Reaction: The Compromise of 1877 and the End of Reconstruction* (New York: Oxford, 1966), 110–12; *New York Tribune*, January 7, 1877.

EPILOGUE

1. "An Attempt to Create a Riot." Clipping. Nash Scrapbook.
2. On black political mobilization in Natchez, see Justin Behrend, *Reconstructing Democracy: African Americans in the Making of Democracy in the Post–Civil War South* (Athens: University of Georgia Press, forthcoming). Kidada E. Williams discusses black resistance to white violence in *They Left Great*

Marks on Me. On the Redeemers' continued reliance on political fraud, see Hahn, *A Nation Under Our Feet*, 312–13.

3. Fitzhugh Brundage suggests a linkage between Reconstruction violence and later acts of mob violence in *Lynching in the New South: Georgia and Virginia, 1880–1930* (Urbana: University of Illinois Press, 1993). Other recent works explore the connections across both space and time, such as Christopher Waldrep, *The Many Faces of Judge Lynch: Extralegal Violence and Punishment in America* (New York: Palgrave, 2002); William Carrigan, *The Making of Lynching Culture: Violence and Vigilantism in Central Texas, 1836–1915* (Urbana: University of Illinois Press, 2006); and Michael J. Pfeifer, *Rough Justice: Lynching and American Society, 1874–1947* (Urbana: University of Illinois Press, 2004).

4. B. R. Tillman, *The Struggles of 1876* (n.p., 1909), 2, 29. See also Kantrowitz, *Ben Tillman*; and Baker, *What Reconstruction Meant*.

5. Lawrence Powell, "Reinventing Tradition: Liberty Place, Historical Memory, and Silk-Stocking Vigilantism in New Orleans," *Slavery and Abolition* 20 (April 1999): 127–49.

6. J. H. McNeilly to the editor of the *Confederate Veteran*, 1916, in *Confederate Veteran* Papers, Duke University Special Collections. McNeilly's letter was a response to the critique offered by the expatriate Tennessean living in Canada, which he included with his editorial. McNeilly took issue with the Canadian's dismissal of the film, arguing that he didn't understand the true nature of Reconstruction or the Klan. McNeilly reported to have been an original member of the Klan in Tennessee. On the backlash against the film, see Melvyn Stokes, *D. W. Griffith's "The Birth of a Nation": A History of the Most Controversial Film of All Time* (New York: Oxford University Press, 2008).

7. Raiford, *Imprisoned in a Luminous Glare*. "Unfinished revolution" refers to the subtitle of Eric Foner's standard on the period, *Reconstruction: America's Unfinished Revolution*. See also Timothy B. Tyson, *Radio Free Dixie: Robert F. Williams and the Roots of Black Power* (Chapel Hill: University of North Carolina Press, 1999); Lance Hill, *The Deacons for Defense: Armed Resistance and the Civil Rights Movement* (Chapel Hill: University of North Carolina Press, 2004); David Fort Godshalk, *Veiled Visions: The Atlanta Race Riot and the Reshaping of American Race Relations* (Chapel Hill: University of North Carolina Press, 2005); Chrystal Feimster, *Southern Horrors: Women and the Politics of Rape and Lynching* (Cambridge, MA: Harvard University Press, 2009); Danielle McGuire, *The Dark End of the Street: Black Women, Rape, and Resistance; A New History of the Civil Rights Movement from Rosa Parks to the Rise of Black Power* (New York: Vintage, 2010); and most recently, Kidada Williams, *They Left Great Marks on Me*.

8. *Christian Recorder*, May 1, 1873.

9. Jacqueline Jones Royster, ed., *Southern Horrors and Other Writings: The Anti-Lynching Campaign of Ida B. Wells, 1892–1900* (Boston: Bedford Books, 1997), 81.

10. Charles Chesnutt, *The Marrow of Tradition,* in Henry Louis Gates, Jr., ed., *Three Classic African-American Novels* (New York: Vintage, 1990), 492, 678.
11. Woodward, *Origins of the New South,* 324–25; William McKinley, *Speeches and Addresses* (New York: Doubleday, 1900), 370. For more on Chesnutt's anti-imperialism, see Harilaos Stecopoulos, *Reeconstructing the World: Southern Fictions and U.S. Imperialisms, 1898–1976* (Ithaca: Cornell University Press, 2008); and Gunning, *Rape, Race, and Lynching.*
12. Frederick Douglass, "The Fate of the Negro," in *Life and Writings,* vol. 4, 411–13. On the relationship between imperialism and black manhood, see Michele Mitchell, *Righteous Propagation: African Americans and the Politics of Racial Destiny after Reconstruction* (Chapel Hill: University of North Carolina Press, 2004), 51–75.
13. Ida B. Wells, *The Red Record* (1892), 77; *Colored Tribune,* April 8, 1876; Kidada E. Williams, "Resolving the Paradox of Our Lynching Fixation: Reconsidering Racialized Violence in the American South after Slavery," *American Nineteenth-Century History* 6, no. 3 (September 2005): 323–50. See also Williams's longer work, cited above. On black masculinity at the turn of the century, see Mitchell, *Righteous Propagation,* and Theresa Runstedtler, "The New Negro's Brown Brother: African American and Filipino Boxers and the 'Rising Tide of Color,'" in *Escape from New York: The 'Harlem Renaissance' Reconsidered,* ed. Davarian Baldwin and Minkah Makalani (Minneapolis: University of Minnesota Press, forthcoming).
14. James Cobb, "Reflections on the Politics of Regional and National Identity at the Millenium," *JSH* 66, no. 1 (February 2000): 5. On the killings of Michael Griffith and Tyisha Miller, see "Koch Comments on 'Deep South' Angers Mayors," *New York Times,* 25 December 1986; "Officers' Killing of Woman Leads to Dispute Over Facts and Motives," *New York Times,* 30 December 1998. Both events also discussed by Larry Griffith in "Southern Distinctiveness, Yet Again, or Why Americans Still Need the South," *Southern Cultures* (September 2000): 57–59. On the spread of "Southern values," some good and some not so good, including but not limited to racism and racial violence, see Stephen Cummings, *The Dixiefication of America: The American Odyssey in the Conservative Economic Trap* (Westport, CT: Praeger, 1998); Peter Applebome, *Dixie Rising: How the South is Shaping American Values, Politics, and Culture* (New York: Times Books, 1996); and Earl and Merle Black, *The Rise of Southern Republicans* (Cambridge, MA: Belknap Press, 2003).
15. Griffith, "Southern Distinctiveness," 59; George Brown Tindall, *The Benighted South: Origins of a Modern Image* (Charlottesville: University of Virginia, 1964). See also Sheldon Hackney, "The Contradictory South," *Southern Cultures* 7, no. 4 (Winter 2001): 65–80. For more recent work taking on the idea of Southern exceptionalism see Matthew D. Lassiter and Joseph Crespino, eds., *The Myth of Southern Exceptionalism* (New York: Oxford, 2010). See also Leigh Ann Duck, *The Nation's Region: Southern Modernism, Segregation, and U.S. Nationalism* (Athens: University of Georgia Press, 2006).

16. Griffith, "Southern Distinctiveness," 70.
17. On the white Americans' ambivalence toward revolutionary violence, see R. Blakeslee Gilpin, *John Brown Still Lives! America's Long Reckoning with Violence, Equality, and Change* (Chapel Hill: University of North Carolina Press, 2011). Gilpin argues that in the case of John Brown, even America's commitment to revolutionary violence for whites was compromised when a white man initiated a violent revolution in the name of racial justice. On the persistence of institutional racism and violence, see Michelle Alexander, *The New Jim Crow: Mass Incarceration in the Age of Colorblindness* (New York: New Press, 2010).
18. For a detailed description and history of the memorial, see its website: http://www.mlkmemorial.org/.
19. "Weighing Race and Hate in a Mississippi Killing," *New York Times*, August 22, 2011. In March 2012, the driver of the truck and two others present at the murder pleaded guilty to the charges. Mississippi authorities continue to investigate the case, and the possibility of bringing charges against other "co-conspirators" remains. See "Three Plead Guilty to Hate Crimes in Killing of Black Man in Mississippi," *New York Times*, March 22, 2012.
20. "Weighing Race and Hate in a Mississippi Killing," *New York Times*, August 22, 2011. On criticism of *The Help*, see the open statement by the Association of Black Women Historians: http://www.abwh.org/index.php?option=com_content&view=article&id=2:open-statement-the-help&catid=1:latest-news.
21. Interview with Clara Allen, *Weevils in the Wheat*, 8; James Baldwin, "Of the Sorrow Songs: The Cross of Redemption," in *The Cross of Redemption: Uncollected Writings*, ed. Randal Kenan (New York: Pantheon Books, 2010), 124.

Index

Page numbers in italics refer to figures.

abolitionism: black abolitionist writers and, 246–47n5; black soldiers and, 108–9, 113, 125–26; black suffrage and, 145; black women abolitionists and, 110–11; bloody imagery and, 109–10; fantasies of rebellion and, 248n13; literature of, 40; martial manhood and, 140; Nat Turner versus Uncle Tom and, 111–16; "negro hate" and, 70; passivity of slaves and, 108, 109–10; universal personhood and, 86; unmanning of enslaved men and, 109–11; "white manism" of, 18
Adams, Doc, 196–97
Adams, John, 143
Adams, Samuel, 136
Adamson, Frank, 178
AFIC. *See* American Freedman's Inquiry Commission (AFIC)
Africa, racial violence in, 188
African Americans: bodily markers of inequality and, 55; centennial celebrations and, 194, 195; continued struggles of, against white violence, 207; control over representations of own suffering and, 210; docility versus rebelliousness of, 166–67; double standard for, 168; emigration by, 212; as feminine people, 109; habeas corpus and, 23; martyrdom versus self-defense for, 214; objectification of, in images of suffering, 52; as object of pity, 55; passivity of, required for sympathy, 52; politics of suffering for, 5, 223n11; preferential treatment and, 57; protection and dependency and, 69; redemption of black manhood and, 213; religious practice of, 4; stereotypes of, 32, 87; subaltern political culture of, 4. *See also* black conventions; black elected officials; black militias; black soldiers; freeborn blacks; freedpeople
Agassiz, Louis, 66
agriculture, freedpeople and, 59, 78
Alcorn, James Lusk, 64
Alcott, Louisa May, 36–37, 55, 115
Allen, Clara, 95, 98, 216
Allen, William, 112
Amar, Akhil, 256–57n29
American Equal Rights Association, 86
American Freedman's Inquiry Commission (AFIC), 66, 113, 115–18, 119
American Indians, 4, 71, 210, 212
American Revolution: black soldiers in, 108, 119; civic millennialism and, 221–22n4; freedom and violent resistance and, 106; as inspiration for white supremacists,

271

INDEX

American Revolution (*cont.*)
  201, 208; legitimation of violence and, 194–95; right to vote and, 142–43; sectional reunification and, 194
Ames, Adelbert, 54, 166, 181–82
Anderson, Claude, 96
Anderson, James Craig, 215, 270n20
Andrew, John, 121
Andrews, Sidney, 80
anthropology, responses to violence and, 7
Argentina, 211
Arnold, Isaac, 21
Associated Press, election of 1868 and, 161
atonement: atonement trials, 3, 213; in Christian theology, 4; Civil War as, 18–19; emancipation and, 21; Lincoln's assassination and, 16; moral suasion and, 17; radical Reconstruction and, 3–4; redemption and, 216; rituals of redemption and, 24–25
Attucks, Crispus, 108

Babcock, Orville, 203
Badger, A. S., 185
Baker, Jean, 142
Baldwin, James, 216
Ball, William, 178, 183–84
Banks, John, 122
Barber, Ed, 178
Bates, Edward, 119
"Battle Hymn of the Republic" (song), 228n23
Baynton, Douglas, 242n30
Beckwith, J. R., 188
Beecher, Henry Ward, 130–31, 145
Bercaw, Nancy, 240n19
Berry, Mary Frances, 105
Bhabba, Homi, 8
Birth of a Nation (film), 209, 268n6
Black Codes, 23–24, 45, 85
black conventions: apocalyptic redemptive vision and, 128–130; citizenship and military service and, 127–28, 131; Congressional testimony and, 52–53; male leadership and, 131–32; petitions to Congress from, 150; right to vote and, 128
black elected officials: candidates for office and, 91; caricature of, 164; in Louisiana, 160, 183; in South Carolina, 164–65, 172, 196; white desertion of, 190
black militias: attempts to form, 87–92; black leadership and, 135; in caricature of black legislators, 164; centennial celebrations and, 195–96; elections and, 156, 172; end of Reconstruction and, 195–97; importance of, 243n34; martial culture and, 101; men and women in, 243n34; racial emasculation of white men and, 169; survival of Reconstruction and, 105; varied duties of, 149; white supremacist press and, 179–80. *See also* black soldiers

black soldiers: in American Revolution, 108, 119; American West and, 213; black masculinity and, 105; burning of Darien, Georgia, and, 114–15; as cannon fodder, 125–26, 134; centennial celebrations and, 194, 195; as Christlike characters, 128; civil and political rights for, 127–28; coercion and violence in military and, 105; commanders of, 114–15, 120; Confederate forces and, 123, 249n27; control over, 112–13; controversy over, in Civil War, 111–12, 115–16; cost of freedom and, 134; discipline of military life and, 116; families of, 116, 133–34; fealty versus ferocity of, 131; gun ownership and, 147, 255n23; as hardened, 113, 115; images of, 102–4, *103*; impressment of, 121–25; legal status of, 105; limitations of martial manhood and, 104–5, 120; manly duty of taking white lives and, 108; manumission and, 119; Massachusetts 54th Regiment and, 114, 121, 194; menial duties and, 120, *121*; of mixed race, 115–16; numbers of, 126; political rituals and, 89–90; racial emasculation of white men and, 169; recruitment of, 107, 112, 120–21, 165; revolutionary violence threatened by, 130; rights-talk of, 119; right to vote and, 138–140; savagery of army life and, 120–22; spirituality of, 22–23, 113; unfair treatment of, 120; in War of 1812, 119. *See also* black militias
Blackstone, William, 143
Blair, Frank, 154, 161, 254–55n17
Booman, Erasmus, 90
Booth, John Wilkes, 11–12, 203
Bourdieu, Pierre, 233n6
Boutwell, George, 163
Bragg, Braxton, 186
Bram, Henry, 73–74

Britain. *See* Great Britain
Brooks, Preston, 194
Brown, Elsa Barkley, 150–51n52, 243n34
Brown, John, 110, 111, 114, 135, 270n18
Brown, Kathleen, 55
Brown, Orlando, 61
Brown, William Wells, 109, 134
Brownlow, William G., 160
Brown's Ferry killings, 49
Bryant, William Cullen, 203–4
Bullock, Rufus, 156, 161–62, 203
Burgh, James, 143
Burke, Edmund, 36, 37
Burton, Vernon, 13–14
Burwell, Hester Ann, 80–81
Butler, Benjamin, 166
Butler, Matthew C., 174
Butler, M. C., 197
Butler, R. J., 196

Camp, Stephanie, 240n16
Canby, Edward, 177
capital punishment, 12–13, 26
Caribbean, labor control in, 224n13
Carmichael, Peter S., 259–260n3
Catholic Messenger (periodical), 173
Caucasian (newspaper), 170, 174, 179
centennial celebrations, 171, 192–96, 198–99, 201
Chamberlain, Daniel, 174–75, 182, 193, 195, 197
Chaney, Ben, 2, 216
Chaney, James Earl, 1–2, 216
Chesnutt, Charles, 168, 210, 212
Chicago Tribune, Philip Sheridan and, 204
Chikunda (southern Africa), 118
children: men's military service and, 133–34; men's protective authority over, 132; orphanages and, 89–90; vulnerability of, 77
Childs, Rhoda Ann, 150
Chile, 211
Chilton, Sarah, 186
Christian Recorder (periodical), 144, 164, 210
Christian theology: language of redemptive suffering and, 22–23; Redeemers' civic millennialism and, 221–22n4; redemption in, 3, 16
cities and urbanization, 79, 239–240n15
citizenship: as abstract, universal notion, 86–87; Bible, bayonet, and ballot, 130;

birthright, 23; dependency and, 69; *Dred Scott* decision and, 86–87, 108, 119, 143; economic versus political, 132; freedpeople's claims on government and, 83; freedpeople's worthiness of, 166–67; historical narrative of vulnerability and, 87; individual rights and, 119–120; manhood and, 8–9; meaning of, 24, 105, 119; military service and, 104–6, 108, 117–19, 126–27, 135; pity versus, 55; protection and, 75; right to bear arms and, 161–62, 167; right to vote and, 167; self-ownership and, 86; social, 57; Southern violence and, 188; voting as defining action of, 141–42, 143–44; whites as idealized public body and, 87; women and, 86, 131–32
civil rights: anthems of, 73; atonement trials and, 213; dangers of withholding, 34; federal enforcement powers and, 265n43; foundations of, 76; images of suffering undermining, 52; long movement for, 2, 224n14; lynching photographs and, 234n21; male leadership and, 131–32, 150–51n52; for men versus women, 151; Philadelphia, Mississippi, killings and, 216; right to bear arms and, 151–53; segregation and, 207. *See also* human rights; right of self-defense; rights, individual; right to vote
Civil Rights Act of 1866: arguments in support of, 150–51; black inferiority as reason for, 69; contents of, 23–24; Darwinist opposition to, 67; limits of federalism and, 57; passage of, 23; right to bear arms in, 153
Civil War: American political culture and, 214; as atonement for slavery, 18–19; black contrabands in, 231–32n42; black veterans of, 42; blurring between battlefield and home front during, 28; conditions for veterans after, 29–30; controversy over arming blacks in, 111–12; demobilized soldiers of, 28–29; extreme violence of, 13; horrified fascination with, 26; individual and nation-state and, 13; militarization of civilian life and, 29; national amnesia about, 194; national purification and, 13; redemption narratives and, 2, 4–5, 31; as sanctifying event, 18; shared suffering and, 5; soldiers' righteousness and, 26

Clansman (Dixon), 209
Clapp, Dexter, 49
Clark, Elizabeth, 39–40, 223n11
Clark, Kathleen, 87
Clark, Sidney, 151
Clark, William, 91
Clausewitz, Carl von, 154
Clinton, Catherine, 240n19
Cobb, Howell, 157–58, 159, 161, 168
Cobb, James, 213
Colby, Abram, 79
Colfax, Louisiana, Easter massacre, 186, 188–89, 190–92, 210. *See also* Louisiana
Collins, Jonathan, 157
colonialism, black emigration and, 212
colonization, 78
Colored Soldiers and Sailors, 130
common law. *See* English common law
Confederacy: Andrew Johnson's amnesty plan and, 30–31; black soldiers and, 123, 249n27; slavery as cornerstone of, 21
Constitution, U.S., 19, 20, 21. *See also specific amendments*
contrabands: appearance of, 36–37; families of, 116; in literature, 36–37, 55, 115; military recruitment among, 116–18, 121–22; question of what to do with, 117–18, *117*; as social threats, 231–32n42; "A Typical Negro" (illustration) and, 102–3, *103*; women and children as, 116, 117, 133–34
Cornelius, J. E., 58
corporal punishment, 48. *See also* whipping
corruption, 17
Cosby, Martha, 81
Cramer, Clayton, 256–57n29
Crawley, Charles, 95–96, 98
crime: blaming of victims of, 53–54; conflated with poverty, 60; convict labor and, 64; fears of, in electoral politics, 33; freedmen's courts and, 82; hate crimes and, 215, 270n20; journalistic reports of, 155–56; postbellum rates of, 26–29, 30, 32–33; as pretext for racial violence, 211, 263n24; racist ideas about, 34–35
Cromwell, Oliver, 177, 202
Cruikshank case, 265n43
Cuba, 211
culture versus race, 215
Cutler, William, 82

Dana, Richard Henry, 34
Darien, Georgia, 114–15
Darwinism, 66–68, 71, 72, 237n44
Davis, Barry, 81
Davis, Ben, 81
Davis, D. F., 91–92
Davis, Edmund, 91–92
Davis, Garrett, 112
Dawson, Frances Warrington, 197
Debro, Sarah, 95
Declaration of Independence, 20
DeClouet, Alexandre, 172
De Forest, John W., 59–60, 163
Delany, Martin, 121
Deming, Henry Champion, 17
Democratic Party: black voters and, 146, 163, 191–92; cooperation versus resistance in, 168; Democratic clubs and, 173; economic modernization and, 168; election of 1868 and, 154–58, 160–62; election of 1872 and, 171; former Confederates in, 254–55n17, 262n19; new departure of, 169, 172; North and South, 191; People's Party and, 191; political violence and, 144–45, 168; Republican papers' portrayal of, 44; white counter-narrative and, 158; white supremacists and, 144, 154, 160, 254–55n17
dependency: versus autonomy, 238n7; black soldiers versus, 103–4; freedpeople's political claims and, 87; ideological dilemmas and, 225–26n19; patronalism and, 238n7; women and children and, 134
Devens, Charles, Jr., 193–94
disability rights, 87, 242n30
Dix, John, 121
Dixon, Thomas, 209
domestic violence, 80–81, 240n19
Donnelly, Ignatius, 69, 163
Douglas, H. Ford, 122
Douglass, Frederick: on blacks' self-liberation, 135; Covey the overseer and, 106–7, 247n7; on dangers of white benevolence, 69–70; on day of judgment, 110; delegation to Andrew Johnson and, 145; on *Dred Scott* decision, 108; on equal protection under the law, 69–70; on fighting and citizenship, 106–8; military recruitment and, 112, 121; on military service and citizenship, 108, 118, 119–

INDEX

120, 126; on necessity of force, 102; on "negro hate," 70; on shortcomings of Reconstruction, 38; specter of slavish passivity and, 108
Downs, Greg, 225–26n19, 238n7
Downs, Jim, 133–34, 235–36n31
Dred Scott decision, 86–87, 108, 119, 143
DuBois, W. E. B., 100–101, 102, 135, 212, 238–39n8
dueling, 34, 35
Dunning School, 240n19

Eaton, John, 115
Edisto Island, South Carolina. *See* Sea Islands
education, 10, 67
Edwards, Laura, 120, 132, 151n53, 240n19
Eldridge, Stuart, 61
election of 1868: black voters criticized after, 162–63; Democratic Party in, 160, 161, 254–55n17; economic intimidation and, 159; expected results of, 156–57, 161; federal and local races in, 136–39; future of white South and, 158–59; journalistic accounts of, 161; Ku Klux Klan and, 154–55; line between war and politics and, 154; political tensions and, 153–55; Republican Party in, 161–62; violence and, 52, 155–161
election of 1872, 171
election of 1874, 172–73
election of 1876, 10, 174–75, 192–93, 195–98, 204–5
elections: ballots and bullets and, 141, 166; black militias and, 89; ceremonies and rituals and, 142, 144; challenged results of, 141, 166; civic millennialism and, 142; martial language and imagery and, 141; as test of manhood, 141; violence during, 52, 138–145, 155–161, 166; voting as emblematic of citizenship and, 141–42, 143–44; voting as manly sport and, 254n11. *See also* right to vote; *specific elections*
Ellet, Robert, 97
emancipation: atonement and, 21; bonds of white society and, 32; celebrations of, 15–16; "evils" of, 64; freedpeople's violent end and, 187; as great crime, 31–35; ideological dilemmas and, 225–26n19; as Jubilee, 6; labor control and, 224n13;

necessity of suffering and, 36, 61; redemptive language and, 21; reuniting of families after, 94; violence and, 4–5; women and children after, 77
Emancipation Day, 10, 82–83
Emancipation Proclamation, 81
emigration of Southern blacks, 212
Enforcement Acts, 174
English common law, 19, 24
Equal Rights League of Pennsylvania, 128–29
Equal Rights League of Wilmington, North Carolina, 82, 87
expansionism, U.S., 140, 210–12
ex-slaves. *See* freedpeople

Faulkner, William, 206
Faust, Drew, 5
fear, liberalism of, 238n7
federalism, limits of, 57
Fifteenth Amendment, 5, 163
Fisk, Clinton, 130–31
Fitzhugh, George, 32–33, 35, 65–67
Folkes, Minnie, 97
Foner, Eric, 82, 168, 238–39n8
forgiveness, difficulty of, 99
former slaves. *See* freedpeople
Forrest, Nathan Bedford, 91, 144, 154, 160, 254–55n17
Forten, William, 128
Fort Pillow massacre, 91, 128, 154, 160
Foster, Hickory, 80
Fourteenth Amendment: civic theology and, 14; Darwinist opposition to, 67; discourse of black predation following, 155; justification for, 5; political illustrations and, 52; right to bear arms and, 256–57n29
Frank Leslie's (periodical), 160, 258n45
Franklin, Celia, 80–81
Frazier, Garrison, 78
freeborn blacks, 79, 93
Freedmen and Southern Society Project, 104
Freedmen's Bureau: abuse investigation and, 61–63; admonishments to freedpeople by, 55–56; agents' duties and, 82; agents of, as plantation owners, 61–63; assessments of worthiness by, 58–60; attacks on agents of, 48, 49; black militias and, 88, 89; civilizing mission and, 58, 69; conditions among freedpeople and, 58–60;

275

Freedmen's Bureau (*cont.*)
Darwinist opposition to, 67; Democratic Party indictment of, 160; domestic violence and, 240n19; Fitzhugh's exposé of, 65–67; freedmen's courts and, 82; freedpeople as assailants and, 80–81; freedpeople's appeals to, 84–87; gun ownership and, 147–49, 152; impressment and, 125; labor compulsion and, 60–62; legislation supporting, 150–51; limits of federalism and, 57; as Negro Nursery, 65–72; outrage reports of, 79–80; politics versus economics for freedpeople and, 163; rations and, 57–58, 60, 235–36n31; triumphant freedom narrative of, 69; violence and compulsion by, 6; weakness of, 225–26n19; white fears of insurrection and, 81–82; white Southerners' complaints to, 31–32; women and children and, 77

freedom: black convention delegates' vision of, 131; Constitution as charter for, 21; control over meaning of, 26; as a curse, 69; Darwinist redefinition of, 66–68; discipline and suffering as conditions for, 38; ensuring the conditions of, 19; exaggerated ideas of, 57; fighting and, 8; language of, 38; line between slavery and, 75, 125; militarization of, 105–6; military service and, 104, 108–9, 118, 126; negated by violence, 61; Northern versus Southern views of, 6; price of, 133–35; versus protection, 66; reclamation of lost voices and, 76; right of self-defense and, 143; triumphant narrative of, 69; as worse than slavery, 56; worthiness of, 166

freedpeople: agency of, 76; allegations of laziness of, 56–57; aspirations of, 56; as assailants, 80–81; as authors of own story, 100; civilizing process and, 38; civil rights protection and, 224n13; compromise of sympathy for, 35; compulsion of labor among, 60–62; contract system and, 57; criticized as voters, 162–63; Darwinist critique of aid to, 66–68; demands of, 55–56; demise of, predicted, 66, 70; desperate conditions among, 58–60; disarmament of, 149–152; emancipation celebrations and, 16; extralegal forums and, 89; family and community for, 77, 216; former masters and, 78; Freedman's Bureau admonishments to, 55–56; government's obligation to protect, 3; gun ownership among, 147–49; infantalization of, 65–67, 131; Joint Committee on Reconstruction and, 52–53; land redistribution and, 74; letter writing among, 94–95; literacy and, 90; living conditions of, 79; militancy of, 212–13; as passive, 165, 166; physical security and economic welfare of, 57; politics versus economic recovery for, 163; protection versus discipline for, 5–6, 38–39, 56, 60–61, 64; radical political discourse of, 87; rape and, 224n14; rations for, 57–58, 60; reciprocity sought by, 85; reconciliation urged on, 93; redemptive vision of, 128–130; resistance to impressment by, 123–24; responses to violence of, 7; as responsible for own freedom, 166; retribution not sought by, 81–82, 84–85, 113; revision of Reconstruction by, 76; rural-to-urban movement of, 79, 239–240n15; self-description of, 84–85; stereotypes of, 246–47n5; testimony of, about violence, 6–7; as uncontrollable, 31–32; U.S. debt to, 16; voices of, before Congress, 53; vulnerability of, 24. *See also* African Americans; contrabands

Free Soil Party, 18
French Republic, 118–19
Fugitive Slave Law, 23
Fullerton, J. S., 61–63
Furstenberg, Francois, 106

Gaines, Matt, 91, 92
Galloway, Abraham, 130
Garnet, Henry Highland, 110
Garrison, William Lloyd, 18, 21
Garrisonians, 17, 18, 20
Gary, Martin W., 174, 175, 196, 197
George, James Z., 174
Georgia: Camilla election riot in, 138–140, 154–55, 157, 161–62, 252n5; land redistribution in, 73–74
Gerber, David, 94–95
Gettysburg Address, 18
Gibson, James, 177, 179
Gilpin, R. Blakeslee, 270n18
Glassman, Jonathan, 188, 263n24

Glymph, Thavolia, 244n48
Godkin, E. L., 67
Goldberg, Chad, 60
Goodman, James, 1, 216
Gordon, John Brown, 144, 154, 254–55n17
government: consent of the governed and, 92; first object of, 19–25; force required for, 92; weakness of, in Reconstruction, 85–86
Grant, Ulysses S.: on arms for black veterans, 255n23; black militias and, 88; campaign motto of, 154; campaign to elect, 52; election of 1868 and, 136–38, 154, 156; election of 1876 and, 205; New Orleans crisis and, 184, 201, 203; promises of, 168; on public exhaustion with Southern violence, 54; white leagues and, 191
Great Britain, 103
Greece, ancient, 118–19
Greeley, Horace, 161, 162
Greenberg, Amy, 226n21
Greene, Arthur, 98
Griffin, Larry, 213–14
Griffith, D. W., 209
Griffith, Michael, 213
Grimsted, David, 144, 254n11
Grinnell, Josiah, 151
gun ownership: citizenship and, 161–62, 167; dangers of, for whites versus blacks, 153; disarmament and, 149–152; Fourteenth Amendment and, 256–57n29; historians and, 256–57n29; hunting and, 148; Independence Day celebrations and, 88; manhood and, 175; proliferation of guns and, 152; restrictions on, 152; rifle clubs and, 174–76, 183–84, 204; right to vote and, 146–47, 150–51, 167; safeguards of liberty and, 151

habeas corpus, 23
Hahn, Steven, 237–38n3, 238–39n8
Halbrook, Stephen, 256–57n29
Hale, John Parker, 46–47
Hall, Thomas, 99–100
Halleck, Henry W., 125
Hamburg, South Carolina, massacre, 196–98, 201, 208
Hamlin, John, 80
Hampton, Wade, III: black vote and, 192; Democratic Party and, 154, 161; election of 1868 and, 159; election of 1876 and, 195, 197; Hampton Days and, 183; physical prowess of, 182; political violence and, 208
Hardy, William, 176
Harlan, John Marshall, 241–42n29
Harper's Ferry raid, 110, 111, 135
Harper's Weekly: on degradation of former slaves' manhood, 34; images of black suffering in, 40, 43–44, *43*, *44*; Jotham Horton death scene in, 50, *51*; as Republicans' favorite, 40; "A Typical Negro" (illustration) in, 102, *103*
Hartman, Saidiya, 39, 92–93
Hartog, Hendrik, 75, 238n7
Hatch, Nathan, 221–22n4
hate crimes, 10, 215
Haven, Gilbert, 16–17
Hawkins, James, 81
Hawley, Joseph, 202
Hawthorne, Nathaniel, 29
Hay, John, 29–30
Hayes, Rutherford B., 10, 204–5, 206, 253n8
Hays, Charles, 267n66
Help, The (film), 215
Henry, Patrick, 194
Higgenbottom, Joseph, 187
Higginson, Thomas Wentworth, 111, 112–13, 114, 120
Hill, Benjamin H., 157
history: African Americans' struggles against white violence and, 207; empirical ideal of, 7; limitations of, for writing about violence, 76; as mode of redress, 238–39n8; oral, 95–100, 244n48; overcoming and not overcoming in, 238–39n8; regional isolation of studies and, 253n7; revisionism on Reconstruction and, 238–39n8, 240n19
Hobbes, Thomas, 19
Hofstadter, Richard, 237n44
Holmes, George, 177
Holocaust, 186–87, 188, 265n36
Horton, Jotham, 50
Houston, Ulysses, 79
How, Storer, 32
Howard, Jacob, 24, 151
Howard, Oliver Otis: on freedpeople's idleness, 57; land redistribution and, 73–74; naïveté of, 86; plantation owners in Freedmen's Bureau and, 63, 236n38;

Howard, Oliver Otis (*cont.*)
  rations halted by, 58; reparations and, 83; on suffering and emancipation, 36, 61; sympathetic portrayal of Southern whites and, 56–57; war wound of, 83
Howe, Julia Ward, 228n23
Howe, Samuel Gridley, 66, 113
human rights: legal revolution in, 40; liberalism and, 238n7; theory of, 39–40. *See also* rights, individual; *individual rights*

immigrants, 28
imperialism, 210–12, 265n36
integration, freedpeople's rejection of, 78

Jackson, Andrew, 144
Jackson, Stonewall, 176
Jacobs, Harriet, 109
Jacoby, Karl, 76
Jamaica, 33
James, Horace, 62–63
Jenkins, Caroline, 81
"John Brown's Body" (song), 26, 228n23
Johns, James, 139
Johnson, Andrew: African American delegation to, 145; on black suffrage, 145; Confederate amnesty plan of, 30–31, 43–44, 73, 128, 203; Freedmen's Bureau investigation and, 61; freedpeople's appeal to, 83; Radical Republicans' denunciation of, 40; Radical Republican struggle with, 49–50, 52, 63; restoration plans of, 40; soldiers after the war and, 30; Thomas Nast engravings and, 41–42
Johnson, Herschel V., 161
Johnson, Katie Blackwell, 98
Johnson, Walter, 238–39n8
Joint Committee on Reconstruction, 48, 52–53
Jones, Beverly, 96
Jones, Charles Colcock, 187
Jones, Mary, 148, 187, 265n37
journalism: fascination with crime and, 26–28; images of black suffering and, 40; outrage mills and, 267n66; racist newspapers and, 179–180; white league movement and, 173
judiciary, 82, 84, 89
Julian, George, 21, 204

Kansas, 110
Kayssar, Alexander, 141–42
Kelley, William D., 152
Kellogg, Henry Pitt, 184–85, 191, 192, 207
Kerr-Ritchie, Jeffery R., 243n34
Keyes, Crawford, 49
Killen, Edgar Ray, 1–3, 10, 213, 214, 216
King, Henrietta, 98
King, Martin Luther, Jr., 215
Kirkwood, Samuel, 125
Knights of the White Camellia, 173
Koch, Ed, 213
Ku Klux Klan: *Birth of a Nation* (film) and, 209, 268n6; in caricature of black legislators, 164; Congressional testimony on, 53, 165, 239–240n15, 256n27; Democratic Party and, 144–45, 160; disarmament of freedpeople by, 149–150; disguises of, 174, 209; economic intimidation and, 159; election of 1868 and, 154–55, 159–162; federal prosecution of, 172, 173; media response to, 162; militia to combat, 160; Nathan Bedford Forrest and, 154; national attention to, 67; in North, 203; origins of, 31; political illustrations and, 52; sexualized attacks and, 256n27; victims of, criticized, 162–63; white league movement and, 173
Kyle, George, 141

labor: antebellum workers as freemen and, 231n40; apprenticeship of children and, 60; compulsory, 60–62, 233n6; contract system and, 57–58, 59, 71–72; of convicts, 46, 64; debt peonage and, 68; dependency and, 72; "free," 38, 57, 62–64, 75, 126, 233n6; free labor acolytes' hypocrisy and, 63–64; restorative power of, 78; sharecropping and, 59; work-or-starve choice and, 58
Lamar, Lucius Q. C., 191
landownership, 73–74, 76–78, 83, 151
Langston, John Mercer, 132
Latimer, Edwin O., 90
Latin America, 211
Lawson, Melinda, 13, 227n10
LeConte, Emma, 25
Lee, Andrew, 90
Lee, Fitzhugh, 193–94
Lee, Robert E., 15, 25

Lennox, Charles, 81
Levi, Primo, 186
Lewis, Charlotte, 58–59
liberalism, 238n7
Liberty Party, 18
Liberty Place, battle of, 186, 194, 201, 208. *See also* New Orleans
Liedtke, F. W., 59
Lincoln, Abraham: advice to freedpeople from, 81; assassination of, 16–17; on Civil War as sanctifying event, 18; Declaration of Independence invoked by, 20; freedpeople's letters to, 125; George Washington and, 17; Gettysburg Address and, 18; as martyr, 14; postemancipation engravings and, *22*; promise of new national state and, 227n10; punishment of assassins of, 11–12; second inaugural address of, 16, 18. *See also* Gettysburg Address
literacy, 90
literature, 7, 10, 99–101, 223n11
Locke, John, 86, 143
Longstreet, James, 185
Lost Cause movement, 158, 161
Louisiana: black elected officials in, 160; Democratic Party in, 171–72; duel governments of, 184; election of 1876 and, 206; mobilization against fusionists in, 172–73; white leagues in, 174–75, 183, 191, 194–95, 201–2; White Man's Party in, 174, 189, 191. *See also* Colfax, Louisiana, Easter massacre; New Orleans
Lowell, Charles Russell, 114–15
Lynch, James, 78, 93–94, 98, 100, 190
lynching, 207, 213, 222n7, 234n21, 264n29

Madison, James, 19
Malcolm X, 136, 139
Malthusian theory, 71
manhood: abolitionism and bloody imagery and, 109–10; American nationalism and, 192–93; citizenship and, 8–9; defense of native whites', 172; discourse of, and civil rights, 127–28; election day as test of, 141; exclusion of women and, 131; feminized image of enslaved men and, 108; fighting back and, 107; gun ownership and, 139, 175; as hinge on door to the future, 111; historiography of, 9; imperialism and, 212; military service as path to, 117–18; Nat Turner versus Uncle Tom and, 111–16; obsession with, 104; reconfiguring of, in black soldiers, 105; in Reconstruction-era politics, 261–62n14; redemption as respite from gentlemanly self-discipline and, 171; right to vote and, 132, 140, 142; violence as litmus test for, 170; voting as performance of, 144, 254n11; white leagues and, 173, 174, 177–78, 183; for whites, 169; white supremacist attacks and, 201. *See also* martial manhood
Manifest Destiny, 140
Manigault, Gabriel, 148–49
manumission, military service and, 118–19
Markell, Patchen, 222–23n8
Marshall, T. H., 57
martial manhood: American identity and, 139; American political culture and, 214; black soldiers and, 103–5, 131; boyhood and, *137*; centennial celebrations and, 195; citizenship and, 119, 151; language of, 154; limits of, 104–5, 120, 207; methods and ideology of, 135; militaristic patriotism and, 260n8; narrative power of, 127; nationalism and, 193, 195; radical abolitionism and, 140; redemption of black manhood and, 213; for whites versus blacks, 9. *See also* manhood
Massey, George S., 133
Masur, Kate, 231–32n42
McCurry, Stephanie, 151n53, 179
McEnery, William, 206
McKaye, James, 113
McNeilly, J. H., 268n6
Melville, Herman, 4–5, 11, 135
Millard, Josiah, 44–45
millennialism, 142, 221–22n4
Miller, Tyisha, 213
miscegenation, 66
missionaries, 26
Mississippi: black grassroots politics in, 207; Democratic Party in, 171; hate crime in, 215, 270n20; as metaphor for violence, 213–14; mobilization against fusionists in, 172–73; Philadelphia killings, 1–2, 216; white leagues in, 174–75, 179, 181–82, 191; White Man's Party in, 191; white paramilitaries in, 54

Mississippi Plan, 190, 207, 211
Montgomery, James, 114–15
Moore, Dosia Williams, 179
moral suasion, 17–18
Morant Bay rebellion, 33–34
Morgan, Albert, 176, 179, 180, 181, 189
Morgan, Edmund, 92
Moses, Charlie, 99, 100
Moultry, Ishmael, 73–74
music, 26, 101

NAACP, 209
Napoleonic Wars, 154
Nash, Christopher Columbus, 174
Nast, Thomas: "Andrew Johnson's Reconstruction and How It Works" engraving by, 41–42, *42*; bloody-shirt politics and, 40–41; "The 'Bloody Shirt' Reformed" engraving by, 197, *198*; "Emancipation" engraving by, 21–22, *22*, 40–41; "Franchise. And Not This Man" engraving by, 128, *129*; "He Wants a Change Too" engraving by, 198, *200*; "Is This a Republican Form of Government?" engraving by, 197–98, *199*; "One Vote Less" engraving by, 52, *53*; "Slavery Is Dead" engraving by, 41, *41*
Nation (periodical), 29–30, 68, 163
National Equal Rights League, 128
National Republican (periodical), 163
Native Americans, 4, 71, 210, 212
natural law, 71
New Orleans: armed takeover of, 172, 184–86; end of Reconstruction and, 206; governor's private army in, 137–38, 184; Liberty Place monument in, 208; prolonged battle for, 201–5; riot in, 50–51, 79. *See also* Louisiana
New South ethos, 259–260n3
New York City, draft riots in, 144
New York Times, 162, 204
New York Tribune, 161–62
Nicaragua, 211
Nicolay, John G., 29–30
North Carolina, 82, 87–88, 210–11
Nye, James, 153

O'Brien, Edward, 58, 59
O'Donovan, Susan, 77, 240n19
Ogden, Frank Nash, 186
O'Leary, Cecelia, 260n8

oral history, 95–100, 244n48
Oshinsky, David, 64
Owen, Robert Dale Owen, 113

Panama, 211
panic of 1873, 172
Parker, Theodore, 70, 109
Parsons, Elaine, 162
Patterson, Delicia, 77
Peloponnesian Wars, 118
Penningroth, Dylan, 88
People's Vindicator (newspaper), 173, 179, 190, 194
Philbrick, Edward, 124
Philippines, 211
Phillips, Wendell, 15
Picayune (newspaper), 173
Pierce, William, 138–39
Pierpont, Francis H., 88
Pike, James S., 164–65, 166
police brutality, 50
Pollard, Edward, 158–59
Pomeroy, Samuel, 151
Poore, Mumford S., 138–39, 161
Pope, Ann, 187
Portuguese colonialism, 118–19
poverty, 60, 63, 70
Prince, Jim, 1–2
Prosser, Gabriel, 106
protection: antebellum legislation for, 20; black militias and, 89–91; blaming of victims of crime, 54; citizenship and, 75; Darwinist challenge to, 72; dependency and, 69; versus discipline, 5–6, 38–39, 56, 60–61, 64; economic welfare and, 57; end of Reconstruction, 207; enslaved men's inability to provide for women, 109; equal, 69–70; federal versus state roles in, 19–20, 23; versus freedom, 66; freedpeople's petitions for, 75; freedpeople's responsibility for their own, 32, 166; government's obligation and, 19–20; growing aversion to cruelty and, 40; gun ownership and, 176; as impulse behind slavery, 66; inferiority versus equality as reason for, 69; institutional unreliability and, 84; law versus impunity and, 82; obedience as condition for, 72; postbellum civil rights legislation and, 20; as right of citizenship, 24; right to vote and, 145–46; rural-to-urban

movement for, 79; under slavery versus freedom, 83–87; US imperialism and, 211; white leagues and, 179–180; for whites as well as blacks, 34–35; of whites from blacks, 157–58; of wives and children, 132

Puerto Rico, 211

Pulitzer, Joseph, 204

Puritans, 4

race versus culture, 215

racism, personal versus institutional, 213–15

Radical Reconstruction: conservative argument against, 145; efforts to discredit, 61; fears about dependency and, 69; images of black suffering and, 40; justification for, 5; *Nation* (periodical) and, 68; preferential treatment of freedpeople and, 57; versus race war, 153; social distance between whites and blacks and, 39. *See also* Reconstruction

Radical Republicans: Andrew Johnson and, 40, 49–50, 52, 63; civil rights legislation and, 150–53; compromised mission of, 224n13; goals of, 3–4; images of suffering and, 52; right to bear arms and, 151–53

Raiford, Leigh, 209–10, 234n21

rape: by armed assailants, 150; freedmen charged with, 81; Ku Klux Klan and, 256n27; in oral history accounts, 97; testimony about, 53–54, 224n14; useless violence and, 188; white supremacist allegations of, 180

Raymond, Henry, 151

Reconstruction: *Birth of a Nation* (film) and, 209; black elected officials and, 160, 164–65; black militias and, 105; conflicting narratives of, 166–67, 209; election of 1876 and, 206–7; election riots during, 139–140; end of, 10, 206–7; fear of race war and, 198; force versus consent and, 243n41; freedpeople's revision of, 76; inconsistencies in ideology guiding, 8; journalistic mocking of, 163–65, 258n45; Ku Klux Klan and, 162; labor question and, 224n13; meaning of Second Amendment and, 256–57n29; Northern withdrawal of support for, 202–5, 267n67; precariousnes of federal authority during, 49–50; revisionist histories of, 238–39n8, 240n19; state's structural weakness and, 225–26n19; terrorization as torture during, 76; unfinished redemption and, 10; unfinished revolution of, 210; violence and American culture and, 209; white counternarrative of, 158–59; white Southerners' early response to, 258n43. *See also* Radical Reconstruction

Reconstruction Acts, 146, 154, 155, 158, 163

redemption: amid rather than from violence, 10; atonement and, 216; autumnal outbreaks in, 201; in the Bible, 11; black versus white versions of, 101; as cash payment, 3; in Christian theology, 3, 16; Civil War and, 2, 4–5; competing narratives of, 72, 214; as contentious political project, 171; divisions within Redeemer elite and, 261n9; election of 1876 and, 192–93; end of Reconstruction and, 10, 13, 165; as gendered movement, 170; as historical trope, 3–4, 215, 221–22n4; historiography of, 10; language of, 2–4, 13–14, 21, 25, 38; Lincoln's assassination and, 16–17; in North versus South, 9, 25; Philadelphia, Mississippi, murder conviction as, 1–2; post-Reconstruction narrative of, 208; racial reconciliation and, 215; redemption of, 208; as respite from gentlemanly self-discipline, 171; revolutionary romanticism and, 205; rituals of, 15–18, 21; small-scale strategies for, 10; as Southern whites' retaking of control, 4, 5; suffering and, 18, 35; from and through violence, 4, 14; title of present volume and, 9–10; unfinished, 10; untrue narrative of freedom and, 100; whites as protagonists in stories of, 215

Red Shirts: election of 1876 and, 195, 197, 199, 201; martial displays of, 207; pranks and disruptions by, 182; reunion of, 208; straight-out campaign of, 209; uniforms of, 177, 184

Red String League, 160

reform movements: antebellum evangelicalism and, 17–18; Constitutional amendments and, 20–21; journalism and, 40; new postbellum impetus toward, 17; postbellum free labor and, 39; prison reform and, 48, 64–65; sympathy for imprisoned veterans and, 30; vulnerability versus autonomy and, 75–76

281

reparations, 83
Republican Party: black elected officials in, 91; crisis of legitimacy of, 8; election of 1868 and, 161; in North versus South, 162–63; Philip Sheridan and, 204; politics versus economics for freedpeople and, 163; Reconstruction violence and, 162; recruitment black soldiers and, 165; self-interest and, 18; souring of, on black suffrage, 164; white leagues' ridicule of, 181–82
Revis, Adam, 80–81
Revis, Charlotte, 80–81
Revolution, American. *See* American Revolution
Revolutionary War. *See* American Revolution
right of self-defense, 143
rights, individual, 120
right to bear arms. *See* gun ownership
right to vote: abolitionists' worries about, 145; Andrew Johnson and, 145; ballots and bullets and, 136, 139, 140; as bugbear of Reconstruction's opponents, 24; dangers of withholding, 34; in Democrats' 1868 platform, 154; disenfranchisement laws and, 207; economic security versus, 133; growth of, for whites, 139, 142–43; journalistic souring on, 163; manhood and, 132; military service and, 127–28, 138–140, 142–43, 253n8; as panacea, 133, 164; political illustrations and, 128, *129*; Republican Party's souring on, 164; right to bear arms and, 146–47, 150–51, 167; as safeguard of liberty, 151; self-defense and, 143, 145–153; Southern readmission to Union and, 146; as tutelage, 130–31; Ulysses S. Grant's promise and, 168; white fears and, 130, 145. *See also* civil rights; elections
Rivers, Prince, 124
Robbins, Frank L., 17
Robison, E. S., 90
Roediger, David, 231n40
Rose, Anne, 26
Rosen, Hannah, 53, 188, 224n14
Royster, Charles, 4

Saint-Domingue, 34, 112
Sampson, Yates, 73–74
Saville, Julie, 149

Saxton, Rufus, 113, 147
Scarry, Elaine, 76
Schurz, Carl, 34, 145, 154–55, 203
Schwerner, Michael, 1, 216
Scott, Robert K., 164, 172
Sea Islands: armed freedpeople on, 148, 149; Edisto Island, 74, 76–77, 83, 86, 237–38n3; Fenwick Island, 88; impressment on, 123; James Island, 148; Skiddaway Island, Georgia, 79
Second Amendment, 150–51, 153, 161–62, 256–57n29
sexuality, images of pain and, 39
Seymour, Horatio, 52, 137–38, 144, 154, 156, 159, 161
Shaler, Nathaniel, 67–68
sharecropping, 59
Shaw, Robert Gould, 114–15
Sheridan, Philip, 201–4, 255n23, 267n64, 267n67
Sherman, John, 112
Sherman, William T.: on black enlistment, 253n8; on black suffrage, 140, 253n8; northward movement of, 15; Savannah's black ministers and, 78; scorched-earth policy of, 163–65; Special Field Order No. 15 and, 73–74
Shreveport Times, 173
Shulman, George, 3
Sickles, Daniel, 152
Simone, Nina, 206
Sinclair, William, 152
Sklar, Judith, on liberalism of fear, 238n7
slave auctions, 15–16
slavery: arming of slaves and, 147; badges and incidents of, 86, 241–42n29; Civil War as atonement for, 18–19; compensation for, 3; as cornerstone of Confederacy, 21; family separations and, 98; family structure in, 116; historical arming of, 118–19; as institutionalized torture, 76; line between freedom and, 75, 125; masters' financial interest in slaves' welfare and, 83–84; national amnesia about, 194; oral history accounts of, 95–99; painful history of, 92–101; passivity and, 108, 109–10; paternalistic view of, 65–66, 181; reparations for, 83; resistance and, 106–8; slaves as threat to free laborers and, 231n40; slaves' rival geography in, 79, 240n16; suicide and,

106; testimony of brutality under, 74; versus tyranny, 231n40. *See also* African Americans

slave trade, 16

smallpox, 58, 235–36n31

Smith, Caroline, 159

Smith, Charles, 149–150, 159

Smith, George, 187

Smith, Gerritt, 135

social contract theory, 19, 222–23n8

Soule, Charles, 55–57

South Carolina: armed employment negotiations in, 88; black elected officials in, 164–65, 172; Democratic Party in, 172; emancipation celebrations in, 15–18, 25–26; end of Reconstruction and, 195–97, 201, 204; land redistribution in, 73–74; rifle clubs of, 174–76, 183–84, 193, 262n16; white leagues in, 174–75, 178–79, 181–82, 191. *See also* Hamburg, South Carolina, massacre; Sea Islands

Southern Relief Commission, 158

Southern whites: alienation of, from political leaders, 172; Democratic Party's new departure and, 169; divisions among, 171; elitism among, 169; failure of, to support white leagues, 189–190; feelings of racial emasculation and, 169; genocidal violence of, 186–89; Northern white men and, 171; white liners and straight-outs among, 170; winnable cause of, 191; yeomen's concerns and, 169–170. *See also* white leagues; white supremacy

Sparks, Elizabeth, 96

Spelman, Elizabeth, 38

Spencer, Herbert, 66–67, 71, 237n44

spirituality of black soldiers, 113

Stanton, Edwin, 89, 90, 122–23, 253n8

starvation, 58, 59

Stauffer, John, 248n13

Stearns, George L., 122–23

Steedman, James, 61–63

Stephens, Alexander Hamilton, 21, 159

Stevens, Chany, 81

Stewart, Maria, 110–11

Stockton, Robert F., 47

Stowe, Harriet Beecher, 31, 99–100, 109

Sturtevant, J. M., 71

suffering: avoidable versus unavoidable, 40; creative, 215; in cultural memory, 101; emancipation and, 36; hierarchies of, 38; human rights theory and, 39–40; images and representations of, 5, 38–40, 50–52, 54–55, 72, 210; imaginative distance from, 55; as imaginative vehicle for transformation, 51; inevitability of, 56, 61, 68, 69; as instructive, 72; literary representations of, 37, 55; Martin Luther King Jr. on, 215; political commodification of, 52; politics of, 38; Reconstruction-era politics and, 49–50; redemption and, 18, 22–25, 35, 57, 214–15; shared, 5; in slavery's historical record, 95–96; in social Darwinism, 66; voyeurism and, 54; white counternarrative of, 158; for whites versus blacks, 48, 55

suicide, 106

Sumner, Charles, 34, *47*, 146, 194

Surratt, Mary, 11–12, 27

sympathy, white. *See* white sympathy

Taney, Roger, 86, 108, 119, 143

Tennessee, Memphis riot in, 50–51, 79, 187–88

terrorism, 207

testimony: about rape, 53–54, 224n1; by freedpeople, 6–7, 79–80, 239–240n15; freemen's courts and, 82; of slavery's brutality, 74; torture's silencing of, 76. *See also* oral history

Thayer, Martin Russell, 21

theology, civic, 13–14, 221–22n4. *See also* Christian theology

Thirteenth Amendment, 21–24, 43, *43*, 52, 64

Thomas, A. G., 16

Thomas, George, 49

Thomas, Gertrude, 154, 156–57

Thomas, James, 169

Thomas, Lorenzo, 88

Thornton, J. Mills, 231n40

Tilden, Samuel, 160–61, 197, 204

Tillman, Ben "Pitchfork," 208

Tillson, Davis, 61

Tilton, Theodore, 109

Toombs, Robert, 159

torture, 76

Trumbull, Lyman, 23–24, 151

Turner, Henry McNeal, 79, 89, 93–94, 132

Turner, Nat, 106, 111, 112

Uncle Tom's Cabin (Stowe), 99, 109, 111

Underwood, John C., 187

INDEX

Union Leagues, 155, 159, 160
United States Colored Troops (USCT), 15, 88, 122
urbanization. *See* cities and urbanization
USCT. *See* United States Colored Troops (USCT)

Vesey, Denmark, 112
Vicksburg, Mississippi, attacks, 175, 177, 201. *See also* Mississippi
violence: African Americans' continued struggles against, 207; ambivalence about, 4; ambivalence about black men's capacity for, 246–47n5; American culture and, 209; American revolutionary tradition and, 192; black resistance and, 212–13; civilization of freedpeople and, 38; Darwinist view of, 72; during elections, 52, 138–145, 155–161; everydayness of, 75; extreme brutality and, 187–89, 207; federal indifference to, 165–66; force and democratic governance and, 92; force versus consent and, 243n41; formative role of, 7–8, 225n16; Freedmen's Bureau's outrage reports and, 79–80; freedpeople and Republicans blamed for, 180–81; freedpeople's redemptive vision and, 128–130; genocidal, 186–89, 265n36; government lack of power and, 85; history's limitations and, 76; imaginative distance from, 55; importance of, in Southern thinking, 6; legitimacy of Civil War and, 13; liberal imagination and, 222–23n8; line between war and politics and, 154; military conquest of American nation and, 225n16; military service and, 105; national identity and, 31, 205; national ideological imperatives and, 9; national unity and, 194; as necessary, 70, 102; negation of freedom and, 61; postbellum attacks on Union soldiers and, 49; race and citizenship and, 188; rationale for, 155; redemption amid rather than from, 10; redemption from and through, 4, 14; regional versus national, 171, 213–14; Republican Party and, 8, 162; risks of speaking about, 6–7; self-defense and, 56, 157; sexualized, 54, 188, 256n27; songs of retribution and, 26, 228n23; South as metaphor for, 213–14; Southern cultural patterns, 9; state legitimacy and, 222–23n8; symbolic versus direct, 233n6; testimony about, 224n14; theatrical aspects of, 264n29; useless, 186–88; valorization of, from whites, 181; victimization in history of, 210; white control of discourse of, 6–7; of white leagues, 179–180; white supremacy and, 191; for whites versus blacks, 164–65, 214. *See also* crime; domestic violence; lynching; rape; whipping

Violence Against Women Act, 10
Vogler, Candace, 222–23n8
voting. *See* right to vote

Walker, David, 110, 111
Ware, Harriet, 123, 124
Warmoth, Frank, *137*
Warmoth, Henry Clay, 137, 184
War of 1812, 119
Washington, George, 17
Weiss, John, 13
Welke, Barbara Young, 151n53
Wells, Ida B., 212
whipping: caning of Charles Sumner, *47*; as challenge to federal authority, 48; Congressional debate over, 46–48; as emblem of white mastery, 44–46; flogging in the navy and, 46–48; in iconography of black suffering, *41*, 43–44, *43*, *44*, *54*; illustration of, *103*; national commitment to white supremacy and, 46; slaves who cannot be flogged and, 107; in Southern states' legislation, 45–46; spectators for, 46; of whites versus blacks, 48. *See also* corporal punishment

Whitaker, Tobe, 177
white leagues: assaults on local governments by, 183, 184–86; Colfax, Louisiana, Easter massacre and, 189, 190–92; end of Reconstruction and, 206; former Confederates in, 174, 176–77; fusionists and, 172–73, 189; martial displays of, 182, 207; martial fantasies of, 177; Northerners' sympathy with, 201–3; Northern public and, 191; popular will and, 183; racist beliefs in, 180–81; Republicans mocked by, 181–82; rifle clubs and, 174–76; rite of passage, 177–78; roots of, 173–74; social events and, 178–79; takeover of New Orleans by, 172; violence of natural world and, 179–180;

284

white opponents of, 189–190; women as recruiters for, 179. *See also* white supremacy

White Man's Party, 174, 189, 191

white militias. *See* Ku Klux Klan; Red Shirts; white leagues

white supremacy: American Revolution as inspiration for, 201; Colfax, Louisiana, Easter massacre and, 190–91, 192; Confederate veterans and, 174; danger to uncooperative whites and, 190; Democratic Party and, 144, 154, 160, 254–55n17; discourse of, 160; Enforcement acts and, 174; genocidal fantasies and, 265n36; good government as code word for, 194; intimidation and violence within, 173; national centennial celebrations and, 171; pageantry and spectacle of, 182–192, 201; poor whites and, 178; tenuousness of white identity and, 208; whipping and, 46; white unity and, 190–91. *See also* Southern whites

white sympathy: black passivity and, 52, 165; dangers of white benevolence and, 69–70; images evoking, 39–40; precariousness of, 210; problematic nature of, 37; racial animosity and, 70; social distance between whites and blacks and, 39; stories of black redemption and, 215; unoffending freedman and, 240n19; unreliability of, 54–55; for white Southerners, 56–57

Whitman, Walt, 183–84

Whittlesey, Eliphalet, 62–63

Whittorne, Washington, 152

Williams, Kidada, 213, 224n14

Wilson, Hawkins, 94, 98–99

Wilson, Henry, 36

women: black women abolitionists and, 110–11; capital punishment and, 12–13; citizenship and, 86; domestic violence claims and, 240n19; enslaved men's inability to protect, 109; gendered discussion of civil rights and, 151; increase in crime by, 27, 28; male civil rights leadership and, 131–32; medical examinations and, 58–59; men's frivolous amusements and, 110–11; men's military service and, 133–34; men's protective authority over, 132; obsession with manhood and, 104; in postbellum black politics, 150–51n52; rape and, 53–54, 150, 224n14; right to vote and, 132, 142; segregation by sex, 151n53; sexual availability of, 54; sexual vulnerability of, 109; state as a woman and, 157–58; vulnerability of, 77; white leagues and, 178–180

Wood, Amy Louise, 264n29

Wood, Marcus, 50–51, 73

Woodward, C. Vann, 211, 261n9

Works Progress Administration (WPA), 96, 98–100, 244n48

WPA. *See* Works Progress Administration (WPA)

Wright, Ellaine, 98

www.ingramcontent.com/pod-product-compliance
Lightning Source LLC
Chambersburg PA
CBHW021937290426
44108CB00012B/876